The Land Question
in Palestine, 1917–1939

The Land Question
in Palestine, 1917–1939

By Kenneth W. Stein

The University of North Carolina Press

Chapel Hill and London

Manufactured in the United States of America

First printing, July 1984
Second printing, April 1985
Third printing, February 1987

Library of Congress Cataloging in Publication Data

Stein, Kenneth W., 1946–
   The land question in Palestine, 1917–1939.

   Bibliography: p.
   Includes index.
   1. Land tenure—Palestine—History—20th century.
I. Title.
HD850.S78   1984   333.3′23′095694   83-21872
ISBN 0-8078-1579-9
ISBN 0-8078-4178-1 (pbk.)

Maps prepared by Karen L. Wysocki

To My Parents and Grandparents

Contents

Tables and Maps

Illustrations

Preface

In 1972, I was eager to write a study on some aspect of Palestine in the twentieth century. A renaissance in Palestinian historiography had resulted from the June 1967 war. Many scholars and other researchers were inquiring again about the foundations, origins, evolution, and development of the Arab-Israel and Palestinian Arab-Israel conflicts. I was not averse to doing another political history, but I decided to find something in the socioeconomic-cum-political realm. Then luck struck.

While using incomplete files of the British Mandatory government's chief secretariat, I stumbled across several dusty boxes in the hall outside of the library of the Israel State Archives. After perusing some 250 files, I discovered very interesting data about the cultivation rights of Palestinian Arab tenants. One thing led to another, and, soon thereafter, Paul Alsberg, the Israel state archivist, granted me permission to review a large number of similar dusty boxes that had come into the possession of the Israel State Archives after the June 1967 war.

Apparently, files from former Mandatory subdistrict offices had remained intact, huddled in corners and basements of what later became West Bank administrative centers under the Jordanian regime. These files included records of correspondence, dispatches, reports, and memoranda from the Palestine Land Registration Department, Lands Department, Commissioner of Lands, and Survey Department. Some of these records were carbon copies of dispatches sent by and to the chief secretariat in Jerusalem and ultimately passed to the high commissioner's office. But another portion of these records was never duplicated either for the high commissioner or for the Colonial Office, which oversaw Palestine's affairs for His Majesty's Government. The boxes of documents concerning all aspects of Palestine's land regime and culled by subdistrict officials enticed my interest. Clearly, those charged with reviewing Palestine's land regime wanted to know who owned what so that proper tax evaluations could be made for revenue purposes. Dr. Alsberg concurred that the data in these documents warranted a thorough historical inquiry.

After nine months of work on these two thousand boxes with ten to fifteen files per box, I realized that these files on land matters were perhaps one of the few chronologically complete archives for the Mandate. Many files had been destroyed by violence, including the King David Hotel blast of July 1946; others had been removed intentionally by Great Britain when withdrawing from Palestine in 1948. The accuracy of these files was confirmed by the concomitant use of British Colonial and Foreign Office documentation, Cabinet Papers, Jewish Agency files, Jewish National Fund documents, League of Nations–Mandates Commission Minutes, and the Palestinian Arab press, as well as memoirs, personal papers, unpublished manuscripts, and secondary materials. This wealth of documentation became the source material for the present work.

The first chapter of this book describes Palestine's demographic, social, political, and economic setting from the perspective of landownership, which was a barometer of prestige and authority in Ottoman and early Mandatory times. Land was and is the key focus of Zionist–Arab Palestinian tension and struggle. Without land, there could not have been a Jewish national home. Without land, there appears to be no acceptable means for the expression of Palestinian sovereignty and national identity. But administrative, economic, and social processes already at work in Palestine in the late Ottoman period and the few British changes facilitated Jewish land acquisition during the Mandate.

Chapter 2 focuses on the land question from 1917 to 1929. This was a formative and important period of Jewish territorial growth in Palestine. The methods and processes of land acquisition under British purview were refined and established. Zionists used their consultative prerogative to influence matters in the land regime. How Jews bought land from Arabs and what the motivations of Palestinian and non-Palestinian Arabs were for selling land are partially answered here.

Chapters 3, 4, and 5 focus on the period from 1929 to 1933. In this four-year period, the real possibility of stopping the growth of the Jewish national home emerged. Under the influence of the third high commissioner, Sir John Chancellor, the land question became a central issue in Palestine politics. In this period, the British issued six reports, all of which were concerned with land—the Shaw Report, the Johnson-Crosbie Report, the Hope-Simpson Report, the Strickland Report, and Lewis French's two reports. They all suggested that there was limited cultivable land available in Palestine. After this series of reports, which culminated in the 1930 White Paper, the British threatened to alter, postpone, and truncate the Jewish national home and, consequently, to abrogate the special nature of the Palestine Mandate. Zionist efforts thwarted that intent and the Jewish national home continued to develop. The period is important because it witnessed the first British application of a defensively protective policy toward the Palestinian Arab peasant. Moreover, the combination of changing British policy and the 1929 communal disturbances forced the Jewish Agency and its affiliated institutions to establish priorities that would assure Jewish control of the lands they considered the most strategically and politically important.

While Palestinian Arab despondency grew during the 1930s, Jewish and Zionist commitment to a national homeland was enhanced by their political successes. Most revealing were the means and mechanisms that the Zionists employed in order to manipulate the British bureaucracy. The Zionists exerted enormous influence in drafting local ordinances and policy statements, in lobbying investigatory commissions, and in making politically sensitive appointments. Chapters 4 and 5 particularly analyze the intense Zionist efforts at neutralizing the intent of the Passfield White Paper and disproving Zionist responsibility for Arab landlessness. Zionist bureaucratic victories are described in the context of a deteriorating agricultural economy and continuous Arab land sales to Jews.

The Zionist successes clearly demonstrated that the British government had committed itself to a dual obligation that it fulfilled inconsistently. This dual obligation had been made to both Jews and Arabs, strikingly different groups whose attitudes, patterns of behavior, and customs were worlds apart. Success in purchasing land and in offsetting British claims reinforced Zionist perceptions of the righteous nature of their cause. Conviction and zeal propelled the Zionists. Two national movements proceeded along parallel tracts, but the Zionists acted with a resourcefulness and at a pace unfamiliar to the Arab community.

Chapter 6 describes how Jewish land-purchase methods and geopolitical priorities changed in the period from 1933 to 1939. Though cultivable land was at a premium, the continued economic distress of the Palestinian Arab community allowed Jewish land-acquisition efforts to proceed. In this period, Jews sought to purchase land in Transjordan, Syria, and northern Palestine far from the areas of previous purchases in the coastal and valley regions. By the late 1930s, Zionists were buying land strictly to reinforce geostrategic requirements.

Finally, the concluding chapter summarizes the purpose of the book, which was to ask the question, How did the Zionists purchase the core of a national territory by 1939? Jewish land acquisition was an accumulative process. It began under an imprecise and changing Ottoman administration; it went unimpeded because the Arab population of Palestine was economically impoverished, politically fragmented, and socially atomized; and it received stimulus through the British Mandate, which protected the Zionist minority and the national home concept. From 1917 to 1939 Zionists refined their understanding of the complexities found in Palestine's land regime. The Zionists applied their skills toward obtaining more land. Organizational cooperation and internal cohesion emerged only after ominous British policy and Arab violence threatened the national home's development from 1929 to 1933. As Palestinians sold land, they steadily lost control over their own destiny while Zionists grasped at greater control of their own fate. Palestine was being transformed into a Jewish state. Recognition of that reality came with Great Britain's issuance of the May 1939 White Paper, which sought to stop by then an unalterable process. After 1939, the question really was not if a Jewish state was to come into being; rather, the question was when.

Acknowledgments

Many individuals and institutions have made the research and writing of this book possible, and I am now delighted to thank them all.

I am particularly grateful to Paul Alsberg, the Director of the Israel State Archives, and his attentive staff for their valuable assistance. Dr. Alsberg had the courage and sense of history to let me use materials and documents whose contents were originally unknown to both of us. Special thanks are due to Michael Heymann and his staff at the Central Zionist Archives, to the helpful librarians and archivists at the Public Record Office in London and at Rhodes House and St. Antony's College, Oxford University, and to the interlibrary loan and reference staffs at the Jewish National Library and the Hebrew University Library in Jerusalem, the Harlan Hatcher Library at the University of Michigan, and the Robert W. Woodruff Library at Emory University.

To the many colleagues who sat with me at the archives, who gave encouragement and criticism to the research as it progressed, and who never grew tired of the topic, let me now take the opportunity to thank you for your suggestions, time, and nourishment. While my family and I were resident in Jerusalem, the Adlers, the Carmis, and the Malkas gave unselfishly in order to make our stay more companionable and more meaningful; in Ann Arbor, the Dykstras, the Lassners, the Mirmelsteins, and the Ramsburghs made the winters more bearable and the sports interludes more relaxing; and in Atlanta, the Emory History Department showed a confidence and faith in me that will always be appreciated.

Without the continued financial support of the Near Eastern and North African Studies Center at the University of Michigan, my research would not have been completed. I will always remember the confidence and direction given to me by the center directors, Allin Luther and William D. Schorger. Other funding agencies helped finance this decade of research, including the American Friends of the Hebrew University, the National Foundation for Jewish Culture, Emory University's Summer Research funds, the Andrew S. Mellon Foundation, and the National Endowment for the Humanities. My thanks are extended to them.

I owe special thanks to several people who have contributed to my education. John Joseph of Franklin and Marshall College started me in the proper Middle Eastern direction; M. Yrtle taught me the virtues of maintaining a low profile; Sara and Yehoshua Porath shared their thoughts and home so freely; Andrew S. Ehrenkreutz made me focus on the mechanisms of change in history; the late Ernest Abdul-Massih radiated compassion, wisdom, and understanding; and the late Richard P. Mitchell guided me through graduate school.

I sincerely appreciate the efforts of Patsy Stockbridge, who painstakingly typed the manuscript, and Richard Calabro and Kathy Scott, who prepared the computer tape. Sandra Eisdorfer and Lewis Bateman at the University of North Carolina Press were encouraging, patient, understanding, and very helpful in shaping the manuscript. The unselfish advice of Professors Keddie, Main, Rabinovich, Rosenbaum, and Shaked is warmly acknowledged. John Palms, Alan Shaw, and Jerry Wright gave needed support. My thanks also go to Karen Wysocki, who prepared the maps, and Ron Maner, who compiled the index.

To my parents, I hope the wait has not been in vain. To J. N., Raymond, Mae, and Pappy, thank you for being supportive. To Jason and Todd, thanks for being patient and letting me correct that extra footnote or phrase before catching a baseball or throwing a football. We all thank Andrew in advance. To my dear wife Ellen, thank you for enduring my nocturnal restlessness and the very frequent early morning mania.

Note on Translation
and Transliteration

Most of the archival information found at the Central
Zionist Archives in Jerusalem is in Arabic, French, German, and Hebrew. In the bibliography, English-title equivalents are given for the reports and memoranda that were found in the Jewish Agency's Political
Department files housed at the Central Zionist Archives. The sensitive
nature of the topic made heavy footnoting necessary so that the reader
may confirm details from the original sources.

Transliteration of Arabic and Hebrew personal names and place-
names was made using the Government of Palestine's *Transliteration and
Transliterated Lists of Personal and Geographical Names for Use in
Palestine* (Jerusalem, 1931). Where Arabic and Hebrew names and
words require indication of the guttural, the *ayn* (') is used in the Arabic,
as in 'Abdullah and Isma'il, and in the Hebrew, as in Ya'acov and
'Aravit. The Arabic *hamza* is noted with an apostrophe ('), as in Ra'is.
Where appropriate, Arabic rather than Turkish spellings of terms, institutions, and administrative units are used. For commonly used words
such as fellah, *hamula*, and *multazim*, the term that corresponds most
closely to the popular pronunciation is used rather than a transliteration
that is faithful to the script.

Linear Measures and Currency

MEASURES		
	1 Turkish dunam	= 919.3 square meters
	1 metric dunam	= 1,000 square meters or ¼ acre
	1 square mile	= 640 acres or 2,560 metric dunams
	1 feddan	= varying between 100 and 250 metric dunams
	1 kilometer	= 0.62 mile

CURRENCY		
	1 Palestine pound (£P) (1927)	= 1 English pound (£)
		= 1,000 Palestine mils
		= 97½ Egyptian piastres
		= 1 Egyptian pound (£E)
		= 975 Egyptian mils
		= 5 American dollars
	1 French franc (1918)	= 40 Palestine mils

The Land Question
in Palestine, 1917–1939

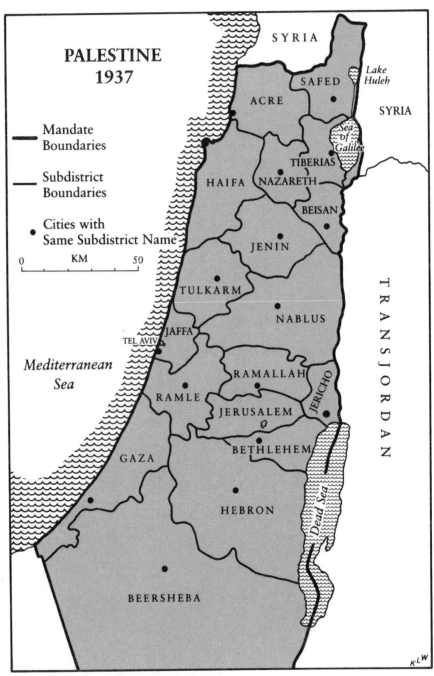

PALESTINE
1937

Mandate
Boundaries

Subdistrict
Boundaries

Cities with
Same Subdistrict Name

0   KM   50

SYRIA

Lake
Huleh

SAFED

ACRE

SYRIA

Sea
of
Galilee

TIBERIAS

HAIFA   NAZARETH

BEISAN

JENIN

TULKARM

NABLUS

JAFFA

TEL AVIV

Mediterranean
Sea

RAMALLAH

JERICHO

RAMLE

JERUSALEM

BETHLEHEM

GAZA

HEBRON

Dead Sea

T R A N S J O R D A N

BEERSHEBA

KLW

1. Palestine's Administrative Boundaries, 1937

Chapter 1

The Land Regime in Late Ottoman and Mandatory Palestine

Introduction

Palestine in the nineteenth and early twentieth centuries was a predominantly agricultural region. Man-made impositions and natural impediments restrained Palestine's economic growth. Rapacious tax demands, the malfeasance of local Ottoman officials, and traditional methods of land utilization discouraged agricultural development. The decline in plow and grazing animals, the dearth of investment capital, and World War I's disruption of foreign and domestic agricultural markets, all exacerbated by the retreating Turkish armies, left Palestine's agricultural economy devastated by 1918.[1]

The strength of Palestine's economy was limited by the land areas capable of cultivation. The land in the Palestine region, like other areas of the Fertile Crescent, was under heavy agricultural use for millennia. Soil quality declined because of salination of water tables, deforestation, predatory raids, and a wide variety of other factors. Though the total land area of Palestine was estimated at 26.3 million dunams,[2] less than a third of it was considered cultivable (see Table 1). The remainder was dotted by intermittent mountain ranges, sand dunes, bleak terrain, alkaline soils, semiarable regions, obstructed water courses, and marshlands. Palestine's topographical features and poor soil contributed to paltry crop yields on which its rural population barely subsisted. In a society in which control or ownership of land was the chief source of relatively stable wealth and position, control of this limited amount of fertile and cultivable land also became the essential criterion for prestige and influence. One's relationship to land reflected one's political, economic, and social weaknesses and strengths.

In the emerging effort to establish a Jewish national home, the area of Jewish land acquisition focused almost exclusively on the cultivable plain and valley regions of Palestine. Thus, in the quest to establish a territorial nucleus for a state, the Zionists sought to purchase a substantial portion of these regions totaling about 9 million dunams of land. By 1948, at the end of the British Mandate in Palestine, Jews had ac-

TABLE 1

Total Cultivable Land Area (in Metric Dunams) of Palestine in 1931

Region	Cultivable Area	Total Area	Percentage Cultivable
Hills of Galilee	1,054,000	2,083,300	51
Acre plain	203,300	315,900	64
Plain of Esdraelon	302,800	351,100	86
Jezreel Valley	636,000	648,000	98
Huleh basin	173,500	261,600	66
Jordan Valley	255,700	681,200	37
Coastal plain	2,302,600	2,928,300	79
Hills of Judea and Samaria	2,165,000	6,005,300	36
Wilderness of Judea	—	1,050,900	0
Beersheba subdistrict	1,160,000	12,300,000	9
Total	8,252,900	26,625,600	33

Source: The statistics for Table 1 were gathered by Maurice Bennett, who was seconded to Sir John Hope-Simpson's staff in 1930. As commissioner for land and surveys, Bennett sent these statistics to the Jewish Agency in 1936. See his dispatch of 9 October 1936, Central Zionist Archives, S25/6562.

quired approximately 2 million dunams of land, mostly in the valley and coastal areas.

In 1918, the economic outlook for Palestine's rural Arab population, estimated at 440,000,[3] was very uncertain. The cultivated land was not very fertile or sufficiently irrigated. The failure or inability to use modern agricultural techniques such as manuring and mechanization kept yields to a minimum.[4] Crop rotation was rarely practiced. A severe shortage of livestock had resulted from a prewar epidemic and Turkish requisitioning of camels and sheep from 1914 to 1917. Conscription had depleted the agricultural labor supply. The massive destruction of olive trees by the retreating Turkish forces compounded the agricultural population's woes. Uncertain validity or absence of land titles hindered the granting of loans, particularly in the administrative turmoil created by World War I. Historically, during periods of economic and physical insecurity, the Palestinian agricultural laborers, or *fellaheen* (*fellah*, sing.), migrated from the coastal or maritime plain to the central range of hills running from the Galilee in the north through Hebron in the south.[5] Jewish immigration and land purchase occurred at a time when the cultivated regions suffered a measure of depopulation resulting from economic hardships, conscription, and local instability.

In 1918, the nature of Palestine's land regime derived from Ottoman inheritance. Most patterns of behavior and social norms within the Arab community transcended the shift from Ottoman to British administration, and it was attended by very little change in the political, economic, and social status quo of the Arab community living in Palestine. No new elites emerged. The loose and unexacting authority of the Ottoman central government had slowly enabled local administrators, merchants, religious leaders, and others to control the administrative structures in "Greater Syria" and therefore in Palestine as well. Arab politics in Ottoman and early Mandatory Palestine relied upon kinship, close family ties, village identity, and personal connections.

What changed, however, with the advent of British administration was the institution of a more efficient and watchful administrative structure, which had an ultimate impact upon the evolution of the Arab community of Palestine. British control over the land regime deprived large landowning families of their customarily unchecked means to financial advancement. British administration blocked individuals who had previously accumulated land during the Ottoman regime through privilege, access to information, and informal political structures. Tax collection and land registration under official British purview denied this segment of the notable class their uncircumscribed means of acquiring more land. The severely damaged agricultural sector and diminished yields had resulted in a decrease in rental incomes and therefore less capital accumulation. No longer able to use the Ottoman modalities of operations, numerous Arabs in Palestine chose to sell land to individual Jews and immigrant Zionists as a convenient alternative for ready cash.

But only gradually did the British presence and administration in Palestine alter the fabric and relationships within Arab society and contribute to increased Jewish presence. Change came slowly in the early 1920s for several reasons. First, the habits inherited from the Ottoman land regime were deeply entrenched in custom and tradition. The fellaheen population had shown a clear aversion to government association because of an abusive and unchecked taxation system. Fellaheen distrust of government was compounded by the fear of conscription. These fears were carried over into the Mandate by an overwhelmingly illiterate and unsophisticated peasantry that had no interest in political involvement, was not cognizant of its legal rights, and did not have any promise of financial betterment. At the other end of the Arab social spectrum, there were relatively few large landowners from whom the early Jewish immigrants bought land. According to the *Census for Palestine, 1931*, out of the total Muslim earning population, only 5 percent was engaged in intensive agriculture and only 4 percent derived its livelihood from the

TABLE 2

Occupations of Religious Groups in Palestine in 1931 (in Percentages)

Occupations

Religious Groups	Agriculture	Industry	Commerce	Transport	Professions
Muslims	90.0	46.0	59.0	69.0	29.0
Jews	5.0	37.0	30.0	19.0	49.0
Christians	3.5	16.5	11.0	12.0	22.0
Others	1.5	.5	—	—	—
	100.0%	100.0%	100.0%	100.0%	100.0%

Occupation by Professions

Religious Groups	Law	Medicine	Literature, Sciences, and Arts	Instruction (Teaching)	Public Administration	Total Population
Muslims	45	17	28	22	37	75
Christians	13	20	8	56	27	8
Jews	42	63	64	22	36	17
	100%	100%	100%	100%	100%	100%

Source: These statistics have been culled from various portions of the *Census for Palestine, 1931*, because it was the most complete data assembled during the Mandate.

rents of leased agricultural lands.[6] Table 2 provides additional information about the relationship between occupation and religious affiliation in Palestine for 1931.

Second, the Zionist community in Palestine, though buoyed by the Balfour Declaration of November 1917 and the prospects of a Jewish national home, was only in the incipient stages of organizational development. Resources were scarce and Jews constituted only 10 percent of the total population of Palestine. Though the Jewish community received through the articles of the British Mandate special consultative privileges not enjoyed by the Arab community, its relationship with the British required definition and refinement.

The establishment of a Jewish national home was part of the context within which His Majesty's Government (HMG) was attempting to protect its strategic interests in the Middle East. Maintaining its presence in Egypt, assuring access to the Suez Canal and the East, preventing French ambitions in Lebanon and Syria from drifting south, and creating a land bridge from the Mediterranean Sea to the oil fields of Iraq all entered HMG's calculus. But in securing and controlling Palestine, HMG demonstrated little understanding of the Zionist commitment to create a Jewish national home or of the Arab community's economic plight. This lack of understanding contributed directly to a hastening of communal separation, physical violence, the idea of creating separate Arab and Jewish states in 1937 and 1947, and the creation of Israel in 1948.

Elite Continuity

Up to 1839, Ottoman administration in Palestine had concentrated on the preservation of Ottoman supremacy, revenue collection, and security for the *hajj*, or pilgrimage to Mecca. The gradual decline of the central government's power, accompanied by the development of autonomous authority in the provinces, forced the Ottoman administration to reform its provincial administration. The *tanzimat*, introduced to spark state building in the Ottoman Empire, involved a variety of reform efforts including the assurance of revenue collection and its successful remittance to Istanbul. Stability in any region of Palestine meant establishing an atmosphere that would encourage continuous cultivation of land and effective collection of taxes. In the past, local officials had siphoned off tax revenue before it reached Istanbul.[7] Specifically, abuses in the tax-leasing system had to be removed from the revenue assessment and collection process.

Prior to the promulgation of the *Hatti Sherif* of Gulhane in November 1839, which outlawed tax farming, the long-term office of the *wali*, or regional administrator, permitted the incumbent virtually unchecked accumulation of power and wealth through tax collection. However, in the rural areas of Palestine, particularly in the hill regions, *shaykhs*, who were village or tribal chiefs and influential heads of families, continued to control local administration. This local elite exercised control in a feudal and somewhat despotic manner. In the Carmel mountain range near present-day Haifa and in the environs of Jenin and Nablus, individuals and particular families had achieved local jurisdiction over particular villages or land areas through economic and political dominance. In the late nineteenth and early twentieth centuries, families locally prominent particularly in the *sanjaqs*, or districts, of Nablus and Acre, solidified their accumulated local authority by serving in bureaucratic positions of municipal and regional administrations.[8] The administrative units of Ottoman Palestine are shown in Table 3.

The leadership of the Palestine Arab community during the early years

TABLE 3
Administrative Units in Palestine Prior to World War I

Administrative Units		
Regional	District	Local
Wilayet (Wali)	Sanjaq (Mutsarrif)	Qaza (Qaimmaqam)
Beirut, Jerusalem	Acre, Nablus, Jerusalem	Acre, Haifa, Nazareth, Safed, Tiberias, Jenin, Nablus, Tulkarm, Beersheba, Gaza, Hebron, Jaffa, Jerusalem

Source: Royal Institute of International Affairs, *Great Britain and Palestine, 1915–1945: Information Paper no. 20*, p. 178.

of the Mandate came from this landed elite or were tied directly to them through familial and social bonds of mutual self-interest. A close review of administrative positions previously held under the Ottoman regime for the *sanjaqs* of Acre and Nablus indicates continuity of these families in politics during the first fourteen years of the Mandate. From the nine subdistricts including Acre, Haifa, Tiberias, Beisan, Safed, Nazareth, Jenin, Tulkarm, and Nablus, forty-one different individuals were elected regional representatives to the Arab Executive at the Third, Fourth, Fifth, Sixth, and Seventh Palestinian congresses. Of these, twenty-six representatives either had served in Ottoman *qaza* (local jurisdictions), were *sanjaq* administrators, or were immediate relations to these administrators.[9]

In order to counter the autonomy of regional officials and rural tax collectors, the Wilayet Law of 1864 redefined the role of the local administrative councils. But instead of eradicating abuses in tax collection, the duties and composition of the established *majlis idara*, or district administrative councils, merely perpetuated them. To participate in these local councils a candidate had to pay a yearly direct tax of at least 500 piastres. This restriction limited participation to those who had previously owned or worked land and who were not fearful of contact with the central government. The Ottoman Electoral Law of 1876 solidified political control in the hands of taxpayers and particularly those who sat on the *majlis idara*. As a result of the tax qualification, the majority of the rural population had no voice in the management of their own affairs in Palestine during the late Ottoman period.[10]

By the Wilayet Law of 1864, the *majlis idara* was vested with local

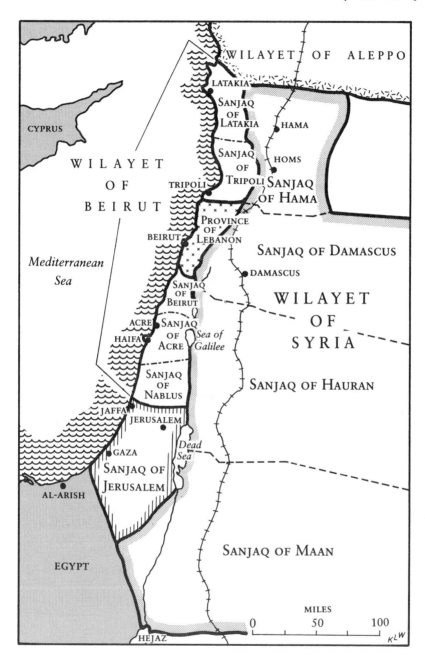

2. Syria and Palestine, 1915

authority over land and land taxation. With the institution of the Ottoman Land Code of 1858 and subsequent registration of land, members of the local *majlis idara* authorized the assessment and collection of taxes, approved land registration, decided questions of landownership, and expressed influential opinions about the ultimate fate of lands that reverted to the state. Each local *majlis idara* was to have a *mufti* and a *qadi* (Muslim religious and judicial officials) in addition to the four government-appointed officials, four nongovernment-elected officials, and four representatives of the non-Muslim religious communities. But, in fact, the non-Muslim communities were underrepresented while Muslim religious leaders and landowners were represented in much greater proportion to their population, thus reinforcing their political position and furthering their private interests.[11]

In addition to the *majlis idara*, there were other commissions, boards, councils, and committees at the *qaza* level which gave their members considerable prestige and access to control of local politics through land accumulation. Membership of governmental units at the *qaza* level at least in 1893, 1900, and 1908 suggests that certain local families dominated varying facets of local administrative activity. In the *sanjaqs* of Acre and Nablus the local administrative elites tended to remain constant. The administrative offices included positions for civil servants on the municipal councils, tax or finance commissions, courts of the first instance, agricultural and commercial committees, chambers of commerce, education committees, land registries, and the commissions for procurement of military transportation. Other civil servants had positions with the revenue commissions, the monopoly offices, the telegraph and postal services, and the local police; others were quarantine officers and the secretaries and recorders for all of the above commissions, boards, councils, and committees.[12]

Continuity of local authority rested with this small elite who staffed local administrative bodies, although there was some mobility within this elite. During certain periods, some of the families dominated; at other times, different families were influential. Basically, however, the membership pool of these elites did not change. The fellaheen barely subsisted and had little, if any, opportunity to be upwardly mobile. The abuses in land registration and in tax assessment and collection spawned and maintained the dominance of the few families.

Land Classification

In order to assume full control of state lands and to check the growth of large private-land ownership, the Ottoman regime promulgated the Land Law of 1858. Yet, over the next sixty years, private-land ownership increased and the attempt to estimate accurately the amount of the state-owned land, at least in Ottoman Palestine, was not achieved.[13] The objectives of the Land Law were not realized because there were insufficient numbers of trained officials to oversee and enforce the law. Simultaneously, local government administration predominated in the absence of a strong central authority. Moreover, the economic pressures on the fellaheen, coupled with their traditional unwillingness to associate with a government that taxed and conscripted them, made registration and certainly accurate registration of land very difficult.

The Land Law enumerated six classes of land: *mulk, miri, waqf, mawat, mahlul,* and *matruka. Mulk* lands were those held in complete freehold and exempt from the tithe. The owner of *mulk* land could dispose of his land as he saw fit, through sale, mortgage, and bequeathal. In Palestine most of the *mulk* land was confined to urban sites, mostly buildings and gardens. It constituted a negligible fraction of the agricultural land in Palestine. In the immediate vicinity of Jaffa, a certain number of orange groves were on *mulk* land, but most of the agricultural land was of the *miri* category.[14]

The owner of *miri* land did not hold the land by title deed but rather by usufruct, which gave him the legal right to the land and to the profits from it. He could not mortgage or sell it without the consent of the state, which was obtained from the Land Office. Even though such consent was usually routine, the aversion to associate with the government spawned unofficial land transfers and influenced those seeking loans to go to moneylenders rather than to the official agricultural bank. But the Ottoman government sought administrative control of *miri* land in order to assure the productive nature of the land, which provided the central government with tax revenue. Prior to 1913, *miri* land could not be used for brickmaking, planting vineyards, orchards, building houses, or for creating enclosures without the consent of the Ottoman government. Such restrictions were intended to keep the largest amount of land available for agricultural production. In fact, these restrictions hampered the intensification of agricultural holdings. In 1913, the Provisional Law of Immovable Property conferred on the holder of *miri* land the right to use the land for any purpose, though still requiring the owner to register any improvement with the government. When *miri* land remained uncultivated for three consecutive years without lawful excuse, such as absence of the holder because of military service, the land reverted back to the state. Similarly, if an owner of *miri* land died without heirs, it also reverted to the state, so that it could be sold at public auction and again be made tax productive.[15] For fear that the fellaheen population would become landless because of its poor economic status at the conclusion of World War I, the Palestine administration did not enforce the provision for reversion of land to the state.[16]

Ottoman state land comprised 4 percent of the total land area of Palestine north of Beersheba. Throughout the course of the Mandate a considerable portion of state lands were slowly alienated into private ownership. Vast areas of vacant land were sold outright to private interests for speculative purposes. Extensive areas of state land suffered from uncontrolled grazing and woodcutting. State lands were often systematically denuded of their natural vegetation and subjected to soil erosion.

In 1930, the total amount of state land (exclusive of land south of Beersheba) amounted to 959,000 dunams of the 26,325,600 dunams in Palestine. Approximately 70 percent of this state land was leased to Arab cultivators.[17] In January 1930, the director of lands noted that all government land capable of cultivation without additional heavy-capital expenditure was under cultivation.[18] In 1936, the area worked by Arab cultivators on state land was reduced to 532,397 dunams. Jews cultivated 175,545 state-land dunams.[19] The reduction of cultivated state land, though still under lease to Arabs, was due to a worsening economic situation that made continued involvement in agricultural pursuits more tenuous. For example, lease-tenancy privileges and cultivation rights to state land in the Beisan area gradually found their way into Jewish possession in this period, further reducing the area of state land cultivated by Arabs.

There were two kinds of *waqf* land in Palestine: true (*waqf sahih*) and untrue (*waqf ghar sahih*). True *waqf* lands were those that were endowed on *mulk* lands to some religious or charitable purpose or to a family trust. With small amounts of *mulk* lands in Palestine, the amount of true agricultural *waqf* lands was also small, restricted instead mostly to houses, shops, and religious areas. *Waqf sahih* land in Palestine approximated 80,000 to 100,000 dunams. *Waqf ghar sahih*, constituted from *miri* land and allotted by special act and with the dedication or permission of the sultan, approximated 600,000 to 1,000,000 dunams in Palestine.[20] During Ottoman times some *waqf* lands were purchased by Jews.[21] *Waqf* properties during the Mandate were administered by the Supreme Muslim Council.[22]

Mawat lands were those comprising unoccupied, hilly, scrub woodland and grazing grounds not held by title deed. Prior to the Mawat Land Ordinance of 1921, persons who assumed possession and cultivated these previously vacant lands could gain title upon payment of the unimproved value of the land. Under the Ottoman regime many Arab cultivators benefited by the provisions regarding this class of land. The sites of many towns and villages were extended and enlarged, giving an active farmer the means to increase his holdings. Because the Palestine administration had little knowledge of which lands belonged to the state and because it wished to retain full control of the state lands, the Mawat Land Ordinance was passed. It was considered an offense to break up or cultivate these wastelands, and no title deed was issued for such lands. By the early 1930s, this ordinance curtailed prior rights of customary and sometimes indiscriminate cultivation for those cultivators who had used *mawat* lands previously but had not registered them. Trespass was a perennial problem in agriculturally predominant Palestine, and boundaries between land areas were not properly defined. In an effort to delimit boundaries between privately held and state-owned land, the Mawat Land Ordinance was kept in force. In 1921, *mawat* lands were estimated at between 50 and 60 percent of the total area of all of Palestine, with much of this wasteland in the south and southeast and comprising the sand dunes along the coast.[23]

Mahlul lands were *miri* lands that were left uncultivated because of persistent neglect or absence of heirs. When left uncultivated for three years, these lands escheated to the state. If the previous possessor paid the unimproved value of the land, as on *mawat* lands prior to 1921, he could redeem possession of the land. When the escheat was not redeemed, other neighbors or individuals could claim the right to the land upon payment of the unimproved value. On 1 October 1920, the Mahlul Land Ordinance was issued in anticipation of the cadastral land survey. This ordinance required both the village authorities and the parties concerned to report the illegal occupation of all such land within three months. Since the cadastral survey was not conducted, all the abandoned and illegally occupied state land defined under *mahlul* was not discovered. The Land Settlement Commission, which investigated and made recommendations regarding the land situation in Palestine in 1920 and 1921, estimated that *mahlul* lands were approximately 87,233 Turkish dunams of which 85,193 were considered cultivable.[24]

Zionists at the Paris Peace Conference hoped that vacated *mahlul* land would come immediately into Jewish ownership. Ultimately, Zionists were disappointed that the provisions of the Mawat Land Ordinance and the Mahlul Land Ordinance were applied only sporadically, and usually not to large landowners who left parts of their land uncultivated.[25]

Matruka lands were those left for general public use such as highways and those lands assigned to the use of a community for a particular purpose. Lands of the latter type were communal pastures, woodlands, village threshing floors, and places of worship. The ownership of these lands rested solely with the state, which did not allow transfer of ownership. No encroachment by another community was allowed on *matruka* lands nor was it legal for members of a particular community to plow or cultivate *matruka* land. No reliable estimate for the amount of *matruka* lands in Palestine exists, and possibly the *matruka* category did not exist in Palestine.[26]

Two other classifications of landownership and tenure were known in Palestine: *mudawara*, or *jiftlik* lands, and *musha'*. *Mudawara* lands were originally those held in private possession and then turned over to the possession of Sultan Abdul Hamid. The largest area of *mudawara* lands in Palestine was in the Beisan area. The tenants there had their cultivation rights reaffirmed by the Palestine administration under the *Ghor Mudawara*, or Beisan Agreement, of November 1921. Other *jiftlik* lands in Palestine included 75,000 dunams in the environs of Jericho. Absolute ownership of *mudawara* lands was vested in the state. Under the Ottoman regime tenants on government lands were not liable to eviction as were tenants on *miri* or *mulk* lands. But later in 1933 cultivators were prevented from acquiring tenancy privileges on a holding in which the Palestine government was the landlord.[27]

The *musha'* land system had at its core collective village ownership or collective tenure of a land area, with each qualified participant in a village or other designated area entitled to shares, generally not parcels, in a particular land area. On a periodic basis of usually one, two, or five years, shares were redistributed allowing each qualified shareholder the opportunity to use the more fertile and arable lands which corresponded to particular shares within a collective unit. The *musha'* land system evolved from tribal organization in which there were common grazing rights over a certain territory. When the tribe settled down, agricultural land was communally owned and worked.[28] The *musha'* system was maintained to prevent land alienation to strangers and to foster village cooperation. Yet these goals proved illusory, as *musha'* land was sold to nonresidents. When the *musha'* shareholder in Palestine dealt directly with the tax farmer or creditor and not through his village, the shareholder's financial condition became less tenable, as did his ability to retain his area in the village lands.[29]

The most harmful aspect of the *musha'* system was its process of periodic redistribution. Most fellaheen lacked interest in improving their temporarily held land when the fruits of the improvement would be taken from them. As a result, manuring, weeding, terracing, or crop alternation was rarely employed, and the already nutrient-deficient soil was further depleted. In 1933, High Commissioner Arthur Wauchope estimated that there were between 4 and 5 million dunams of *musha'*-held land, mostly in the plains and valley regions.[30] Even though fellaheen all over Palestine in 1921 favored dividing the *musha'* shares into individually owned parcels, the partition of *musha'* shares, or *ifraz*, did not occur. Local notables and landowners who were most often entitled to large percentages of village-owned shares were unwilling to give up the local economic and political leverage that they maintained over a *musha'* community. When *musha'* shareholders fell into debt, they often remitted their shares as debt payment and remained as tenants on the land they once owned collectively. By 1923, nearly 75 percent of *musha'* lands were owned not by fellaheen but by individuals who lived in towns.[31] Somewhere between 2.6 million to 3.3 million dunams of *musha'* land were owned by landowners resident outside of the village community. High Commissioner John Chancellor described the process of *musha'* share alienation as follows: "The fellaheen vendors were in many cases in debt to money lenders for money borrowed at usurious rates of interest. When pressed by their creditors they sold their (*musha'*) share in village land in order that they might discharge their liabilities . . . [and] the Arab cultivators were usually allowed to remain in occupation on the lands as tenants."[32] Out of a desire not to pique the Arab landed elite with whom the British had informal but essential political contacts, compulsory partition of *musha'* shares was not implemented during the Mandate.[33] During the process of land settlement, however, when HMG undertook the triangulation and survey of land in Palestine, some *musha'*-held shares were consolidated. But the impression had to be avoided that any overt legal instigation of *ifraz* could be construed as an intentional British effort to make blocks of land available to Jewish purchasers.

Those who held *musha'* shares found it extremely difficult to obtain a mortgage on their land since there was rarely a title deed that could be offered as collateral. Often, even if the land were registered, a nominee or nominees held it in the name of the entire village. *Musha'* shares that devolved through inheritance forced a fixed amount of land area to be divided among a geometrically increasing number of heirs. Typical of this was the *musha'* village of Zeita in the Tulkarm subdistrict. There, twenty-three persons were registered as co-owners in 1871. During the process of litigation for ownership, in April 1923 the District Court of Samaria found that there were in fact 906 claims to ownership.[34] The sheer diminution of parcel size in *musha'* and non-*musha'* areas through inheritance further reduced existing economic potential. The *musha'* land system was described by every major authority on land in Palestine as the most debilitating factor affecting the economic betterment of the Palestinian fellaheen.[35]

The Tithe

In combination with the land regime, the tithe and the tax-collection systems were extremely deleterious to the economic well-being of the agricultural population in the Ottoman Empire after 1839. In 1913, almost 90 percent of the state's direct income came from agriculture; more than half of this resulted from the tithe.

In Palestine, the methods of tithe assessment and collection varied, depending upon the power of local officials and the cunning of the local fellaheen population. The entire tithe system in Palestine was open to wide abuse and fraud. At each bureaucratic level, a government official was able to skim an amount off the top for personal needs.[36] When tax-collection responsibility was contracted to the highest bidder—a local official, *shaykh*, speculator, moneylender, or *mukhtar*—the fellaheen invariably had to deal with the tax collector, the creditor, or an intermediary directly. This the fellaheen dreaded. In the coastal plain and in the valley regions of Palestine such as Gaza, Ramle, and the Jericho Valley, taxing privileges remained in the hands of a few families. In the mountainous regions around Hebron and Jerusalem, villagers sometimes collected the tax themselves. In areas close to the city, where the produce could be easily watched and assessed, a collector under fixed salary would collect the tax with the profit accruing to the state and not to a tax farmer. In the Gaza area, the fellah rarely had recourse for his complaints, though in the mountainous regions the peasants sometimes did challenge unjust taxation.[37]

Until the early 1880s, the tithe was 10 percent of the gross produce; thereafter taxes totaling 2.63 percent were added. The additional payment was used primarily for providing capital to make agricultural loans. Loans ceased during World War I. Loan registers were destroyed and funds were either appropriated by the retreating Turks or seized by the army as booty.[38]

Little incentive existed to produce large quantities of a crop. The tithe was assessed on a fixed basis of the gross yield of the harvest, so the more one produced, the more one was taxed. Until 1935, the tithe weighed more heavily upon poor-quality land. Fallow land went untaxed during the Mandate. As property values rose because of the Jewish demand for land, it became more profitable for landowners to deny tenants use of land areas and then sell the land to an interested buyer. Moreover, nontenanted land during the Mandate relieved landowners of the financial burden of paying compensatory obligations to tenants.

At the time of tax estimation, when the grain was in sheaves, the assessor could only guess the yield and its worth. He could, therefore, deliberately increase or decrease the valuation depending upon his own interests. Sometimes the harvested crop had to be moved to a central village to be estimated, which might take it far from its local markets. Often the tax collector would not arrive until at least several days after the harvest was threshed and winnowed, forcing the fellah to leave his harvest exposed to the attack of birds, insects, rats, and other vermin as well as to the depredation of thieves and the damage of occasional showers. Sometimes there was a delay in moving produce to market early in a season, preventing fellaheen from obtaining the best possible prices for their yield. In general, if a peasant paid a tithe on only 30 percent of the crop yield, he considered himself fortunate.[39]

While it was the purpose of the Wilayet Law of 1864 to circumscribe local authority, the *mukhtars*, who were established as the government's representatives in the villages, continued to enjoy varying degrees of local autonomy. *Mukhtars* were elected theoretically, but in practice they were chosen sometimes by the governor or subdistrict (*majlis*) officers. The *mukhtar* was entitled to receive 2.5 percent of the tithe when he collected the tithe and the land tax. Hence, the larger the amount the *mukhtar* assessed, the larger was his own share. The *mukhtar* enhanced his authority after land registration was introduced into Palestine in 1871. Until 1934 local legal authority regarding ownership, dispositions, and registrations of lands was vested in the *mukhtar*. Often he would not report transactions that he carried on outside of the Department of Land Registry office.[40] During the Ottoman regime, the *mukhtar* augmented his power over many fellaheen because he enjoyed the right to register them on military conscription rolls. Agreements in which the local notable was bribed were common. Arrangements were sometimes made between the local *shaykh*, the *mukhtar*, and the moneylender to the long-term detriment of the fellaheen. Oliphant describes one such ruse in which the moneylender is addressing the *mukhtar* or *shaykh*: "You and your village are unable to meet the government demands; if you will persuade your village to borrow from me at fifty percent, I will give you so much commission, and if at the end of three years you can manage irretrievably to ruin your village so that I can come down upon them and obtain possession of the village in satisfaction of my debt for half of its value, your profit shall be so much, and you shall retain such a share of the village lands."[41]

The process of arbitrary tax assessment and the abuses related to it continued during the early years of the British Mandate in Palestine as well. Many fellaheen hid their crops, causing a considerable loss of tithe revenue to the administration. In an effort to eradicate this abuse, the Palestine administration passed the Tithe Law Amendment Ordinance in 1922, which imposed penalties for concealing crops; this abuse, nevertheless, continued. In 1922, the Palestine director of agriculture reported, "As a result [of taxation], the average fellah's margin of profit is being reduced almost to a vanishing point, and . . . in cases where a cultivator is not the owner of the land this point has been reached."[42]

During the early years of the Mandate, *mukhtars* continued to collect the tithe, but they did not always ascertain whether the person who paid the tax was the actual landowner or cultivator. A tenant would often use an agricultural laborer to pay the tax for him; then the laborer's name would appear on the tax-registry rolls.[43] When tax-payment records were later used to determine the legal status of an agricultural tenant, they were found to be inaccurate.

In order to make the tithe more equitable, the Palestine administration in 1927 based the tithe on the average yield for the previous four years. Syria and Lebanon instituted similar tithe reform in 1929.[44] However, in Palestine, during the period 1930 to 1935, a large portion of the tithe had to be refunded because the average yield was based on the period from 1925 to 1929 when production was much higher. In the agriculturally poor years that followed, the amount of the computed tithe remained the same, thereby not relieving the fellaheen's obligation to the administration. After the implementation of the Commutation of Tithe Ordinance in 1927, the collection of the tithe became impossible because of family feuds in areas around Nablus, Jenin, and Tulkarm. In the Huleh plain, there was difficulty collecting it from reputed owners who lived in Syria. Some villagers very easily moved crops around to areas where the commuted tithe did not apply. Such evasions disappeared gradually. By 1929, all Palestine was subject to the new arithmetic of tithe payment, except the Bedouin of Beersheba. By 1931, the fellaheen population began to experience the serious adverse effects of the tithe payment. The continued indebtedness of the fellaheen caused villagers in the Northern District to believe that even if the Palestine administration had no desire to injure them, it certainly took no interest in helping them.[45] Finally, in June 1935, after a long investigation into the structure of the tithe and tax system, the administration promulgated the Rural Property Tax Ordinance, which replaced both the Ottoman House and Land Tax and the Commutation of Tithe Ordinance instituted by the British administration in 1927. Land was now classified in sixteen groups with the property tax calculated according to soil category. Citrus land was taxed the most. The last three groups were exempt from payment so as to relieve the sagging economic condition of the poorer fellaheen. Villagers who had been accustomed to incessant taxation by the Ottomans grew suspicious of the administration's intent when they were not required to pay any tax. Some believed a policy of no tax payment was a prelude to government confiscation of their lands. So prevalent was this perception among fellaheen that an amendment to the

Rural Property Tax Ordinance was immediately passed to allay that apprehension.[46]

Fellaheen debt was not a phenomenon of recent origin. For at least three-quarters of a century prior to the British civil administration, the fellaheen had borrowed for seeds, new plows, fresh horses, donkeys, mules, oxen for plowing, and repayment of other debts, taxes, or private loans. Local landowners, moneylenders, and merchants charged anywhere from 10 percent to 50 percent per annum interest.[47] Moneylenders often made loans based on a certain percentage of a future crop as collateral. When time came for payment, the moneylenders would appear at the threshing floor during harvest to make sure the fellaheen did not hide a portion of the yield as they tried to do when the tax collector came. Usually the fellah was unable to repay the loan; sometimes he took out a larger new loan. Creditors of the indebted fellah found it easy to acquire the debtor's land as compensation for the outstanding loan.[48] The turmoil in Palestine caused by World War I compounded the fellaheen's economic insolvency.

Until the Anglo-Egyptian Bank ceased granting agricultural loans to Palestinian fellaheen in 1923, a large number of the loans were used to pay off moneylenders. Just prior to this time of generally high agricultural prices, merchants extended credits to small owners of land. By 1930–31, prices of agricultural produce had fallen, making it practically impossible for the small owner to make the payments due on his loans taken out seven and eight years earlier. For some, the only means of removing their outstanding debt was through the sale of their small parcels of land.[49] Several consecutively poor agricultural years in the late 1920s and early 1930s heightened the fellaheen's economic hardship.

The Palestine fellah had a lifelong personal and ancestral attachment to his land and was philosophically opposed to selling it. But oppressive taxes, enormous debt, inefficient land usage, and climatic vicissitudes were the burdensome pressures that forced the fellah to relinquish his independence as an owner. An independent owner-occupier sometimes became a tenant and then, in some cases, an agricultural laborer. This process, which had its recorded beginnings in the nineteenth century, did not cease with the inception of the Mandate. As claims submitted to the Palestine administration by individuals seeking legal-tenancy status under the Protection of Cultivators Ordinance of 1933 (POCO) indicate, the one-time owner-occupiers often became agricultural laborers.[50] The *Census for Palestine, 1931* included the observation that "indebtedness to the money-lender may quickly reduce the ordinary cultivator to the status of agricultural laborer."[51] According to that census report, 465,-000 earners and dependents, or two-thirds of the Muslim Arab population of Palestine, were dependent for their livelihood upon ordinary cultivation and pasturing of flocks. Of these 115,913 earners, 50,552 were owner-occupiers, 29,077 were agricultural laborers, 12,638 were agricultural tenants, 7,889 raised, bred, and herded flocks, 7,530 were growers and pickers of fruits, flowers, and vegetables, 2,000 were orange growers, 43 were agents-managers of estates and rent collectors, and the remainder hunted, fished, and raised small animals.[52] More than 25 percent of this Muslim agricultural population earned less than a subsistence income.[53]

Profound social and economic changes occurred in Palestinian society as a result of small landowners' defaulting on their lands or selling them. A large tenant and agricultural laboring class and a small landowning class with large holdings evolved over a lengthy period of time. Where owner-occupiers did not initially lose the right to use their land, they lost control over their land's future disposition. They became increasingly less independent and more the wards of notables, an estranged bureaucracy, and politics beyond their control. Under the Ottoman regime and during the early years of the Mandate, the beneficiaries of this social process were local village leaders, merchants, bankers, moneylenders, and larger landowners who could personally profit from the fellah's indebted condition. Some fellaheen retained their owner-occupier status, especially in areas where the musha' land system was practiced. But eventually many holders of musha' shares sold their rights as well. By varied and cumulative means the fellaheen of Palestine were further forced into economic dependency, enabling others eventually to acquire their lands and forcing former owner-occupiers to become more and more dependent upon seasonal, occasional, and part-time labor. This proletarianization process was hastened and aided by Jewish land acquisition, without which Palestinian fellah disenfranchisement would only have been delayed, not discontinued.

Land Registration

The complex land system, the tithe, and estrangement from and distrust of governmental authorities resulted in little, if any, registration of Palestine land. In order to increase agricultural production and, therefore, tax revenues, the Tabu (Turkish, *Tapu*) Law of 1858 attempted to define land holdings precisely. Title deeds became obligatory for all lands. However, land seems to have been actually registered in Palestine only after 1871. Prior to registration there were no official deeds proving ownership. Tradition determined boundaries. Yet the right of might forced weaker villagers to give their customary rights to outsiders and stronger intruders. Most villagers already suffering from unrestrained tax imposition failed both to register their rights to a given land area and to acquire a deed. In pursuing such a conscious course, villagers avoided paying the cost of the deed and the additional tax valuation that would have been assessed upon registration. In particular, the inhabitants of the coastal plain, who were reckoned as the small proprietors of the country and who sometimes practiced the *musha'* system, strenuously denied that they had any landed property whatever, simply to save the cost of title deeds. Others parted with their property for a nominal sum to landowners. In this way, many fellaheen lost legal control of their patrimony.[54] Even in 1921, during the British administration, many cultivators believed as they had in Ottoman times that registration would obligate them for military service. Most were uneducated fellaheen, unfamiliar with the laws of Palestine generally and unaccustomed to the restrictions and requirements of the Department of Land Registry.[55] So disliked and feared were the subdistrict Land Registry offices that in 1925 three-quarters of all land in Palestine was held by unregistered title.[56] The failure to register land and acquire clear title to it meant that the fellaheen rarely had recourse to the formality of a regular mortgage. The director of lands in 1932 estimated that less than 5 percent of the fellah's land was mortgaged formally; instead, money was borrowed from local creditors and merchants.[57]

Registration of land in Palestine was one of deed and not of title. Possessing a deed was not a guarantee of title; thus, registration was personal and not territorial. When areas *were* registered in the Land Registry offices in the Ottoman *qazas*, which later comprised Palestine, they were usually registered as a fraction, or as one-third to one-fourth of the true land area. For example, the Wadi Hawarith lands located near Hadera, which the Jewish National Fund purchased in April 1929, actually measured 30,000 dunams but were registered as only 5,500 Turkish dunams. Yehoshua Hankin, the purchasing agent for the Palestine Land Development Company, noted that especially in the Nablus and Tulkarm areas, lands were recorded in the Land Registry as much less than their actual size.[58] Similarly in Syria, land was often registered under a pseudonym or the name of an influential person or notable who promised protection against oppression from the state, tax farmers, and moneylenders.[59] Tibawi has summed up the consequences of this process:

> Thus when a beginning at land registration (tabu) was made some of the city merchants, moneylenders, and absentee landlords sought to divert its benefits to themselves. They misrepresented the measure as a device both to register the men for military service

and to increase the taxes. The peasants, who dreaded both contingencies, were easily persuaded to sell their prescriptive rights to the land they cultivated for nominal prices, to the rich who grew richer in the process. It was members of this rich class of absentee landlords who made large profits by selling to the early Zionists extensive lands acquired in this way or by other means.[60]

Lands held in *musha'* ownership did not have the shares recorded reliably, if at all. When registered, *musha'* lands were often recorded in the name of a local landowner, merchant, moneylender, or other notable, with the village's inhabitants continuing to practice the *musha'* system on a tenure or cultivation basis.[61]

Possession of land in the Bedouin tribal areas south of Beersheba and Gaza was based on factors of periodic grazing and cultivation rights acquired during the Ottoman regime. In some cases, if land had not been cultivated for more than three years, it did not revert back to the state. The Bedouin there genuinely feared that women would inherit property on the death of their parents or husbands. Moreover, in the event of daughters marrying into another tribe, lands might be alienated from the original tribe by inheritance if the land were registered. Because of a lack of firm Ottoman administrative control over the Beersheba region, title deeds for the lands south of Beersheba town were not available in late Ottoman times. Only 50,000 of the more than 12 million dunams of what later comprised the Beersheba subdistrict under the Mandate were registered, and these were mostly close to Beersheba town. Even the lure of exempting the Bedouin from registration fees did not assuage their fears about eventual Palestine-administration encroachment on their lands. Administration attempts to have them register their lands failed.[62]

In addition to the lack of registration and underregistration of property, no map or cadastral survey accompanied the description of the lands registered. Boundaries in many instances were identified by roads, buildings, or referenced to a local piece of history such as the "land of the great fight" or "land of the big rock." During the 1920s, the director of lands stated with complete frankness and accuracy that he was unable, from registered information and the isolated plan that sometimes accompanied it, to locate the piece of land that a registered transaction purported to concern.[63]

In Palestine, lands were registered either in the *yoklama* (census) or *daimi* (perpetual) registers. *Yoklama* registers were established for those persons without previous deeds in one village. They contained a serial number of a plot in a given locality unrelated to any map, estimated land area, judicial category of land, or boundary description. Reference points in the boundary description usually contained names of neighbors, holders of adjoining parcels, and mention of physical features such as the sea, a valley, or sand dunes. Sometimes an entry was followed by mention of all the parcels purchased by a particular owner in a specified locality. The *daimi* registers recorded the names of persons in possession of land by virtue of old titles issued originally by local notables such as *sipahis* and *multazims*, or the names of those who had lost their title deeds. The *daimi* registers became journals of reported land transactions entered chronologically for an entire area rather than registers of title ownership for one village.[64] Both registers together were a patchwork of incomplete, inaccurate, and unfaithful representations of the true nature of landholdings and landownership in Ottoman Palestine.

For the British administration in 1918 the problem was not merely the imprecision of Land Registry documentation caused by deliberate circumventions and administrative inefficiency. Those few existing registries disappeared. Along with the agricultural bank registers, tax registers, and maps of state land in Palestine, the land registries were either destroyed by the Turks in Palestine or removed to Damascus during their retreat. Some of the registries for Jerusalem were destroyed beyond all chance of recovery. A portion of these registries and some of those from the subdistricts of Nablus and Gaza were returned to Palestine in February 1919, while the registries for the subdistricts of Acre, Haifa, Hebron, Jenin, Nazareth, Safed, Tiberias, and Tulkarm were found intact, but not complete.[65] As a combined consequence of the administrative turmoil and a desire to maintain the status quo, the British military administration closed all the Land Registry offices on 18 November 1918. All land transactions were forbidden. An important consideration in closing the registries was the prevention of fellaheen mortgage foreclosure. In an effort to avoid conscription, many peasants in Palestine before and during the war purchased military exemptions using their lands for collateral. The Land Registry offices were reopened on 1 October 1920.

The closing of the local Land Registry offices and the cessation of related functions deprived local officials of a major prerogative. The administrative scrutiny of the Land Registry offices fell to the legal secretary (later attorney general) and the director of lands. Obtaining personal power through fraudulent registration of lands or lackadaisical administrative action was now made more difficult with a centralized authority in Palestine. The local *majlis idara*'s preview over land matters was terminated. However, the introduction of British organization and procedure over the land regime in the *qaza* subdistricts did not quickly undermine the accumulated landed power base of former officials, merchants, moneylenders, landowners, or religious officials. What slowly came to a halt was the growth of land accumulation by a relatively few individuals.

Landownership and Rental Agreements

Under the Ottoman regime, the fellaheen of Palestine had minimal access to local centers of political authority. Most feared the urban-dominated administrative taxation and conscriptive apparatus. Seeking to protect their anonymity, they refrained from properly registering land they habitually worked. In addition to the lack of political influence, the economic prospects of the fellaheen were poor. In the absence of regular commercial-loan institutions, perennial insolvency necessitated private borrowing at usurious rates. A fellah's land could have been collateral for a loan or eventually the loan grantee's satisfaction for a debt not repaid. Physical absence from one's land for military duty allowed some land to revert back to the state, whereupon it was publicly auctioned. Alternative occupations in commerce, industry, or in manual labor were few in Ottoman Palestine. The fellah, therefore, remained on land he had cultivated by prescriptive right and tradition, but his ownership of such land passed to others more economically solvent, financially stronger, and administratively in league with local governmental officials.

At the conclusion of World War I, the fellaheen concerned themselves with survival first and with paying their debts and the tithe second. Most were not interested in politics, and the influence of the *effendi*-notable on the village remained despite a prevalent indebted condition of some large Arab landowners.[66]

The war had drained villages of their younger members, leaving the scattered parcels of land to be cultivated by older people, children, and women. The large stocks of grain held over from 1921 and the selling of wheat on the Palestine market from the Hauran region of Syria and from Transjordan hindered Palestine's postwar recovery. In October 1922 in the Hebron and Gaza areas, the fellaheen found it difficult to dispose of their crops at a reasonable price. In the Northern District a month later, villagers everywhere had difficulty in getting money to pay their debts. The fellaheen resented the British administration because they could not obtain fair prices for their produce while having to pay the tithe. The director of agriculture, writing from Haifa, reported that the governor of Galilee said cultivators there were "being compelled to sell their wives to pay their tithes," while others in the Acre subdistrict were using their most recent agricultural loans to pay the tithe on the last crop that failed. Farmhands in Ramle were leaving the villages for the towns in the hope of receiving higher wages.[67]

For economic reasons alone, antagonism among the fellaheen population toward the British administration continued throughout the 1920s. The fellaheen placed the responsibility for their excessive burden of taxation on the British administration, which was faulted for not providing them with the necessary means to break the stranglehold of usurious moneylenders.[68] The fellaheen did not make immediate contact with Jewish land purchasers. During the first decade of the Mandate, the fellaheen did not directly benefit from Jewish land purchases as did the large Arab landowner. Some fellaheen did receive fair sums from Jewish purchasers as compensation for leaving their lands and did benefit indirectly through health care and other social services from the injection of Jewish capital into Palestine.

The fellaheen attempts at political organization failed for several reasons, including insufficient funds. They received very limited support from the landed Palestinian Arab political leadership, who did not wish to undermine their own landed power base by speaking in favor of fellaheen financial needs. The Palestinian Arab political leadership meant to keep their accumulated power and prestige under the new British administration. In fact, most urban merchants, religious officials, village notables, and prominent families retained their social and political status in the transition from Ottoman to British rule. Bureaucratic posts held by some notable families during the latter part of the Ottoman period in Palestine insured the control and facile accumulation of land. During the Mandate's first decade, at least, scions of these families formed the political leadership of the Palestinian Arab community. Large Arab landowners, real estate investors, and creditors such as doctors, lawyers, civil servants, merchants, and members of the religious hierarchy, continued their uncontested political and social authority over a village or group of villages. Previous methods of land registration, the *musha'* system, and fellaheen indebtedness cemented the dependency of the fellaheen to landowning interests. Descendants of landowning families who had accrued their landed wealth during the late Ottoman times inherited Palestinian Arab leadership positions in the 1930s and 1940s.

The urban landowner viewed the fellah as inferior. In 1881, Reverend Klein noted, "The towns people naturally consider that they reached ne plus ultra of civilization and pity the stupid, boorish fellaheen. The very name has become a term of reproach, and is used to describe a stupid, uneducated man."[69] Commenting on the social bonds between the notable-*effendi* and the fellaheen in January 1923, Sydney Moody of the Colonial Office wrote that "the mass of people whose interest is to agree with the Government are afraid to speak. A village is at best a personal union and at worst a personal disunion."[70] In October 1935, a Palestinian intellectual, Afif I. Tannous, commented that "the fellah until recently has been the subject of oppression, neglect, and ill treatment by his own countrymen and the old political regime. The feudal system played havoc in his life, the *effendi* class looked down upon him, and the old Turkish regime was too corrupt to be concerned with such a vital problem."[71]

Large estates, whether owned by Palestinians resident within or outside the geographical boundaries of Palestine, tended to lie in the lowlands and plain regions and less in the mountainous regions of Judea and Samaria. In 1907, peasants were estimated to own completely or partially or enjoy cultivation rights to approximately 20 percent of the land in the Galilee and 50 percent in Judea.[72]

At the end of 1932, approximately 80 percent of the land in the coastal and Acre plains belonged to fellaheen and 20 percent to large landowners, or 2,560,000 dunams belonged to fellaheen and 640,000 dunams to large landowners.[73] Accordingly, in 1930 some 250 Arab landowners, mostly Palestinians, *owned* more than 4 million dunams of land in or near the Beersheba and Gaza subdistricts, and the fellaheen owned an equal amount in those areas.[74] A partial list of landowners possessing 5,000 Turkish dunams or more in 1919, exclusive of the Beersheba subdistrict, indicates that 405,000 Turkish dunams were in the hands of owners residing outside of the boundaries of Palestine and 455,000 Turkish dunams were owned by individuals resident in Palestine as it came to be geographically defined by the Mandate after 1922.[75] Thus, less than 2 percent of the total land area of the British Mandate, excluding Transjordan, was legally owned by nonresident absentee Arab landlords. Much of the land that these landlords held, however, was among the most fertile and cultivable land areas in Palestine.

Many absentee landowners resident in Palestine had lands situated far from their actual domiciles. These lands were cultivated by tenants, but the landowner usually employed a manager, contractor, or agent who leased the land and collected rents and taxes. For example, the Tayans of Jaffa owned land in Rehovoth and at Wadi Hawarith south of Hadera; the Ra'is and Abyad families lived in Haifa primarily but had some lands in Shatta village in the Beisan subdistrict; and the Saad family from Haifa owned areas in the Nazareth subdistrict and near Ras al-Naqura, not far from the present border between Lebanon and Israel. Predominantly urban families and their familial branches such as the al-Husaynis and al-Nashashibis owned lands close to Jerusalem where they lived but also had lands in their possession as far away as Gaza, Jaffa, and in Transjordan. Landowners living outside of the geographic borders of

Palestine were predominantly residents of Beirut, Damascus, Alexandria, and Cairo.

In 1930, evidence collected from 104 of the more than 800 Arab villagers in Palestine shows that the average holding of an owner-occupier was 56 dunams. While this holding was not deemed sufficient for the maintenance of an average family,[76] it was only an average taken from 13 percent of all Arab villages. However, confirmation of the accuracy of this Johnson-Crosbie estimate is available for at least the Safed, Acre, and Haifa subdistricts as per the Rural Property Tax records of 1936. Table 4 suggests that 81 percent of the taxed Arab owners in Safed, 83 percent in Acre, and 79 percent in Haifa owned less than 40 dunams. There is, of course, no way of knowing whether an Arab owner in one of these subdistricts possessed a parcel that was 20 to 40 dunams in one locality and another parcel of 50 to 99 dunams elsewhere. Since it was not uncommon for an owner to have several parcels scattered about in a particular area, an owner, depending on the quality of his land and the size of his family, might have possessed an area sufficient for his maintenance. But the heavy preponderance of owners with less than 100 dunams and particularly with 40 dunams or less suggests cause for a very precarious economic existence for the fellaheen in the early 1930s.

The lease agreement made between the tenant and the landowner or his agent varied according to the quality of the land cultivated, the amount cultivated, the crop grown, and the value of the agricultural materials (seed, stock, etc.) provided to the tenant by the landowner.[77] Rental for a specific sum was always confined to house and commercial property. Yet while cash rents were uncommon in the first decade of the Mandate, this method of payment increased in the 1930s. Where cash rents for cereal lands were made, payment per dunam per year was made as follows: 40 to 50 mils for bad sandy land, 50 to 100 mils on good sandy land, 100 mils on average land, and 100 to 150 mils for good land.[78] In addition to the rental payment in kind, calculated from one-sixth to as much as two-fifths of the gross yield, the tenant was usually responsible for the tithe payment, though often he paid this to the landlord or his agent who in turn paid the tithe to the administration. In the lands of Wadi Hawarith, for example, 'Abdullah Samara paid the taxes to the Ottoman government and acted as the agent to the Tayans who owned the land. In such a capacity, Samara possessed local political influence.[79] On state lands administered by the Palestine administration, such as those in the Beisan area, only 10 percent of the crop was collected as rent; this was generally commuted for a monetary payment. While the administration did not move its tenants from plot to plot each year, tenants frequently changed their cultivation areas voluntarily. In some cases, they sold their cultivation rights to other incoming tenants

TABLE 4
Arab Land Ownership According to Size of Owner's Holding, 1936

Number of Dunams

Owners by Subdistrict	1–4	5–9	10–19	20–40	50–99	100–499	Over 500	Total
Safed	2,302	493	420	563	358	445	76	4,657
Acre	2,909	1,356	1,349	1,891	905	571	57	9,038
Haifa	1,255	415	400	517	397	267	25	3,276

Source: These statistics were culled from the rural property tax registers of 1936, Central Zionist Archives, A202/file 150. For comparative remarks about the maintenance area of an Arab owner, see Chapter 6, pp. 000–00.

or Jewish farmers. If the *musha'* land system were practiced on a tenancy basis, tenants were accustomed to moving around from one parcel to another. Sometimes, however, during the Mandate, landlords or their agents moved tenants around from parcel to parcel particularly to prevent them from gaining legal tenant-protection rights.[80]

Lease agreements were usually made for a period of one year, or for the summer and/or winter cultivating seasons. Some agreements were written, but most were verbal with tithe receipts serving as the only evidence a tenant had (if he retained them) of past association with a particular land area. Agricultural laborers were sometimes hired by tenants when the land leased was more than 120 to 150 dunams. For his efforts, the agricultural laborer received one-quarter of the produce and sometimes paid a portion of the lease agreement and the tithe. An example of one division of the gross yield was: 20 percent to the landlord as rent; 10 percent to the administration for the tithe; 3 percent to the shepherd; 3 percent to the reapers; 3 percent to the threshers; 45.5 percent to the tenant; and 15.5 percent to the agricultural laborer. On land owned by the Palestine Colonization Association, where Arab labor was hired to work Jewish-owned lands, lease agreements were concluded in writing with individual tenants for one-year periods.[81]

The Status Quo and the
"Politics of Notables"[82]

Despite its general political opposition to the contents and implications of the Balfour Declaration, the British military administration had time only to concern itself with the status quo. Unsure of their longevity and future financial status, the British made no effort to reform landholdings, create educational or credit facilities, or engage in other attempts at social and economic reform. The military administration had to content itself with maintaining the peace, reviving monetary credibility, and seeing to it that the population did not starve. The land-accumulation interests of the large landowning classes were not furthered by the closing of the Land Registry offices that precluded mortgage foreclosure. Fellaheen interests were aided somewhat by tithe exemptions for 1918–19 and the distribution of cash, cattle, and seeds by the military administration.

After the Balfour Declaration was issued in November 1917, the Zionist Commission was established in March of the following year to look after Jewish interests in Palestine. It acted as a liaison with the British and the Arabs, evolved into the Palestine Zionist Executive in 1920, and became the expanded Jewish Agency in 1928–29. The Palestine Zionist Executive and its successor the Jewish Agency formulated and implemented daily decisions regarding Jewish development in Palestine. A second Jewish Agency Executive in London maintained communication with British politicians and Colonial Office and Foreign Office officials in London. Affiliated with the Jewish Agency were land-purchasing and settlement organizations such as the Jewish National Fund and the Palestine Land Development Company, financial institutions such as the Keren Hayesod and the Anglo-Palestine Bank, a Jewish self-defense force known as the *haganah*, a Jewish labor organization known as the *histadrut*, and numerous other agencies working to build the Jewish national home.

The British military and civil administration, in seeking to establish organizational counterweights to these Jewish organizations, stimulated Palestinian Arabs to mobilize politically. Thus, the Muslim-Christian associations and the Supreme Muslim Council were formed. Out of the Muslim-Christian associations evolved the Arab Executive in December 1920. The Arab Executive became the unofficial voice for Palestinian Arab remarks, complaints, and protestations to the high commissioner and other British officials until its demise in the early 1930s. The Supreme Muslim Council and Arab Executive continuously refused to accept the Mandate and the Balfour Declaration in its preamble. This deliberate boycott of the Mandate denied the Arab political community close contact with and the confidences of British officialdom. Nevertheless, these two organizations gave the Arab community an opportunity to express itself vehemently against the Mandate and the establishment of the Jewish national home, while preserving the political status for those less than one hundred members in both organizations. But organizational development did not hide the deep personal differences between notables within the Palestinian Arab political community. These differences greatly hindered a uniform and effective reply to the Zionist enterprise. In fact, the retention of local family prestige, authority, and influence was repeatedly spliced into larger quests for the control and direction of the Palestinian Arab national movement on a countrywide level.

Throughout the Mandate, notables continued to dominate Arab society because of their economic and social position. Despite being denied real power in national, municipal, and local government, the notable class had its political status officially sanctioned on the social level during the Mandate by many governmental proclamations and ordinances, which had the quality of binding law. For example, the *mukhtars* and notables of a village or in a group of villages were police constables. The regulations governing the Muslim Sharia courts and the Supreme Muslim Council placed the notables in significant roles on local *waqf* committees. In all localities of Palestine, socially recognized notables, usually large landowners, were employed to help verify boundary claims. Most revealing in land matters was the decision on the part of the administration to accept the names of nominees who appeared in the Ottoman Land Registry records as legal liaison between the administration and a village.[83]

Sir Herbert Samuel, the first high commissioner, turned to these notables in his attempt to gain official Palestinian Arab participation in the Mandate. Even when they refused Samuel's invitation to participate in a legislative council and an Arab agency, the notables remained as the de facto representatives of the Arab community. In December 1921, the administration succumbed to the pressures of Arab landowners and removed the size and area restrictions imposed on all dispositions of land when the Land Registry offices were reopened in October 1920. The civil administration and the Zionists, for that matter, carefully guarded the prestige of the landowning class by never publicly faulting it for collaborating with Jews in land sales. Only in internal memoranda of the Jewish Agency and its affiliated institutions, which remained out of the public eye, was there any mention of Arab landowner participation in the alienation of land. Later, especially after 1929 when the administration paid particular attention to the land question, the official onus of responsibility for Arab displacement was publicly placed on the shoulders of Jewish land purchasers.

Aside from political reasons for pursuing a policy that favored landowning interests, there was also sufficient reason from an administrative point of view for not reforming the land regime. Politically, any abrupt reorganization of the land regime would have been construed by the Arabs of Palestine as an overt attempt to turn the country over to the Zionists at once. Administratively, there was neither the trained staff nor the budget necessary to reassign or reallocate landholdings, institute a needed cadastral survey, or partition *musha‘*-held shares in a compulsory manner.

The civil administration's budget was based on the revenue collected locally without subventions from the British Exchequer. The bulk of expenditures went toward maintaining the garrison in Palestine. Annual budgetary expenditures thereafter were dominated by costs for strategic requirements such as railway, port, telephone, telegraph, and road development. In the fiscal years prior to 1922–23, expenditures involving land administration and regulation went almost exclusively toward establishing the subdistrict Land Registry offices and salary payments for junior staff. In the fiscal years 1922–23 and 1923–24 less than 1 percent of the yearly Palestine budget went collectively toward the Land Registry Department, the Lands Department, and the Survey Department. More than half of the administration's expenditures continuously went toward supporting the gendarmerie and strengthening Britain's strategic presence in Palestine.[84]

Instead of revamping the land regime through land reform, the civil administration tended to recognize the validity of the existing method of land use, extralegal procedures of land transfer, and the past circumventions used in land registration. For example, Article 8 of the Ottoman Land Code of 1858 had expressly forbidden *miri* land from being held as a whole by the inhabitants of the village. But the widespread use of the *musha‘* system forced a Palestine Land Court in 1926 to recognize this village custom and further ordered the *musha‘* shares to be registered in the Land Registry offices.[85] During the Ottoman regime, owners of property often avoided land registration and the assessments of land-registration fees and subsequent tax payment by transacting land transfers outside of the Land Registry offices. The Palestine administration gave recognition to unofficial transfers by unregistered title deed.[86] But legal recognition of transfer by an unregistered title did not imply administration recognition of ownership. When the Land Registry offices were reopened, the reluctance to register dispositions remained. The assistant director of lands noted the following about unregistered transfers in 1923: "In many cases it will be found that the present beneficiary owners of properties did not come into possession by virtue of private purchase direct from the registered owners, but from first, second or third transferees to whom the properties passed by private sales after the first registration."[87] Private transactions continued throughout the Mandate period, particularly after the outbreak of the Arab general strike in 1936. The institution of the Land Transfer Regulations in 1940 forced many sales agreements between Arab vendors and Jewish purchasers to take place outside of the Land Registry.[88] In December 1947, the director of land settlement reported that "the Arab rural cultivators, unless they are transferring land to townsmen or to some non-Arab who insists on registration, keep clear of the Land Registry."[89]

During the late Ottoman period, out of fear of creating another minority problem in already religious-sensitive Palestine, Jews were restricted from purchasing land. Nevertheless, Jews managed to acquire land by bribing local government officials, local Arabs, consuls, consular agents, and by registering land in fictitious names or in the names of Jews resident in Istanbul.[90] Those purchases made unofficially by Jews were entered into land books held by the Jewish settlements. An exact record was kept of the transactions that took place between Jews during the period of Ottoman restriction and later when the Land Registry offices were closed between 1918 and 1920. As in subdistrict Land Registry offices, the names appearing in these land books were sometimes not representative of the real owners. Often lands failed to be cultivated because of an owner's absenteeism. Instead of the lands being subjected to public auction through escheat to the state, lands were transferred to third parties.[91] Since these land books were respected as credible representations of landholdings within a given Jewish settlement, financial arrangements such as loans and second mortgages were predicated on the authenticity of their contents. In early 1924, a fall in land values caused some Jews, who were financially encumbered on lands so recorded, to believe in the possibility of repudiating their obligations and escaping the liabilities of their contracts. With some concern that the economic downturn might cause harm to the Jewish community's financial institutions, the Palestine Zionist Executive sought to have these land books legally recognized.

In 1920, under the Land Registers Ordinance, the administration recognized the presence of a large number of occupiers or landowners whose lands were not registered but were entered in the Land Registry offices in the name of a nominee or trustee. Individuals were given the opportunity through 1924 to correct registration through the Land Courts, but fee receipts collected by the Land Registry Department indicate that few people corrected their registration. Nominees or trustees continued to have land, which at one time had been entrusted to them merely as a ruse, registered in their names. While the opportunity was provided for the fellaheen to correct their holdings, the Land Court adjudicating these rights required either proof of a nonappealable judgment by a court, a private document attesting to one's rights to the land, or proof of tax payment—all unlikely to be in the possession of a small owner who had been interested for so long in anonymity from government. Nonwritten or oral evidence was heard in the Land Courts, but rarely was it accepted against the existence of a title deed.[92]

Since a precedent had been set for making transactions valid even though they were not registered, the Palestine administration, interested in creating uniformity in its record keeping in land, acknowledged the validity of the Jewish land books as well by the enactment of the Correction of Land Registers Ordinance of April 1926. Moreover, transactions, which were carried out and entered in these books between November 1918 and October 1920 when the Land Registry offices were closed, were not illegal, though they were not recorded in the official registers. While the exact amount of land transferred from Arabs to Jews and recorded in the Jewish land books during this period is not known, the actual drafting and refining of this ordinance was largely handled by members of the Palestine Zionist Executive and particularly by Harry Sacher, a Zionist and official of the Anglo-Palestine Bank.[93]

The new precision in record keeping and the consultative lawmaking process gave the Zionists an additional advantage over a more traditional and unschooled Palestinian Arab community. Within the Arab community the economic lien that notables had on the fellaheen in the early 1920s transcended the establishment of the British administration. Past debt accumulation, the dominant presence of a large sharehold in a *musha'* village, and the social and religious prestige enjoyed by local village *shaykhs* and *mukhtars* did not dissipate quickly. But in the early 1930s the process of Jewish land purchase tore at already fraying traditional relationships.[94] By the early 1940s those bonds were weakened, if not destroyed, in some parts of Palestine.

For at least the first decade of the Mandate, most of the large landowners were able to retain considerable socioeconomic influence over the fellaheen classes. Gradually, the ties between the fellaheen and the landlord-merchant-creditor were reduced. As land slowly came into Jewish ownership and occupation during the Mandate, Palestinian Arab social relationships were altered to the detriment of Palestinian Arab unanimity. Already splintered by the regional, local, religious, economic, and social differences, the land-sale process created additional cleavages among Arabs that ultimately aided Jewish nation building.

In administering Palestine through the Arab landowning notables, the

British did not attempt to reorder rights to land. They generated misapprehension among the fellaheen regarding land reform. Such distrust militated against any active land policy. The introduction of British administration and scrutiny over the land regime permitted proper and accurate registration that sanctioned past and accepted customary practice, including the extralegal ploys, ruses, and abuses of Ottoman times. Reluctance to register land and the *musha'* system continued. Especially during times of political uncertainty and potential or actual restraint against free transfers, unregistered transfers were employed. It took fifteen years for tithe reform in Mandatory Palestine, which happened coincidentally when the administration had a large budgetary surplus.

The Zionist ability to create a national home was significantly aided by the poor economic status of the Palestinian peasant during the Ottoman and Mandatory periods. Insufficient rainfall and draft animals, inefficient management of agricultural land, small parcel size, lack of investment capital, indebtedness, and a general disillusionment with government aided Jewish nation building. Lack of interest in the majority of the fellaheen agricultural population by a socially distanced Palestinian Arab landowning elite also aided the development of the Jewish national home. The Palestinian Arab community was unquestionably a numerical majority throughout the Mandate, but its own financial distress gave the Zionist minority a distinct advantage in the struggle to control Palestine.

At the precise time when the British administration inherited the Ottoman legacy in Palestine, the Jewish national home concept received its official sanction from the British. It was a most propitious occasion for the Zionists. As the British initiated their own means and priorities for governance, the Zionists simultaneously developed an infrastructure, organizations, and methods for continuing immigration and land settlement in Palestine. From 1917 to 1939 the Zionists created a territorial nucleus for a Jewish state. They also developed the conviction, confidence, and enthusiasm that their goal could not be thwarted by either a splintered Arab community or a British administration that became increasingly paternalistic toward the Palestinian Arab.

Chapter 2

The Land Question, 1917–1929

The Zionist intention at the Peace Conference in Paris in 1919 was to give statutory effect to the implications of the Balfour Declaration. Zionists wanted a trusteeship or mandate system for Palestine that would protect and enhance the rights of the Jewish minority. The wording of the British Mandate's articles reflected the Zionists' success. But British policy objectives were more encompassing: they wanted to strengthen their strategic presence in the Middle East while finding compromise solutions to Arab aspirations for independence in the Levant and in the Arabian peninsula. Both Ibn Saud and Sharif Husayn, rivals for ascendancy in the Arabian peninsula, were tethered by British subventions. Having courted Sharif Husayn during World War I, the British maintained their relationships with him and his son Faysal, who emerged as the diplomatic spokesman of Arab independence at the conclusion of the war. Since the French made no secret of their aim to control all of Syria, Husayn and Faysal had little choice but to cast their lot with the British.[1] But in so doing, they reluctantly but tacitly accepted the attendant political ramifications of Britain's Zionist entente.

In his memorandum of January 1918, though mentioning a Jewish return to Palestine, Commander D. G. Hogarth of HMG's Arab Bureau in Cairo reaffirmed Britain's intent to see the formation of an independent Arab nation. In June 1918 similar assurances were given to seven Arab leaders in Cairo. The following October, General Edmund Allenby restated this pledge to Faysal. Affirmation of principles based upon the consent of the governed, the "complete and definite emancipation of the peoples so long oppressed by the Turks," and the establishment of governments based upon self-determination were included in the Anglo-French Declaration of 7 November 1918. Where the British had been vague about the inclusion of Palestine in the Husayn-McMahon correspondences of 1915 and 1916, now the British and French failed to mention Palestine specifically as a geographic area where indigenous governments would be encouraged. Meeting in London in the early days of November 1918, the Advisory Committee on Palestine discussed the concepts of trust and mandates with the Zionists.[2]

While the British were courting Faysal and developing carefully worded agreements, the Zionists continued to give their goal political substance in London and practical reality in Palestine. The dispatch of the Zionist Commission in March 1918 provided the Zionists an institutional vehicle to translate policy into reality. In addition to seeking amicable relationships with the British military administration and the Arab community in Palestine, the Zionist Commission coordinated relief work for the Jewish community that complemented its political activity. However, the British hope that the Zionist Commission's efforts would lead to improved relations between Jews and Arabs proved illusory. Certainly the individuals who staffed the military administration did little to foster cordial Arab-Jewish understanding, let alone amiable intercommunal relations.[3]

While the Arabs of Palestine lacked a distinctive and cohesive nationalist movement at this time, they had no illusions about Zionist development or its intent in Palestine. Before the outbreak of World War I, some Arab notables protested against Jewish immigration, against Jewish land purchases, and against the unavoidable consequence of fellaheen dispossession from the land. But land disputes among Arabs and discontent between Arab tenants and their landlords predated Jewish settlement. Encroachment onto a neighbor's land, brigandage at the threshing floor, and uprooting of olive trees were standard manifestations of discontent. When Arab privileges or cultivation rights were interrupted or terminated by the transfer of land into Jewish ownership, intercommunal friction widened. Jewish purchasers and settlers unfamiliar with the local custom of allowing grazing after the harvest antagonized both the sedentary and nomadic Arab rural population by denying that right.[4] Most Arab protests were confined to the urban, educated, and landowning elite, who possessed unchallenged voices of economic and social authority. Several historians have noted that a few rich, landowning families were happy to see Jews buy land at almost any price, and further, when protests were made for restrictions of Jewish immigration and land sales, the protests benefited the landowners by driving up the price of land.[5]

In early 1918, politically involved Arabs in Palestine did not believe that the ultimate ambitions of Zionism could be anything but the expropriation of land, recovery of the Holy City, and the establishment of self-governing Jewish institutions in Palestine.[6] In April 1918, Chaim Weizmann, the individual most responsible for directing the Zionist movement, tried to persuade Isma'il al-Husayni and Kamel al-Husayni (the latter was the mufti of Jerusalem) that these were not Zionist intentions. Weizmann found particular antagonism to Jews in the environs of Nablus, Tulkarm, and Qalqilya where few Jews had lived. He noted existing hostility to the Jews in the Upper Galilee, though he ascribed this to the activity of French agents presumably eager to derail British claims to parts of Palestine's northern frontier.[7]

Weizmann sought to explain and neutralize Arab opposition to Zionism. In June 1918, north of Aqaba and twice again within six months in London, Weizmann met with Faysal. Weizmann wanted to prove that Zionist development in Palestine would be beneficial, not injurious, to the Arab population. In December 1918, Weizmann told Faysal that the Jews would try and revive Palestine's economy without encroaching on the ownership rights of the Arab peasantry. Weizmann stressed the need to reform the land laws in Palestine so that land in the control of large landowners and usurers could be made available for Jewish settlement. Faysal concurred with Weizmann that there was no scarcity of land in Palestine.[8] Although Faysal signed the agreement with Weizmann in January 1919 with reservation, once again both men agreed to uphold the rights of the Arab peasantry to remain on the land they cultivated.

Unlike the British, who began their contact with the Arabs of Palestine in 1917 and 1918, some Zionists had attitudes colored by more than four decades of political and economic contact with them. Prior to World War I, the Jews who had immigrated to Palestine often did so under restriction and injunction against them.[9] The ability to overcome the personal hostility of Ottoman officials in Palestine and to circumvent edicts against Jewish immigration and land purchase had important perceptual consequences. During the Ottoman period, Jews and committed Zionists clearly realized that restrictions and regulations could be circumvented, that despite vocal protests sellers were willing and even eager to sell their land, and that therefore political opposition to the Zionist enterprise was insincere and artificial.

These realities did not change during the Mandate. In 1918, when Weizmann was told of Arab opposition to Zionism, in June 1930, when land-transfer regulations were officially broached, in 1934–35, when public condemnation of land sales to Jews rose in crescendo, and in 1940, when the Land Transfer Regulations were enacted, Zionists continuously received offers to purchase from large and small landowners.[10] The *only* factor limiting the pace and scope of Jewish land purchase prior to and after the institution of the Mandate was insufficient funding. Zionists in Palestine during the Mandate believed that no amount of legislative prohibition could prevent the establishment of a Jewish national home and that Arab opposition to Zionism was inauthentic and inconsistent as far as land sales were concerned. Most important, Zionist successes in the land sphere convinced them that land redemption as a part of Zionist philosophy was not a dream but a concept capable of immediate realization.

While Zionism was still in its incipient stages of intellectual evolution, epitomized in part by the writings of Moses Hess, Leo Pinsker, and later Theodore Herzl, practical insight into the complexion and structure of Arab society was accumulated by both the prewar Jewish immigrants and the members of the Sephardic community already living in Palestine. They found that Arab politics in the *sanjaqs* of Acre, Nablus, and Jerusalem were dominated by a small coterie of Arab landowning notables, living either within these administrative boundaries or in Alexandria, Cairo, Beirut, or Damascus. Because of land transfers during the late Ottoman period from such families as the Sabbaghs, Habibis, and Tueinis (Beirut), the Abyads, Khuris, Kitrans, Saads, and Khalils (Haifa), the Beyduns (Acre), the al-Fahums (Nazareth), the Khatibs (Safed), and the al-Tabaris (Tiberias), Jewish settlements were established at Hadera, Zichron-Ya'acov, Kinneret, Metullah, Ayelet Hashachar, Rosh-Pina, Tel-Hai, and at least fifteen other locations.[11] By 1914, from predominantly private purchases and not through institutions of the Zionist organization, Jews had acquired more than 400,000 dunams by title-deed transfer.[12] This amounted to approximately 20 percent of all registered land transferred into Jewish ownership by the end of the Mandate on 14 May 1948. In 1914, the acquisition of an additional 838,000 Turkish dunams was in various stages of negotiation with Jewish purchasers.[13] Demographically, by 1914, the number of Jews in Palestine had increased to 65,000 from 24,000 in 1882.[14] At the Eleventh Zionist Congress in September 1913 principles for the continuation of practical settlement work in Palestine had been carefully outlined by a leading Jewish settlement expert, Arthur Ruppin.[15]

For Zionists in Palestine in 1917, the Balfour Declaration merely confirmed British support for a process initiated forty years earlier. Drawing upon previous years of Zionist experiences, the Zionist Commission was not shy about intruding its thoughts into the Mandate's formulation. Comparing the Zionist Commission's land proposals with the Mandate's articles on land sharply reveals the Zionists' ability to have some general concepts adopted, while other specific requests were either denied or postponed.[16] The Zionist Commission's suggestions for intensive cultivation, settlement of the Jews on the land, Jewish access to state, vacant lands, and wastelands, and the introduction of a land system suitable to the needs of Palestine were replicated in Articles 6 and 11 of the Mandate. On the other hand, the Zionist desire to enjoy preemptive rights to purchase holdings in excess of a "maximum" area possessed by any one individual, the wish to have all Jewish land purchased by a central Zionist agency, and the attempt to fix the price of land required for public purposes at its August 1914 value were never formally consented to by the British government. However, the Zionist plea for control of speculation in land was sanctioned in the Land Transfer Ordinance of 1920.

In a strictly secret internal memorandum, the Zionists expressed the belief that they could acquire more than 5 million dunams by 1925. Much of this intended area was to include state lands and lands to the east of the Jordan River, lands not yet included by the creation of Transjordan in 1921.[17] Before the end of the Mandate, Jews acquired approximately 2 million registered dunams, a figure far short of their projection for 1925. Although the total registered area acquired by Jews was small in relation to the total mandated area or in relation to the area later to encompass Israel's 1949 armistice lines, the area acquired from Arabs was strategically essential for the growth and establishment of a geographic nucleus for a Jewish national home.

Zionists in London and Palestine experienced great hope in the immediate aftermath of the Balfour Declaration. Though the declaration was a carefully worded compromise document, which included the seed of the future dual-obligation policy, the term "national home" for most Zionists was merely a diplomatic euphemism for "Jewish state."[18] For Zionists in the Palestine Office, the euphoria of the moment was tempered by the reality of the scarce financial resources available for their ambitious land-purchase and immigration goals. What fears the Arabs of Palestine had about the ultimate purpose of Zionist intent was generated from past experience and direct personal contact. Though Arabs in Palestine were not privy to the detailed land-purchase plans established by the Zionists in 1919, some Arabs believed that the Zionists were ready to displace them. Arabs in Palestine feared the Jew as a competitor. Gradually, they came to see the Jewish immigrant not only as a menace to their livelihood but as a possible future overlord.[19]

More immediate than this apprehension at the conclusion of World War I was the dire Arab need at all social levels to maintain economic and financial solvency. Although political attention was riveted on Arab nationalist quests in the Levant, Egypt, and the Arabian peninsula, the British sought to arrest the destitution of Palestine's rural population via legislative methods without committing large-scale British spending.

Closure of the Land Registry Offices, 1918

In April 1918, in his first report as Britain's liaison with the Zionist Commission, William Ormsby-Gore strongly urged the suspension of all purchase and sale of land in Palestine.[20] His primary reason for this action was the growing impoverishment of the local population. He argued that land transfers in which tenant occupants would be displaced could lead to the creation of a sizable landless class whose welfare would become an unwelcomed British responsibility. Both large landowners, whose rent went uncollected during the war, and small landowner-occupiers, who in many cases were deeply in debt, eagerly offset their deteriorating financial condition through land sales. In May 1918, land transfers were unofficially prohibited, especially in cases where the seller (owner) was not a Jew. Yet land continued to change ownership. Where fictitious debt creation and irrevocable powers of attorney were not employed, potential vendors received monetary advancements as collateral for a future commitment to sell.[21] Realizing that unofficial sanctions against land transactions were not effective, Major General A. W. Money, the chief administrator of the Occupied Enemy Territory Administration (OETA) South, issued two official proclamations on 18 November 1918 to halt land sales.

Proclamations No. 75 and No. 76 forbade all owners of immovable property from making any dispositions affecting them in the *sanjaqs* of Acre, Nablus, and Jerusalem. Dispositions pertaining to sale, mortgage, transfer of mortgage, gift, and dedication of *waqf* in the *sanjaqs* of Jerusalem, and carried out prior to 18 November, were to be considered valid pending the registration of such dispositions at the reestablished Land Registry offices. Any disposition carried out after that date anywhere in the jurisdiction of the military administration was invalid. Existing mortgagers could receive their entitled payment in the presence of a notary public, but, by a prior proclamation of 24 June 1918, no court could order the sale of any land in execution of a judgment debt or in satisfaction of a mortgage. The land market was legally closed as a means to acquire and borrow capital. As a consequence, the economic development of the country was "cramped."[22] In April 1921, the courts again had the authority to order the sale of immovable property in satisfaction of a mortgage debt. However, the president of the District Court could postpone a sale if he believed that either the debtor had reasonable prospects of paying within a given time, or if the debtor would be caused undue hardship by the sale of his land.[23]

The military administration's concern for the condition of the agricultural population went further than maintaining fellaheen on their lands as cultivators. Prompt relief was sought through an agreement with the Anglo-Egyptian Bank (not the British taxpayer). Long- and short-term loans totaling more than £E500,000 allowed fellaheen to buy draft animals, seeds, and agricultural implements. The loans saved the British from becoming the direct financial guardians of the fellaheen population. Equally important, the availability of these loans gave some fellaheen at least a temporary alternative to their traditional dependence upon the notable landowning class, which was itself in financially depressed times. In fact, the loans had a profound salutary effect upon the fellaheen attitude toward the administration.[24] That goodwill eroded even before the loans were discontinued in 1924, primarily because of the inability of the fellaheen population to recover fully from the grave economic disruptions that occurred prior to and during World War I. In 1923, some fellaheen in the Northern District, despondent over their poor economic situation and disenchanted with the administration, blamed Jewish settlement penetration of the country as the root cause of their problems. Agricultural loans were discontinued because more than half of them were not repaid.[25]

Initially, Zionists at the Peace Conference and in Palestine favored closing the Land Registry offices for the same reason they opposed loans for fellaheen: they desired acquisition of the most amount of land at the lowest possible price. Members of the Zionist Commission believed that keeping the Land Registry offices closed could act as a temporary brake on speculation in the land market. The politically inspired but unofficial military-administration directive to postpone land transfers to Jews, effective from April–May 1918 to the following November, had the advantage from the Zionist point of view of limiting land speculation. Yet the closure of the Land Registry offices after November had the effect of creating a scarcity in land availability that in turn drove up the prices in the unofficial marketplace. On land of similar quality situated in close proximity to existing rural Jewish settlements, the price increased from an average of £E1–2 per dunam in 1914 to £E2–5 per dunam in 1920–22.[26] In addition, the sums used as key money to initiate transactions increased.

The existing practices of land registration further prompted the Zionists to opt for a closure of the Land Registry offices. They were fearful that Arab land brokers would acquire vast amounts of underregistered or unregistered land, conduct a survey of this land, and then sell the larger actual area to Jewish purchasers. The Zionists preferred, if possible, to engage in this practice themselves without having an Arab broker or intermediary siphon off already-scarce capital.

In addition, the Zionists, particularly Weizmann, feared the consequences of massive dedication of land into *waqf* endowments. In the past, land dedicated to religious authorities had found its way into Jewish ownership. But now, Jewish purchasers were apprehensive that large amounts of land would be removed from the open market. If this happened, previous Arab landowners might have the land returned to them on a long-term lease. Whether true or not, rumors were abundant in 1919 that vast areas were to be dedicated as *waqf*. These rumors caused the Zionists to seek continued support for the closure of the Land Registry offices.[27]

The Zionists wanted no land transfers while their proposals were being acted upon at the Peace Conference, and they also strongly opposed the granting of loans to the fellaheen. Such an attitude was not completely consonant with the statement made by Weizmann to Faysal concerning Jewish sympathy for the Arab peasant. Since the granting of loans required the offering of equivalent collateral, the Zionists feared that loan forfeiture would see the eventual passing of title or ownership to a financial institution outside of Palestine whose directorate might be potentially unfriendly to the Zionist movement. Furthermore, the Zionists did not want any legal determination of land titles required upon the granting of a loan or mortgage. Granting official recognition to a land area previously worked without boundary delimitations would have given a large number of fellaheen title or ownership rights that otherwise might have remained undefined. The Zionists reasoned that if the administration accepted mortgages as collateral for a loan, then it would simultaneously sustain the validity of a title. Lastly, because many Jewish purchasers had acquired their land through legitimate though unregistered transfer, they too did not possess title deeds that could be given as collateral for loans. Weizmann believed that the loan proposal would have worked more to the advantage of the fellaheen than to the Jewish cultivator. Weizmann was so antagonistic to the loan proposal that he believed it was "life and death" for the cause of the Jewish nation in Palestine.[28]

Weizmann placed the blame for the origin of the loan proposal on the shoulders of Colonel Vivian Gabriel, financial adviser to the military administration. Gabriel was characterized as an open enemy of the Jews.[29] Weizmann and the Zionist Commission were not against financial aid to the fellaheen, but they feared the impact that loan forfeiture would have upon Jewish land acquisition. Because the Zionists failed to make clear why they opposed the loans to the fellaheen, some Arabs in Palestine believed that Zionist opposition was due to a willful intent to further impoverish them.[30]

Before the topic of agricultural loans was first aired in June 1918, the military administration withdrew the prerogative of giving judgments over landownership and title from the civil courts. At the end of 1919 that policy remained unchanged. The willingness of the military administration to keep a hands-off attitude regarding ownership and title determination eventually caused Weizmann to modify his opposition on the loan question.[31] During the Mandate, the civil administration continued the policy of overseeing land transfers without guaranteeing title acquired in the Ottoman period.

By late spring 1919, the military administration was actively engaged in the reestablishment of the Land Registry records removed or destroyed by the Turks. Some of the records were returned from Damascus with the help of the French in Syria while others were restored locally. At the same time, a Draft Land Transfer Ordinance was written. Weizmann continued to be vexed by the possibility of massive *waqf* dedications. (That option was in fact not exercised by Arab landowners.) As a consequence he argued for a continued cessation of registration in September 1919.[32] Weizmann's anxieties notwithstanding, the Land Registry offices were not administratively capable of handling dispositions of land at that time. The decision not to reopen the offices was a matter that required administrative and bureaucratic resolution. Only after Weizmann received assurances that the Anglo-Egyptian Bank had no interest in the land given as security for loans did he consent to the agricultural-loan scheme that began in late 1919. He wanted to be sure that the military administration would not give any bank or syndicate the mortgaged securities for repayment of the loans.

By late 1919, Weizmann and his colleagues on the Zionist Commission had seen the Draft Land Transfer Ordinance. Earlier in July, the British delegation at the Peace Conference said that it had no objections to reopening the Land Registry offices, provided that preferential consideration be given to Zionist interests. Both Arthur Balfour and Lord Curzon were ready to give preferential rights to the Zionists under the terms of the Mandate. In particular, Zionists had great expectations for gaining access to state lands.[33] There is no evidence available to suggest that notables from the Arab community of Palestine were privy to the Draft Land Transfer Ordinance as the Zionists were. The British did make it clear to Arab notables that they would not be compelled to give up their property to the Jews.[34] In fact, it was reported that some Arabs in Palestine viewed the embargo on land transfers as an intentional check upon the Zionist movement, achieved through Arab pressures exerted upon officials of the military administration in Palestine.[35]

The degree of concern that the Zionists showed for land acquisition in 1918 and 1919 is indicative of the priority they gave to influencing the Mandate's operations in general. The Zionists had a very decided advantage over a politically amorphous and unsophisticated Arab community. They incorporated their goals into policy, anticipated and deflected damaging consequences in the land sphere, drafted opinions, lobbied the British in London, Paris, and Jerusalem, and wrote legislation in Palestine. A process of direct consultation and debate was established that sometimes caused great consternation among British officials. Whether the British enjoyed the frequency of this contact or not, the Zionists shrewdly utilized their access to policymaking to influence the development of the Jewish national home.

The Land Transfer Ordinance (LTO)
of 1 October 1920

No formal or informal guideline or precedent existed requiring the British to consult with the Zionists about policy formulation for Palestine. Yet the appointment of the Zionist Commission plus the foreign secretary's request of Weizmann to prepare confidential reports on the land regime enabled the Zionists to establish the consultative prerogative officially affirmed later in Article 4 of the Mandate. Moreover, the British tended to become reliant and then dependent upon Zionist material and cooperation concerning land. The British lacked such information, but Zionist officials possessed vast amounts of it based upon more than four decades of official and unofficial experience in land acquisition.

In 1919, after the Draft Land Transfer Ordinance was written and submitted to British officials in Egypt for comment, those sympathetic to Zionist growth, such as Lord Rothschild and Norman Bentwich, commented on the modified draft. In an effort to curb land and price speculation, the Draft Ordinance required an individual to obtain written permission from the military administration for any disposition of immovable property. Consent was to be withheld if an excessive amount of land was obtained by one individual in a particular area. The area of disposition could not exceed 300 dunams in size or £E1,000 in value. Despite Weizmann's apprehension, *waqf* dedications, along with sales, mortgages, and gifts, were defined as dispositions. Because agricultural loans were not yet considered or allocated when the Draft Land Transfer Ordinance was written, the proposed land-transfer law intended to give financial assistance to the small landowner. It was reasoned that the fellaheen might sell only a portion of their land in order to obtain the cash required for agricultural supplies and equipment. Neither the Zionists in Palestine nor the members of the Foreign Office believed that circumventions by speculators could be prevented when Zionists attempted to acquire large areas of land.[36]

Then Bentwich as the senior judicial officer under the military administration wrote a memorandum on the Draft Ordinance. He stated quite clearly that it was desirable to restrict the creation of large estates and to prevent the larger landowners of the country from extending their holdings.[37] In the draft, which was submitted to the Foreign Office for comment, no mention was made of protecting the cultivation or tenancy rights of the fellaheen. Yet Bentwich in his memorandum referred to a clause generally stipulating tenant and owner-occupier protection and specifically the retention of a maintenance area sufficient for the fellah and his family in the event of a transfer. There were precise area and size restrictions in the proposed draft to enable the fellaheen to acquire minimally required capital. Bentwich hoped that retention of a maintenance area would keep small owners from selling all of their land while discouraging landlords from selling tenanted land. Who was responsible for the deletion of the fellaheen protection clauses is unclear; Bentwich nevertheless stressed the importance to the military governors of the necessity for keeping the fellaheen on their land. Here Bentwich was replicating Weizmann's wish to protect the fellaheen and to support the military administration's policy of maintaining the status quo with regard to land by not raising ownership or title questions. Bentwich hoped that the bulk of the intended Zionist land would be purchased from the large landowning and land-connected notable classes, thereby diminishing their political and social prestige. Later, Bentwich became the legal secretary and then the first attorney general under the civil administration.

By March 1920, the issue was no longer whether the Land Registry offices would be reopened, but rather when and under what conditions. During Weizmann's visit to Palestine in November–December 1919, he realized that land transfers would enhance the economic development of the country. He still favored transfers on a limited and controlled scale. Until the negotiations with former premier Georges Clemenceau regarding the future status of Palestine were completed, the Foreign Office, unlike the War Office, favored maintaining the status quo. The War Office believed that small transfers would immediately help both Arabs and Zionists. The military administration felt that any further postponement would create undue hardship for the population and be a disappointment to the people.[38] In March, with the status of Palestine unofficially confirmed as a British Mandate, Curzon advocated a reopening of the Land Registry offices but with *waqf* dedication excluded from the term disposition. Curzon unsuccessfully opposed Bentwich's proposal to give the senior judicial officer oversight of the Land Registry Department and control over all of its functions.[39]

At the San Remo Conference in April 1920, the mandates of the former Turkish territories were allotted. Britain became trustee for Palestine, and Sir Herbert Samuel was appointed high commissioner. The civil administration replaced the military administration the following June. Military governors, who after June changed their titles to district governors, received copies of the proposed Land Transfer Ordinance in July. In September, the ordinance was signed by Samuel, and it became effective on 1 October 1920.

The general goals of the Land Transfer Ordinance were identical to those of the proposed 1919 draft: prevent speculation, afford the small owner and tenant protection against eviction, and provide access to a minimum amount of capital. All transactions had to be made at the Land Registry Department and receive the consent of the administration. Consent to a disposition that included *waqf* dedication was provided if (1) property value did not exceed a value of £E3,000 or 300 Turkish dunams of agricultural land or 30 Turkish dunams of urban land; (2) the person acquiring the property was resident in Palestine (thereby precluding speculation by landowners and land brokers outside of Palestine); and (3) the person acquiring the property intended to cultivate or develop the land immediately. The consent of the administration or registration of the deed did not imply guarantee of title. The high commissioner possessed the authority to give consent to larger purchases in size and amount if it were deemed to serve some public utility. District governors were to withhold their consent to a disposition if they were not satisfied that the person transferring the property, or a tenant in occupation, would retain sufficient land in the district or elsewhere for the maintenance of himself or his family.[40] The fellaheen protection clause omitted from the revised Draft Land Transfer Ordinance in 1919 was reinserted into the ordinance. Actions for the partition of *musha'*-held property were permitted but not quite encouraged. Because general supervision of the Land Registry offices was vested in the legal secretary (attorney general), Bentwich enjoyed unparalleled influence over land matters until High Commissioner Chancellor included these offices under his purview in 1929. There is no doubt that in the 1920s Bentwich's Zionist sympathies neutralized administration opponents to the Jewish national home concept. While Bentwich was in office, the Palestine administration neither prohibited land transfers nor contemplated prohibitions.

After the promulgation of the ordinance, the expected rush to transfer land at the Land Registry offices did not materialize for several reasons. The administrative mechanisms introduced to scrutinize a transfer took as long as three months. Although they expressed a wish to partition their lands, many *musha'* shareholders had no desire to approach the administration even if they possessed title deeds, which many did not. Small landowners who were receiving agricultural loans were not yet confronted with the absolute necessity of selling a portion of their lands for needed capital. Others had received monetary payments from potential Jewish purchasers, who did not wish to reveal an inordinate desire to purchase land lest land values be driven up by demand. Perhaps most important, those interested Zionist purchasers preferred acquiring larger areas of land despite the existence of the Land Transfer Ordinance's size limitations.

For Zionists interested in proving to themselves and the British their intent to establish a homeland, a very large land sale would demonstrate not only commitment but also competence. To be sure, negotiations for land purchase had not ceased with the proclamations of November 1918, as evidenced by the contacts maintained by Jewish purchasing agents with the Sursock family in Beirut from the early 1900s throughout the 1920s and with other potential vendors in and outside of Palestine. Larger land purchases inevitably meant having to give considerable thought to tenants and to decisions about whether the vendor or purchaser would see to their future location. The acquisition of larger land areas also required protracted planning because of the large amounts of money needed to effect a transfer.

Most of the transfers during the first six months of the ordinance's existence took place in three urban areas: Jerusalem, Jaffa, and Haifa. Of the 3,365 petitions for land transfer made in this period, only 26 were refused. Until June 1921, with the exception of the previous February, Jews purchased fewer dunams than did the Arabs. As recorded by the Department of Land Registry, the absolute increase of land into Jewish hands during the first nine months after the offices were opened amounted to a mere 13,453 dunams.[41] For purposes of preventing or limiting land speculation, the initial half year of the ordinance's operation proved reasonably successful.

Reaction to the Land Transfer Ordinance and Its Emendation

Almost immediately after its promulgation, the ordinance was criticized by all segments of the population, both for what it included and for what it omitted. Vocal Arab reaction, though perhaps not representative of all Palestinian Arab interests, was most pronounced. In an open letter to High Commissioner Samuel, the Muslim-Christian Association of Jaffa questioned the unlimited authority given to the high commissioner, especially in the absence of a legislative council.[42] While the Zionist Commission had similar reservations, their proximity to the drafting of the ordinance enabled them to have a clause inserted into Article 8 of the Land Transfer Ordinance that allowed the high commissioner the option to refer any application for a disposition to a commission that he might appoint.[43] Although the presence of such a clause diminished the absolute prerogatives of the high commissioner in ruling on a disposition, he was able to retain control over the appointments to such a commission. The Palestine Arab political community, interested in majority self-rule and wary of Samuel's pro-Zionist sympathies, believed that such a commission would serve only Zionist interests.

A second reason for Arab objection to the Land Transfer Ordinance was the noticeable omission of punitive action against those involved in land dispositions during the previous twenty-two-and-a-half-month period of transfer prohibition. The Zionist Commission was opposed to sanctions imposed upon organizations or individuals who purchased land during 1918–20.[44] The Muslim-Christian Association of Jaffa asserted correctly that prior to the ordinance many fellaheen had entered into agreements to sell their land to Jewish purchasers. Those agreements to sell were set at specific prices. But when the Land Registry offices reopened, the Jewish purchasers retracted their original commitments, informing the Arab sellers instead of their willingness to pay only half of the price agreed upon earlier. Some fellaheen, already suffering economically, sold their land at lower prices. There is evidence to indicate that advance loans were issued by Jewish purchasers to small landowners. Promissory notes were also written as collateral for the eventual transfer of title deeds. Sometimes promissory notes were given to Jewish purchasing agents in return for cash outlays or even for volume equivalents of cooking oil. Ultimately, land sold or negotiated for sale during the prohibition period was given legal recognition by the Correction of Land Registers Ordinance of 1926.[45]

The Land Transfer Ordinance required that a person be a resident of Palestine in order to acquire land. The Muslim-Christian Association of Jaffa considered such a restriction distinctly pro-Jewish because it specifically excluded Egyptian and Syrian residents from purchasing land in Palestine. It is not clear whether such a reservation was voiced in the vague hope or active anticipation that there might be financial and political defense of Arab land in Palestine by Egyptians or Syrians. At this time approximately 500,000 dunams of land in Palestine were held by absentee Arabs. Such a restriction meant the denial of future acquisitions motivated by speculative or commercial reasons. The Muslim-Christian Association acknowledged that the Jewish population was the only financially viable segment of Palestine's population at the conclusion of World War I.[46] In 1920, the impression held by an overwhelming majority of politically active Arab politicians in Palestine was that the Land Transfer Ordinance was a covert mechanism to aid Jewish land purchase.[47] This image eventually contributed to the emendation of the Land Transfer Ordinance in December 1921.

The ordinance was further censured on the grounds that it contained restrictive legal provisions. Article 7 of the Land Transfer Ordinance provided the district governor with the right to withhold consent to dispositions of land that had previously been sold within the year. Director of Lands James N. Stubbs believed it was the acquisition and not the disposal of land that had to be subject to control. Stubbs wanted to prevent the aggregation of large estates, as did many Zionists.[48] In addition, he noted that the administration would have to provide the fellaheen with a more generous supply of draft animals and agricultural equipment if the administration meant to keep "unsuccessful" farmers on their land. A Palestinian Department of Lands official, Amin Rizk, believed that the purchaser-speculator hesitated to acquire land because he could not relinquish it to his advantage in the future.[49] Some tenants were using the ordinance as a refuge, realizing that the landlord was prevented from free disposition of his land.

The ordinance had been in effect for only two months when Bentwich discussed possible revisions of it with two Zionist officials.[50] Because the Zionists were in the final stages of negotiations for large areas of land primarily from the Sursocks in the Jezreel Valley, the administration and the Colonial Office believed that retention of the size restrictions would ultimately prove futile. Moreover, the Palestine administration had no jurisdiction over land sales by absentees and could control only the registration of such sales. Because of the size and area limitations for owners residing in Palestine, the Jewish National Fund and the Palestine Land Development Company were encouraged to continue purchase negotiations with owners not living in Palestine. The troubled financial condition of the Zionists was sufficient for one Colonial Office official to believe that the removal of the provision for a maintenance area would not greatly endanger the future of the Arab agricultural population.[51] No Colonial Office official or any member of the Palestine administration supported any notion that hinted at the relocation of Arab cultivators across the Jordan or elsewhere.

When the Jaffa disturbances occurred in May 1921, the Land Transfer Ordinance was already a contentious piece of legislation. The Haycraft Commission, which investigated the causes of this intercommunal unrest, reported that the Arabs of Palestine considered the Land Transfer Ordinance a cause for the disturbances.[52] The "Arabs" to whom the commission referred were not the majority engaged in agriculture, but the numerically small notable landowning and land-benefiting class who strongly believed that their livelihoods were constrained by the ordinance's restrictions. Buying and selling land for speculation was limited by British intercession. It was believed that the land market was being managed by the government to help develop the Jewish national home. Yet the contents of official Arab protests to High Commissioner Samuel focused almost exclusively against Jewish immigration. Curiously, when Winston Churchill came to Palestine in June 1921, he did not find Arab notables identifying the sale of land to Jews as an equivalent grievance against British policy.[53] From mid-1921 on at least, it seems that public protest from Arabs in Palestine was more forceful, frequent, and vocal against Jewish immigration than against land sales to Jewish purchasers.

There were at least three reasons why immigration was an issue that roused greater protest than the land issue. First, physical Jewish increase by immigration was visually apparent and dramatic. The political and economic consequences of land transfers were not so immediately apparent. Second, in 1921, High Commissioner Samuel responded to Arab protests and violence by suspending Jewish immigration, albeit temporarily. The British gave the issue of Jewish immigration a more important policy status than that of land sales. Third, the political consequences of Arab land sales to Jews was not yet understood by the British. And fourth, the land market, which was very important financially to Arab landowners, was a protected domain in which a customary livelihood and life-style could be maintained if it was manipulated properly. Certainly, protests against Arab land sales and Jewish purchasers in the 1920s did occur. But the protests were more infrequent, especially after the constraints on dispositions found in the Land Transfer Ordinance of October 1920 were almost eliminated by amendments in December 1921.

After the May 1921 disturbances, Samuel intensified his efforts to enlist Arab participation in the Mandate. Some argue that he capitulated to their anxieties.[54] From June 1921 until February 1922, the Draft Palestine Constitution and proposals for advisory and legislative councils were aired. Samuel also urged his Colonial Office colleagues to encourage Arab participation in the Mandate. In late June 1921, the first Arab delegation to London shunned Samuel's advances. The delegation maintained its avowed policy of seeking to abrogate the Mandate and to rescind the Balfour Declaration. After discussions with Colonial Office officials in August, the delegation's attention focused on larger issues of principle, and less on individual pieces of legislation, such as the recently drafted Land Transfer Amendment Ordinance (LTAO). When representatives of the Arab delegation and Weizmann met with Colonial Office officials on 29 November 1921, both were aware of the administration's decision to remove the restrictions in the Land Transfer Ordinance.[55] Significantly, neither Palestinian Arabs nor represented Zionists opposed the proposed changes to the 1920 Land Transfer Ordinance. On 6 December the first Advisory Council met and decided to remove the various impediments to unrestricted land transfers contained in the Land Transfer Ordinance. Only the provision for the protection of tenant cultivators was retained.

The Advisory Council unanimously passed the LTAO with the belief that its effect would be popular throughout the country. Samuel and the

Palestine administration responded directly to Arab (landowning) criticism and pressure to amend the Land Transfer Ordinance.[56] Such responsiveness was commensurate with the administration's policy of seeking the Arab political community's acceptance, cooperation, and involvement in the Mandate's operation.

When the amended Land Transfer Ordinance came into effect on 15 December 1921, it removed value and size restrictions as well as qualifications on a purchaser's residency. District governors could no longer object to the purchase of property for speculative purposes. While there had been no recorded instance under the Land Transfer Ordinance in which consent was withheld because pure speculative intent was assumed, the administration recognized now that it could not legislate against land speculators or speculation. The Palestine Land Development Company initially suffered from the free rein given to speculation. For example, when a vendor signed a preliminary contract to sell at £E3 per Turkish dunam, it was sometimes found that at delivery of the title deed, the seller had abrogated the initial agreement and entered into a second contract to sell at £E9 per Turkish dunam. For this reason land-acquisition contracts drawn up by Jewish purchasers with Arab vendors frequently contained "specific performance" clauses. This insured against the loss of initial monetary advances given at the signing of preliminary contracts and guaranteed the acquisition of a particular parcel of land under negotiation.

Instead of the high commissioner or the district governor, the director of land registries was charged with giving assent to a particular land transfer. He had to be assured only that the seller had a title and "in case of agricultural land which was leased that he be satisfied that the tenant in occupation retain sufficient land in the district or elsewhere for the maintenance of himself and his family."[57] The overwhelmingly larger classes of agricultural laborers and small owner-occupiers were not entitled to any legal protection under the Land Transfer Amendment Ordinance.

The phrase "tenant in occupation" was amorphous and not given to official legal interpretation until the Protection of Cultivators Ordinance of 1929. Because of collusive arrangements between Arab landlords and Jewish purchasers and the willingness or necessity of Arab tenants to accept monetary compensation, the right of the tenant in occupation to a maintenance area was repeatedly and enthusiastically abridged after December 1921. Unlike the Land Transfer Ordinance, the Land Transfer Amendment Ordinance did not force the small landowner to retain a maintenance area. The prohibitions on all land dispositions made in November 1918 were intended to keep the fellaheen owner and tenant on the land in order to prevent the creation of a landless class ultimately dependent upon British financial sustenance. The Land Transfer Ordinance, before amendment, was also designed to protect the Arab owner "in spite of himself in matters where he [was] perhaps none too well fitted to protect himself."[58] The belief that an owner-occupier should be required to maintain a minimum area necessary for the support of himself and his family was repeated in September 1922 by the governor of the Galilee District.[59] Though given a political airing by Sir John Hope-Simpson in 1930, the concept of a maintenance area or "lot viable" was not considered again seriously by the administration until late 1935. Planned implementation and application of the "lot viable" concept was postponed indefinitely in April 1936 because of the outbreak of communal disturbances that month.

Compensation to Tenants in Occupation

The official Jewish purchasing institutions such as the Palestine Land Development Company and the Jewish National Fund favored the acquisition of land that could be easily settled by Jewish immigrants. There was, therefore, a priority interest in purchasing land where tenant encumbrances would be minimal or nonexistent. The Land Transfer Amendment Ordinance required that provision of a maintenance area be made for a tenant in occupation. A tenant not in occupation at the time of transfer was not legally entitled to a maintenance area. Through intricate arrangements made between the Arab landlord and the Jewish purchaser, tenants in occupation were offered compensation *prior* to actual transfer. The Arab vendor, aware of the Jewish purchaser's preference to acquire land free of tenant occupants, made considerable efforts to persuade former tenants to accept monetary compensation. Tenants who were often deeply indebted to their landlords or other moneylenders rarely had much choice but to succumb to financial pressures. Jewish purchasers wrote clauses into preliminary sales agreements or purchase contracts that specifically stipulated that the land had to be delivered free of occupying tenants. Even though the landlord might coerce his tenants into accepting monetary compensation when they did not do so voluntarily, the landlord sometimes insisted that the Jewish purchaser or purchasing organization be accountable for the actual disbursement of this compensation. By so doing, the Arab landlord was able to maintain his physical distance from those tenants who undoubtedly loathed his actions, protect himself from incurring undue public disdain, and place the visible onus of unsavory responsibility upon the Jewish purchaser.

When the Protection of Cultivators Ordinance was passed in 1929, it was admittedly enacted to bring legal requirements into line with actual practice. This ordinance confirmed the use of monetary compensation. Further, it removed any stipulation for the provision of a maintenance area for the vast majority of Arab-tenant earners. In effect, the landlord after June 1929 was given the legal right to terminate his tenants' occupancy by merely providing written notice that he wished the tenant to quit the land for monetary compensation. Not only did this ordinance of 1929 apply to a mere 10 percent of all earners engaged in ordinary cultivation or herding, but it stipulated that a tenant had to be in occupation of a holding for two consecutive years to qualify for compensation.[60']

Between 1929 and 1933, several amendments to this ordinance were passed in an effort to plug the loopholes used vigorously by Arab landlords and Jewish purchasers to circumvent its application. In 1933, a revised Protection of Cultivators Ordinance stipulated that land could be provided as compensation and made the definition of a tenant more encompassing.

Between 1921 and 1929, the total compensatory amount offered to tenants and others in residence was usually equivalent to 15 or 20 percent above the agreed purchase price. It was difficult for an Arab tenant whose net income was between £E9 and £E20 a year to refuse immediate compensatory amounts that were equivalent sometimes to two years' income. Compensatory sums given to tenants and grazers of livestock at Wadi Hawarith, after its purchase by the Jewish National Fund in 1929, were in the vicinity of £P30 per feddan,[61] or a little less than an owner-occupier's yearly net income. Since contracts for sale were often signed three or more months prior to the actual transfer, the director of land registries (later the director of lands) or the district officer often could not locate the previous tenants when registration was applied for at the Land Registry offices.[62] Hence, there was no way of enforcing the tenants' provision for compensatory land as stipulated in the Land Transfer Amendment Ordinance of 1921.

However, District Office officials knew that a complex compensatory process was being implemented. The agreements between Jewish purchasers and Arab tenants were officially notarized at subdistrict offices in anticipation of the transfer. The apparent silence of these officials about such agreements suggests tacit awareness at a minimum or active collusion at a maximum. At times these officials received "hush" money. Whether they understood the ultimate impact and effects such agreements would have upon a considerable segment of the Arab agricultural population is unclear. These agreements specifically provided the tenant with a certain amount of money. In return the tenant agreed to quit the lands he was working prior to a given date. Failure to quit the lands within the prescribed time forced tenants to pay an indemnity to the Jewish purchaser or agent, who as of that specified date might not become the legal owner of the land or possessor of the title deed.

No Ottoman law or any British ordinance required payment of monetary compensation to tenants. Few tenants who were offered monetary compensation refused it. Many left agricultural pursuits and even refused to work on alternative land offered by the purchaser or vendor. A few tenants who received monetary compensation did retain areas for cultivation and for grazing temporarily in the immediate vicinity of the land they formerly tenanted. (See Document 1.)

DOCUMENT 1

Translated from Arabic

Undertaking
Mr. Yehoshua Hankin
through the District Officer, Nazareth.

WE, the undersigned, cultivators of the lands of the village of Affula, as shown by the Register of the Commuted Tithe for 1924, hereby admit and acknowledge that the lands and houses situated in the village of Affula are from old times the property of Nicola and Michel, sons of Ibrahim Bey Sursock, late of the city of Beirut, and that after the death of the said Michel his share devolved by way of succession according to Miri Law to his heirs, viz., his widow Lisa Sursock and to his sons and his said wife, who being still infants are under the lawful guardianship of their mother, and that the said lands and houses are still their property to this day, without any objection of adverse claims by another person, and no other person has any rights to the said properties:

AND WHEREAS, you have purchased the said lands and houses with all the rights and benefits appurtenant thereto on behalf of the Palestine Land Development Company, and the American Zion Commonwealth, and you caused the said properties to be surveyed and to be registered in the names of the said two companies,

AND WHEREAS, we are not in a position to purchase the said properties or any part of the same owing to our inability to pay the price, and you have offered us sufficient land for cultivation,

WE THEREFORE, of our own free will do hereby inform you that we decline your offer, as we have obtained lands for cultivation elsewhere, and we are not in need of land, and we undertake that by the 5th of January 1925, we shall evict and deliver for your use our houses and remove from the said houses our families and our cattle, and we shall leave the lands of Affula, its houses and other buildings and deliver the same to you,

AND WE FURTHER UNDERTAKE to deliver to you four camel-loads of fodder per feddan.

AND WE ACKNOWLEDGE WITH THANKS the receipt from you of £E.50 for two feddans, and I, Salam al Saadi, received from you £E.25 for one feddan; and I, Mustafa al-Shari, received from you £E.25 for one feddan; and I, Ali al-Khalaf, received from you £E.25 for one feddan; and I, 'Abdullah Muhammad Jawish, received from you £E.50 for two feddans; and we, Ariefeh and Arfeh, heirs of Kamal Assad, for ourselves and in our capacity as guardians of our infant brother, (?) and the other heirs, received from you £E.50 for two feddans, and this by way of compensation for the tilth and any other work done by us on this land, and as consideration for our refusal of your said offer of land for cultivation, and we hereby waive by way of full and irrevocable waiver any rights which we may have had to the said lands and houses, and we declare that we have no further right to demand the purchase of the said land or any part of the same, nor do we demand land for cultivation nor any rights to the tilth, nor any other rights whatsoever.

If we fail to comply with the above terms or if we fail to deliver the said lands and properties (viz., the said houses) and to leave the said village within the aforementioned period, we shall be liable to pay you by way of rental for the said houses and lands at the rate of half-a-pound per day for each feddan, and in addition to this if we fail to leave and deliver or we fail to comply with any of the terms herein mentioned, we shall be further liable to pay you the sum of £E.50 per feddan by way of damages for the damage caused to you and of any Court or other fees which you may incur without the necessity of any Notarial or other notice, and our failure to deliver or our default shall be deemed to be sufficient notice within the meaning of Article 107 of the Ottoman Code of Civil Procedure.

Yours, etc.

28th December
1924.   (Signed)   'ABDULLAH MUHAMMAD JAWISH
        Fingerprint of ——   Ali al-Khalaf al-Adad
                    Salam Mahmud (al)-Saadi
                    Salim Mahmud (al)-Saadi
                    Mustafa Omar Shari

Arifeh bint ? Kamal Assad

Arfeh bint ? Kamal Assad

We personally know the above five men and two women and they have signed the above document in our presence after it was read over to them.

Witness (Signed)   Hassan Mubari

Mahmud al 'Abd-al Hassani (?)

Certified by the Notary Public of Nazareth under number 338 of 26/12/24.

Source: Central Zionist Archives, S25/3368.

The most detailed and representative documentation available pertaining to Arab tenant compensation as a result of Jewish purchases in the 1920s relates to the Jezreel Valley and the sales made there by various members of the Sursock, Karkabi, Tueini, Farah, and Khuri families mostly of Beirut residencies.

The lands sold by these families, mostly to the Jewish National Fund and the American Zion Commonwealth, were represented by approximately twenty agreements for a total of about 240,000 dunams. Most of the purchase agreements were signed between 1921 and 1925 between the vendors and the Palestine Land Development Company acting on behalf of the Jewish National Fund. Well over £E800,000 was spent for the purchase of this land. There were 688 tenant families occupying 130,000 of the total 240,000 dunams. Thus about 45 percent of the area purchased was unoccupied or unused by permanent Arab tenants or agricultural laborers. The 688 tenant families received more than £E27,000 in monetary compensation or an average of £E39 per tenant family. (See Table 5.)

When the Nuris block of land in the Jezreel Valley was sold by the Sursocks in 1921, 38 tenant families or approximately 224 total inhabitants worked 5,500 dunams of the 27,018 total dunams. Each tenant family worked an average of approximately 144 dunams before the sale. Some of the tenants at Nuris decided initially to remain there after the sale and accept land as compensation; others accepted monetary compensation and left Nuris immediately. There is no information available regarding the number of dunams occupied by the tenants who remained. But those tenants who did remain at Nuris acquired land for a period of six years with an option to purchase the land originally leased to them. The rental of this land was fixed at 6 percent of the published purchase price, a sum equivalent to £E8,000. At the request of the tenants the rental was changed to one-fifth of the yield. The tenants who remained neither left Nuris at the expiration of the six-year lease in 1928 nor did they make an effort to purchase the land. In 1928, the Palestine Land

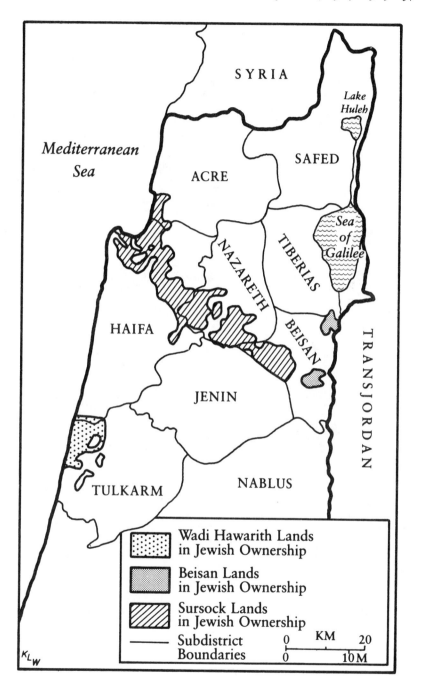

SYRIA

Lake
Huleh

Mediterranean
Sea

SAFED

ACRE

Sea
of
Galilee

NAZARETH

TIBERIAS

HAIFA

BEISAN

TRANSJORDAN

JENIN

TULKARM

NABLUS

Wadi Hawarith Lands
in Jewish Ownership

Beisan Lands
in Jewish Ownership

Sursock Lands
in Jewish Ownership

Subdistrict
Boundaries

KM
0   20

0   10 M

K_L_W

3. *Wadi Hawarith, Beisan, and Former Sursock Lands, March 1930*

1. *Sursock lands in the Jezreel Valley,* 1920
Courtesy of Central Zionist Archives, Jerusalem

2. *Jewish settlers clearing the swamps in the Jezreel Valley on former Sursock lands,* 1921
Courtesy of Central Zionist Archives, Jerusalem

Development Company transferred the land to the Jewish National Fund, which was then obliged to extend the lease to the tenants for another three years before it could obtain permission from the Palestine Land Department for the transfer to be completed and registered in the Jewish National Fund's name. Had all the Nuris inhabitants retained the 5,500 dunams they had been cultivating before the sale, the more than fivefold population increase in this area from 1922 to 1929 would have dramatically reduced the average amount of land per inhabitant. Where there were 24 dunams per inhabitant on the 5,500 dunams worked by the tenants in 1921, in 1929 there were only 4.4 dunams per inhabitant.[63]

Sale of lands in the Jezreel Valley had important significance, but certainly not the political value given to it by many writers. These land sales attracted notoriety because of their collective size, the importance that this fertile valley had for Palestinian Arab agriculture, and the fact that these were the first sales by official Jewish purchasing organizations during the Mandate. However, these so-called Sursock sales have become like a shibboleth supposedly characteristic of all land sales in Palestine. Palestinian Arabs claim that non-Palestinians predominated in land sales to Jewish purchasers, thus removing any implied onus of responsibility from Palestinian actions. Zionists and Israeli sympathizers assert that the Sursock sales had the effect of focusing Jewish purchases away from Palestinian fellaheen and the politically sensitive issue of dispossession. These sales were important not for future polemical purposes but for the depth and scope of negotiations that they portrayed; they established procedures for a tenant's compensation under British tutelage; they proved how a tenant's rights could be circumvented under the pliant eye of subdistrict officials; and they provided precedents in tenants' protection that were hammered into law by the Protection of Cultivators Ordinance in 1929.

The Beisan Agreement

There were at least three factors that contributed to the unobtrusive nature of the land question in the 1920s. First, Arab landowning interests were served with the passage of the Land Transfer Amendment Ordinance. No land reform or redistribution of land occurred. Second, fellaheen tenants gladly took what they viewed as exorbitant amounts of money to vacate land prior to transfer. Third, HMG in London responded to the urging of the Palestine administration and assuaged some of the fears of the Bedouin and the fellaheen population by legally conferring upon them traditional cultivation and grazing

TABLE 5

Sales Information on Tracts Acquired by Jews in the Plains of Esdraelon (Jezreel Valley) and Acre

Land	Sellers	Area in Metric Dunams Purchased	Previous Tenanted Area	Number of Tenants	Compensation Paid £E
Nuris Block	Sursock	27,018	5,514	38	615
Nahalal Block	Sursock	20,034	6,433	64	333
Jinujar	Sursock	10,568	5,927	20	256
Tall al-Adas	Sursock	19,758	8,271	34	492
Harithiya					
Sheikh Bureik					
Harbaj	Sursock	23,894	14,244	59	3,314
Jabata					
Khuneifis	Sursock	22,056	11,028	57	2,032
Jeida	Sursock	9,465	9,190	54	3,338
Tall					
al-Shaummam	Sursock	6,341	5,973	22	1,103
Qusqus-Tab'un	Farah	9,281	6,984	40	1,628
Affula	Sursock	14,244	12,406	47	2,603
Shuna	Sursock,	9,373	5,514	14	1,051
	Ra'is, Atala				
Abu-Shusha	Karkabi	4,870	1,929	17	432
Waraqani	Karkabi	3,308	2,757	9	513
Jidru	Sursock, Tueini	40,976	14,704	117	3,568
Majdal	Sursock	19,023	18,380	96	6,156
Totals		240,209	129,254	688	27,434

Source: Central Zionist Archives, S25/7620.

rights. This in combination with the simultaneous establishment of the Supreme Muslim Council created a good impression among Muslims, suggesting positive intentions by the British toward the Arab community as a whole in Palestine.[64]

Since there were no title deeds correspondent to the vast areas of land south of Beersheba town, HMG permitted tribal custom to prevail in these Bedouin areas. In March 1921, Churchill told several *shaykhs* from the Beersheba region that their special rights and customs would not be interfered with by the Palestine administration.[65] Churchill's promise was kept. Article 45 of the Palestine Order in Council confirmed that legal jurisdiction in the Beersheba area would be governed according to tribal custom. By not requiring the Bedouin to pay Land Registry fees, the administration hoped that they would not be reluctant to acquire title deeds. The administration's benevolence had the desired effect of quieting Bedouin anxieties about the disposition of their land.

At the Peace Conference the Zionists voiced an ardent interest in acquiring state lands, unoccupied lands, lands of uncertain ownership, and uncultivated lands. The belief that there was easy access to these lands became an integral element in the Zionist land-acquisition plans for the period to 1925. The secretary of the Zionist Commission as early as May 1918 requested that the British set up land commissions in order to determine the extent of *jiftlik*, *mudawara*, *mawat*, *mahlul*, and state land. In August 1920, Samuel appointed a land commission with a two-fold responsibility: to identify the exact dunam amounts of the above land categories and to recommend means to increase agricultural productivity so that dense settlement of Jews could be encouraged.[66]

Though published in the same month, the Land Commission's findings were not influenced by the May 1921 disturbances.[67] The commission upheld the administration's policy of protecting agricultural tenants but not at the expense of forfeiting administration latitude in controlling the disposition of state land for tithe and rent revenues. Tenants on state land at that time were required to sign contracts obliging the tenant lessee to follow administration instructions concerning cultivation practices. A tenant's failure to sign such a contract meant forfeiture of his lease agreement without compensation. Tenants in the Beisan region were cultivating state lands that had been previously owned by the sultan. Since the 1880s, these tenants had been considered by the Ottoman government as tenants holding perpetual leases. Signing these new agreements with the Palestine administration was construed by the tenants to mean that the British could terminate their status at will.

In early 1921, apprehension among these Beisan tenants was high since the administration had stipulated that no state land could be cultivated for summer crops unless a lease was signed.[68] Arab cultivators feared that the administration was about to encourage Jewish settlement in Beisan. This would have fulfilled Zionist goals and been compatible with British promises in Article 6 of the Mandate. Some fellaheen believed that Samuel intended to divide up the state lands and hand them over to incoming Jewish immigrants.[69] But at a meeting with local *shaykhs* and notables in Beisan in April 1921, Samuel reassured them that the administration had no intention of prejudicing their rights. The *shaykhs*, however, refused to enter into lease-tenancy agreements with the administration because they did not wish to confirm the notion that the British, as the inheriting governmental authority, had prerogatives over their land.[70] The tribal leaders were all the more uncompromising in their position when a special administrative subcommission was established in March 1921 to deal especially with the 302,000 dunams in Beisan. Despite the administration's assurances, possible governmental interference in their affairs worried them. But by July 1921, Samuel and the Arab notables and *shaykhs* from Beisan reached a compromise in which the Colonial Office concurred: the resident tenant cultivators and tribal members would be given the option to purchase the lands they had worked as "occupancy tenants."

Ghor Mudawara, or the Beisan Agreement, was signed on 1 November 1921.[71] During the period when the cultivators had the right to purchase these lands, their position as occupancy tenants was protected. Over a period of fifteen annual installments, the tenants purchased their land at a rate of 150 Egyptian piastres per dunam of irrigable land and 125 Egyptian piastres per dunam of nonirrigable land. The purchase price requested was approximately one-seventh to one-fourteenth of the prevalent market price per dunam of rural land in the area. At the end of the fifteenth year, if the tenant failed to pay the full transfer price, he was to forfeit his right to a title deed as well as to any legal rights then available to a government tenant. It was the administration's policy not to alienate state lands. However, in an effort to establish a relationship of confidence with these tenants, the administration believed that this accommodation was necessary. The administration was not giving up its ownership rights to these lands immediately. During the term when the transfer price was to be paid, the land assigned to the tenant could not be transferred except by succession or mortgage to the administration. Tenants' occupancy on these lands was in the administration's best interest because it assured continued tithe collection.

In 1921, the Land Commission formed the Beisan Demarcation Commission. It determined which areas would be allotted to the tenants residing in the twenty-two villages and tribes under the agreement's purview. By the end of 1931, 2,614 Arab tenants had been allotted lands averaging 101 metric dunams each. More than 87 percent, or 264,000 of the original 302,000 dunams, had been assigned.[72] For reasons of local politics or favoritism, some tenants received areas far in excess of the amount they could cultivate themselves. Some, in fact, hired additional agricultural laborers. Others preferred to sell their excess land to Jewish purchasers even though it was in direct contravention of Article 16 of the Beisan Agreement.[73]

Representation on the Beisan Demarcation Commission became a politically contentious issue among Arab notables and *shaykhs* in Beisan. Initially Jubran Kazma (also the Beisan representative to the Fourth Arab Congress) and Mubarak Zu'bi represented the cultivators' interests on the commission. Both men were accused by Mustafa al-Khatib, Salih al-Qasim, and Rushdi Yusuf ʿAbd al-Hadi, *mukhtars* of Tira, Jabul, and al-Ashrafiyiah respectively, of denying the cultivators the right to sell excess land to Jewish purchasers.[74] Mustafa al-Khatib in the early 1920s received 30 Egyptian piastres a month from a Jewish land-purchasing agent to rid Kazma and Zuʿbi from the Demarcation Commission. The purpose of the subvention was to have these men and their opposition to the selling of excess lands to Jews removed from the commission.[75] By 1932, at least 47 percent of the original 2,614 transferees from eighteen of the twenty-two villages and tribes had disposed of some of their land to Jewish purchasers.[76] By 1 June 1938, some 77,000 dunams, or almost 30 percent of the land originally assigned to Arab tenants in Beisan, had been sold to Jewish purchasers.[77]

Through the intercession of the tenants' representatives on the Demarcation Commission, the second high commissioner, Lord Plumer, decided in May 1926 that the scale of payment initially assigned to the tenants through the agreement was an economic burden to some. After consulting with them, Plumer recommended extending the time of payment from fifteen to twenty-five years.

The Beisan Agreement, revised in September 1928, further extended the payment period to thirty years. After the Zionists protested their exclusion from this state land by the original Beisan Agreement, the administration acceded to the Zionist demand that state lands be provided to them as specified in Article 6 of the Mandate.

Article 16 of the revised agreement now permitted the transfer of any land allocated by the government under the original agreement to any group as long as payment of the annual installment was made to the government. Explicit rights and privileges to these state lands were not granted to the Zionists. However, the revised agreement did give them the opportunity to procure land legally, which they had been acquiring irregularly since the implementation of the agreement in 1921. Once again the administration was giving legal recognition to established reality, this time to land transfers between Beisan tenants and Jewish purchasers.

The administration was not willing to provide necessary long-term loans to alleviate the indebted condition of these tenants. The severe drought in the Beisan area in 1928 and the drop in cereal prices in 1929 offset any economic advantage the Beisan tenant might have achieved in selling a portion of his land. Because of the tenants' poor economic situation and their extensive farming methods, it was estimated that the transferee would pay off this purchase price in seventy-five years.[78] In anticipation of the 1940 Land Transfer Regulations' implementation, many Beisan transferees exercised the option to sell their lands. In July 1940, only 1,073 Arab tenants remained signatories to the original agreement.[79] Almost 60 percent of the Arab tenants in Beisan, who were to be protected explicitly by HMG and given exclusive aid for the retention of their land, relinquished that land for monetary equivalents.

When the Transfer Regulations went into effect after February 1940, Jewish purchasers continued to acquire land within the geographical area defined by the original agreement. The purchase methods included execution of irrevocable powers of attorney before the notary public in the name of Jewish purchasing agents and Jewish purchasing organizations and the use of Arab representatives, who, as land brokers, made purchases at public auctions of land that had been collusively prearranged.

The Beisan Agreement greatly angered Zionists who felt that the Mandate was obligated to make state lands available to them. Not to have their right circumscribed, Jews went about actively buying land in Beisan as early as 1922.[80] Like the situation in late Ottoman times and during the period of land-transfer prohibitions in 1940 and after, legal restrictions were not impediments to Jewish land acquisition. The Beisan Agreement epitomized the nature of the British approach toward the Arab fellah: employ and expect legal, legislative, and bureaucratic means to maintain the Arab peasants on their lands. But British custodianship failed to provide the alternative source for money, so necessary if the tenant were to free himself from the control of moneylenders, merchants, landlords, and the debilitating rural economy. Instead, the Arab tenant and the owner-occupier, regardless of the administrative protection offered, became dependent upon Jewish land purchase as a main means to money and capital. Furthermore, an unintentional effect of the Beisan Agreement was the denial of free access to state land to private Jewish and Zionist purchasers. This was a factor that influenced Jewish land purchasers to concentrate on acquiring land from independent Arab owners. It may be argued that the Beisan Agreement, though publicly assuring Arab cultivators of their rights, helped make the land question a political issue. Had state lands such as those around Beisan been more freely provided to Jewish land purchasers in the 1920s, scarce Jewish capital might have been spent developing the Beisan area more fully, and the land question might not have emerged so quickly as a contentious political problem in 1930 and after. However, the 1920s did see the development of mutually beneficial contacts between Jewish purchasers and Arab owners, who in part comprised the political elite and leadership in the Palestine Arab community.

Palestinian Arab Land Sales: Motives

The apparent concentration of Jewish land-purchase efforts in the Galilee in the period prior to 1914 and in the Beisan area, Jezreel Valley, and coastal plain during the first decade of the Mandate did not reflect the planning and successful pursuit of a coherent or systematic Zionist land-settlement policy. Until 1929, no methodically planned national-land policy existed, though attempts were made by the Palestine Zionist Executive to promote coordination between the disparate public land-purchasing companies and their separate settlement objectives.[81] No scheme or plan existed for bringing a specific area of land under Jewish ownership in the early 1920s. Geostrategic concerns only became apparent—and then almost immediately paramount—in 1929–30 when the development of the national-home idea was physically threatened by the 1929 disturbances and politically endangered by HMG's policy to truncate Jewish immigration and land settlement.

Prior to 1929, and specifically before the August disturbances, there was not only an absence of coordination in establishing land-purchasing objectives, but there was also fierce competition among Jewish purchasing organizations for areas and parcels of land. Competition between private purchasers and public organizations had the unpalatable result for the Zionists and Jews of driving up land prices. Although the Jewish National Fund was the most prominent public land-purchasing organization in the late 1930s and 1940s, it was hindered in its attempt to influence the establishment of uniform Jewish land-purchase policy in the 1920s because of financial limitations, organizational problems, and internal ideological disputes. Had it not been for the disturbances of 1929 and the political aftermath of 1930, Jewish land-purchasing efforts might not of their own initiative have concentrated on the creation of geographically contiguous Jewish land areas.

Although rural land prices had risen over the previous years, the rise in the price of land was particularly noticeable in the urban areas. For example, in 1921, the Sursocks sold rural lands in the Jezreel Valley to the Palestine Land Development Company–Jewish National Fund for forty to eighty times the price they had originally paid. In 1921, that was equivalent to 3 to 6 Egyptian piastres per dunam.[82] Eighty percent of the Fourth Aliya, or wave of Jewish immigration into Palestine (1924–29), with its predominance of Jewish middle-class urban-oriented families, settled in towns and cities such as Jerusalem, Tel Aviv, and Haifa.[83] Inevitably, urban land prices soared. As a consequence, more money was spent per urban dunam of land than per rural dunam. The rise in urban land prices gave fuel to considerable speculation that spread to rural areas as well. The relatively small land purchases by Jews in the period

1926–28 reflected in some degree the high prices, rampant speculation, and insufficient funds. In determining whether rural land should be purchased, the variables that were considered included soil, fertility, cultivability, price, availability, the number of occupying tenants, pace of the transfer, and the number of owners with whom a sale had to be negotiated.

The absence of an enunciated Jewish land-settlement policy with precisely stated political objectives contributed to keeping the land question in a politically nascent form. Moreover, during the Mandate's first decade, the Palestinian Arab political community almost exclusively was consumed with financial, organizational, definitional, and leadership matters. The Arab delegations' attempts to abrogate the constraints imposed on national independence inherent in the Balfour Declaration were primarily directed at immigration, that is, the physical increase of Jews into Palestine. In addition, the land question did not enjoy the focus of local political attention because most of the land transfers to Jews in the period to 1929 were made by nonresident Palestinians, and there were minimum numbers of tenants or agricultural laborers on those lands. The policy adopted by the Palestine Zionist Executive, the Jewish National Fund, and other private purchasing organizations to refrain intentionally from publicly embarrassing those Palestinians who sold land added to the noticeable absence of Arab protest. The Palestine Zionist Executive's purpose was clearly designed to keep past vendors interested in future sales, to neutralize Palestinian Arab opposition to Zionism, and to preserve the land-benefiting classes' financial reliance upon Jewish sources for access to capital.[84] Moreover, Jewish land-purchasing agents took particular pride in their profession and guardedly maintained the confidentiality of their clients.

Nevertheless, from data presented to the Shaw Commission by Mr. Farrah of the Arab Executive, it appears that more than one-quarter of the land (116,000 dunams) that Jews legally purchased during the Mandate's first nine years came from Palestinian *effendis* and fellaheen.[85] Palestinian Arab politicians who were landowners selling land to Jews did not dwell on the land issue lest their own deep involvement become part of public discussion. Militant protests against land sales, brokers, and intermediaries, which had been absent during the Mandate's first decade, developed considerable intensity in the early 1930s.

In the struggle for control and direction of the Palestinian Arab nationalist movement, Arab politicians were eager to protect themselves against self-incrimination. It is not clear whether certain Palestinian Arabs even realized the obvious inconsistencies between their public demands for self-government, majority rule, and independence and their private actions in land sales. Some Palestinian Arab political leaders in the 1920s damaged the nationalist cause, and it is not clear whether Palestinian Arabs were concerned about the long-term disadvantages they were bequeathing future generations. Perhaps the existence of local or regional rivalries for political control in and around Tulkarm, Jenin, Jaffa, Nablus, Jerusalem, Gaza, and elsewhere stifled a conscious national appraisal of the scope of local individual involvement in land sales. Certainly, the magnitude of land sales to Jews after 1930 awakened the Arab political leadership to the reality that vast areas of Palestine were passing out of their hands, never to be reclaimed.

The overwhelming contribution of Arab land sales to the creation of a geographic nucleus for a Jewish national home was not only astonishing in the amount of land transferred by Palestinians (which continued to rise after 1930), but was also marked by the preeminent role of Palestinians who guided the nationalist cause in the 1920s and early 1930s. It is not to be argued here whether the Arab Executive did or did not effectively represent or reflect the interests of the entire Palestinian Arab population. In fact, the Arab Executive accepted the responsibility of representing Palestinian Arab interests to the Palestine administration and to HMG in London. Of the eighty-nine members elected to the Arab Executive between 1920 and June 1928, at least one-quarter can be identified, personally or through immediate family, as having directly participated in land sales to Jews. Of the forty-eight members of the Arab Executive in attendance at the Seventh Arab Congress in June 1928, at least fourteen had by that date been involved in land sales.[86] Members of the various Palestine Arab delegations to London appear to have been deeply involved in the land-sale process. For many of these individuals who sold land, their participation at an early juncture did not preclude the development of overwhelming hostility to land sales at a later date. A detailed, but neither exhaustive nor complete list of Palestinian Arabs involved in land sales to Jews appears in Appendix 3.

Musa Kazim al-Husayni, a former *qaimmaqam* of Jaffa under the Ottoman regime, mayor of Jerusalem from 1918 to 1920, president of the Muslim-Christian Association of Jerusalem, president of the Arab Executive from 1920 to 1934, and head of the Arab delegations to London in 1921–22, 1922–23, and 1930, sold an unspecified amount of land in the village of Dilb in the Jerusalem subdistrict to Jewish purchasers before the Mandate. In addition, Musa Kazim apparently took an unspecified amount of money from a Jewish purchasing agent in the period 1920–22.[87] Another member of the first Arab delegation was Amin al-Tamimi, who was also a member of the Supreme Muslim Council from 1926 to 1938. Amin was the brother of Muhammad al-Tamimi, who defended Jewish land-purchasing agent Yehoshua Hankin in a civil court appeal in 1925, and earlier in 1921–22 successfully defended the

Palestine Land Development Company in its attempt to have the Arab tenants at Jinujar vacate the lands they had been occupying.[88] Mu'in al-Madi, formerly the head of intelligence for Faysal in Damascus and then a member of the Arab Executive from Haifa to the Seventh Arab Congress, sold land to Jews near Atlit in the Haifa subdistrict.[89] A fourth participant of the six-member first Arab delegation, Shibli al-Jamal, later a Jaffa representative to the Fifth Arab Congress in August 1922, sold lands to Jews near Beisan.[90] No evidence has appeared to suggest that 'Abd al-Qadir al-Muzaffar or Wadi al-Bostany, also members of the various Arab delegations to London, were involved in land sales to Jews, directly or indirectly.

The Arab delegation that visited London in March–April 1930 was composed of Musa Kazim, Raghib al-Nashashibi (the mayor of Jerusalem from 1920 to 1934), Alfred Rok (a Greek Catholic and close associate of the mufti and later a member of the Arab Higher Committee), Jamal al-Husayni (the secretary to the Supreme Muslim Council and the Arab Executive from 1922 to 1934 and later head of the pro al-Husayni-dominated Palestine Arab party), and 'Awni 'Abd al-Hadi (a lawyer, legal adviser to the Supreme Muslim Council, the Jenin representative to the Fifth and Sixth Arab congresses, and later a leader of the Istiqlal party).

It appears that all of these men except Jamal al-Husayni were involved in land sales to Jews. Raghib al-Nashashibi, along with 'Omar al-Baytar, the president of the Muslim-Christian Association of Jaffa, and 'Asim Bey al-Said, the mayor of Jaffa, sold 1,200 dunams to the Jewish National Fund in the late summer of 1924. The transaction was handled by an Arab land broker who was paid 5 piastres per dunam for his services. The vendors demanded and received an immediate payment of £E500.[91] Alfred Rok's family sold approximately 10,000 Turkish dunams to Jews in the late 1880s and early 1890s. Later in the 1930s and 1940s he and other family members sold land to Jews at Rantiya and Fajja in the Jaffa subdistrict.[92] In 1943 Alfred Rok sold land to the Jewish National Fund that later became part of Tel Aviv's central bus station. 'Awni 'Abd al-Hadi received a very handsome retainer for performing legal duties for the Palestine Land Development Company–Jewish National Fund in its purchase of 30,000 dunams at Wadi Hawarith in April 1929.[93]

Arab political infighting complicated and delayed the choice of the Palestinian Arab delegation to the London (St. James's Palace) Conference in 1939. There is no question that the Palestinian Arab political leadership, though rife with personal animosities, was unalterably opposed to the concept of the Jewish national home. Jamal al-Husayni headed this delegation, which included 'Awni 'Abd al-Hadi, Musa al-Alami, George Antonius, Dr. Husayn al-Khalidi, Alfred Rok, Amin al-Tamimi, Raghib al-Nashashibi, and Yaqub Farraj. 'Awni 'Abd al-Hadi and Alfred Rok had been involved directly in previous land sales. Musa al-Alami sold 900 dunams to Jewish purchasers in Beisan. One-third of this delegation might be described as somehow having personally compromised their nationalist goals.

Perhaps for more than any other reason Arabs sold land to the Jews during the Mandate for economic reasons.[94] High, sometimes exorbitant prices during times of economic distress was for some Arab landowners an enticement they could not refuse. The Jewish demand for land answered an Arab need for cash in financially troubled times. In fact, the quantity of Arab land offered for sale was far in excess of the Jewish ability to purchase.[95] Jewish buyers turned down purchase offers of small-tract land areas in the 1920s when it was in their interest and easier to buy larger tracts.[96] Even during times of extreme tension between Arabs, Jews, and the British, the Jewish National Fund never lacked numerous offers though it suffered from severe shortages of funds. In December 1937, in the midst of the Arab revolt, the Jewish National Fund was offered between 200,000 and 300,000 dunams by potential Arab sellers. In December 1940, after the application of the Land Transfer Prohibitions, the Jewish National Fund could not, because of financial constraints alone, effect all the purchase offers tendered.[97]

Landownership was the last surviving political prerogative for many of the Arab elite, whose privileges were slowly circumscribed by the British presence and Jewish settlement. Acquisition of capital via land sales became a vehicle for temporarily retaining one's declining social and economic prominence. Land accumulation had always contributed to status, prestige, and wealth. Acquiring, buying, selling, and speculating in land was a norm of behavior for landowners; whether land sales caused alienation and whether that alienation generated personal shame, disgrace, and remorse requires investigation of each sale. Certainly the acts of selling, brokering, or association with land sales became valid and recurring means for indicting political adversaries or deviant family members.

To be sure, the incongruencies between public and private actions were not representative of all Palestinian Arabs or of all those who sold to Jewish buyers. Yet the following exemplary cases betray an obvious dissonance. (There are scores of others as demonstrated in Appendix 3.) Mayor 'Omar al-Baytar of Jaffa was a member of the Arab Executive from 1921 to 1934. In May 1921, he severely attacked Attorney General Bentwich for his pro-Zionist sentiments and his influence over the courts of Palestine.[98] Yet al-Baytar sold land to Jews in Yahudiya in the Jaffa subdistrict. In March 1933, 'Awni 'Abd al-Hadi, responding to the newly written French report on agricultural development, said, "The question of land, in every nation, is not one which affects the individual citizen only. [I]n a country like Palestine . . . the land is insufficient for the requirements of the population which is rapidly increasing."[99] At that time, 'Awni 'Abd al-Hadi was a leading member of the Istiqlal party but four years earlier he had received a very large sum from the Jewish National Fund in the Wadi Hawarith sale.[100] Along with Rashid al-Hajj Ibrahim of Tulkarm, 'Awni 'Abd al-Hadi addressed a meeting of the Young Men's Muslim Association in January 1936 in Haifa. There, both men noted the incipient rebel movements of 'Izz al-Din al-Qassam as a natural outcome of the Judaizing policy adopted by the British government in Palestine.[101] Al-Hajj Ibrahim, too, had previously sold land to Jews.[102] Similar apparent inconsistencies existed with Yaqub al-Ghusayn, who was a Ramle citrus grower and member of the Arab National Fund. Al-Ghusayn in May 1936 remarked that "the nation forms a united front which will continue the [Arab] strike, and more than the strike; we shall not yield to threats, nor to force."[103] Six years later he and a close relative sold 306 dunams to the Jewish National Fund in the Gaza subdistrict for £P4,000 and received as balance for the land a loan of £P5,000 from the Jewish National Fund.[104]

Whether it was avarice or need, self-preservation or greed, Palestinian Arab land sales breathed life into Jewish aspirations and advanced Zionist goals. Indeed, Jews purchased only a small percentage of the total area of Palestine under the Mandate. The critical variable for Zionist motivation was Arab readiness to part with a portion of their patrimony. Palestinian Arab land sales meant the absence of true commitment to Palestinian nationalism. At a time of feverish anti-Zionist and anti-British sentiment, Palestinian Arab land sales to Zionists showed that individual priorities were equal to or more important than an emerging national movement. For the less-educated small-tract Palestinian landowner who was more likely to alienate his land in the 1930s, economic survival was his paramount motivation.

Jewish Land Purchase: Methods

The incomplete and inaccurate Land Registry records restored by the British in 1919 and 1920 facilitated the land-acquisition process for Jews and Zionists. Previously underestimated land areas were now registered in their larger actual sizes. Nasty and bitter boundary disputes were frequently forgotten in exchange for materials or money provided by the Jewish buyer to the Arab seller. Often land-sale contracts were written with the boundary stipulated as "not less than so

and so many dunams."[105] In another fashion Jewish land purchase benefited from the desire to establish accurate land records. Jewish buyers
often bought *musha'* shares during the land-settlement process. Often
the schedule of rights to *musha'* shares was posted to allow potential
claimants the opportunity to challenge the schedule before it was actually recorded. At that point, land was sometimes transferred into Jewish
ownership. When the time came for official registration of the shares or
the designation of rights to those shares, these unofficial transfers were
entered in the Land Registry books and legalized, since they now appeared in the posted schedule. Some former Arab occupants or owners
of these *musha'* shares continued to occupy the newly purchased Jewish
lands temporarily until arrangements were made for the establishment
of Jewish settlements.[106] At that point, the Arab occupants left the *musha'*-land areas they once owned, usually with monetary compensation
in hand.

It seems that the rewards and benefits accruing to the Arab seller and
Jewish purchaser were mutually beneficial at that time. This symbiotic
relationship stimulated the evolution of mechanisms that protected the
land-sale/land-acquisition process. Various ruses were devised to guarantee the anonymity of the seller, to expedite the transfer procedure, and to
circumvent the legal rights of tenant cultivators.[107] Avoidance of public
ridicule was a major priority for Arab politicians who may have been
simultaneously at the vanguard of the emerging Palestinian Arab national movement and involved in land sales. An important class of intermediaries grew in an effort to allow the Arab notables to protect their
reputations and fend off characterizations of traitor to the nationalist
cause. Not surprisingly, this group of speculators, brokers, and middle-
men grew wealthy from land sales and drove up land prices considerably
as a result of applying their fees. Both Jewish and Arab brokers made
little, if any, distinction between the sources of their income and the
political ramifications of their actions. Brokerage activity was more active in the 1930s because land sales in that decade involved the collection of smaller parcels of land from numerous owners prior to transfer
into Jewish ownership. In the 1920s, the landowner himself sometimes
acted as a broker or middleman as he briskly coerced his occupying
agriculturalists, who were otherwise indebted to him, to vacate lands in
anticipation of a land transfer. Clauses in land-purchase contracts often
specified this middleman role for the seller as he sought his tenants'
removal from lands prior to Jewish purchase.[108] In these instances, the
landowner's anonymity was obviously not completely protected. From
the vantage point of Jewish land purchases, the central motivational
factor governing "silence" about Arab complicity was the belief that
public exposure would jeopardize both future sales possibilities and the

practice of utilizing *effendi* intermediaries in land sales. Although the Palestine Land Development Company and the Jewish National Fund had carefully drawn up a list of Arab political leaders involved in land sales and intermediary activity as land brokers,[109] the list was intentionally kept from the Shaw commissioners in 1929 and 1930.

In most Jewish land purchases some amount of money was paid to a potential Arab vendor in anticipation of a land sale. These sums were outright loans, grants, or subventions made as part of the land-purchase process. Some form of liberal financial lubrication easily neutralized a *mukhtar*, local *shaykh*, or religious official's recalcitrance.[110] Though *mukhtars* were adjudged to be utterly incompetent in discharging their duties of registering all local land transactions, for which they were responsible until March 1937,[111] their assent or signature on a transfer, registration, or mortgage document was essential. Not surprisingly, the *mukhtar, shaykh,* or religious official who was so inclined could utilize his local social or religious stature to persuade villagers to leave their lands.

Protection of the Arab vendor's name and reputation was easily achieved through various land-purchase methods. One such method enabled the seller to borrow money from the Jewish National Fund, fail to repay the loan, and therefore be "forced" by the courts to sell a specified land area to the Jewish National Fund in order to satisfy the accrued debt. Some Arab vendors mortgaged their portion of *musha'*-held shares to Jewish mortgagees, failed to pay the principal due in thirty days, and, therefore, had to submit their lands to public auction. According to Documents 2–4, on the following pages, this entire process was preplanned so that the Jewish National Fund would obtain the land, the prestige of the seller would be protected, the rights of cultivators would be summarily circumvented, and the seller would obtain a price for the land well above the price set by the court. This same process was utilized in the sale of the Wadi Hawarith lands noted below.

DOCUMENT 2

District Offices
Jenin

Confidential
In reply please quote
J. 200/1/1   Date 16 August 1930
Administration Officer
Nablus Area

Subject: Sales of Land Zirin village
Reference: Your 200/4/j of 8.8.30.

1. The lands of Zirin village are *musha'*. They are divided into

85 shares of which 11 shares are owned by the original inhabitants of the village; the rest are owned by the 'Abd al-Hadi family.

2. The approximate area of each share is estimated to be 250 standard dunams.

3. The shares owned by 'Abd al-Hadi are cultivated by one of the undermentioned methods:

a) partnership with one or two of the inhabitants of Zirin, i.e., the owner and the cultivator share all expenditures and benefits, or

b) the owner gives his share by agreement of taking a certain percentage of the yield after the payment of the tithe and expenses; sometimes tenants from other areas are employed.

4. The tenants of Zirin village are either originally from the village or are outsiders who have come to Zirin in the last 10–30 years. Therefore, these tenants are affected by the change of the ownership.

5. Wajih Abdul Karim 'Abd al-Hadi of Nablus mortgaged and sold by public auction his share, which is about 1/85, to a certain Mustafa Shahin of Nablus [a middleman for the Jewish National Fund], who mortgaged the same lot in the name of the Jewish National Fund for one month. The mortgage is about to be due.

6. There are now three transactions in hand for mortgages which are owned by Yusuf Abdul Karim (1/85), Fouad Kassem 'Abd al-Hadi (1/85), and Afif 'Abd al-Hadi (1/2 /85); also Hilmi 'Abd al-Hadi and brothers of Arraba are proceeding to Jaffa to make the preliminary agreement with Hankin for mortgage and sale of the shares.

7. It is believed that every one of the 'Abd al-Hadis is going to sell to the Jewish National Fund or any other person whom they will find, but owing to the fact that they are afraid to lose their moral prestige amongst the inhabitants because of such sales, they are borrowing the money from the Jewish National Fund and making secret arrangements in which they agree to sell their mortgaged share by public auction, simply to show the public that they were unable to refund the money borrowed and that they were obliged to accept the sale which was affected through the court. And in the meantime [this process] relieves them from the rights of the cultivators which will be claimed, should the lands be sold in the ordinary way.

HH/BM   (Signed) H. Husayni
                           DISTRICT OFFICER

Source: Israel State Archives, Box 3511/file 1.

DOCUMENT 3

5 September 1930

Chief Secretary   Subject: Zirin village

1. The above village is situated on the Jenin-Affula road about ten kilometers south of Affula.

2. It is owned by the 'Abd al-Hadi family and partly by the fellaheen. I recently received information that the former were mortgaging their shares to Jewish mortgagees on terms requiring the repayment of the principal in thirty days. There was, however, an understanding that the mortgagor would default in payment and that the property would be submitted to auction and bought in by the mortgagor at an agreed price. I asked the District Officer for a report and his reply bears out my information.

3. The village is stated to comprise about 20,000 dunams divided into 85 shares of which 74 belong to the 'Abd al-Hadi family and 11 to the fellaheen. The population is about 900.

4. The District Officer reports that all of the 'Abd al-Hadis are believed to be entering into agreements for sale with the Jewish National Fund and that the relevant documents are being signed in Tel-Aviv. The vendors fear loss of their prestige if they execute official sales to a Jewish organization and they are therefore proceeding by way of short-term mortgage, default and compulsory sale. Four mortgages have been registered, of which one has been foreclosed and the share purchased by the Jewish National Fund.

5. These are compulsory sales in which the Government cannot intervene and if the reported arrangement is carried to a conclusion we will find ourselves faced with a second Wadi Hawarith for which reason I bring the matter to your notice.

6. I would add that Mr. Hankin, of the Jewish National Fund, agrees that my information is substantially correct.

(Signed) J. N. Stubbs

DIRECTOR OF LANDS

Source: Israel State Archives, Box 3511/file 1.

DOCUMENT 4

No. 287/268

District Commissioner's Office
Haifa
1st October 1930

Confidential
Chief Secretary,
Jerusalem

Subject: Zirin village
Reference: Your 3761/30 of 8.9.30.
The Nablus Administration Officer confirmed the state of affairs at Zirin village recorded by the Director of Lands.
I quote an example of the transactions described. Yusuf 'Abd al-Karim borrowed from the Jewish National Fund in July 1930 the sum of £P350 repayable in August 1930. When the debt fell due, Yusuf by arrangement failed to pay, and the Courts, on application, ordered the sale of the land mortgaged as security. This was acquired by the highest bidder, Mr. Hankin, for £P350. It is believed, however, that the figure was privately adjusted to £P750 per share.
The arrangement relieves the vendor in some degree of the odium that would attach to a voluntary sale to the Jews, while the purchaser escapes the restrictions of the Protection of Cultivators Ordinance, 1929, and possibly those rising from prior rights of purchase. In addition, the fictitious sale price is likely to affect the future valuation of the land for purposes of taxation.
The tenants, ploughmen, and laborers and their families at Zirin are estimated at some 900 souls, and the shares at the disposal of the tenants have dwindled from 74 to 11. They are therefore obliged to rent land from the 'Abd al-Hadis. If the 'Abd al-Hadi shares are transferred to the Jews, this resource will, of course, be lost to them, and a considerable landless population will result.
As the Area Officer points out, the tactics adopted at Zirin may become general throughout the country, and the position would be very serious. It would therefore appear necessary for Government to consider legislation to safeguard cultivators' rights and prior rights of purchase affected by forced sales of land through the Execution Officer.

(Signed) A. N. Law
FOR ACTING DISTRICT
COMMISSIONER.

Copy to: Director of Lands
Administrative officer, Nablus

Source: Israel State Archives, Box 3511/file 1.

Methods employed either to expedite a land transfer or to assure the transfer of a particular parcel, and not another, included irrevocable powers of attorney and penalty or specific performance clauses. When a Jewish purchaser anticipated that for some reason a vendor might in the future become dilatory in transferring a parcel of land, or refuse to do so in hopes of obtaining a higher price in the spiraling land market, irrevocable powers of attorney were used to bind the seller to a particular transfer within a precise time period at a fixed price. Additionally, the penalty or specific performance clauses stated that if a vendor failed to meet the obligations of the contract, he would be compelled to pay an indemnity to the purchaser. For example, if the vendor failed to deliver his land by a given time or under certain circumstances, such as "without tenants in occupation," the purchaser might be entitled to as much as ten times the land value. The penalty clause was aimed at the seller who might continue to shop for a purchaser willing to pay a higher price. Once the penalty clause appeared in the contract, the clause became a negotiable element for the Jewish buyer's purposes. If the seller owed a large sum of money to the buyer because of failure to adhere to the penalty clause, the buyer could cancel or reduce the penalty-clause amount in exchange for a more advantageous schedule of payments, or receive a greater area of land than was originally negotiated.[112]

Most if not all land-purchase methods described above were used throughout the Mandate. Many were refined to account for local political events, such as the 1929 and 1936–39 disturbances or the implementation of the 1940 Land Transfer Regulations. Collectively, these methods in the 1920s helped to keep the land question a nonpublic issue. More important, however, the purchase of land from large single owners, many of them not resident in Palestine, afforded the land issue a minimum of political prominence. Bentwich's handling of land matters, the Arab landowner's need for capital, the Beisan Agreement, fellaheen willingness to take monetary compensation, and a land regime in need of reordering helped obliterate the rancor that characterized the land issue in the 1930s. The present but dormant state of the land question as primary political focus for confrontation changed noticeably with the advent of Sir John Chancellor as Palestine's third high commissioner. His influence upon the Shaw Report, the Hope-Simpson Report, and the Passfield White Paper gave the very sensitive issues of land availability and landless Arabs their first thorough public airings. The denouement of the Wadi Hawarith affair, which lasted through the late 1930s, provided graphic examples of both issues and kept the land question alive in the Palestine Arab press.

The Wadi Hawarith Affair

In April 1929, the Jewish National Fund purchased 30,000 dunams of land at Wadi Hawarith, an area lying approximately thirty miles south of Haifa. Its purchase partially connected Jewish-settlement activities near Tel Aviv in the south and Haifa in the north. The thirteen vendors were all members of the Tayan family, six of whom had Jaffa addresses. In November 1928, in anticipation of the transfer, Yehoshua Hankin agreed with the Tayan sellers to acquire the land at public auction in order to preserve the latter's anonymity. On behalf of the Jewish National Fund, Hankin signed an agreement stipulating that the Jewish National Fund would pay the difference between the higher prearranged sale price and the expected lower price to be paid at the court-ordered public auction. The purchase price announced at the public auction was £P41,000; the real amount eventually paid to the thirteen Tayans approximated £P136,000.[113]

Prior to the actual sale, Hankin offered monetary compensation to the Bedouin and the fellaheen inhabitants who numbered about 1,200. The Jewish National Fund paid compensatory sums amounting to £P6,154 to cultivators, agricultural workers, grazers, and officials in surrounding villages, such as *mukhtars* and *shaykhs*, in an effort to ease the transfer process.[114] Before the sale was effected, the Jewish National Fund through Hankin served notice on the eighty-six cultivators at Wadi Hawarith to quit the land within one year. The Jewish National Fund and the Palestine Zionist Executive believed that unsavory political repercussions could be avoided if the land could be vacated before the Jewish National Fund took possession. In June 1930, after several lower court judgments, the chief justice of Palestine ruled that the order for eviction due in October 1929 stood. His important decision indicated that the landlord could not take steps to avoid future obligations that might be imposed upon him, such as compensation to the tenants.[115]

Before the publication of the Shaw Report in March 1930, a segment of the Wadi Hawarith inhabitants claimed that 6,000 dunams sold by the Tayans were not represented by title deeds and, therefore, were the property of the inhabitants. High Commissioner Chancellor, favorably disposed to Arab over Jewish rights in Palestine, wanted the order for eviction stayed pending determination of the ownership claims to the 6,000 disputed dunams. Ultimately, the Wadi Hawarith inhabitants were evicted from this area as well.

Short of preventing the eviction order, Chancellor wanted 6,000 dunams designated as state lands so that they could be leased to the Bedouin and the fellaheen.[116] In June 1930, after the eviction order was upheld by the chief justice, Chancellor turned to the Jewish National Fund in hopes of achieving a compromise. He suggested that the Jewish National Fund provide a portion of its recently purchased land to the Wadi Hawarith inhabitants. The Jewish National Fund, with the prodding of the Jewish Agency, recognized that failure to compromise with the high commissioner over the future of the Wadi Hawarith inhabitants would exacerbate Chancellor's anti-Jewish-settlement attitude. In the aftermath of the Shaw Report, but prior to the writing of the Hope-Simpson Report, the Jewish National Fund thought it wiser to demonstrate that it was not creating a landless Arab population as claimed in the Shaw Report. The Wadi Hawarith inhabitants chose to accept the Jewish National Fund offer, which allowed them to remain on 5,000 to 6,000 disputed dunams for a twenty-two-month period. When this agreement was reached in October–November 1930, the Jewish National Fund became increasingly adamant about the protection of its legal rights. The publication of the Passfield White Paper and the rumored land-transfer prohibitions in 1930 caused the Jewish National Fund trepidations. The Jewish National Fund wanted express guarantees from the administration that the land would be vacated at the end of the twenty-two-month period and that the Jewish National Fund would not be subject to new tenants' protection legislation. Such guarantees were not given, as Chancellor clearly sided against the legal rights of the Jewish National Fund. Instead, Chancellor found himself paternalistically bound to the Bedouin and the fellaheen inhabitants.

The Jewish National Fund continued to admonish the administration for its failure to find a satisfactory compromise that would not impinge upon the Jewish National Fund's legal rights. The twenty-two-month Jewish National Fund lease made to the administration was in turn transferred to the Wadi Hawarith inhabitants until the end of October 1933. On 15 November 1933, the Wadi Hawarith inhabitants, after failing to gain tenancy privileges under the newly promulgated Protection of Cultivators Ordinance, were evicted for a second time. During the period from September 1930 through December 1931, when the cultivators and grazers were on Jewish National Fund land without legal rights, the Jewish National Fund did not collect either rent or the tithe from them. When offered resettlement on land in Beisan as suggested by the administration in May 1933, the Wadi Hawarith inhabitants refused. Instead the Jewish National Fund was asked for a third time to lease land to the administration, this time for a five-month period that ended in May 1934.[117] By August 1934, a parcel of 2,000 dunams of state land near Wadi Hawarith was drained and readied for resettlement by the Wadi Hawarith inhabitants. Other Wadi Hawarith inhabitants in early 1934 purchased back 150 dunams of the recently acquired Jewish National Fund land while leasing an additional 1,000 dunams at nearby Wadi Qabbani.

By 1941, when the administration signed long-term leases with some of the Wadi Hawarith inhabitants, less than 300 persons of the original occupants of the Tayan lands remained. Some had moved south of Beersheba; others were employed as seasonal laborers on neighboring Jewish settlements; still others had obtained employment from the Public Works Department in building the Haifa-Jaffa road, a road that eventually cut through their small remaining parcels of land in 1939.[118]

The administration's repeated efforts to seek compromise from the Jewish National Fund had numerous effects. The Wadi Hawarith inhabitants grew to believe that, regardless of their economic situation, the administration would not ultimately abandon them. The sense of paternalism invoked by Chancellor's attitudes and actions was accepted by the former Tayan cultivators and grazers and expected by other Arab fellaheen as well. The belief grew that despite their legal right to the land the Jewish National Fund could be forced to yield to strong pressure from the administration. The repeated evictions and cumbersome court procedures provided the Palestine Arab political leadership a cause célèbre with which to indict and flog the Jewish-settlement process.

Like the Sursock land sales, the Wadi Hawarith purchase had an effect far greater than the acquisition itself. The Sursock sales created the false notion that absentee landlords predominated in the land-sale process to Jews during the Mandate. The Wadi Hawarith purchase and its duration contributed to the false perception that the Zionists and Jewish land purchase were the sole reason for the creation of a class of landless Arabs. Both perceptions were incorrect. On the other hand, the delicate handling of the Wadi Hawarith purchase provided the Jewish Agency and Jewish National Fund a certain immediate political advantage. The repeated compromises to which they agreed helped postpone the imposition of land-sale restrictions advocated by Chancellor and expressed in the October 1930 Passfield White Paper.

Chapter 3

The British Threat to the Jewish National Home, 1930

Sir John Chancellor

A major reason for the ultimate success of the founding of the Jewish national home was the Zionists' ability to influence policymaking for Palestine. Zionist officials helped draft the Balfour Declaration, the Palestine Mandate, ordinances and legislation, and other important documents; influence was exercised over the appointment of individuals and officials who played pivotal roles in Britain's design and management of the Mandate. In the 1920s, Zionists were accustomed to being sympathetically heard by High Commissioners Samuel and Plumer and Attorney General Bentwich. They were instrumental in assisting the Zionist enterprise, though their relationships with leading Zionists were marked by disagreement over particular policies. Never did Samuel or Plumer oppose the development of the Jewish national home. Members of the Palestine Zionist Executive became accustomed to a close, positive, and synchronized relationship with the key decision makers at the highest levels of Palestine's civil administration.

The atmosphere changed in 1929 and 1930. Zionists were severely challenged and tested by individuals, policy, and potential legislation that were antithetical to Zionism, the Balfour Declaration, the nature of the Palestine Mandate, and the concept of the Jewish national home. Staunch, vocal, and committed advocates of Arab political rights in Palestine took control of the Palestine administration and sought to steer it in a radically different direction.

High Commissioner Chancellor (1928–31), the Shaw Commission findings, Sir John Hope-Simpson, and Colonial Secretary Lord Passfield (Sidney Webb) made Palestinian Arab rights a priority. Jewish settlement was put on the public defensive. The land question became as politically sensitive as the immigration issue had been in the 1920s. Proposals were made in the 1929–31 period for land-transfer controls and additional tenant's legal protection. This frontal attack against the physical growth of the Jewish national home resulted in several investigative committees that studied land availability and the number of landless Arabs. In addition, several detailed reports were written concerning rural development, agricultural practices, and the fellah's financial condition. Recognition was given to the legitimacy of Arab protests that self-determination and majority self-government had been denied. Slowly but consistently in the 1930s, HMG drifted from the status of umpire to that of advocate and finally to paternal defender of Arab rights. Such a policy was valid within the confines of the dual obligation as interpreted by High Commissioner Chancellor.

The challenge to Zionist growth and development eventually subsided. Restrictions on the growth of the Jewish national home were debated and then postponed for a decade. In the 1930s, Jews acquired more than 300,000 dunams of land. This was less than the 500,000 registered dunams acquired from 1920 to 1929, but more than the 200,000 dunams acquired via legal purchase from 1940 to 1947. But the increment in the 1930s gave credible substance to a geographic and demographic nucleus for a Jewish state; secondly, Jewish demographic growth in the 1930s reached new levels, with the number of Jews in the total population more than doubling from 164,000 to 370,000 from 1930 to 1936 alone.[1]

Equally important, the Zionists were challenged physically by the Arabs in the August 1929 disturbances, and politically by the British. The Mandate's political atmosphere became more emotionally charged and the Zionists' political future was threatened. Yet the Jewish Agency and its affiliated institutions were successful in derailing the ominous British proposals initiated by Chancellor and his colleagues. That success gave the Jewish Agency collective self-confidence, added conviction that their goal could be achieved, and forced the emergence of coordinated political tactics and strategy. Without the anti-Zionist British attitudes generated from the 1929 disturbances, it is doubtful whether Jewish leaders would have begun to consolidate and harmonize their geopolitical efforts for creating a Jewish state. Perhaps the stimulation to action would have come later in the 1930s or 1940s, but the events of 1929–31 were critical to the ultimate evolution of the Jewish state.

The British threat catalyzed action. It stimulated the development of methods and refinement of procedures for disproving British claims against the Zionist enterprise. Reams of information were collected, processed, and turned out in rebuttal to British suppositions. Jewish Agency counterstatements were issued, public testimony was largely and deftly provided for visiting British investigatory commissions, lobbying efforts in London and at the League of Nations were increased and augmented, and frequent expressions of distress against the portended turn in British policy were made.

No less affected by the possible shift in emphasis in British policy was the Arab community in Palestine. A genuine feeling emerged among some Arab leaders that majority self-government was not far away. But hopeful expectations fell short of being realized. In fact, the Zionists' success at neutralizing the threats posed to its development confirmed to some Arab leaders and fellaheen just how empty, insincere, and ineffective British promises and actions were. The combination of increased dissension within Arab political leadership circles and poor economic years made many Palestinian Arabs despondent and frustrated.[2] The rapid decline in control of their own future and destiny led many to despair and violence; for some, this meant angry participation in the 1936–39 disturbances.

No single person influenced the ideological shift more in 1930 than did Sir John Chancellor. The high commissioner made recommendations to further Palestinian Arab self-government, to restrict Jewish immigration to the limits of economic absorptive capacity, to protect Arab land alienation, and to prevent Arab fellaheen displacement. His personally strong anti-Zionist disposition helped formulate the majority conclusions of the Shaw Report's inquiry into the 1929 disturbances, the Hope-Simpson Report on Immigration, Land Settlement and Development, and the Passfield White Paper.[3]

Following the disturbances of August 1929, Chancellor forcefully made his political views regarding Palestine known to the Colonial Office. In a very lengthy dispatch in January 1930, he lucidly recounted the history of Great Britain's first decade in Palestine. He paid particular attention to the "bitter hostility of the Arabs toward the Jews" and recommended solutions to existing and potential problems. Chancellor attributed the outbreak of the 1929 disturbances to several factors long festering beneath the surface. These explanations included the pledges given by HMG to support the independence of the Arab peoples in 1915; the existence of the Balfour Declaration; the failure to uphold the promise inherent in the Anglo-French Declaration of 18 November 1918; the growth of Arab nationalism both inside and outside of Palestine; the Arab belief that the British Mandate in Palestine was inconsistent with Article 22 of the League of Nations' Covenant that promised eventual independent status to communities formerly in the Turkish Empire; and the Arab-held notion that certain Mandate articles gave the British justification to act contrary to the second half of the Balfour Declaration which protected Arab rights.[4]

Chancellor contemplated two ways to prevent further communal conflict: either continue the present policy of de facto recognition of Zionist over Arab rights and maintain a sufficient military force in Palestine to protect the Jews from the Arabs, or withdraw the special privileged positions granted and enjoyed by the Zionists within the Mandate's structure. To Chancellor, the first option was repugnant. Because of his sympathy with Palestinian Arab grievances and his growing dislike for the Zionists and their enterprise, he sought to implement the second alternative. He endeavored to create an Arab focus for the Mandate. In order to realign the Mandate's emphasis, he advocated abrogating certain parts of it.

While the Jewish Agency developed cogent and rational arguments for continuing Jewish settlement in 1930, the inescapable fact remained that there was an increasing scarcity of unoccupied or partially occupied land. Zionists were confronted by this reality, Chancellor's philosophy, and the loss of life and property as a result of the 1929 disturbances.

For Chancellor, the 1929 disturbances were critical in shaping his political attitudes. Prior to the disturbances, he did not possess a desire to shift the balance of power in favor of the Arab population. At the time of his appointment in 1928, he had had little contact with Jews in general except for personal friends among the English Jewry. Also, he knew little of Arab sentiment against the Jews or of Arab resentment based on promises made and breached during World War I.[5] In July 1929, he was optimistic about the continued improvement of communal relations between Arabs and Jews.[6] After the disturbances his animosity toward the Zionists and his deepening empathy for the Arabs of Palestine developed simultaneously. The disturbances and their aftermath moved him to a pronounced anti-Zionist and pro-Arab position. Specifically, he disliked the Jewish verbal attacks against Palestinian civil servants and the British police during and after the disorders. He took particular offense at the Jews gaining access to all secret documents that passed between the secretary of state and himself. There was a certain amount of bitterness between Chancellor and the Jewish Agency head, F. H. Kisch, both former lieutenant colonels in His Majesty's Army.[7] In their day-to-day relationship, neither one greatly enjoyed receiving orders, instructions, or suggestions from the other. Chancellor's identification with the Arab community and its rights, vaguely alluded to in the Balfour Declaration and the Mandate, appears to have developed more out of an antipathy for the Zionists than from an inherent or intrinsic ideological identity with the Arabs.

Central to Chancellor's views was his distaste for the Balfour Declaration. He considered the declaration to be unjust and detrimental to the interests of the British Empire.[8] Underlying his deliberations was a genuine concern for other parts of the Empire with large Muslim populations. The question was how best to effect an immediate departure from the declaration's intent. He could, and did, influence the Shaw commissioners sitting in Palestine from late October to late December 1929. But the Shaw commissioners refrained from suggesting constitutional changes for Palestine. Chancellor strongly believed that if some concessions to the Arabs were not made and the ambitions of the Zionist Jews not curbed, then a real rebellion against the government and the Mandate policy would be imminent.[9] Hence, he drafted his January 1930 dispatch in order to aid the Arab population through legislative means at least.

The views of Chancellor and Samuel about Arab disturbances during their respective tenures in office were similar. In the August 1929 disturbance—just as in the May 1921 unrest—each man noted that a spirit of nationalism in Palestine among the Arabs was evident. Both thought that Arab grievances had to be appeased or pacified.[10] Both sought and accomplished a temporary suspension of Jewish immigration. But Chancellor was not overjoyed about his position as high commissioner in Palestine. He neither liked the Zionists with whom he was in contact nor was he sure that HMG would support him in his effort to alter the Mandate dramatically. He expressed a willingness to leave Palestine if HMG truckled to Jewish pressure.[11] He ultimately stayed on in Palestine until the middle of 1931 in order to obtain his pension from HMG. But the issuance in February 1931 of the MacDonald Letter, which neutralized his anti-Zionist policy options, greatly distressed him and contributed to his departure from Palestine.

Chancellor proposed total suspension of Jewish immigration. He believed it was also critical to stop land sales, thereby protecting the rights of the Arab agricultural population. Conclusions 5 through 8 of his lengthy dispatch to the Colonial Office revealed the scope and magnitude of the land measures he wished to institute. They said, inter alia, that "all cultivable land in Palestine was occupied; that no cultivable land now in possession of the indigenous population could be sold to Jews without creating a class of landless Arab cultivators; that legislative measures be taken in order to insure that the indigenous agricultural population shall not be dispossessed of its land and to prevent the creation of a class of landless peasantry."[12] To effect the successful implementation of these goals, Chancellor proposed the promulgation of two laws by the Palestine administration. They were the Transfer of Agricultural Land Bill (TALB) and the Protection of Cultivators Amendment Ordinance. The former legislation was aimed at the Jewish purchaser and the latter was directed at the Arab vendor. To his son Chancellor wrote, "If the Government agree[s] to them [the legislative land proposals] it will be a great blow to political Zionism."[13]

Inherent in TALB was the concept of nonalienation of Arab land. The transfer of Arab agricultural land and the creation of rights over such land were to be subject to the consent of the high commissioner. Chancellor wanted to reinstitute the high commissioner's control over land transfers. As a conciliatory gesture to Arab landowning interests, the high commissioner gave up this right in the Land Transfer Amendment Ordinance of 1921. He wished to blunt the practice of buying agricultural tenancy with monetary compensation. Protecting the Arab tenant agriculturalist by providing him with land instead of money would also reduce the prospects of the per diem agricultural laborer being removed from the land. The high commissioner feared that unless the entire Arab agricultural population remained on the land it worked, most of the dispossessed would become brigands.[14] In addition, Chancellor's proposed bill included the potentially explosive and politically sensitive issue of codifying legal discrimination between Arab and Jew. By taking the responsibility for determining whether a vendor was an Arab or not,[15] Chancellor was in fact seeking to change legally the concept embodied in the phrase "non-Jewish population," which appeared in the articles and preamble of the Mandate. Chancellor wanted Arab rights positively stated rather than referred to in an offhanded, secondary manner. Legal discrimination between Arab and Jew was finally applied ten years later when the Land Transfer Regulations of 1940 were implemented.

Since the Jewish purchaser was generally interested in having his newly acquired land delivered free of tenant encumbrances, Chancellor proposed that the administration receive prior notification of eviction proceedings. Chancellor hoped to prevent through legal injunction the collusive agreements signed between Arab vendor and Arab tenant *prior* to a new land-transfer registration. Chancellor did realize that there was no way the proposed bill could be made totally impenetrable to evasions by Arab landlords.[16] His support for the tenants went even further. A tenant was to be given legal recourse to challenge an increase in rent. It was not uncommon for a landlord to increase the rent on leased land in order to force a tenant to vacate it. An increase in rent or a threat of an increase contributed to the landlord's local authority, as the tenant had no option except to succumb to the landlord's pressures. Under Chancellor's proposals, the tenant had an opportunity to appeal a rent increase. A board composed of administration officials as arbiters was to decide whether a rent increase was justifiable. Such legislation, if promulgated, could have far-reaching social and political implications. Unprecedented administration support for a tenant against his landlord would have disturbed the traditional relationship between the two. In short, Chancellor wanted to prevent unwarranted rent increases.[17]

In an effort to reduce the number and size of land transactions, Chancellor proposed severe limitations on transfers. Transfers in land parcels over 1,000 metric dunams were to be forbidden without the high commissioner's consent. Clauses were inserted into Chancellor's proposed bill to prevent vendors and purchasers from arriving at agreements for areas smaller than 1,000 dunams in size. The concept of a subsistence area was also to be reinstated. No tenant was to be evicted if the high commissioner felt hardship would ensue unless the tenant received sufficient land elsewhere as compensation.

Chancellor considered the tenants' situation critical. In his estimate, the solution to their plight was to be found in shutting down Jewish settlement and particularly Jewish land purchases. Chancellor wanted to stop the alienation of Arab land. But his proposed legislative measures did not receive support from the Colonial Office. In fact, they encountered considerable resistance. Lord Passfield, the colonial secretary, did agree that a grave situation was developing in regard to land. Sir John Shuckburgh, a Colonial Office bureaucrat, believed that some effective measures would be necessary to protect Arab villagers.[18] But Colonial Office officials in London had broader and much deeper considerations to take into account without having to contend with the inevitable expected criticism emanating from either the Zionist or Arab communities in the event that Chancellor's proposals were adopted. The potential domestic political repercussions expected from the publication of the Shaw Report in late March 1930 were considered. Discussion of the Palestinian issue in the House of Commons was to be avoided lest a division in the House cause the minority government of Ramsay MacDonald to falter. In a tight domestic situation the Colonial Office could not sanction the obviously discriminatory legislation advocated by Chancellor.

Officials in the Palestine administration also questioned the wisdom of the proposed land legislation. Some, however, defended the legal distinction that Chancellor was seeking to make between Arab and Jew. R. H. Drayton, who drew up the proposed Transfer of Agricultural Land Bill, believed in a narrow interpretation of Article 15 of the Mandate that forbade discrimination of any kind on the grounds of race, religion, and language among the inhabitants of Palestine. Article 15 was purposely restrictive, he argued, and was not applicable to other matters,[19] such as land. Attorney General Bentwich on the other hand believed that the draft of such legislation was contrary to Article 6, which called for high density or "close settlement" of the Jews on the land.[20] The acting chief secretary of the Palestine administration, Eric Mills, not only took issue with the fact that the proposed bill tended to advocate political segregation of Jews and non-Jews, but also questioned the wisdom of the administration's encouraging divisive legislation even though such segregation might be inevitable.[21]

Chancellor wanted to put the onus of responsibility for the poor economic condition of the Arab agriculturalist on the shoulders of Jewish land purchase and immigration. He glossed over the reasons for the large indebtedness of the fellaheen class, namely, their uneconomic methods of land usage, the burden of agricultural taxes upon them, and the uncontrollable but periodic presence of natural setbacks such as drought, field mice, plague, locusts, and earthquakes. Chancellor was looking for political causation while others in Palestine officialdom saw the roots of the problem embedded elsewhere. The commissioner of lands, Albert Abramson, took direct issue with any restriction in the sale of land. He believed it would interfere with the economic life of the country and would be resented by the majority of landowners.[22] Mr. Bennett of the Palestine Lands Department, like the commissioner of lands, considered excessive taxation and indebtedness as the two burdens weighing most heavily upon the agriculturalist.[23] No one in the Palestine Lands Department, Chief Secretariat, or Colonial Office mentioned the debilitating nature of the *musha'* system practice, which reflects a lack of informed comprehension of, or attention to, the socioeconomic mechanisms at work in Palestine. British officials could easily pinpoint political sensitivities that had to be watched. They were likewise consumed with fiscal and monetary stringency with regard to Palestine. However, officials of HMG were not likely to cite their own errors of commission or omission.

Yet the British knew that if they instituted land-transfer restrictions, they would forfeit needed tax revenue and Jewish immigrant-introduced capital into the Palestine economy. HMG relied heavily upon Jewish capital to fuel the economy and, more particularly, to fund the requirements of the Jewish population's social services. Without making Palestine a burden to the British taxpayer and with Palestine's self-generated tax revenue, HMG could direct its attention to bolstering its strategic presence in Palestine. To be sure, not every Jewish land purchaser found a vendor in Palestine, but even the ancillary input of Jewish capital into the administration's revenue collection was more than significant. In 1928, while the Jewish population was only 17 percent of the total population, Jewish revenue contribution to the Palestine administration amounted to 44 percent of the administration's revenue.[24] In June 1936, a member of the Permanent Mandates Commission noted that the Jews in Palestine contributed more to the Palestine public treasury than did the Arabs.[25] Land-sale restrictions undoubtedly would have been a very severe blow to Jewish immigration and land settlement in general and land purchase in particular. Political considerations had to be weighed against the desired financial input of the Zionist enterprise into Palestine's economy.

The Colonial Office and the MacDonald government, while acknowledging the problems of land settlement in Palestine, could not for larger political and economic considerations act positively on Chancellor's proposal to stop all land transfers immediately.

The Shaw Report

When Sir Walter Shaw and his three colleagues were asked to investigate the immediate causes that led to the August 1929 disturbances, they were also charged with making recommendations about the steps necessary to avoid their recurrence. With the Shaw Commission's appointment, there was no question of any reconsideration of British tenure in the Mandate or of British abandonment of its international pledges because of the 1929 disturbances. HMG agreed to Weizmann's demand that the only possible modifications that the Shaw Commission might suggest would pertain to methods of administration. The Zionists had a sanguine feeling that the commission would show that certain Arab leaders, particularly the mufti of Jerusalem, al-Hajj Amin al-Husayni, had planned the 1929 disturbances. But after the later sessions of the Shaw Commission were completed, the Jewish community in Palestine sensed that the commission would be pro-Arab and anti-Zionist.[26] The mufti was vindicated by the majority of the Shaw commissioners, who only rebuked him mildly for arousing religious passions during the disturbances.[27] The Shaw commissioners were unwilling to find fault with senior administration officials in Palestine for either being outside of Palestine during the disturbances or for the untimely reduction of the Palestine police force in 1928. According to the *Times*, the majority of the commissioners had a sense of solidarity with the Palestine governing caste and tended to justify the actions of Palestine officials while implying the Zionists were to blame.[28]

The issues of immigration and land, both critical components in Jewish settlement, were singled out in the Shaw Report as underlying causes for the 1929 disturbances. The report noted: "The feeling of Arab apprehension caused by Jewish immigration was a factor which contributed to the outbreak."[29] With regard to land, the report correctly specified that the Protection of Cultivators Ordinance of 1929 did nothing to check the tendency of Arab cultivators to become landless. "Their position," it said, "is now acute. There is no alternative land to which persons evicted can move. In consequence a landless and discontented class is being created."[30] The report recommended precisely what Chancellor had requested in his January dispatch—that the transfer of land to other than Arabs be restricted.

The Shaw Report was the first public statement by HMG on Palestine that categorically put the Zionists in a defensive position. The Shaw

Report advocated the introduction of some form of restriction to prevent the alienation of Arab land. The Zionists reacted by advising candor in future discussions about their settlement activity. They reasoned that frankness with British officials would yield an inescapable positive evaluation. But the Zionists also lost little time in criticizing the Shaw commissioners' findings. They said that the commission had exceeded its terms of reference and had expressed views of subjects like economics for which there was no sufficient evidence.[31] The Shaw Report made a strong case for establishing practical limits on Zionist settlement in Palestine. The issue of Arab landlessness was raised publicly. Arabs in Palestine felt that for the first time since British occupation their case had been given an unexpectedly full hearing. The Arab press said that the Shaw Report was a "brilliant victory for the Arabs and a death blow for Zionism." Alfred Rok, a secretary to the Arab Executive, remarked, "We consider the report seventy percent favorable to the Arabs."[32] But before the restrictions on land transfers could be implemented, the commissioners suggested further examination of the problems.

At precisely the time that the Palestine Arab Executive's delegation reached London to discuss the working of the Mandate, the Shaw Report was made public. Arriving on 30 March, the Arab delegation sought HMG's assurances for the cessation of Jewish immigration, for protection of the Arab agriculturalist, for the prohibition of land sales, and for institution of self-government. Ramsay MacDonald, hoping to hold the government together, had to maneuver between Arab demands and Jewish criticism. On 3 April 1930, he enunciated a middle policy, taking some edge off Arab hopes and Jewish fears. In the House of Commons he said, "It is the firm resolve of HMG to give, in equal measure, to all sections of the population in Palestine."[33] Restating the dual obligation was a far cry from amending the Mandate as recommended by Chancellor, or from restricting Jewish immigration as suggested by the Shaw Report, or of giving in fully to Arab demands. Duality had become an avowed policy for HMG in Palestine. On 27 May 1930, HMG issued a White Paper on Palestine essentially reaffirming the findings of the Shaw Commission and postponing any statement of future policy pending a thorough investigation of immigration, land settlement, and development.[34]

The day before MacDonald's affirmation of HMG's dual obligation, the Cabinet discussed the Palestine question. In order to assist the government in deciding future Palestine policy, a fresh inquiry was deemed necessary to clarify and expound upon the Shaw Commission's findings. Lord Balfour, David Lloyd George, and General Jan Smuts, all gentile Zionists, had recommended that a second commission go out to Palestine to "correct" the Shaw Commission's findings.[35] But there were objections to another investigatory commission. HMG did not want to cast dark shadows over the findings of the Shaw Report, but more important, it did not wish to appear to be inconsistent. Also, Chancellor's sensibilities could not be blatantly ignored. The high commissioner did not want anyone going over his head, suggesting policy for the Cabinet to consider. Yet the Cabinet wanted to know the facts on economic questions that were "behind the political questions."[36] As a result, the Colonial Office made it abundantly clear that an appointed expert on land settlement would always be in consultation with the high commissioner.

Hope-Simpson's Appointment and Arrival

Several people were considered by HMG before Sir John Hope-Simpson was asked to take charge of the investigation. Two of the individuals considered were believed to be too pro-Zionist for the task. They were General Smuts and Sir John Campbell.[37] On the other hand, Hope-Simpson had spent twenty-seven years in the Indian Civil Service and was the vice-chairman of the Greek Settlement Commission that had settled over one million refugees in Greek Macedonia. His personal knowledge of Palestine was limited to what he learned after his appointment.[38] He had read the Shaw Report in its summary in the *Times* of 1 April 1930 and the *Report of the Joint Palestine Survey Commission* of 1927–28, a composite agricultural and settlement survey of the needs and directions of Jewish growth in Palestine. Hope-Simpson accepted the position offered him by Passfield and the remuneration of £E200 per month.[39]

His appointment met with mixed reaction from both Arab and Jewish circles. The Arab delegation who met with the prime minister and Colonial Office officials in April and May were not entirely satisfied with HMG's pronouncements on duality. Lord Passfield, secretary of state for the colonies, told the delegation that "with regard to land, we are very busily engaged in endeavoring to secure for the Arab cultivator that he should be protected and should not be turned adrift even with compensation."[40] MacDonald assured al-Hajj Amin al-Husayni that "HMG would safeguard Arab interests in land and that, pending the results of the (Hope-Simpson) survey, the present tendency toward the eviction of peasant cultivators off land should be checked."[41] Passfield made no promises to the Arab delegation to prohibit land sales, but he did give assurances that legislation was already being drafted to restrict land transfers. In Palestine, the Arab press warmly greeted the administration's interest in aiding the economic condition of the fellaheen.[42]

Jewish reaction to Hope-Simpson's appointment was varied. It noticeably lacked the profound hostility shown for the Shaw Report. Members
of the Jewish Agency in London expressed complete confidence that an
inquiry conducted by a man of Hope-Simpson's experience in the resettlement of populations would be favorable to Jewish colonization in
Palestine. Hope-Simpson had been instrumental in the exchange of
populations between Turkey and Greece; some Zionists hoped that he
would transfer some of the Palestinian Arab population to Transjordan
or Iraq, thereby making more room for Jewish settlement.[43] In 1930, the
discussion of effecting an Arab population transfer remained exclusively
within Zionist circles, although both Chancellor and the Colonial Office
were keenly aware of the Zionist wish.

The Jewish Agency Executive in London was willing to facilitate
Hope-Simpson's mission but Weizmann was less hopeful. He was troubled by Hope-Simpson's "capture" by British officials in Palestine and
elsewhere.[44] In Palestine some Zionists feared that Hope-Simpson would
have the narrow outlook of a Colonial Office official, "lacking the
ability to penetrate the larger cultural and dynamic ideals of Zionism."[45]
Other members of the Palestine Jewish political community eagerly
awaited the chance to justify the Zionist enterprise. Weizmann wanted
to be sure that Hope-Simpson left London with the "proper orienta-
tion." He sought an interview with him prior to his departure for Palestine. Passfield is reported to have promised Weizmann such an interview,
but Shuckburgh said that Passfield did not see any reason why Hope-
Simpson would want to see Weizmann before he took up his duties in
Palestine. Hope-Simpson himself did not wish to see an Arab or Jew
prior to his departure.[46] The presence of the Arab delegation in London
may have provided Passfield the reason to display HMG's independence
from Jewish pressures.

Chancellor's legislative proposals calling for severe restrictions on
land transfers and for the protection of agriculturists were still held in
abeyance. But partial suspension of Jewish immigration was effected
pending Hope-Simpson's findings. Colonial Secretary Passfield and not
Chancellor's anti-Zionism instigated this immigration suspension. Chancellor approved the labor immigration schedule of 2,300 men and 1,000
women for the six-month period ending September 1930. The category
of working men and women and their families was deemed by Chancellor to have prospects of available employment.[47] But Prime Minister
MacDonald had already committed himself more forcefully to the Arab
delegation's immigration requests than to land-sale prohibitions. He had
told the Arab delegation, "We have put that [immigration] question already to the High Commissioner as to how far it is possible to stop
immigration pending the report of the expert."[48] Chancellor had seen a

decrease in Jewish unemployment from April to May 1930. Passfield, however, thought that the implied promise made to the Arab delegation had to be at least partially fulfilled. On 13 May he ordered Chancellor to suspend all but fifty labor-immigration certificates. Passfield came under immediate pressure to rescind the immigration suspension. As a result, Passfield told Chancellor that the suspension should not be unduly prolonged.[49] Only after the decision had been taken to suspend part of the labor schedule did Chancellor steadfastly refuse to give in to Jewish pressures. Chancellor did not want any further confirmation of the widely held belief that Jewish pressures exercised in London could procure reversals of decisions taken in Jerusalem.[50] Even though Passfield had originated and advocated the suspension, Chancellor wanted all appearances to show that Palestine was the epicenter for administration decision making.

Hope-Simpson arrived in Palestine on 29 May 1930. Prior to his departure he was informed by Passfield that immigration was not to exceed the economic capacity of the country to absorb new immigrants. This definition and the concept of the dual obligation was first stated publicly in the Churchill White Paper of 1922 but had originated with High Commissioner Samuel. Like duality, the definition of economic capacity was amorphous and flexible enough for successive high commissioners and Colonial Office officials to maneuver between present perceived requirements and tugging political pressures. Hope-Simpson upon his arrival in Palestine was supplied with massive amounts of documentation. Data prepared by the Palestine Lands Department for the Shaw Commission was put at his disposal. This included information on Arab land alienation from both individual proprietors and large landowners. He was made privy to Chancellor's two legislative proposals regarding land and given reports concerning proposed agricultural loans, irrigation potential, and surveys undertaken and planned. However, the thrust of the content and information supplied to him emphasized Chancellor's primary interest for the precarious economic condition of Arab agricultural laborers and tenants.[51]

Like the Shaw commissioners and Chancellor, Hope-Simpson's impressions about land availability were influenced by the effects of the Jewish National Fund's Wadi Hawarith purchase. Both the legal proceedings involving a claim by the 1,200 Bedouin and fellaheen to preemptive rights to portions of the 30,000 dunams and the decision upheld by the Palestine chief justice for their eviction were contemporaneous to his inquiry.

With all the information provided him, Hope-Simpson, because of the time demand put upon him by the Colonial Office, could not, would not, and did not find time to make judgments independent of either

Passfield's or Chancellor's influence. The Colonial Office needed the expert to arrive at conclusions capable of incorporation into HMG's evaluation of future Palestine policy. The scope of his inquiry precluded fact finding and statistics gathering on a firsthand basis. He was forced to rely upon projections and appraisals made by officials for whose accuracy and competence he could not vouch.[52] Since the Colonial Office had already promised Chancellor that Hope-Simpson would be in direct consultation with him, Hope-Simpson could not help but be influenced by Chancellor's ideological view. The final factor acting upon Hope-Simpson was personal. It had an immeasurable effect upon his findings. Although he had reservations, he wanted to be the next high commissioner of Palestine. Exactly when in the employ of the Colonial Office Hope-Simpson first considered this idea is not clear, but his intentions seem to have been well hidden from the Zionists in Palestine.[53]

The Jewish Agency's Rationale to Hope-Simpson

In the aftermath of the Shaw Report, the Jewish Agency in Palestine realized the political importance of Hope-Simpson's inquiry. The preparations for his visit were extensive. A committee was set up to detail concrete plans for Jewish colonization and industrial development. Set up partially in reaction to Hope-Simpson's inquiry and partially to evaluate the needs of Jewish settlement in general, the Colonization and Immigration Committee of the Jewish Agency, as it came to be called, adopted priorities for future Jewish settlement. Those priorities were for further development of the coastal plain, the Jezreel Valley, the Huleh basin, and the Lower Jordan Valley. Little if any emphasis was placed upon settlement in Transjordan, the Negev, in the environs of Haifa, Galilee, near the Jerusalem–Tel Aviv road, or in the hill areas of Judea and Samaria.[54] This committee clearly wished to take the sting out of the implications of the Shaw Report. The committee forcefully reminded Hope-Simpson that Arab tenants had been dealt with fairly in the past. The need for agricultural credits, lower taxes, more Jewish immigration, incentives for industrial development, and intensification of agricultural methods were also discussed in the committee's report to Hope-Simpson.

The importance that the Jewish Agency attached to the Colonization and Immigration Committee's recommendations to Hope-Simpson was reflected in its composition. On the committee were Dr. Arthur Ruppin, who had been involved in land matters in Palestine since 1908 and who in 1930 headed the Jewish Agency's Colonization Department; Dr.

Chaim Arlosoroff, then editor of a monthly journal, *Ahdut Ha-Avodah*; Eliezer S. Hoofien, general manager of the Anglo-Palestine Bank; Dr. Abraham Granovsky, managing director of the Jewish National Fund; Yitzhak Vilkansky, an agronomist and chief advisor on agriculture to the Jewish Agency; Shabtai Levi, a Palestine Colonization Association employee with considerable knowledge and expertise about the life of the Arab fellah; Moshe Smilansky, chairman of the Jewish Farmers Federation of Judea and Samaria; and several other consulting members.

The committee emphasized the positive contributions of Jewish settlement in Palestine both in the past and for the future. In order to reply properly to Arab claims, the committee asked that Arab grievances submitted to Hope-Simpson be passed on to the Jewish Agency for reply. If the administration refused to show the Jewish Agency material it was preparing for Hope-Simpson, "other ways to become acquainted with it" were found.[55] The practice of acquiring statistical data and departmental reports prepared by the Palestine administration continued during the period of Hope-Simpson's inquiry. (During the 1920s, the Jewish Agency, through at least Attorney General Bentwich's office, was repeatedly aware of the various ordinances being drafted. Later administration officials favorably disposed to Jewish development, such as Max Nurock and Lewis Andrews, frequently made administration reports on land matters available to the Jewish Agency.)

Special efforts were made by the Colonization and Immigration Committee to show that the "economic crisis," i.e., the diminution of Jewish immigration in 1926–27 only affected the Jewish community and had no reverberations upon its Arab counterpart. In an effort to paint an optimistic picture of Jewish land-purchase procedures, the Jewish Agency requested land purchasers to be sure that no deed of sale be executed without first gaining authorization from the administration. The Jewish Agency wanted Hope-Simpson and Chancellor to be satisfied that tenants and owners were being adequately provided for with either land or money. It seems that this pledge may have helped to mollify the Colonial Office sufficiently to the point that it postponed implementation of Chancellor's land legislation.[56]

In June the Jewish National Fund through Kisch's discussions with Chancellor was made aware, though not for the first time, of HMG's contemplated land-transfer restrictions. The Jewish National Fund was divided as to which policy to adopt in meeting this challenge to Jewish settlement. Berl Katznelson, a leading personality in the Jewish labor movement, wanted to purchase as much land and as quickly as possible before the effective implementation of any restrictions. Kisch wanted to enter into new contracts so that the Arab vendors would be forced to bring pressure on the government to rescind any new constraints. Gra-

3. Dr. Arthur Ruppin and Dr. Jacob Thon, 1908
Courtesy of Central Zionist Archives, Jerusalem

4. Colonel F. H. Kisch, 1923
Courtesy of Central Zionist Archives, Jerusalem

5. Dr. Abraham Granovsky, 1947
Courtesy of Central Zionist Archives, Jerusalem

6. *Yehoshua Hankin, 1943*
Courtesy of Central Zionist Archives, Jerusalem

7. Menachem Ussishkin, 1919
Courtesy of Central Zionist Archives, Jerusalem

novsky strongly believed that the non-Jewish landowners wanted the Jews to buy land. For that reason they did support the Jewish National Fund's opposition against the proposed restrictive legislation. Granovsky also made it clear that the long tedious process of acquiring title deeds militated against entering into new negotiations. Yet the entire Jewish National Fund Directorate considered it unwise to contract for large purchases lest initial payments be lost to prospective vendors when the restrictions came into force. Since funds were not available to complete large purchases quickly, it was decided not to enter into any new agreements. All outstanding small purchases were to be completed with the utmost speed.[57]

Now, the Jewish Agency's public argument for continued Jewish settlement was no longer solely linked to the benefits of the settlement per se on the Arab fellah; it introduced the concept of upgrading the economic condition of the fellah through administration assistance. This was to be accomplished in two ways, by establishing access to financial loans so that fellaheen could cast off their indebtedness and by intensifying their agricultural holdings. The key thrust in the Jewish Agency's presentation to Hope-Simpson was designed to show that there was sufficient land in Palestine for both the continued Jewish settlement and an increasing Arab population.[58]

The Jewish Agency wanted its settlement activity to diminish the dependency status many fellaheen had with landowners and moneylenders. Straining these ties, it was reasoned, might also create conditions favorable to the intensification of agricultural holdings. By making the fellaheen more economically solvent, they might not be so readily forced to forfeit their *musha'* shares or land as debt payment to Arab landowners, but instead might wish to sell land to Jewish purchasers. Reducing or breaking the ties to local landowners, politicians, and moneylenders might also enhance the development of an independent political force not tied to the prestige of the landowning classes. An economically viable fellaheen class in Palestine might at least note the benefits of Jewish settlement and development, though perhaps not appreciate it wholeheartedly. Nevertheless, attempts made by the Jewish Agency and its affiliated land-settlement organizations to establish an agricultural bank for fellaheen failed several times for lack of sufficient capital.[59] The fraying of the economic and social bonds between the Arab merchant or landowner and his tenants or other owner-occupiers came not as a result of ploys designed by the Jewish Agency but because of the several consecutive poor harvests that diminished the landowner's (moneylender's) percentage of the yield. Landowners who were not residing on their tenanted lands in 1930 were not benefiting financially from their property as they once had. Poor yields in the agricultural sector from 1931 to

1935 made it increasingly difficult for owner-occupiers to retain their small parcels of land. And, increasingly, landowners found it economically unsound to retain tenanted lands.[60]

The Jewish Agency also hoped that the adoption of intensive methods of agriculture would provide excess land for Jewish acquisition. The idea of fostering intensive cultivation of land was not new. It was especially mentioned in Article 11 of the Mandate and clearly present in Zionist settlement policy prior to and immediately after World War I.[61] Because the Land Registry offices had been immediately closed and the alternative of purchasing numerous large areas of unoccupied and uncultivated land existed, the Zionists did not dwell then on the concept of agricultural intensification. But in 1930 with a growing scarcity of available cultivable land, promoting intensive agriculture was necessary from practical, political, and ideological viewpoints.

Some Jewish Agency officials reasoned in 1930 that if the owner-occupier was solvent he would be more inclined to part with some of his land. They advanced the argument that the fellaheen could part with half of their land and use the money they received to reinvest and upgrade their remaining holdings. In theory, this concept seemed plausible and perhaps even beneficial to segments of the fellaheen population. Not only could Jewish settlement continue unabated, but fellaheen could increase their living standards.

But the Jewish Agency was myopic in its belief that centuries of customary tenure and land usage by the fellaheen would be swept aside in favor of more efficient methods of agricultural production or establish habits of thrift, savings, and investment. An administration committee investigating the protection of tenant agriculturists in 1927 noted that the introduction of modern scientific methods of cultivation frightened the fellaheen.[62] Mechanized agriculture required modern skills and knowledge to which the average fellah did not have access. The change from dry farming of cereals to the employment of intensive irrigation entailed a complete change of cultivation habits. In place of the short cultivation period between January and April, followed by a few weeks' activity at the harvest in July or so, the cultivator would find himself compelled to work hard almost the entire year. Instead of the portion of heavy labor being performed by draft animals, cultivation under irrigation sometimes involved a greater degree of manual labor. Even the marketing process involved in irrigation cultivation or in poultry or dairy farming necessitated greater daily attention than did the leisurely annual disposal of cereal crops in day-to-day farming.[63]

The Jewish Agency, nevertheless, repeatedly pointed to its own successes using intensive agriculture to reclaim land that had been malarial swamp a decade previously. Some Zionists noted that Arabs living in the coastal plain had successfully invested the money they had received from the sale of their surplus lands. But those Arabs who had been successful in converting their capital into eventual remunerative agricultural output were sufficiently solvent to risk the contingency of failing in new agricultural endeavors. In fact, the number of fellaheen who sold a portion of their lands and then reinvested the capital was a very small minority. The suggestion that Arab agriculturists undertake citrus farming was also unrealistic. It took five to seven years for citrus trees to become fruit-bearing, and in the meantime, without other income, the small owner-occupier did not have the economic means to survive. Some fellaheen in the coastal plain or in other citrus-growing districts did sell portions of their land and did reinvest their surplus capital in orange and vegetable cultivation. But the evidence suggests that the fellaheen who engaged in upgrading their holdings were few. Prior to 1930, less than five hundred fellaheen who sold portions of their land were successful in reinvesting their newly acquired capital in citrus cultivation.[64]

Hope-Simpson's Attitude toward the Land Issue

The presentation of the Jewish Agency's position to Hope-Simpson was aimed at proving that there were still available cultivable lands for both Arab and Jew in Palestine. Noticeably absent from the Jewish Agency's argumentation to Hope-Simpson was reference to the total cultivable land area of Palestine. Intentionally, the Jewish Agency did not wish to disturb the prevailing estimate made by Lord Stanhope, the civil lord of the Admiralty, in the House of Lords in 1925. Stanhope estimated that there were 12,500,000 Turkish dunams still available for Jewish settlement.[65] This inflated assessment essentially meant that almost all of Palestine exclusive of the Beersheba subdistrict was cultivable. Since Jews had acquired only approximately one-tenth of the area that Stanhope said was available to them, it was believed wiser not to raise the issue. In fact, there was some anxiety on the part of Dr. Ruppin, the chairman of the Colonization and Immigration Committee, that the results and implications of any new estimate would show that the amount of cultivable land available was in fact very little. He told Weizmann this in late January 1930, when he wrote, "Ich fürchte das Resultat einer solchen Untersuchung wurde am Schluss darauf hinaus laufen das von überhaupt bearbeitbaren Boden in Palästina nur wenig unbesetzt und unbearbeitet ist."[66]

There were of course Zionists who believed that infusions of vast amounts of capital would continue to increase the cultivable land area.

While the notions of agricultural intensification and possible transfer of the Arab population to Transjordan and elsewhere were not entirely new, they were once again emphasized by the Zionists in the 1930s.[67] But even Ruppin's recognition that there were only limited amounts of land available for their settlement did not deter public and private purchasers. Arab vendors continued to approach Jews with offers to sell. As soon as rumors spread in June 1930 that land-transfer restrictions were contemplated, more than 50,000 dunams were offered to Jewish buyers by Palestinian and non-Palestinian Arabs.[68]

The Jewish Agency's contact with Hope-Simpson was frequent. For Hope-Simpson, these exchanges were very revealing. Rafts of information, position papers, and personal interviews were provided him. Initial impressions by Ruppin and Kisch of Hope-Simpson were that he was an honest man who had come to undertake an impartial study from a strictly economic perspective. Ruppin's positive impression of Hope-Simpson did not diminish as his inquiry pressed on; Yehoshua Hankin, an otherwise astute and shrewd land-purchasing agent for the Jewish National Fund and the Palestine Land Development Company, hoped that Hope-Simpson's report would prove to be a second Balfour Declaration showing the progress made by the Jews since Balfour's letter to Lord Rothschild.[69] From Hankin's frank discussion with Hope-Simpson, both he and Chancellor became aware of the offers then being tendered by prospective Arab vendors to the Jewish National Fund. Arlosoroff, later the head of the Political Department of the Jewish Agency, believed that Hankin and Menachem Ussishkin, the head of the Jewish National Fund, were too candid with Hope-Simpson and had unfortunately allowed him scrutiny of files no one should have seen.[70] Hope-Simpson's report was clearly anti-Zionist.

The Jewish Agency's future candor was tempered by the experience with Hope-Simpson. Subsequent eagerness to make administration officials privy to confidential memoranda, purchase contracts, and dispatches on land matters was restrained. The Jewish Agency's guarded cooperation with the Development Department in the assessment of "landless" Arabs in the period 1931–36 was the most noticeable immediate case in point. Again in January 1933, as a result of the Hope-Simpson experience, the constraints upon free transfers posed by the Protection of Cultivators Ordinances caused the Jewish Agency to be circumspect with its information. Hope-Simpson and the land issue's emergence made the Jewish Agency, Jewish National Fund, and other Jewish land-purchasing organizations considerably more discreet about their settlement plans, acquisition procedures, and land information in general.

As the length of Hope-Simpson's stay in Palestine increased, general

Jewish Agency confidence about the positive nature of his projected conclusions began to diminish. Kisch began to have some misgivings. Would Hope-Simpson be able to see through the "fog of misrepresentation" in which he was expected to be enveloped by High Commissioner Chancellor and others? Kisch noted as early as 29 May that Hope-Simpson "had already developed a strong feeling of sympathy for the poor Arab whom he believes to be the underdog—a characteristically English tendency."[71] Hope-Simpson was not receptive to Kisch's claims that the Jews came to Palestine to create a new way of life, nor did he agree with Kisch's views that Palestine should not be the geographical focus through which Arab nationalism was to express itself. Hope-Simpson contended that the Zionists had created hatred between themselves and the Arab fellah, causing Arab cultivators to leave their land. Smilansky, the least optimistic member of the Colonization and Immigration Committee, believed that Hope-Simpson would have restrictive legislation instituted that would forbid land sales by villagers and large landowners.[72]

There is no doubt that Hope-Simpson's sympathy, like Chancellor's, rested with the Arab cultivator. Accounts of fellaheen poverty shocked him. He was dismayed by their inextricable ties to Arab moneylenders and the eventual transfer of their lands to large landowners. When he came to the Jewish National Fund's headquarters in Jerusalem in the middle of June, his conversation with Ussishkin was repeatedly punctuated by his concern about the Wadi Hawarith Arabs. Hope-Simpson feared that "if the Government [had] to send troops to remove the [Wadi Hawarith] Arabs, there might be shooting and the whole world would be aroused because Arabs were killed for refusing to leave the land they had cultivated."[73] Ussishkin blamed Arab politicians for the difficulties at Wadi Hawarith because of their intervention on behalf of the soon-to-be-evicted eighty-five Bedouin families.

While in Jerusalem, Hope-Simpson was Chancellor's houseguest. They fully discussed all aspects of the land question. In a letter sent to Chancellor at the end of June 1930, Hope-Simpson summarized his attitude on several related issues. "*We* [my emphasis] cannot allow land to pass into Jewish hands without the knowledge of the Government. For the time being the Zionists have bitten off as much as they can chew. It is the duty of the Government to see that the Arabs get a fair chance of development. At present they have none. Until a scheme is evolved, the Government must have rigid control of all sales of land."[74] As Hope-Simpson crisscrossed the country, whatever tension existed in Arab villages subsided at least temporarily. He was greeted warmly by the Arabs with cups of coffee and by Zionists with cold statistics. The latter did not impress him greatly. He disliked the Zionists and their use of land. He characterized the Jewish desire for land as the "prophylactic of the

Jewish disease."[75] In August 1930, he described his personal feelings in a letter accompanying his completed report. He summed up by saying, "All British officials tend to become pro-Arab, or, perhaps more accurately anti-Jew. . . . Personally, I can quite well understand this trait. The helplessness of the fellah appeals to the British official with whom he comes in touch. The offensive self-assertion of the Jewish immigrant is, on the other hand, repellant."[76]

Hope-Simpson's Findings: Cultivable Land Estimates

Hope-Simpson departed Palestine on 24 July and completed his report in Athens by the middle of August. The report was simultaneously published in London with the Passfield White Paper on 21 October 1930. With respect to land, Hope-Simpson touched on three major points: the extent of cultivable land in Palestine; the issue of the creation of a landless Arab class; and a proposal to establish a Development Department to oversee Palestine's economic development.

Assessing the amount of cultivable land area had the greatest political implications. The Palestine administration defined cultivable land as "land that could be brought under cultivation by the application of the labor and financial resources of the average Palestinian cultivator."[77] This definition was unacceptable to the Jewish Agency, which viewed cultivable land as any land capable of farming regardless of the financial input required for amelioration. The administration's comparatively restrictive definition excluded marsh areas, the coastal sand dunes between Rafah south of Gaza and Acre, all of the wilderness of Judea, and the area south of Beersheba town. Because no land survey had been completed by the administration covering the total land area of Palestine, Hope-Simpson chose an existing estimate that he found philosophically compatible.[78]

Lord Stanhope's estimate of 1925 accounted for 11,487,500 metric dunams of cultivable land. Although he knew that the figure was inaccurate, Dr. Ruppin intentionally used this statistic when he gave evidence before the Shaw Commission on behalf of the Jewish Agency. In his January dispatch, Chancellor estimated 11,000,000 cultivable metric dunams.[79] Of the other estimates offered, two stood out for Hope-Simpson's consideration: one by the director of surveys and one by the commissioner of lands. In metric dunams, these were divided into geographic regions.[80] (See Table 6.)

Hope-Simpson used the estimate by the director of surveys and subtracted the plain of Beersheba, arriving at a figure of 6,544,000 metric

TABLE 6
Cultivable Land Area Estimates for Palestine

Area	Estimates	
	Director of Surveys	Commissioner of Lands
	(in Metric Dunams)	(in Metric Dunams)
Hill country	2,450,000	5,376,000
Five principal plains	4,094,000	5,216,000
Total cultivable land	8,044,000	12,233,000
Total for all of Palestine	26,000,000	

Source: *Palestine: Report on Immigration, Land, Settlement, and Development* [Hope-Simpson Report], Cmd. 3686, pp. 21–25.

dunams for the total cultivable land area.[81] He was criticized by the commissioner of lands and others, in and outside the administration, for making no more than another erroneous estimate.[82] Jewish Agency officials took issue not only with his estimate, which was based on partial aerial photographic surveys, but with the fact that the photographs were made in June or July when most crops were harvested and cultivated land had an uncultivated appearance.[83]

The Jewish Agency had to discredit Hope-Simpson's estimate if the greater question of continued Jewish settlement was not to be jeopardized. The Jewish Agency and its affiliated land-purchasing and land-settlement organizations were aware of the scarcity of unoccupied and unworked land still available for Jewish settlement. Yet to admit to the accuracy or even the semi-accuracy of Hope-Simpson's estimate would have politically endangered the entire Zionist enterprise. The Jewish Agency knew that, despite the lack of available land, they could continue Jewish settlement. The key in their minds was the unceasing Palestine Arab willingness to sell land.

Publicly, the Zionists in Palestine and London were able to discredit Hope-Simpson's estimate, although only indirectly. The Passfield White Paper based an overwhelming amount of its content, information, and phraseology on Hope-Simpson's report. Through Zionist diplomatic skill, HMG repudiated the Passfield White Paper and its threats to Jewish settlement by issuing the MacDonald Letter in February 1931. Then, in the middle of 1931, HMG announced that new statistics and facts had to be gathered.[84] So successful and shrill was the Jewish Agency attack against the cultivable land estimate presented by Hope-Simpson that HMG did not publicly raise the question of cultivable land availability again.

The fact remained that Hope-Simpson with all his guesswork came very close to the actual amount of cultivable land in Palestine. In preparation for the introduction of a rural property tax to replace the commuted tithe, the Palestine administration tried to assess the total cultivable land area. That survey showed that the irrigable and nonirrigable ground-crop land was 5,855,584 cultivable dunams; tree-planted land other than citrus amounted to 1,083,218 dunams, with citrus amounting to 146,758 dunams. Exclusive of the Beersheba subdistrict the total amount of cultivable land in Palestine was said to be 7,086,560 dunams.[85] The Peel Commission Report, which investigated the 1936 disturbances, stated that the total cultivable land from the Rural Property Tax rolls owned by Arabs and Jews totaled 6,076,000 dunams exclusive of the Beersheba subdistrict.[86] Village statistics culled in the 1940s put the total taxable agrarian cultivable area exclusive of state land and the Beersheba subdistrict at 6,973,335 dunams.[87]

The Jewish Agency maintained that deriving figures for the cultivable-land areas based upon the Rural Property Tax rolls was an inaccurate measurement. Their protests were valid on at least two points. The Rural Property Tax rolls placed land in sixteen categories for the purpose of having the rural-tax burden fall upon land with the greatest economic potential. The last three categories were classified incapable of being farmed and therefore the owners or tenants of such land did not have to pay any rural property tax. It was the Jewish Agency's argument that local *mukhtars*, who did the assessment of local land areas for the administration, tended to give their own villagers the benefit of the doubt in classifying land in categories lower than their actual agricultural potential. Hence, some tillable land was classified uncultivable in order to avoid tax payment. The second point of contention was the exclusion of state lands from the Rural Property Tax rolls.

The statistics Hope-Simpson used for determining state lands were prepared originally for the Shaw Commission by the Palestine Lands Department.[88] Those statistics indicated that there were "approximately" 959,000 metric dunams of state land.[89] Of this area, 47,000 dunams were considered uncultivable because the land area was an antiquity, it was occupied by a government school, it consisted of sand dunes, or it was otherwise not capable of cultivation; 65,000 dunams were in disputed ownership between the government and either Arab or Jewish claimants; 98,000 dunams were on lease to Jews, Jewish-owned companies, or were soon to be turned over to Jewish settlement organizations; 397,000 dunams were originally set aside for Arab cultivators and grazers in the Beisan area under the Beisan Agreement (only 302,000 were to be allocated); 300,000 dunams were leased to Arab cultivators on a 10 percent yield per annum basis; and 52,000 dunams were subject to Ottoman concessions in the environs of Lake Huleh, north of the Sea of Galilee.

Hope-Simpson carefully orchestrated his argument against Jewish claims to state lands by mentioning only those areas to which Jews had claim or where Jews were in actual occupation.[90] He did not publish the available statistics, indicating that more than 70 percent of all state land had been allotted or leased to Arab cultivators in 1929–30. Acknowledging that fact would have bolstered the Jewish Agency argument that Jewish settlement on state and wastelands as stipulated in Article 6 was not being facilitated. Hope-Simpson said with regard to state lands, "It cannot be argued that Arabs should be dispossessed in order that the land be made available for Jewish settlement. That would amount to a distinct breach of the provisions of Article 6 of the Mandate, which also ensured the rights and positions of other sections of the population."[91] Like Chancellor, Hope-Simpson wanted to protect the present Arab population from future Jewish settlement.

Hope-Simpson's Findings: Landless Arabs

The Shaw Commission Report cited the figure of 11,-000,000 dunams of cultivable land. Acknowledging that although the land area required to support the average family must vary with the fertility of the soil, the Shaw Commission, nevertheless, concluded that the average holding of the Arab agriculturist had to be increased if he were to maintain his subsistence existence. Hope-Simpson, using a vastly lower estimate of the cultivable land area, came to the same conclusion, stating that the average Arab cultivator was 40 dunams short of the required amount necessary for his and his family's existence.[92] Having determined that there was already a land shortage, Hope-Simpson further noted that "of the 86,980 rural Arab families, . . . 29.4 percent are landless."[93]

Whether Hope-Simpson's estimate of the landless Arab population was accurate will be discussed below, but there is little doubt, as Ruppin and Hankin realized, that the amount of unoccupied or unowned land was virtually nonexistent. The inevitable natural increase of the Arab population, coupled with continued Jewish immigration, portended conflict over possession, access, and use of limited amounts of land. The only mechanisms that would relieve the pressures on land distribution would be the intensification of Arab agriculture as recommended by the

Jewish Agency and eventually by Hope-Simpson,[94] and/or the infusion of large amounts of capital to improve land of marginal cultivability.

The second major issue raised by Hope-Simpson concerned the existence of a landless Arab class. The Shaw Report said: "A landless and discontented class is being created."[95] The Permanent Mandates Commission, while not taking issue with the Shaw Report's assertion, did wonder how such a statement could be made without prior statistical information.[96] Hope-Simpson used statistical evidence, but its accuracy was very questionable. In less than two weeks after arriving in Palestine, Hope-Simpson believed that a large portion of the Arab population was landless. In "proving" that there was a landless Arab class in existence, he relied on the statistics and conclusions of William Johnson and Robert Crosbie.[97]

Commissioned by the Palestine administration to examine the economic condition of agriculturists, Johnson, the Palestine treasurer, and Crosbie, the Southern District commissioner, submitted questionnaires to 104 "representative" villages chosen from more than 1,000 villages in Palestine. A total of 23,573 families representing a population of 136,-044 rural Arabs gave some response to the questionnaires. Heads of 6,940 families were laborers, that is, they were neither owner-occupiers living exclusively on their own holdings nor owner-occupiers.[98] Using their statistics, Hope-Simpson did some dubious extrapolation. He deduced that 29.4 percent of these family heads who did not live directly by cultivation were doubtless all landless men who previously had been cultivators. Accepting this statistic as fact and representative for all of Palestine, he concluded that "it also appears that of the 86,980 rural Arab families in the villages, 29.4 percent are landless."[99] In raw numbers, Hope-Simpson was claiming that 25,572 rural Arab families or approximately 145,760 rural Arabs were landless.[100]

The Johnson-Crosbie Report never equated the laboring class with a landless condition. Nor did the report say that 29.4 percent of the population in the 104 representative villages or among the 86,980 rural Arab families was landless. Hope-Simpson conveniently chose figures to fit his philosophy. Clearly, he wanted to ascribe to Jewish land purchase and settlement the responsibility for the creation of a landless rural Arab class. He mistakenly or deliberately assumed that it was not customary practice in Palestine to have laborers work without owning land. Farm servants, field laborers, crop watchers, manure carriers, ploughmen, threshers, herdsmen, and shepherds sometimes worked on land without possessing either formal title to it or formal written tenancy agreements with a landlord. Hope-Simpson pointed to the need to reform and remit the tithe, as well as to partition *musha'*-owned villages. But nowhere in his report did he describe the very lengthy process of small-landowner alienation and accompanying large-landowner land accumulation that had taken place during the Ottoman period. He did not define the dynamic of socioeconomic transition from owner-occupier to tenant cultivator to agricultural laborer. Lastly, Hope-Simpson intentionally omitted any mention in his report of the complicity of the Palestinian Arab landowner, notable, or *effendi* in hastening the "proletarianization" process.

That Hope-Simpson willfully concealed this aspect of the problem is suggested by his private remarks about Palestinian *effendis*. He considered them to be "an enemy of agricultural progress" and contemplated the forced implementation of lengthy lease agreements so that tenants could rationally work their land.[101] It was not uncommon practice for landlords to draw up lease agreements for a period of less than two years in order to prevent tenants from gaining legal protection under the Protection of Cultivators Ordinance of 1929. Under this law, once a tenant received statutory status, he was entitled to receive compensation for a disturbance and was invariably paid in money, not in land.[102] Lengthy lease periods were not made compulsory for agricultural lands because the administration did not wish to infringe upon the prerogatives of the Arab landowner through whom it had political contacts. Instead, after 1933 tenants could claim compensation in land if they had worked given lands for one year or more. The burden of responsibility rested with the less-sophisticated, less-educated, and politically weak tenant class. For his part, Hope-Simpson intentionally refused to indict the self-serving practices of the Arab landowning class.

The ultimate official but inaccurate estimates of landless Arabs displaced by Jewish land purchase were achieved through the efforts of the Development Department, which operated from 1931 to 1939. That estimate, based upon the narrowest of definitions of what constituted a landless Arab, found that less than 900 Arabs were displaced because of Jewish land purchase. There is little doubt that Jewish land purchase and Arab land sales forced a greater number of fellaheen from land they had traditionally cultivated and used for grazing. But in the absence of accurate information on the former status of cultivators, or of the intermediary activities of Arab landlords, merchants, lawyers, and other individuals who acted as land brokers, no true assessment of landless or displaced Arabs could then, or now, objectively be made.[103]

The Jewish Agency was faced with the administration's officially attributing Arab landlessness to the Zionist presence. Chancellor's position toward the Arab tenant, conceptualized and expounded by the Shaw Report, enunciated in statistical form by Hope-Simpson's report, and announced as policy in the Passfield White Paper, established the foundation for HMG's argument against further Jewish settlement. The Shaw Report asserted, "Palestine cannot support a larger agricultural population than it at present carries unless methods of farming undergo radical change."[104] Hope-Simpson concluded his report with his estimate of the number of landless Arabs, adding, "It has emerged quite definitely that there is at the present time and with the present methods of Arab cultivation no margin of land available for agricultural settlement by new immigrants, with the exception of such undeveloped land as the various Jewish Agencies hold in reserve."[105] The Passfield White Paper slavishly but not unexpectedly repeated Hope-Simpson's conclusions. To ameliorate the condition of the Arab fellaheen, the White Paper called for a policy of land development without specifying precisely how or under what auspices such development policy was to be effected.

Hope-Simpson's Findings: The Development Department

In his report Hope-Simpson had been more exact than the October 1930 White Paper about the nature of land development and the course it should take. He recommended the formation of a Development Department. The White Paper, reiterating HMG's policy of wanting to keep Palestine as a self-supporting economic enterprise and free from the considerable expenditures that were required for economic development, merely said that HMG was "giving earnest consideration to the financial position which arises out of this situation."[106] Hope-Simpson's reasons for creating a Development Department as part of the Palestine administration was threefold: to aid the depressed economic condition of the Arab agriculturist; to curtail the growth of Jewish settlement; and to provide the administrative mechanism through which he could succeed Chancellor and become the next high commissioner.

Hope-Simpson's desire to aid fellaheen agricultural development was aimed at pursuing two distinct purposes: first, to improve their methods of cultivation and extend irrigation wherever possible and, second, to rearrange their holdings in order that land be available for further Arab settlement in accordance with the terms of Article 6.[107] While Article 6 called for "close settlement of the Jews on the land," Hope-Simpson was clearly looking at the first clause of the same article, which called for "ensuring the rights and positions of other sections of the population." "The immediate problem," said Hope-Simpson, "is not how to render Palestine available for Zionist exploitation; on the contrary, it is how to establish the Arabs in a better position than they are in at the present time."[108] As envisaged by Hope-Simpson, the Development Department would not only supervise the development of land, but it would also be responsible for its settlement. All consent for the transfer of land was to rest with the Development Department. He reasoned that the existing Jewish land reserves—land that had been purchased but as yet not settled—would suffice Jewish organizations until a general scheme of development was brought into operation. This was an absurd conclusion manufactured to meet political ends.[109] Hope-Simpson wished to give the Development Department the power to purchase at a set price all land for sale in the open market. He wanted the administration to refuse to sanction land transfers. In such instances, the would-be vendor would have the right to demand that the administration take over the land at a given purchase price. In effect, the administration would act as a landholding company for the Arab population. In addition, he asked that the Development Department be given the right to expropriate land as required for public purposes.[110] The public purpose Hope-Simpson had in mind was the resettlement of landless Arabs.

Hope-Simpson sought to provide the Development Department with unchallenged authority over the growth of the Jewish national home. His uncompromising attitude toward Jewish land purchase was evidenced by what he termed the creation of "Jewish mortmain" by the Jewish National Fund. Making land inalienable prevented land from reverting back into Arab ownership, and, according to clauses in the Jewish National Fund lease agreements with its settlers, precluded the hiring of Arab laborers. He argued that the Mandate contained no provision whatever "contemplating purchase of land by Jews."[111] He wanted all land used by Jews in the future to be leased to them by the administration and on administration terms.

High Commissioner Chancellor's intent to control land transfers was to have its bureaucratic home in the Development Department. In June, before Hope-Simpson had been told by Jewish National Fund representatives about Palestinian Arabs eagerly making offers to sell land, Chancellor impressed on Passfield the necessity of controlling all dispositions of agricultural land.[112] The Colonial Office and Passfield had seen reports from Egypt indicating that some Palestinian Arabs in anticipation of the rumored land-transfer restrictions were seeking to employ Egyptian Jews to act as their land-selling agents. Despite this, Passfield believed that a promise to suspend immigration had been made but that no pledge to institute land-transfer restrictions had been given to the Arab delegation in its March–May 1930 visit. The Colonial Office, ever apprehensive of negative Jewish reaction to policies against Jewish interests in Palestine, stopped short of implementing both of Chancellor's proposals.[113]

The Development Department's exclusive control of land disposition as described by Hope-Simpson's scenario meant essentially providing himself with supreme authority over its calculated direction. Hope-Simpson was keen to Chancellor's dislike of life in Palestine. Chancellor wanted to remain until October 1931 in order to be eligible for his government pension.[114] Hope-Simpson tendered his resignation to the League of Nations as vice-chairman of the Refugee Settlement Commission in the first week of July 1930. After writing his report in Athens, Hope-Simpson returned to London where he served on the Cabinet's Committee on Policy in Palestine. He remained in constant touch with Chancellor and Colonial Office officials about his report's findings and recommendations. On 29 September, Hope-Simpson wrote to Chancellor informing him that he (Hope-Simpson) would head the Development Department only on the condition that he would be the next high commissioner.[115] Then several days prior to the publication of the White Paper and his report, Chancellor "recommended" that Hope-Simpson be "sounded out" as to his willingness to be the director of development.[116] Hope-Simpson replied positively to Passfield's offer. In part he said:

> Still less is it certain that the ideas of his [Chancellor's] successor will coincide with those on which, under the Chancellor regime, the [development] scheme will be initiated. It is impossible to ensure that the new man should accept the views of his predecessor without question. It would be wrong to demand that he should, and I cannot imagine any man of ability accepting the post with such limitations. In my opinion, the correct policy is to propose to Chancellor that he should serve one more year as High Commissioner and to nominate as Director of Development the man whom it is intended to appoint to succeed him as High Commissioner. If His Majesty's Government desires my services in an arrangement such as I have indicated, I shall be very willing to undertake the work and to carry it out to the best of my ability for five years from the date of my original appointment.[117]

In all fairness to Hope-Simpson, he did not greatly relish the possibility of being the next high commissioner, especially with "the Jews in their present and unreasonable temper,"[118] but he believed he could help the British government settle its problems in Palestine. The Colonial Office was quite aware that unfavorable reactions would emanate from Jewish quarters regarding the adverse remarks made about past and future Jewish settlement in the Hope-Simpson Report. Nevertheless, three months was considered enough time for the "storm to blow over" in regard to Hope-Simpson's appointment and by then his duties on the Refugee Settlement Commission would have ended.[119] But the immediate and over-whelming negative Jewish reaction to the White Paper's contents caused Passfield to withhold HMG's appointment of Chancellor's successor.

Hope-Simpson was not ultimately chosen either as the director of development or as Chancellor's successor. Yet his impact, unquestionably generated by his contact with Chancellor, had numerous reverberations on Palestine Mandate politics. The Palestinian Arab community received from the same authority that issued the Balfour Declaration statistical "proof" for their protest claims against Zionist settlement. The estimate of landless Arabs was frequently quoted by adherents of the Palestinian Arab cause in petitions to the League of Nations, by Palestinian Arab political-party representatives to the high commissioner, and in official Arab Executive remarks to the Palestine administration.[120] The Passfield White Paper devoted equal space to the land issue and as such gave it the same political value as constitutional development and the question of Jewish immigration. While the enunciated Passfield White Paper policy only existed temporarily, compromised by the MacDonald Letter, Hope-Simpson's inquiry remained an omnipresent specter in the minds of Jewish Agency officialdom.

Chapter 4

Neutralization of the British Threat:

The Postponement of Land-Transfer

Controls

Chancellor's ideology and Hope-Simpson's statistics had to be immediately and completely refuted if the concept of the Jewish national home was to become a reality. In their quest to establish Jewish sovereignty over Palestine, or at least portions of it, Zionists clearly differentiated between their ability to develop an infrastructure for a Jewish state and their right to build a Jewish nation. Limitations on their ability were mostly financial, but that was often circumvented by dedication to a cause, diligence toward its implementation, and willingness to make some personal sacrifices. Not all Jews or Zionists in Palestine were dedicated, diligent, or self-sacrificing. Yet most agreed that they were in Palestine not by sufferance, whim, or fancy, but by right. Such Zionist motivation deprived the 1930 Passfield White Paper of its political effectiveness.

In the twelve months after the White Paper appeared, its implied threats to the establishment of the Jewish national home and its explicit defense of the Arab population's political position were removed. Because the Jews successfully countered the influence of anti-Zionists in the Colonial Office and in the Palestine administration, and effectively lobbied government officials in London who were already favorably disposed to the development of the Jewish national home, the MacDonald Letter was issued. Its categorical phrasing of positive support for the Zionist enterprise thwarted both Hope-Simpson's and Chancellor's objectives implicit in the White Paper. The chameleon character of HMG's Palestine policy caused the Palestinian Arab community to distrust the British even more. Naturally the Jewish Agency and adherents of Zionist growth in Palestine were pleased by HMG's prompt turnabout.

The economic hardships and political difficulties suffered by the Palestinian Arab community were not caused by Zionists, but were due to a combination of external and internal economic factors, namely, HMG's reluctance to spend money on development, the worldwide economic depression, the decline in Palestine's agricultural sector, and deep social divisions within the Arab community. Palestinian Arab political centers were being torn asunder by intense local competition between families, *hamulas*, and personalities.[1] Village cooperation and harmony were strained. Traditional social relationships between landlords and fellaheen were breaking down. Had the British given what they promised in the Passfield White Paper, some political cohesion might have emerged from within a severely splintered Arab community. Instead, majority self-government was postponed indefinitely while the Jewish national home forged ahead. While the Arab community continued to splinter, the Jewish community continued to grow. It set about to castigate and discredit Chancellor, Hope-Simpson, and Passfield. The Zionists in London and Palestine were relentless in their effort to neutralize the British threat to the Jewish national home.

Composed of a British chairman with Arab and Jewish members serving in advisory capacities, the Development Department was to implement a narrow and restrictive interpretation of Article 6 of the Mandate. The purpose of the department envisaged by Hope-Simpson was the settlement of Arabs and Jews on land through lease, not sale. The projected development activity was to focus on the resettlement of landless Arabs. In fact, the perceived magnitude of the landless Arab problem, derived from Hope-Simpson's estimates, sent HMG's Treasury officials scurrying for a way out of a large financial commitment. They did not want British taxpayers to bear the expense of the millions of pounds recommended for resettlement. Hope-Simpson had believed that since HMG had accepted "this remarkable Mandate . . . money for the development scheme [would] fall upon the British people."[2] But Hope-Simpson's consideration for what he thought right and necessary did not mesh with HMG's willingness to be Palestine's financial benefactor. The Passfield White Paper only made passing reference to a development authority in charge of the control of land transactions.[3] No financial commitment was made in the White Paper.

During the previous July a Cabinet Committee was established whose task it was to consider HMG's policy with regard to Palestine. Initial drafts of Hope-Simpson's report were in Colonial Office hands by the end of August. By 11 September the Draft Statement of Policy was completed; matters dealing with economic and social development were largely based upon it.[4] On 23 September the Cabinet Committee decided that HMG was under no obligation to provide financial assistance for the establishment of the Jewish national home. Yet HMG was morally, if not legally, bound to see that provision be made for those Arab families who had been dispossessed of their land.[5] The decision to look after only the Arab population evolved partially from an erroneous belief that Jewish land reserves were enormous and capable of absorbing

future Jewish immigrants. Using a figure close to Hope-Simpson's estimate, the Cabinet Committee judged that no fewer than twenty thousand Arab families were landless or held precarious tenancies that would
make them landless in the near future. The special Cabinet Committee
proposed several different budgets, varying the number of Jews and
Arabs who might still be settled at government expense with at least ten
thousand Arab families, the minimum number to be resettled. Then the
Cabinet had to determine whether an expenditure of £7,200,000 at British taxpayers' expense was justified by the terms of the Mandate so that
[Jewish] immigration might continue.[6]

The Cabinet basically understood the Palestine problem from Chancellor's anti-Zionist viewpoint. On 24 September the Cabinet Committee on Palestine recommended, and the full Cabinet accepted, five
fundamentals regarding the future of Palestine: HMG was under no
obligation to finance Jewish settlement; HMG was bound to provide for
Arab tenants; occupancy rights were to be given to Arab agricultural
tenants on Jewish land reserves; Jewish immigration should be restricted
to such numbers as could be settled on Jewish land reserves; and legislation should be enacted covering the next five years (1931–36), which
stipulated that no further parcels of land be acquired by Jewish organizations.[7] These principles were designed to gain time for the economic
assimilation of landless Arabs. The Cabinet decided against spending
£7.2 million for resettlement purposes. Instead, it budgeted only £2.5
million. Most of this money was for resettlement of landless Arabs.
Only a very small amount of this appropriation was designated for Jewish settlement and none of it was allotted for specifically upgrading agricultural methods, for improving the economic condition of the fellaheen
population, or for breaking the financial stranglehold moneylenders had
upon many fellaheen. Subsequently, the Draft White Paper was rewritten
to exclude any mention of the previously contemplated massive-develop-
ment scheme.

The Passfield White Paper

During the first week of October, Passfield informed
Weizmann of the main points in the proposed White Paper. Weizmann
preferred to reserve comment until he could see the entire policy statement. On 13 October he wrote to Passfield threatening to resign from
the Jewish Agency if the statement were issued. Last-minute pressure
brought to bear on HMG by the Zionists in London proved unsuccessful, and on 20 October Weizmann resigned.

Issued on 21 October in London and published on 24 October in

Palestine, the White Paper gravely threatened the very existence of the Jewish national home and gave the Palestinian Arabs a chance to applaud HMG's stated policy. The White Paper called for the establishment of a legislative council based on the formula of the 1922 Churchill White Paper—a high commissioner with twenty-two members of whom ten were to be official and twelve unofficial members. Real power still rested with the high commissioner with prerogatives of the council circumscribed. As in 1922, HMG was unwilling to relinquish full constitutional control of Palestine to the Arab population. HMG reminded Arab leaders that its dual obligation was its reason for not granting a constitution as they demanded.[8] Significantly, immigration was no longer to be left to a flexible interpretation of the country's economic capacity to absorb new immigrants; instead, Jewish immigration was to be linked to the total number of unemployed in Palestine. Paragraph 28 of the White Paper suggested that if it were deemed necessary Jewish immigration should be reduced or suspended. HMG admitted that it had pursued a laissez-faire attitude allowing economic and social forces to operate with a minimum of interference or control. But the policies in the White Paper and their attending implication for land dispositions did nothing to inspire Jewish confidence and support for HMG's policy.

Quoting Hope-Simpson's cultivable land statistics and estimates of the percentage of landless Arabs, the White Paper declared, "It can now be definitely stated that at the present time and with the present methods of Arab cultivation, there remains no margin of land available for agricultural settlement by new immigrants, with the exception of such undeveloped land as the various Jewish agencies hold in reserve."[9]

Article 6 had essentially stipulated that insuring the rights and positions of other segments of the population was as important as facilitating Jewish immigration and close settlement on the land. Now the Passfield White Paper made close settlement *subject* to insuring the rights and positions of other segments of the population.

Land transfers were to be permitted only insofar as they did not interfere with the plans for the development authority. State lands, according to the White Paper, were to be reserved by the administration for landless Arabs or Arabs without enough land.[10] The resettlement of landless Arabs was to be considered a public purpose, thereby excluding Jewish settlement from the right to state lands as called for in Article 6.

Since the director of lands had stated in January 1930 that all state land capable of cultivation (without additional capital expenditure) was being cultivated, two explanations exist for the White Paper's comment on the future use of state lands. First, Hope-Simpson and/or those who wrote the White Paper lacked accurate information regarding state lands, suggesting a discrepancy between the true amount of land and the figure used in policy formulation. Second, HMG consciously knew that state lands were occupied, yet deliberately promised to resettle landless Arabs there.

As expected, the Jewish community in Palestine and other supporters of Jewish settlement were distressed by the White Paper's contents. Palestinian Arab reaction was typified by differences in opinion, not uncharacteristic of the varying shades of sentiment concerning the British and the Jewish national home. While there was unanimous discontent with the presence of both the British and Zionists in Palestine, there was a variety of views about the methods and tactics to be utilized in confronting them. Some Arabs adamantly refused cooperation with either the British or the Zionists; others plainly adopted a less militant tack. More extreme elements within the Palestinian Arab community were not about to accept the Passfield White Paper simply because it displeased the Zionists. In spite of the pro-Arab tone of the policy statement, individuals such as Jamal al-Husayni and Subhi al-Khadra, both members of the Arab Executive, continued to demand the abolition of the Balfour Declaration. More moderate members of the Arab Executive, such as Musa Kazim al-Husayni and Raghib al-Nashashibi were fairly satisfied that the White Paper went a considerable distance toward meeting Arab demands against Zionist encroachment. Some members of the Arab Executive were dissatisfied because the legislative-council proposal did not meet Arab nationalist aspirations. Al-Hajj Amin al-Husayni regarded this proposal as a violation of the promise for a full parliament like the one in Transjordan.[11]

The Arab Executive replied to the White Paper on 11 January 1931, two-and-a-half months after the policy statement's publication. The inability or unwillingness of the Arab Executive to reply sooner may have come from a comfortable feeling that its position was congruent with the high commissioner's. Certainly, after the Palestine issue was debated in the House of Commons on 17 November 1930, Arabs in Palestine did not believe that the White Paper would be whittled down.[12] Their reading and knowledge of events in London proved to be inaccurate. The Arab Executive response finally stressed four points that were essential to Palestinian Arab aspirations: abolition of the Balfour Declaration; establishment of a government responsible to elected representatives; prohibition of the sale and transfer of Arab-owned land to non-Arabs; and cessation of Jewish immigration. The Arab Executive also called upon the Palestine administration to ameliorate the distress of the landless Arabs by giving them state lands in the environs of Lake Huleh in northern Palestine.[13] Although the Arab Executive vocally supported fellaheen economic assistance and the institution of land-sale controls, the private actions of many Arabs did not match their public protests.

The proposed land-transfer controls were not in the interest of Arab landowners. Leasing their land to tenants for a fixed percentage of the gross yield was not financially advantageous in years of poor harvests. Hence, the option to sell excess or untenanted land was often contemplated and exercised. In view of Hope-Simpson's recommendations, those landowners who retained leasing tenants were likely to be deprived of substantial revenues because the government was likely to fix lease-hold fees at a low rate. Immediately following the publication of the White Paper with its implied constraints, many Arab landowners who feared losing title to their lands refused to lease land to hitherto permanent tenants. In addition, many landowners feared administration expropriation of privately held estates as the first step toward meeting Hope-Simpson's recommendation that every Arab agriculturist have a maintenance area of 130 dunams.[14] With these possibilities in view some Arab landowners pressed ahead with land sales to Jews. Some vendors concluded their transactions before restrictions were to come into force. The *Times* of 6 November 1930, quoting *Filastin*, reported that the activity of land brokers and landowners threatened to bring about the sale of more land within the next few days than had changed hands in the past ten years. (See Table 7.) Despite the fact that large tracts of Arab land were being offered to Jewish purchasers, transfer could not be effected because of a shortage of capital.[15] The Jewish National Fund, because of its strained financial condition, decided on two parallel courses of action.

The Fund would enter into new land-purchase agreements only if they could be written so that cash commitments would not have to be paid until after an initial three-year period and if land were purchased only from Arabs and not from other Jewish companies, agents, brokers, or speculators. Had the Zionists more available capital, the ominous predictions suggested by *Filastin* might have resulted. Certainly, Arab landowners, mostly resident in Palestine, were not constricting Jewish land-purchase opportunities.

Reaction to the White Paper and to Chancellor's Land Legislation

Zionist and Jewish reaction to the White Paper did not stop with Weizmann's resignation. Felix Warburg and Lord Melchett, both high-ranking Jewish Agency members, immediately submitted their resignations. Melchett, in resigning his chairmanship of the Jewish Agency's political committee, referred directly to the implied sale restrictions. He viewed the Arabs as only too anxious to sell their land, and he

TABLE 7
Land Area Acquired by Jews from Arabs, 1 July 1930–
1 November 1931

Month	Number of Dunams	Status of the Implementation of Land-Transfer Restrictions
July 1930	1,871	
August	978	
September	688	
October	1,723	After the publication of the
November	1,203	Passfield White Paper,
December		
1930	3,333	24 October 1930, but before
January 1931	2,011	the MacDonald Letter,
February	1,011	13 February 1931.
March	5,271	
April	325	
May	2,974	
June	328	
July	660	
August	3,271	Land-transfer restrictions were to
September	1,121	come into effect at the end of
October 1931	390	August and then were rumored once again in mid-September.

Source: Israel State Archives, Box 3390/file 3.

"reminded" the Arab population that it was not because of the Zionists that Arabs would no longer be able to dispose of their land.[16] The American Jewish Congress, holding its final annual session in Washington, reacted with resentment and bitterness to the White Paper and the Hope-Simpson Report.[17] Meanwhile in London, former Cabinet ministers Leopold Amery, Stanley Baldwin, and Austen Chamberlain, gentile Zionists in their own right, characterized the White Paper in a *Times* letter as definitely negative in content and in conflict with the intention of the Mandate and the Balfour Declaration. Chancellor felt that this published letter presaged enormous troubles for HMG if there were going to be acrimonious debate in the House of Commons on the subject.[18] The high commissioner's fear was not unwarranted.

Perhaps most damaging to the White Paper's legality, as perceived by Foreign Secretary Arthur Henderson, was a letter to the *Times* signed by two lawyers, Lord Hailsham and Sir J. Simon. Both argued that the White Paper violated certain terms of the Mandate, particularly those articles referring to immigration and land settlement. In their considered opinion, unless and until a judgment from the International Court at The Hague was made, the White Paper should not be implemented.[19] Finally, on 6 November Passfield in the *Times* and MacDonald in a communication to Weizmann explained the White Paper's contents. Passfield said that the White Paper in no way excluded the possibility of future Jewish settlement through land acquisition or immigration. In order to affirm this very liberal interpretation of the White Paper and to assuage Zionist misgivings, MacDonald offered Weizmann and other Jewish leaders the opportunity to meet a Cabinet subcommittee to discuss the situation in Palestine and especially the White Paper.

On 11 November the Cabinet approved MacDonald's offer to Weizmann to discuss Palestine. Three days later, HMG officially invited the Jewish Agency to confer with HMG on the compatibility of the White Paper and the Mandate. While the invitation to the Jewish Agency indicated that "the *parties* [my emphasis] of the Mandate strongly are desirous of securing its [White Paper's] correct interpretation and impartial administration,"[20] the Arabs of Palestine were not invited to participate in these discussions. Meanwhile, during the three weeks between the publication of the White Paper and HMG's decision to rethink the White Paper's implications, Chancellor's proposed land-transfer legislation still threatened Jewish settlement activity. Immediately following the White Paper's publication, Chancellor received instructions from Passfield to proceed with the land legislation.

Chancellor had no fewer than six pieces of legislation drafted dealing with land, its occupants, and its transfer. Among them, the Transfer of Agricultural Land Bill (TALB) and the Protection of Cultivators Amendment Bill (POCAB), both remnants from his January 1930 dispatch, represented the largest immediate threat to Jewish settlement. The high commissioner was optimistic that their implementation would be valuable for Arab cultivators and would prevent Arab eviction from the land.[21] So consumed was Chancellor with the Arab tenant-occupant's position that he wished, but eventually failed, to expropriate Jewish National Fund land in the Nazareth subdistrict in order to resettle the evicted fellaheen and Bedouin of Wadi Hawarith. The Jewish Agency reacted with expected anger over Chancellor's proposed legislation. For very different reasons, the Arab Executive also took issue with Chancellor's proposals.

Of central concern to the Jewish Agency was the "absolute autocratic character" of TALB. All transfers involving land were to be left up to the discretion of the high commissioner. In the definition of "disposition" of land, dedication of *waqf* land was noticeably omitted, emphasizing

Chancellor's hope or design to encourage Arab land to become inalienable. No time limit was imposed on the high commissioner for his determination on whether a land sale should or should not be sanctioned. Without such a stipulation, the proposed bill was tantamount to empowering the high commissioner with the exclusive right to forbid all land sales. Such control would have cut to the very core of Jewish land-purchase methods and the growth of the national home. Many Arab owners made their agreement to sell small parcels of land dependent upon the immediate receipt of cash payment. Arab land brokers could no longer be given monetary advances to amalgamate widely scattered parcels of land if the high commissioner's approval of a transfer could not be guaranteed. Similarly, monetary prepayment in preliminary sale negotiations to correct boundaries, enact surveys, and reach agreements with neighboring landowners might be jeopardized. Jewish purchases sometimes involved buying up small areas of contiguous land parcels, each owned by a different landowner. Each of these transfers would have required the high commissioner's consent. The Jewish Agency argued that overseeing all transfers would be a physical impossibility, causing the high commissioner to delegate authority to a lower echelon of sub-district administrative officials. The Jewish Agency did not wish to pay once for the land and then be forced to entice an Arab or British official with money so that consent to a transfer would be granted.[22]

Under Section 7 of the proposed TALB, the high commissioner reserved the right to refuse a mortgage sale or foreclosure on a mortgage. The mortgagee could apply to the high commissioner for payment of the amount due. Payment would be made from funds taken directly from general Palestine revenues. In essence, the Jewish contribution to the revenues of Palestine would have been used to prevent Arab lands, mortgaged to Jewish purchasers, from becoming the property of Jews through eventual mortgage forfeiture. Chancellor was very eager to make this section of TALB retroactive to cover mortgage forfeitures that had taken place prior to the bill's effective date. With such centralized power, Chancellor could have legally provided the fellaheen and Bedouin formerly of Wadi Hawarith with the necessary money to re-purchase the 30,000 dunams acquired by the Jewish National Fund in 1929. As mortgage forfeiture was an often-employed mechanism in Jewish land acquisition, Chancellor's proposals would have limited or voided further use of this method. The high commissioner knew that land transfers through mortgage forfeiture, as in the case of Zirin village (see Chapter 2), were taking place at the very time his proposals were under consideration in London. The director of lands informed the chief secretary that the administration could not intervene to prevent these sales at Zirin, even though they might create a considerable landless population.[23] Chancellor made every effort to void such agreements but failed.

The Jewish Agency took no less solace from the proposed Protection of Cultivators Amendment Bill. The administrative entanglement likely to result from this law meant ponderous land-sale negotiations. In a sellers' market with land prices almost continuously on the rise, a potential vendor might renege on a prior agreement to sell if he thought he could obtain a better price by waiting. With the administration making it more difficult for Jews to gain access to land free of tenants, a landowner who was willing to sell was more likely to wait for and demand a better price. Specifically, an Arab landowner wishing to sell his land with tenants in occupation would have had to proceed along very precise guidelines. First, he would have to make his ultimate intention of wishing to sell his land to Jews known to the high commissioner. Second, the vendor was required to make adequate provision for the livelihood of the persons to be evicted by giving them rights on other land. Monetary compensation for eviction, sanctioned by the Protection of Cultivators Ordinance of 1929, was not replaced by compensation in land. Finally, the Arab vendor had to apply to a magistrate, more often than not another Arab, and satisfy him that all the vendor's legal obligations to his tenants were met. An Arab magistrate might prolong the eviction proceedings, thereby further compounding the land-transfer process. The legal advisers of the Jewish Agency not unexpectedly hoped that the law would not be passed. They hoped that Arab tenants would continue to leave the land voluntarily after signing tenancy waiver agreements prior to the Arab vendor's notice to the high commissioner for transfer sanction. Both proposed pieces of legislation were considered by the Jewish Agency to be much more than an administrative hindrance. The Jewish National Fund believed that this legislation would have brought the purchase of land by itself and by the Jews in general to an end.[24]

The Arab Executive also reacted in a negative fashion to these two bills. Publicly, the Arab Executive demanded that all land sales be prohibited entirely. The principle of the high commissioner's retaining control of all land transfers by Arabs to non-Arabs was considered inconsistent with the Hope-Simpson finding that there was no margin of land available for Jewish settlement, save for Jewish land reserves. In the Arab Executive's opinion, any delay on the part of the Palestine administration in issuing land-transfer prohibitions could not be endured in the interests of the Arab population.[25] However, as shown above, personal opportunism or simply the need for money drove members of the Arab political leadership to sell portions of their patrimony. The Arab Executive had, in responding to the two proposed land bills, taken particular notice of the compensation that was being paid to tenants at Wadi Qabbani in the Tulkarm subdistrict. It deprecated *Jewish* monetary payment to the Arab tenants, but did not publicly censure its own members for participation in the Wadi Qabbani land-sale process. Both Mughannam Mughannam, a Protestant Arab from Jerusalem, and Fakhri al-Nashashibi, a personal aide to his cousin the mayor of Jerusalem, had acted as intermediary agents in the sale of 8,000 dunams at Wadi Qabbani.[26] Furthermore, Palestinian Arab landowners were circumventing the Protection of Cultivators Ordinance by ridding their land of tenants and thereby avoiding payment of monetary compensation. In the village of Shatta in the Beisan subdistrict, Chancellor was particularly concerned that the Arab tenants, ploughmen, agricultural laborers, and dependents who numbered more than two hundred, were about to be evicted from their lands. The major landowner of Shatta, Raja Ra'is, was in the process of fulfilling an agreement with the Palestine Land Development Company for sale of approximately 12,000 dunams to be transferred free of tenant encumbrances. Ra'is was utilizing the long-accrued indebtedness of his tenants and their ignorance of the law to remove them from the land.[27]

The Henderson Committee: Repudiation of the White Paper

As the storm of Zionist protest against the White Paper grew, and because Weizmann had been invited by MacDonald to "interpret" it, Passfield was forced to amend his post–White Paper instructions to Chancellor. Still, the high commissioner was adamant against any further delay in promulgating his land bills. He too was aware that there was very considerable activity between Arab vendors and Jewish purchasers. But Passfield insisted, despite Chancellor's protests to the contrary, that all land bills had to be submitted first to the Jewish Agency and then to Arab leaders for their respective comments before they could become law. Weizmann asked the Jewish Agency in Palestine not to communicate with the high commissioner concerning the proposals. Weizmann did not wish to enter into discussions with the high commissioner in Palestine. Instead, he wanted the decision-making process for Palestine subject to effective Jewish pressures in London, where Chancellor's views could be contained, if not ignored. Moreover, by entering into discussions with the high commissioner and suggesting amendments and corrections to the proposed bills, it might be construed that the Jewish Agency tacitly accepted the premise that land-transfer restrictions should be introduced. The Jewish Agency did not wish to legitimize these proposals by giving the Palestine administration the opportunity to claim that the Jewish Agency had been consulted and that the legislation had been passed with its consent. On 1 December Kisch informed Chancellor that the Jewish Agency could not communicate with the Palestine administration about the proposed legislation pending the outcome of the discussions in London.[28]

In mid-November 1930, the Palestine question was debated at length in the House of Commons. Both Jews and non-Jews sympathetic to Zionism raised their voices in protest. Sir Herbert Samuel, James de Rothschild, David Lloyd George, Leopold Amery, and others historically recounted Britain's first decade in Palestine, while taking the government to task for threatening to freeze the development of the Jewish national home. Answering for the government was the prime minister, but the burden of explaining that the White Paper did not really mean what it said fell to the under secretary of state for the colonies, Dr. Drummond Shiels. Shiels defended the White Paper and the obligations of HMG to the Arab population of Palestine. While the debate in the Commons was in progress, HMG's first discussion with the Zionists was also taking place.

In these intimate discussions, the Zionists clearly intended to repudiate categorically the implications of the White Paper and, if possible, to avoid dealing with the philosophies reflected in the thinking of the Chancellor, Hope-Simpson, and Passfield triumvirate.[29] Serving in this advisory capacity (an existing prerogative in Article 4 of the Mandate), the Jewish Agency had the opportunity to degrade Hope-Simpson's statistics while establishing a format to refute his implications publicly. The Zionists reasoned that by retaining decision-making discussions in London, they would not only bypass Chancellor's influence, but they could also transfer Palestine affairs to the purview of a more sympathetic Foreign Office official, Arthur Henderson, and away from Passfield. The Zionists succeeded in discrediting Hope-Simpson but only temporarily neutralized Chancellor's and Passfield's authority. Weizmann was not successful in his attempt to create an administrative committee of Zionists with direct access to the Cabinet. And Palestine affairs were not moved over to the Foreign Office. Henderson did conduct the discussion with the Zionists, thereby reducing Passfield's role to that of an interested spectator.[30] Chancellor too felt his prestige and influence sapped as Palestine's policy formulation remained in London.[31] Shuckburgh of the Colonial Office was so upset by these discussions with the Zionists that he would have resigned except that his "bread and butter depended upon his emoluments."[32] Though Passfield was relegated to an observer, he felt it wiser not to embarrass the government, especially at a time when the Whitechapel by-election was pending. There existed the clear intent of the parliamentary candidates to curry favor with the Jewish constituency. Mindful of the by-election, HMG released 1,500 Jewish immigration certificates for Palestine in mid-November.[33] Domestic British politics did play a role in appeasing Zionist demands.

At the first meeting with the Zionists on 17 November, Henderson assured them that no land legislation would come into effect before negotiations were concluded. Nevertheless, Henderson confirmed that preparations for such legislation were proceeding. The land question and Henderson's remarks were of particular concern to Zionist partici-pants. However, much of their anxiety over such legislation was lessened by the knowledge that they had more than a sympathetic draftsman working on the proposed legislation in the person of Norman Bentwich.

Bentwich's deeply embedded pro-Zionist sympathies were acquired long before he became the nephew by marriage to Herbert Samuel. Not surprisingly, Chancellor disliked Bentwich. The high commissioner and the Arab Executive wanted Bentwich removed from his post, especially after he encouraged the imposition of severe sentences on Arabs found guilty of participation in the 1929 disturbances. Chancellor felt that Palestinian Arabs could not continue to tolerate a situation in which a Jew was the highest legal authority in the Palestine administration. Fi-nally, in 1930 Bentwich went on home leave to London, but he was retained in a consultative capacity by the Colonial Office. Bentwich's replacement in Palestine was R. H. Drayton, someone more inclined to agree with Chancellor's anti-Zionist settlement philosophy.[34] When the Colonial Office decided that Chancellor's land bills would not be en-acted, Bentwich was asked to recommend interim legislation to protect tenancy and occupancy rights.[35] Bentwich had headed the 1927 investi-gatory committee of the Palestine administration that had delved into the means to protect agricultural tenants. He approved of the practices and means employed by the majority of Jewish land purchasers. He was of the belief that land compensation was not practical for a cultivator-tenant because he would dispose of any land he received.[36] When the Protection of Cultivators Amendment Ordinance came into effect in May 1931, compensation in land was not required, as Chancellor wished. In this legislation, the Jewish Agency was able to inject not its preferred method of compensation (that is, landowner responsibility to compensate), but one it could easily tolerate (monetary compensation for tenants).

The Zionists' organizational ability and political commitment to ob-tain a favorable official interpretation of the White Paper prevented any curtailment of Jewish settlement activities. When they submitted their criticisms of the White Paper, HMG did not reject them outright. The

Zionists had a sympathetic ear in Malcolm MacDonald, the prime minister's son and Weizmann's close friend, who lent his name to the Mac-Donald Letter.[37] No fewer than five drafts of the MacDonald Letter were written, the first of which was completed on 29 November. Most of the actual drafting of the letter was done by Zionists. In addition to Weizmann, Leonard Stein, Lewis Namier, and Maurice Hexter made important contributions. The Zionists meticulously expunged from the White Paper all implications that were potentially dangerous to their aspirations.

Chancellor and his ideological disciples wanted full government control of land transfers. By 26 November the Henderson Committee's focus was broadened to include the condition of landless Arabs. In broadening the scope, HMG wished to stop the displacement process and return landless Arabs to agricultural pursuits. The Zionists used the expanded scope to focus on the landless Arab question, consenting to discuss, investigate, and help identify landless Arabs but in a manner that would disengage HMG from imposing the greater threat of government-controlled land transfers or full prohibition of land sales. Ultimately, the Zionists' participation in the landless Arab inquiry became conditional upon the cessation of portended land-transfer controls. The Zionists were able to manipulate HMG into a focus less detrimental to the evolution of the Jewish national home and yet provide HMG with the evidence it desired to show for its concern for the Palestinian Arab fellaheen.

By the end of November 1930, HMG contended that it had an obligation toward landless Arabs displaced by Jewish land purchase. The Jewish Agency representatives objected. They believed that the number of landless Arabs was quite small, and they resented the lack of attention paid to Arab landlord complicity in the creation of landless Arabs.

In order to absolve Jewish responsibility for making Arabs landless, the Jewish Agency sought to adopt a very narrow definition of such a group. Because of Jewish Agency input, the definition of landless Arabs encompassed only "such cultivators as can be shown to have been directly displaced from the land in consequence of the land passing into Jewish hands, and who have not obtained other holdings on which they can establish themselves."[38] The Cabinet Committee accepted the Jewish Agency definition, deleting only the word "directly." Not only did the MacDonald Letter use the Jewish Agency definition for landless Arabs, but it made the definition even more restrictive in scope than the Jewish Agency representatives had requested. It is not clear why HMG went further than the Jewish Agency intent. But the MacDonald Letter's definition, which was employed from 1931 to 1939 by the Development Department to enumerate landless Arabs, defined them as "such Arabs as can be shown to have been displaced from the lands which they occupied in consequence of the lands passing into Jewish hands, and who have not obtained other holdings on which they can establish themselves, or other equally satisfactory occupation."[39] The adoption by HMG of a strict and narrow definition subsequently permitted the Jewish Agency to prove publicly that Jewish land purchase and settlement were not directly responsible for the creation of a large landless Arab class.

The MacDonald Letter

As the MacDonald Letter took shape, Henderson informed the Jewish Agency representatives that the formulation of land legislation was proceeding simultaneously. There was to be some linkage between the centralized control of land transactions and the initiation of the landless Arab inquiry-and-development scheme. This control was to be regulative not prohibitive, already somewhat of a dilution of Chancellor's intent. The Jewish Agency continued to seek postponement of all land-transfer controls. Chancellor had been advised by Passfield to consult with the Jewish Agency regarding such legislation. Weizmann reminded Henderson that the Palestine Jewish Agency Executive had been requested to boycott any discussion with the high commissioner on possible draft legislation. As the discussions in London progressed, Henderson retreated from his initial warning that land legislation was being formulated. He assured Weizmann that no legislation would be enacted without consulting the Jewish Agency. Passfield, while sympathizing with Chancellor's eagerness to enact legislation and plainly committed to HMG's obligations to defend Arab rights and interests, nevertheless had to insist that no legislation be enacted without consultation with the Jewish Agency. All misunderstandings with the Jewish Agency in Palestine were to be avoided, especially as the Whitechapel by-election of December 5 neared.[40] Chancellor was being boycotted through circumvention.

The Zionists wanted HMG's interpretation of the Passfield White Paper issued through an equal format or mode, namely another White Paper. In fact, the Cabinet on 4 February 1931 agreed that the prime minister would issue one. But to mollify Arab opinion, the Cabinet reversed itself a week later. An explanatory statement, it was argued, should not take the form of a White Paper. Furthermore, a White Paper had come to be regarded as a statement of policy and a second White Paper on Palestine in less than four months would cast doubts upon HMG's ability to adhere to an enunciated policy. MacDonald was to send a letter to Weizmann and to make the contents public. The timing for the release of the MacDonald Letter was carefully planned in an effort to avoid expected negative Arab reaction. The letter was not to be made public until the 13th of February in London, thereby avoiding agitation that might have occurred after the Friday prayer in Palestine's mosques.[41]

The letter sent to Weizmann by the prime minister conceded to the Zionists that the Jewish national home was not to be contained. There was no imputation of blame directed toward the Zionists for infringing on the rights and position of the Arab population. Jewish immigration and close settlement of Jews on the land remained a positive obligation of the Mandate, whose fulfillment could be achieved without prejudice to the rights and positions of other sections of the population of Palestine.[42] Jewish settlement was not to take a subordinate position to the rights of other sections of the population as suggested by the White Paper. Although the White Paper had clearly implied that some measure of land-transfer restrictions would be imposed, Paragraph 13 of the MacDonald Letter refuted any such implication by saying that the White Paper contained "no such prohibition nor is any intended." The temporary control of land transfers was announced in order that the projected development scheme be unimpaired. Important to the Zionists was the explanation that control of land dispositions was to be limited, and in no respect arbitrary. At least temporarily, Chancellor's proposed land-transfer bill was effectively muted.

In other spheres of Palestine policy determination, the MacDonald Letter was generous to Zionist practices and aspirations. According to the White Paper, suspension or reduction of Jewish immigrants who could be classified in the labor category was to be dependent upon Arab or Jewish unemployment. In not-so-subtle terms, the White Paper took issue with the practice of exclusive Jewish labor for certain Jewish organizations. The MacDonald Letter vindicated such practice to which the Arab Executive naturally demurred.[43] The MacDonald Letter even went beyond the scope of matters dealt with in the White Paper—commitment was made to Jewish employment on public works in Palestine.

In Paragraph 3 of the MacDonald Letter, HMG recognized that its obligation was to the Jewish people and not just to the Jewish population of Palestine. The Palestinian Arab response to such a clause only fueled the notion that world Jewry possessed rights that the Arabs themselves did not possess in Palestine. Chancellor could not perceive the logic of equality reflected in this idea; he wondered how Jews resident in Poland or Russia could be more entitled to the land of Palestine than was the indigenous Arab population.[44]

Jewish labor was to be given its share of employment on public works projects. With the domestic economic condition reacting to the worldwide depression, Jewish Agency officials wished to provide avenues of work opportunity for unemployed Jewish workers. The Jewish share in the participation of public and municipal works was not to be based upon the percentage of Jewish population to the entire population, which was less than 20 percent, but according to the percentage of the Jewish contribution to the total revenue of the Palestine administration, which was in the neighborhood of 50 percent.

While the official interpretation of the White Paper gave practical and emotional support to the Zionists, the Palestine Arab population and especially the Arab Executive were incensed. If the economic climate of Palestine had not been so precarious, the threatened mass resignations by Arab officials from their administrative, political, and religious posts and a threatened countrywide Arab boycott might have taken place.

But the general economic situation in Palestine dictated restraint. A worldwide overproduction of cereals and subsequent dumping of foreign wheat on the Palestine market generated a fall in the local price of cereals. As a result, the Arab agriculturist had difficulty in disposing of his crop. He found it almost impossible to pay his tithe to the administration and, if a tenant, difficult to pay rent to his landlord. The administration recognized this economic plight by partially remitting the tithe. Landowners and merchants who depended upon the agricultural sector for part of their income through rents suffered too, though to a lesser extent than those whose entire income relied upon agricultural production. The Arab Executive decided upon a partial Arab economic boycott to emphasize Arab self-sufficiency, that is, Arabs were to sell Jews anything except land and buy from Jews nothing but land.[45] But despite the political intent, economic considerations forced some Arabs to continue engaging in land sales in order to maintain themselves. While there were no large Arab land sales to Jews,[46] there was an unusual number of small-landowner transfers recorded in 1931. More small landowners were parting with lesser amounts of land in an effort to meet their short-term economic needs. This process of small-landowner participation in land sales to Jews grew during the decade as the economic condition of the Arab rural population dramatically worsened.

HMG was somewhat shackled by the legislative action it could take with regard to land because of the constraints in the MacDonald Letter. Yet HMG considered the problem of landless Arabs as a potential threat to the political and social stability of Palestine. Instability in the form of communal disturbances as had occurred in 1929 demanded the maintenance by HMG of large military contingents in order to protect Jewish settlements.[47] Military presence in large numbers required expenditures from the British Exchequer and from the British taxpayer. In an effort to reduce military expenditures in Palestine, HMG drew the conclusion that a reduction or elimination of the landless Arab problem would remove one of the main sources of political instability. As their maneuver to impose land-transfer prohibitions had been somewhat circumscribed by the Zionists, HMG chose instead to protect those tenants still engaged in agricultural occupancy and to resettle those Arabs previously displaced. Neither of these two approaches was of recent innovation. Hope-Simpson had alluded to both in his report, and some form of legal tenant protection had existed since October 1920.

Jewish Agency Reaction to the Proposed Land Bills

Although the MacDonald Letter explained that any contemplated land-transfer controls would contain safeguards to assure as little interference as possible in the free transfer of land, the Jewish Agency was not convinced that land-transfer prohibitions would be postponed. Having profound fears about Chancellor's anti-Zionist philosophy, the Jewish Agency moved expeditiously to thwart any prohibition of land transfers. In a concerted two-pronged effort, the Jewish Agency sought simultaneously to dilute the potential effectiveness of both the Protection of Cultivators Amendment Bill and the Development Department. Limiting the number of Arabs who might be classified as landless was a priority, but it was not as important as keeping the Arab need for money dependent upon Jewish land purchases and not HMG's benevolence.

Active Jewish Agency criticism against the POCAB continued to be focused on the Colonial Office rather than on Jerusalem. Fortunately for the Jewish Agency, the Colonial Office was not interested in another round of Jewish criticism; hence many of the Jewish Agency remarks were incorporated into the bill's final form. The Colonial Office's desire to keep the "lid on" was influenced by its impending submission of the annual report on Palestine to the League of Nations. When first approached about the POCAB, the Jewish Agency feared the centralized authority that could be personally exercised by the high commissioner. After successfully countering that threat, the Jewish Agency focused on particular sections of the bill. For instance, the Jewish Agency argued that the definition of a land disposition included in the POCAB was too broad. The definition stipulated that tenants' protection would be extended to land transactions that were effected by options to purchase, foreclosure of mortgages, and land sold in execution of a judgment debt. Since these methods involved collusion with Arab vendors and virtual circumvention of existing statutes for the protection of tenants, the Jewish Agency did not want them included. Indeed, no definition of disposition even appeared in the Protection of Cultivators Amendment Ordinance's final promulgated version in May 1931. Only after the POCAB had been twice redrafted with the incorporation of Jewish Agency recommendations for revisions and deletions was the bill passed on to the Arab Executive for comment. However, the Jewish Agency and the Jewish land-purchasing organizations were not able to influence the wording of the POCAB to the degree that they would have liked.[48] But they were able to have their points of view heard, and the final form of the bill bore small resemblance to the bill proposed by Chancellor in November 1930.

Chancellor still intended to protect the Arab community and in particular the Arab agriculturists. Chancellor wanted no part of Kisch's legal differentiation between tenants of long standing and casual laborers. Chancellor viewed every evicted cultivator as a "highwayman." Any absence of their legal rights, he believed, was due to an "iniquitous Turkish regime."[49] Although he espoused a paternalistic defense for the Arab agricultural classes, Chancellor refused to assign complicity to those Arab landowners involved in land sales.[50] Any public exposure by Chancellor would only have played into the hands of those Zionists who believed that Palestinian Arab demands were nothing less than a front for self-seeking individual aggrandizement. The Jewish Agency, in both official and unofficial contacts with the administration, continued to avoid specific mention of those Arab vendors who were satisfying the Jewish requirement for land. Moreover, the Jewish Agency was keenly aware that any investigation by the Development Department with its avowed priority of enumerating and resettling landless Arabs might secondarily expose Arab landowner complicity as well as brand Jewish land-purchase and settlement activity with an unsavory political label. The task at hand for the Jewish Agency was to repudiate the implication that it was the sole cause for Arab landlessness and yet selectively protect the prestige and public honor of past and future Arab vendors.

After the MacDonald Letter, the Jewish Agency insisted that the Colonial Office make no change in the laws affecting the disposition of agricultural land. Passfield, anxious about the future of the fellaheen at Shatta village in the Beisan subdistrict, told Weizmann that unless the Jewish Agency stopped their eviction, he would find it necessary to recommend immediate implementation of land-transfer restrictions despite the MacDonald Letter's assurances. Weizmann reiterated to Passfield that the evictions of tenants and agricultural laborers at Shatta were being carried out by the Arab landowner and not by the Jews. Passfield was not concerned with who was responsible for the eviction process; he wanted immediate resettlement of the tenants and laborers. Weizmann thereupon told Kisch, who in turn informed Granovsky, the managing director of the Jewish National Fund, that all efforts be made to settle not only the tenants but also Shatta's agricultural laborers.[51] After the order for their dispossession was given by the Beisan Civil Court on 15 April 1931 in favor of the owner Raja Ra'is, the Jewish National Fund purchased the land from Ra'is, but not before all the tenants and agricultural laborers found alternative lands to work. When the political gun was put to their heads, the Jewish Agency made the requisite compromise. Then they inevitably asked for more.

The day after the two hundred former inhabitants (including tenants, agricultural laborers, and dependents) of Shatta were legally removed from their land, Weizmann met with Passfield about the pending draft of the POCAB. Weizmann agreed with Passfield that the POCAB, which was now in a second revised form (after the Jewish Agency had its recommendations included) should be promulgated.[52] The Jewish Agency tactic to weaken the potential effectiveness of the POCAB had succeeded. However, HMG's attention was not diverted from either the potentially more threatening land-transfer controls or the question of landless Arabs. The concept of a Development Department became the bureaucratic focus for both issues.

The Development Department

In March 1931 HMG announced that the Development Department, with its projected £2.5 million budget guaranteed by a loan from HMG, would, as Hope-Simpson suggested, require both an Arab and a Jewish adviser. Proposals were then solicited from both Arab and Jewish representatives concerning the eventual structure and priorities of the new department. Discussions with both sides were to open in London on 13 April. Despite Chancellor's prodding of the Arab Executive to attend the meetings, the Arabs rejected the invitation on two grounds: the failure of HMG to disavow the MacDonald Letter and the inability of the Arab Executive to meet with HMG alone without the presence of Jewish representatives.[53] The Arab Executive decided to discuss the subject unofficially with the administration on the conditions that the meetings did not imply Arab assent to the Jewish national home policy and that they not meet in London. When Chancellor opened contacts with the Arab Executive on 20 April in Palestine, several conditions were laid down by the Arab participants. They included the following: (1) the appointment of advisers in proportion to the total Arab and Jewish population; (2) the appointment of an Arab deputy adviser to the director of development; (3) the adoption of a priority for resettlement of all landless Arabs and not merely those displaced according to the restrictive definition of landless Arabs found in the MacDonald Letter; (4) the withholding of money for Jewish development until all landless Arabs were resettled; (5) the provision of a minimum number of dunams for each Arab family that would consider the natural growth of the Arab population; and (6) the enactment of land legislation that would prevent transfer of land by Arabs to Jews.[54]

These explicit preconditions for participation were extensive enough to make HMG's acceptance of them something tantamount to capitulation to Arab demands. Nevertheless, certain members of the Arab Executive were willing to participate in the Development Department's endeavors whether or not HMG accepted the conditions. The inclusion of the demand for an Arab deputy adviser clearly became a struggle within inter-Arab factions between Jamal al-Husayni, a longtime secretary of the Arab Executive, and Mughannam Mughannam, a Protestant member of the al-Nashashibi opposition. In July, Jamal al-Husayni tendered his resignation as director of the *waqf* in anticipation of possible appointment to the director of development's staff.[55] In addition to reasons of personal advancement, the decision to carry on unofficial contacts with Chancellor about the future of the development scheme was motivated by some genuine feeling that the budgetary allocation for development could benefit the Arab agricultural population.

Even though HMG failed to meet any of the Arab Executive's preconditions for participation, the Arab Executive did not immediately dismiss the development scheme. On 16 August the Arab Executive finally rejected the development scheme after HMG severely reduced its budget to a meager £50,000. The Arab Executive maintained that it was being consistent in boycotting programs that might have given some de facto recognition to HMG's presence in Palestine and the Jewish national home policy. In rejecting the development scheme, the Arab Executive more than forfeited aid to a financially needy Arab agricultural population; it was clearly protecting the individual interests and personal reputations of its members.

Another land inquiry, like that of Hope-Simpson's, did not bode well for those Arabs who had sold land to Jews. Hope-Simpson had not raised this point, and members of the Arab Executive now could not be sure that a new inquiry by the director of development would be equally circumspect. Knowing that HMG was committed to the resettlement of landless Arabs, the Arab Executive could not permit an investigation that might prove that Jewish land purchase was not the sole cause of Arab landlessness.[56] Arab Executive apprehensions were well founded. The director of development's report specifically pointed to the "Arab *effendi* or capitalist landlord" as a factor in the creation of a class of landless Arabs.[57] After the decision not to participate officially in the development scheme, the Arab Executive claimed that the plan's purpose was to force the Arab agricultural population to utilize intensive methods of agriculture in order to make room for more Jewish settlers. Consonant with its anxieties about the investigation of landless Arabs, the Arab Executive refrained from issuing instructions to the fellaheen on whether it was in their interest or not to submit claims as landless Arabs. A thorough investigation of a claim would have revealed the name of a claimant's Arab landlord prior to the land's transfer into Jewish ownership.

While internal, personal, and political considerations kept the Arab Executive from participating in the development scheme, the Jewish Agency decided ultimately to cooperate with the director of development and his staff. Still looming were the proposed regulatory land-transfer controls that were to accompany landless Arab resettlement. If the number of claims could be proved to be small, reasoned the Jewish Agency, then what would be the need to institute even partial land-transfer controls? HMG for its part had two reasons for instituting partial controls: first, to prevent speculation by brokers on land that might be required by the Development Department in resettling landless Arabs; and second, to thwart, if only partially, further acquisition by Jewish purchasers of options to purchase more land.[58] But the very threat of land-transfer controls caused a rush in land transfers in August and September 1931, similar to the increased activity in land sales to Jews immediately after the publication of the Passfield White Paper in October 1930.[59]

When discussions between Zionists and HMG continued in London in April, Kisch considered any further mention of the still-pending Transfer of Agricultural Land Bill as inopportune until after the Seventeenth Zionist Congress met in Basle from 30 June to 10 July 1931. In early June, Colonial Office Under Secretary Shiels made it very clear that regulatory land controls would be instituted in the near future, but he stressed that the first priority of the Development Department would be resettlement of landless Arabs.[60] To avoid Zionist criticism at the Basle World Zionist Congress, HMG's official statement outlining the Development Department's program was not made public until after the close of the Congress, although the program was drafted and dated on 27 June 1931.[61] The Jewish Agency announced its participation in the development scheme on the condition that the share allotted for Jewish settlement be equal to the amount allocated for the resettlement of landless Arabs. The development scheme's proposed budget was so attractive to the Zionists that they felt required to participate in it, especially in light of the Jewish Agency's overall poor financial situation and its drastically reduced settlement budget.

The organizational framework of the Development Department was described in the HMG dispatch made public in the House of Commons on 20 July 1931. The director of development was to be subordinate only to the high commissioner, and he was to be independent of existing administration departments in Palestine. No mention was made of Hope-Simpson's suggestion that the director of development become the successor to the present high commissioner. On the director of development's staff were to be advisers from the Jewish Agency and the Arab Executive, as well as a legal adviser whose duty it would be to scrutinize the claims submitted for landlessness classification. The legal adviser would make the final determination regarding the credibility of evidence presented by each claimant. When the time came to appoint the legal adviser, the Jewish Agency successfully influenced the selection.

The director of development was charged with planning a scheme of resettlement and development within the limits of the available funds. The dispatch in no way committed HMG to the £2.5 million consistently linked to the activities of the director of development's budget. Partially because of the Arab Executive's reluctance to participate officially in the development scheme and partially because of HMG's unwillingness to make large financial subventions available to Palestinian agriculturists when British farmers were suffering economic hardships, HMG decided against authorizing the £2.5 million. Perhaps a more important reason for the postponement of the Development Department's £2.5 million allocation in the summer of 1931 was the uncertainty over the stability of the pound, which dropped in value by more than 25 percent when it was taken off the gold standard in September.[62]

The operational guidelines for the Development Department emanated from Paragraph 11 of the MacDonald Letter, which was drafted mostly by Zionists. HMG affirmed in public for the first time that it had begun to consider a physical partition or division of Palestine into separate demographic concentrations. With considerable Jewish Agency prodding, the development scheme's guidelines noted that "the question of the congestion amongst the fellaheen in the hill districts of Palestine is receiving the careful consideration of His Majesty's Government. It is contemplated that measures will be devised for the improvement and intensive development of the land, and for bringing into cultivation areas which hitherto may have remained uncultivated, and thereby securing to the *fellaheen* a better standard of living *without, save in exceptional cases, having recourse to transfer*" (my emphasis).[63]

HMG wanted to reserve the hill areas of Palestine, namely, Judea, Samaria, and the Upper Galilee, for landless Arab resettlement. HMG also acknowledged that those Arabs previously displaced because of Jewish land purchase had of their own volition resettled in these hill areas.

The seed for the eventual partition of Palestine had been planted. HMG's purpose was clear: resettle landless Palestinian Arabs away from existing Jewish settlements to avoid armed communal conflict. The likelihood of armed conflict might further necessitate HMG's intervention as an unwelcome expense to the British taxpayer. Neither Arab nor Jew was myopic about the implications of such policy. Nahum Sokolow, the newly elected president of the World Zionist Organization, clearly supported a policy whereby landless Arabs would not be resettled in Jewish districts, while 'Awni 'Abd al-Hadi protested against making the coastal plain into a Jewish preserve.[64]

The Defeat of Land-Transfer Controls

The feasibility of the development loan became increasingly unlikely. The issue of parity in expenditures from the loan became secondary to the implementation of immediate land-transfer controls that were to begin with the director of development's arrival on 20 August. There is no doubt that the Jewish Agency perceived such controls as a real threat to increased Jewish growth in Palestine. The Jewish Agency dallied in its contacts with HMG, hoping to gain a more favorable ear with Chancellor's successor, Sir Arthur Wauchope. Knowing that the proposed land-transfer controls were to coincide with the activation of the director of development's tenure of office, the Jewish Agency requested and received the Colonial Office's reluctant concession of more time to consider the proposed TALB. The Jewish Agency was given until 7 September to comment.[65] This delay enfeebled the idea of coordinating land-transfer controls with the beginning of the development scheme. Having won this breathing spell of a fortnight, the Jewish Agency, in addition to commenting on TALB, presented its own conditions for participation in the Development Department's activities. Since the Jewish Agency possessed the most detailed, though perhaps not the most organized, material and information on the previous occupancy status of Arab tenants and agricultural laborers (critical for ascertaining landless Arab claims), HMG conceded to Jewish Agency demands.

In his new capacity as head of the Jewish Agency's political department, Chaim Arlosoroff's first meeting with Chancellor on 19 August dealt with the TALB. Arlosoroff was dissatisfied because only the preamble of the bill mentioned the connection between the proposed land-transfer controls and the Development Department. The Jewish Agency wanted it explicitly stated that any control in the hands of the director of development be limited to resettlement. The Jewish Agency believed it would have greater influence with a newly appointed director of development than with the high commissioner whose control in land transfers would be uncontested. The Jewish Agency reasoned that the appointment of a Jewish adviser on the director of development's staff would give them a voice over any decision to limit land transfers. HMG could not proceed with resettlement of landless Arabs without the Jewish Agency's participation. At the Zionist Congress meeting, the Jewish Agency had decided to appoint its candidate to the director of development's staff if all of the Jewish Agency's demands were met. But as the TALB was still under discussion, the Jewish Agency used the tactical threat of nonappointment of an adviser. The Jewish Agency made it clear to Chancellor that unless the connection between the Development Department and land transfers be explicitly interwoven into the body of the bill, the Jewish Agency would boycott the Development Department and not appoint a Jewish adviser. Arlosoroff believed that the Jewish Agency's use of this "weapon" was quite effective both in London and in Jerusalem.[66]

There were no surprises in the formal comments submitted by the Jewish Agency on 30 August regarding the TALB's contents. The proposed autocratic control of the high commissioner was again severely criticized, and the point was made that not even the Palestine courts had legal jurisdiction over the powers in which the high commissioner could exercise discretion. Raising larger political issues, the Jewish Agency claimed that such a bill was incompatible with the MacDonald Letter and Article 6 of the Mandate. So forceful was the Jewish Agency case that the new secretary of state for the colonies, J. H. Thomas, recommended to Sir Mark Aitchison Young, the officer administering the government in the high commissioner's absence, and to Lewis French, the director of development, that only minimum directives regarding centralized control be implemented.[67]

Since this communication was sent two days after Thomas informed the Colonial Office's Middle Eastern Department that the development loan would not be funded, there is room to believe that the suspension of land-transfer controls was tied directly to the loan's stillbirth. Even though HMG had decided against the land-transfer controls in London, Young and other members of the Palestine administration continued to press for controls. The Jewish Agency did not know at this time that the land-transfer controls would be suspended, but they did know that the development loan would not be forthcoming. The Jewish Agency argued to Lewis French in Palestine and to the Colonial Office in London that without allocations for landless Arab resettlement or for the intensifica-

8. Dr. Chaim Arlosoroff, 1929
Courtesy of Central Zionist Archives, Jerusalem

9. Sir Arthur Wauchope, 1935
Courtesy of Central Zionist Archives, Jerusalem

tion of agriculture, any restrictive land-transfer controls could not be justified and would be meaningless. Having made that point, the Jewish Agency moved to the position of not accepting even temporary controls as long as the register of landless Arabs had not been completed and their number determined.[68] Once more the Jewish Agency continued in London and Palestine to press for parity in the spending of any money that might be made available to the Development Department. The question of when to appoint the Jewish adviser to the Development Department staff also continued to be used by the Jewish Agency as a mechanism to obtain, although unwillingly, HMG's acquiescence to the Jewish Agency's viewpoints.

HMG's inability to provide the financial capital for the development loan, the boycott applied to the development scheme by the Arab Executive, and the regular contacts that the Jewish Agency enjoyed with the Colonial Office prevented implementation of the land-transfer controls implied in the Passfield White Paper and originally suggested by Chancellor in January 1930. After the Jewish Agency criticism of the White Paper, HMG repeatedly capitulated to what it perceived to be potentially embarrassing Jewish or Zionist censure. The MacDonald Letter was the first of at least four recisions; the other three included postponement of land-transfer controls or mention thereof prior to the June 1931 meeting of the League of Nations, prior to the meeting of the Seventeenth Zionist Congress in July, and prior to the arrival of the new high commissioner in November. HMG did not wish to sour relations between the new head of the Jewish Agency, Chaim Arlosoroff, and Sir Arthur Wauchope, the newly appointed high commissioner. When the Jewish Agency in December 1931 persuaded the Jewish National Fund to offer temporary resettlement to the Bedouin and to the fellaheen of Wadi Hawarith and to make provision for the tenants at Shatta village, Wauchope believed that Jewish purchasing organizations were making a genuine effort to defuse the landless Arab controversy. Wauchope's newness to Palestine and his ignorance of land matters, save for information provided him by Palestine administration officials, did not in the least hurt Jewish settlement efforts. Fear of exposure to public culpability kept some members of the Arab Executive from participation in the development scheme. Other Palestinian Arabs maintained their consistent belief that such a scheme was nothing more than another vehicle to enhance Jewish settlement and to confine the Arab population to certain geographical areas. For the Zionist proponents of something more politically definite than just *a* Jewish national home, the defeat of the land-transfer controls was critical.

Chapter 5

The Rural Economy and Lewis French:

The Landless Arab Inquiry

In the early 1930s, Arab land sales and Jewish land purchases contributed to the evolution of an Arab landless class. But the
principal factor influencing Arab landlessness was the fellaheen's deteriorating economic condition. To be sure, the overall condition of the
Palestinian economy was relatively strong in the early 1930s and continued to grow primarily because of increasing imports of Jewish capital.
However, the overwhelming majority of the Muslim Arab rural population, so dependent on agricultural yields, suffered woefully. British regulation had arrested the heretofore unchecked land-accumulation process. Landlords were not disposing of their tenants as freely as they had
in the late Ottoman times. Yet successively poor harvests and the availability of Jewish capital through land sales attracted many small landowners. As Jewish land purchase aimed increasingly at the smaller
holder, many fellaheen left their rural occupations for the urban building trades. For those who depended on rent income calculated according
to a percentage of the yield, poor harvests were financially injurious.
Thus some Arab merchants, moneylenders, landlords, and other profes-
sionals who had liens on segments of a village population forced many
to sell to them or their agents. In turn, sales were made to Jewish purchasers. Not affected by the severe agricultural squeeze in the 1930s
were Arab and Jewish citrus growers, but they comprised only one-tenth
of 1 percent of the total population.[1]

At the other end of the spectrum, the overwhelming majority of the
agricultural population was in dire straits in the early 1930s. In fact,
the fellaheen's economic condition had not appreciably improved since
World War I. According to a Jewish land-purchase authority, the average
annual net income on 150 Turkish dunams for an owner-occupier remained constant at £P68 to £P70 in the two periods 1914–23 and
1924–26 respectively.[2] In the years 1927–30 that income decreased by
40 percent to approximately £P42.[3] From 1929 to July 1930 the average
net income on 100 dunams had fallen from £P27.5 to £P16.5 for an
owner-occupier and from £P20 to £P9 for a tenant farmer.[4] In 1930 it
was estimated that still half of the cultivable land area of Palestine, or

3.6 million dunams, was under some form of the *musha'* system,[5] making the economic potential of the fellah's land all the less amenable to increased productivity. From 1926 to 1936, there were in Palestine severe cattle plagues, recurring periods of drought, a field mice plague in the Northern District, and a locust plague in the Southern District.[6] Because of the grave shortage of indigenous cattle and sheep in Palestine, many were imported in 1929 and 1930; more than 633,000 dunams were partially damaged by the field mice plague in spring 1930. This adversely affected more than 350 villages and settlements, causing a 64 percent loss in the winter cereal crop.[7]

Since cereal-growing was the principal undertaking of a majority of the fellaheen, yield levels and the price of wheat, barley, and lentils were critically important to agricultural subsistence. Wheat was grown in all districts of Palestine on about 30 percent of the total cultivated crop-raising area. It accounted for 40 percent of the cereals raised in Palestine.[8] It was estimated that only one-third of the wheat crop was available for marketing since most was required for the fellaheen domestic consumption. The prices of wheat and flour in Palestine were unfavorably affected by foreign imports. Despite the Palestine administration's efforts at stabilizing locally produced wheat prices, the Palestine-Syria Customs Agreement of 1929 nullified these attempts since commodities produced in either country were not subject to custom duties. By 1935, Palestine's trade deficit with Syria was approximately £650,000, due primarily to the import of Syrian wheat and flour.[9] From 1930 through 1933 wheat production and its price plummeted in Palestine without a comparable increase in other cereal production. The export price of domestically produced Palestinian wheat dropped from £10.81 per ton in 1929 to £6.97 per ton in 1931. In the same period the price of barley dropped from £7.66 per ton to £3.03 per ton.[10]

Chancellor believed in June 1930 that three measures would improve the economic situation of the fellaheen: an early reduction in the tithe; measures to prevent the dumping of foreign wheat and prohibition against the importation of olive oil; and the grant of agricultural loans.[11] The tithe was not reduced, although, as had occurred in 1928, 1930, and later from 1931 to 1934, portions of the tithe were remitted because of very poor agricultural seasons. Loans for fodder, forage, and seeds were granted to fellaheen in the period 1931 to 1935, but little was done to prevent the slippage in the price of olive oil and wheat.[12] Imports of wheat and flour continued.

With a drastic decline in agricultural prices and in the total production of wheat, the indebtedness of the fellaheen was further compounded. The bulk of the wheat crop in 1930 was mortgaged for debt payment to moneylenders, many of whom were grain merchants. Loans

TABLE 8

Citrus and Wheat Production for Palestine, 1929–1937

Year	Total Cases Citrus Production	Total Dunam Areas under Citrus Cultivation	Domestic Wheat Production in Tons	Net Imports of Wheat into Palestine in Tons	Dunam Area of Wheat under Cultivation
1929	2,897,686	70,500	87,873	17,731	—
1930	2,468,937	90,500	87,339	2,207	—
1931	3,734,556	110,000	51,519	13,650	2,358,103
1932	4,498,830	125,000	56,186	27,114	1,723,243
1933	5,526,097	160,000	48,305	59,951	1,768,021
1934	7,330,846	203,500	85,171	45,318	1,930,713
1935	5,897,310	278,000	104,353	17,759	2,251,018
1936	10,790,110	298,000	76,059	21,536	2,320,140
1937	11,408,964	299,500	127,420	36,016	2,258,908

Source: Palestine Government, *Annual Report of the Department of Agriculture, Forests and Fisheries,* 1927, 1928, 1929, 1930, 1931, 1932, and years ending in March of 1934, 1935, 1936, 1937.

Note: The citrus season lasted from October to April, hence years in this case refer to the current and upcoming year, 1929–30, for example. For these nine years, Jewish and Arab ownership of citrus groves was about equal.

were usually expressed in terms of kilos of wheat and included a provision for the proportionate increase in the amount of wheat to be repaid by the fellah, should prices fall below a certain figure. Two options were left to the fellah: either use more wheat for his family's sustenance, which left him with less to exchange for what money he could obtain to pay his debt, or retain enough wheat to meet his loan payments. But moneylenders also realized that there was no market for wheat and often refused to accept payment in kind. Hard currency was apparently so scarce that much of the rural population was resorting to barter. Chancellor feared that regardless of which avenue the fellaheen chose, they would fall deeper into debt and bankruptcy.[13] In fact, in 1930–31 many fellaheen were insolvent and living on the sufferance of their creditors.

Moneylenders were characterized by C. F. Strickland, who came to Palestine in 1931 to undertake a study of introducing agricultural cooperatives, as "greedy Arab merchants who buy their [fellaheen] crops."[14] The destitution and indebtedness of the fellaheen reached such proportions in 1931–32 that one Zionist official described their economic condition as "nauseating poverty."[15] The commissioner of lands portrayed their general personal attitudes as "sullen and indifferent."[16]

Their economic condition steadily worsened. In 1932, there was a drought in the early part of the year that caused particular hardship to the fellaheen in the hill country. The drought caused a failure of 60 percent of the durra crop, 80 percent of the olive crop, and 85 percent of the sesame crop in 1931–32.[17] Not only was the tithe remitted by 25 to 40 percent, but there was difficulty in purchasing fodder since the drought had destroyed grazing pastures. Many draft animals, particularly cattle, were sold at low prices, which forced some fellaheen off their remaining parcels of land. In 1933, in addition to remitting the tithe, the high commissioner set aside the small sum of £P50,000 for seed loans and £P15,000 for fodder loans.[18] The failure of the winter harvest in 1933 meant that the fellaheen found it impossible to provide seed for the 1934 crop year. Wauchope's action was aimed at reducing the fellaheen's additional indebtedness to moneylenders and grain merchants.[19]

In March 1934, the high commissioner waived the collection of arrears from fellaheen amounting to some £P95,000 due from agricultural loans, tithes, and land and animal taxes. The cold winter of 1933–34 and drought caused a high mortality in farm animals. Tithes were again remitted and forage loans made for plough oxen for the summer crop of 1934.[20] In a further administration attempt to aid the fellaheen population, a few experimental agricultural plots were made available in the hill districts after September 1935. But the magnitude of the administration's attempt at helping the fellaheen's depressed economic condition and the timing of assistance was clearly a case of too little too late. The agricultural experiment plots were established in only eighteen of Palestine's more than eight hundred Arab villages. The £P50,000 allotted for long-term agricultural loans only reached 1,125 individual fellaheen by the end of 1934.[21] While there had been much discussion of what had to be done to ameliorate the condition of the fellaheen population, little was translated into actual assistance.

Some owner-occupiers, tenants, and laborers were forced to leave agricultural pursuits solely because of the worsening and untenable economic situation. Those who found seasonal labor were fortunate. In late 1933, more than 5,000 Arab laborers, not all of them landless, were employed by Jewish landowners in the orange-growing districts.[22] By early 1935, the *New York Times* reported a shortage of farmhands in Palestine and an increased migration to the cities.[23] But even the citrus industry, whose production had dramatically increased in the early 1930s, suffered a setback in 1935–36 because of a prolonged sirocco, exchange regulation problems with Germany, and shipping insecurity caused by the Italian-Abyssinian dispute. As a result of the decline in citrus production, the hiring of seasonal laborers and the hours they worked also declined.[24] The boom in the building trades in late 1935 absorbed some of the seasonal laborers who had become landless.

Perhaps the only real beneficiary of these bad economic times was the development of the Jewish national home. Jewish land purchase increased dramatically from 1933 on. Simultaneously, Jewish Agency lawyers and advisers cleverly eliminated the potential adversity emanating from the landless Arab inquiry. The drive, capability, and commitment exhibited by Jewish Agency officialdom on this issue in comparison to the generally despondent and frustrated feelings of many Palestinian Arabs was indicative of the widening distance between the two communities.

The Landless Arab Inquiry: The Jewish Agency's Position

The British government had acknowledged the existence of a landless Arab population in 1930 and had established the Development Department to solve that problem. The original development loan was an appropriation of more than £7 million, but it was twice reduced, once to £2.5 million and then again to £P50,000, when the Development Department began its work. Neither the Palestine administration nor the Colonial Office was interested in committing any of the Palestine administration's surplus revenue of £4.7 million[25] (as of July 1935) toward improving the economic position of the fellaheen. Revenue customs attributed to increased (Jewish) immigration and the import of (Jewish) capital accounted for the surplus.[26] Eventually, most of that surplus was used for military and police expenditures during various stages of the Arab revolt between 1936 and 1939.

HMG acknowledged that it was unwilling to make a large financial commitment to arrest the fellaheen indebtedness; it therefore gave priority to enumerating and resettling landless Arabs.[27] HMG was treating the effects and not the causes. A bureaucratic rather than a financial solution to a socioeconomic problem was chosen. Even limiting the resettlement of Arabs classified as landless required a meager financial commitment. Only 74 of the 899 Arab families ultimately classified as landless were actually resettled on land provided by the Palestine administration's Development Department. The department eventually spent only £P84,000 for resettlement, and 85 percent of that amount was for the purchase of land.[28] Little resettlement activity took place after the outbreak of disturbances in 1936. The Development Department ceased to function in 1939. Its aims were nobly defined, but its effectiveness was appallingly limited.

The Jewish Agency had nothing positive to gain from the Development Department once HMG decided to concentrate on enumeration and resettlement of landless Arabs. Only if the inquiry could show conclusively that Jewish purchases had not contributed to Arab landlessness might the Jewish Agency salvage something politically from the Development Department's activity. Although the Jewish Agency had originally desired parity in the allocation of the development loan, the Jewish Agency was not disturbed when the loan itself failed to materialize. Without the development loan there was little chance that the administration would expropriate Jewish-owned land for landless Arab resettlement, a threat implied first by Chancellor over the Wadi Hawarith resettlement. Also there would not be a ready alternative source of British capital to compete for, which would endanger land transfers that demanded initial monetary outlays by the Jewish Agency. Though publicly advocating agricultural intensification, which could have included the partition of *musha'*-held shares, the continuation of the *musha'* system enabled Jewish purchasing institutions to employ local landlords and land brokers as intermediaries to facilitate transfers.[29]

Arlosoroff believed in the autumn of 1931 that total rejection of Jewish Agency involvement in the Development Department would not be in the agency's best interest. Arlosoroff weighed the benefits and liabilities inherent in appointing a Jewish adviser to the Development Department's staff. In the event that the director of development's report due in December 1931 would grossly misrepresent the Jewish Agency position, a Jewish staff adviser in his official capacity could submit to Parliament an authoritative exposition of the Jewish Agency viewpoint on development and Jewish settlement. An official resignation threat by a Jewish adviser would be an effective means to amend or cancel any contemplated land-transfer controls.[30] Hexter and Ruppin were more eager than Arlosoroff to have a Jewish adviser appointed. Their concern emanated from landless Arab registration that had begun in September. They wanted to halt the inflation of preliminary claims. Both men wanted to be sure that the resettlement of displaced Arabs did not take place in predominantly Jewish districts.[31] Repeatedly, the Jewish Agency officially refused to appoint its adviser and tied its refusal to the department's priority on landless Arab resettlement at the expense of the agency's emphasis on parity. Later, after French wrote his first report, the Jewish Agency withheld the appointment of its adviser until it was assured that land-transfer controls were not included in his report. The agency concentrated its efforts initially on influencing both the choice of the legal adviser-assessor who would ascertain the validity of landless Arab claims and the method in which those claims would be scrutinized. The Jewish Agency's relationship with Lewis French was not characterized by the candor and cordiality Ruppin and Hankin had extended to Hope-Simpson. Soured by Hope-Simpson's anti-Zionist conclusions, the Jewish Agency was more reluctant to share its information.[32] Like Hope-Simpson, French had his baptismal political discussions in Palestine with Chancellor prior to the retiring high commissioner's departure from Palestine. Unlike Hope-Simpson, who the Jewish Agency considered to be sufficiently qualified to investigate Palestine's economic situation, French was assessed as having less ability. Neither the procrastination in appointing a Jewish adviser to French's staff nor Arlosoroff's unveiled threat that French's attitude would be closely watched by Jewish adherents in Parliament endeared him to the Jewish Agency.[33]

The Jewish Agency's preliminary caution in dealing with French and its assessment of his political leanings were fairly accurate. So odious to the Jewish position in Palestine were the contents of French's first report that he was asked by the high commissioner and the Colonial Office to rewrite fourteen of its pages. Moreover, his initial report contained no definite scheme for development. Rather, it was a diagrammatic compendium on how best to stop Jewish land settlement. His one-sided outlook forced HMG to request a supplementary report that appeared in April 1932, four months after the first report.[34] Having correctly anticipated French's position, the Jewish Agency directed its energies toward having a legal assessor appointed who was less antagonistic and even perhaps amenable to Jewish settlement activity.

The legal assessor was assigned the task of making a register of "displaced" Arabs. The register was then submitted to the director of development for final inclusion in the resettlement rolls. Having received HMG's acquiescence to use the very restrictive definition of what constituted a landless Arab, the Jewish Agency made every effort to have someone appointed who would strictly adhere to that definition. Once again, that definition classified one as landless who could be shown to have been displaced from land that he had occupied because it had passed into Jewish hands and who had not obtained other land or other equally satisfactory work.

Among those considered for the position of legal assessor were several Palestine judges, then serving in the local Land Court and District Courts. Chancellor, not eager to pass up an opportunity to influence a pivotal appointment, wanted R. C. Tute, a Land Court judge, for the job. Tute's judgeship was to be phased out in keeping with recommendations to streamline the Palestine administration. Chancellor wanted to provide another job for him. He consulted Chief Justice McDonnell for his opinion on Tute's qualifications. Notwithstanding the Palestine chief justice's approval, Passfield was told that Bentwich considered Tute to be in "imperfect sympathy with Zionism."[35] Tute was not appointed. The Jewish Agency wanted someone who would make his determinations on strictly legal grounds, not on grounds of political preference. More acceptable to the Jewish Agency was a former member of the Nablus District Court, Judge A. H. Webb. Largely because of Jewish Agency pressures, Webb was appointed to the position of legal assessor. Arlosoroff was pleased by the differences between Webb's understanding of Jewish settlement and the more negative opinion held by French. Webb remarked to Arlosoroff that it was "his duty to protect Government and you (meaning the Jews or Jewish Agency) against fraudulent claims."[36] Many British administration officials in Palestine remained displeased with the degree of influence enjoyed by the Jewish Agency.

In late November 1931, the Jewish Agency began its preparations to quash the potential volatility of the landless inquiry. Three separate committees were set up by the Jewish Agency to deal with French and the Development Department. A legal committee had two primary tasks —the investigation of Arab landlessness claims and the determination of which information the Jewish Agency should share with Webb or French. A development committee drew up priorities for Jewish Agency participation in the projected development scheme. A third committee was to discuss the feasibility of establishing agricultural credit facilities in Palestine. The two latter committees' functions were reduced to unimportance because HMG did not provide the necessary capital for either. Similar to the high-caliber composition of the Colonization and Immigration Committee established to inform Hope-Simpson in May– June 1930, the representation on the Jewish Agency Legal Committee reflected its concern and priority for achieving favorable results from the landless Arab inquiry.[37] The Jewish Agency coordinated efforts among the Jewish National Fund, the Palestine Land Development Company, and the Palestine Colonization Association. Arlosoroff wanted the Legal Committee to review each claim of landlessness submitted to the administration. In order to prepare the necessary data, in addition to the tenant information already compiled by the Jewish Agency for the Jezreel Valley and for former Sursock lands, information on other geographical areas was collected through the cooperative use of Jewish National Fund, Palestine Land Development Company, and Palestine Colonization Association records. Joseph Nehemey of the Palestine Land Development Company was put in charge of the districts of Tiberias, Beisan, and Safed; Haifa and Tulkarm were allotted to Shabtai Levi of the Palestine Colonization Association; and Judea and Samaria were charged to the Palestine Land Development Company and Yehoshua Hankin.[38]

Three separate and distinct categories of possible claimants were considered by the Jewish Agency in their preparation of district lists: owner-occupiers who had sold their own lands; tenants whose occupied land was sold by owners; and agricultural laborers. HMG had preoccupied itself with tenant protection in the 1929 Protection of Cultivators Ordinance, its amendment in May 1931, and the Law of Execution Amendment Ordinance of the following month. Emphasis on tenants' protection was transposed by HMG to the landless Arab inquiry. This permitted the Jewish Agency the welcome opportunity of concentrating on this numerically smaller category at a time when Jewish land purchases were acquired predominantly from small owner-occupiers. The Jewish Agency had reliable information from at least one Arab informant that owner-occupiers would be making claims.[39] Jewish Agency officials were deeply concerned that claims would also be made by agricultural laborers. Official acceptance of those claims would have caused severe problems for the Jewish Agency. But Jewish Agency trepidations about the inclusion of agricultural laborers' claims were erased because of HMG's announced unwillingness to make the financial expenditures necessary to resettle them.[40]

In anticipation of possible discussions about the owner-occupier and agricultural laborer question, the Jewish Agency compiled lists of possible claimants in these categories. The lists of tenants by districts who had received monetary or land compensation from Jewish purchasers in the past were compiled with details appended as to whether a tenant owned land or had found equally satisfactory occupation elsewhere.[41]

The Landless Arab Inquiry: Procedures for Enumeration

In order to ascertain the number of Arabs who considered themselves landless, the Development Department distributed a questionnaire. The questionnaire was given to district officials and through them to individual villagers and village *mukhtars*. (Specimens of letters sent to *mukhtars*, individuals considered to be former owners, and declarations of former ownership appear in Documents 5, 6, and 7.) Nowhere on the questionnaire was there mention of the very restrictive definition that would be used to determine who was a landless Arab. Moreover, there is no indication to suggest that district officials either knew that definition or made it clear to the fellaheen in their districts.

DOCUMENT 5
Landless Arab Inquiry—Letter from the District Commissioner to
a Villager via the Village *Mukhtar*

14 October 1931

To _____

c/o The *mukhtar* of the _____ Village,

Sir,

In accordance with information in hand it appears that you have
sold land to Jews. If this information is correct, I am to ask you to
fill out the enclosed form sent to you through the *mukhtar* of the
village. The facts which you are to state in this form must be set
out correctly and have your hand signature or your seal in the special place reserved therefore. The signed form is to be handed to
the village *mukhtar* in order that he should add his observations
and comments. Having secured the *mukhtar*'s signature or seal
with his observations, you are to present this form in person to this
Office, and to secure in return a written receipt signed by the Office Clerk. This form must reach this Office in the course of fifteen
days from the above date, otherwise your application will not be
considered.

Sgd. Nicola Saba
for District Commissioner
Jerusalem-Bethlehem

Source: A copy of this letter was taken from Central Zionist Archives, A202/119.

DOCUMENT 6
Landless Arab Inquiry—Letter from the District Commissioner to
the *Mukhtar* of _____ Village

16 October 1931

To the Mukhtar
of the _____ Village,

Sir,

I forward herewith _____ [figure] forms attached to _____
[figure] letters addressed to _____ [figure] person(s) resident in
your village. You are to hand them to the persons concerned and
secure a written receipt in return. These forms are to be filled out
by the addressees and signed by them. You are to examine the
filled-out forms and give your opinion and observations as to the
accuracy of the information contained. If it is correct, you are to
sign your name in the line reserved therefore. In case the data is
not correct, you are also to add your observations and comments
on the point. Having done this, you are to approve the question-

naire and return it to its signatory so that he may present it to this Office in the course of fifteen days from the above date.

Signed,
District Commissioner

Source: A copy of this letter was taken from Central Zionist Archives, A202/119.

DOCUMENT 7
Landless Arab Inquiry—Declaration Requested from Former Owners of Property Who Sold Their Land to Jews from 1920 Onwards

1. Name of applicant.
2. Number of members of the family of the applicant at the time of the filling out of this form. State names.
3. Name of the village or the present place of residence of the applicant.
4. The present occupation of the applicant.
5. Name of the village where the land sold by him to the Jew is situated.
6. The area of land transferred, in dunams. In case of *musha'* land, state the share which passed to the Jew.
7. Price received by seller for his land.
8. Name of the buyer.
9. Date of sale.
10. The applicant's signature or seal.
11. The area of land in dunams which remained in the applicant's ownership.
12. The crops grown on the land which is in applicant's ownership.
13. Observations and comments of the village *mukhtar*.
14. Signature or seal of the *mukhtar*.

Source: A copy of this form was taken from Central Zionist Archives, S25/7596.

District officials were not at all diligent in explaining to the fellaheen that submission of the claim did not guarantee that the land would be allotted to them. With the approval of the high commissioner's office, local district officials encouraged the fellaheen who did not consider themselves qualified as landless to come forward with claims.[42] Many claims were genuine. However, the fact that only one in ten of the Arab rural population was literate suggests that the filing of most of the claims was done by persons on behalf of claimants. The questionnaire was designed to collect information from former owners who had sold their land to Jews. No distinction was made on the questionnaire between those Arabs who had been displaced either by an absentee landlord sale or by an Arab landlord or land broker who then sold the land to a Jewish purchaser. Although some claimants volunteered such information, including the name of the Arab who ultimately sold land to the Jews, such a claimant was not considered displaced because of the way in which the questionnaire was worded. No separate information was sought as to whether one had been a tenant or a seasonal laborer and was therefore displaced as a result of another's sale. The questionnaire sent by Palestine subdistrict officials did not reflect London's emphasis on tenant protection, but rather it emphasized protection of the owner who had sold his own land. And the definition of a landless Arab excluded persons who had themselves sold their land to Jews.[43]

The discrepancy between the working definition of a landless Arab as it originally appeared in the MacDonald Letter and the questionnaire drawn up by members of the Palestine administration supports the belief that local officials were eager to expand the definitional framework of a landless Arab. Many local subdistrict officials wished to disprove the Jewish Agency's claim that it was not responsible for Arab landlessness. They elicited claims of landlessness from the fellaheen in their subdistricts.[44] In some areas, claims were accepted from persons who sold their land prior to World War I. No penalties were suggested for a *mukhtar*'s inaccuracy in submitting claims. Hence, inflated estimates were made rather easily despite the refusal of the Arab Executive's officials to urge the fellaheen to submit claims or to aid district officials in registering claimants.[45] Many fellaheen believed that the administration was about to distribute land and money gratis. Anyone who had anything to do with Jewish land purchase in the past, and some who did not, entered their names or had their names entered on the *mukhtar*'s lists. The following incidents and remarks relating to claims are illustrative:

In the villages in the environs of Lake Tiberias and in chance meetings with fellaheen the topic of the day was the government's decision to take the land of the Jews back and restore it to its first owners, the Arabs. . . . Arabs who left the country altogether and settled in Transjordan, where they own land, have filed applications as "displaced" Arabs in Tiberias, and are demanding back the land which was sold by their fathers. Here is a specific example. Muhammad al-Khatib, the shaykh of the Dallata Bedouin, whose father together with others sold land upon which Yavneel has now been standing for 33 years, came with his tribesmen and submitted petitions as "displaced" Arabs. He and his tribesmen have been living in Transjordan for 15 years, and he owns about 1,000 dunams of land at Shukir al-Ghor. He is convinced that the Jews have decided to leave Palestine, and he thinks he has a claim prior to other Arabs to the land and to the improvements of the Jews, because his father or grandfather once owned the land. Another Arab, Salim Jalal, whose tribe formerly owned Kinneret and Poriya, encounters Dhib Ibrahim, the Arab, who is cultivating the Poriya land on lease, and says to him, "I say, one of these days you are going to get an order to leave the place and to surrender to me the land and keys of the houses of the Jews to which you are the watchman. My relatives and I already put in a petition about it."[46]

Some tried to speculate on the registration process. In one area, an official working for a Jewish land-purchasing organization was offered land for sale by persons confident that it would be restored to them at an early date. Several Arab landowners offered the same official in Lubya in the Tiberias subdistrict small plots of land totaling 56 dunams in the belief that the administration would give them 150 dunams for the land. Some fellaheen[47] in the Tiberias subdistrict believed that they would be granted state lands. One fellow in the coastal plain, who had once owned 60 dunams of citrus, sold 25 of them in hopes of being classified as landless for not having sufficient maintenance area.[48]

As the legal assessor, A. H. Webb was the first in the Development Department to receive all the claims. Webb knew that the Jewish Agency wanted to keep the list of landless Arabs to a minimum. But more critical to Webb was the detailed information to which the Jewish Agency had access. Such information was used as a control for the submitted claims. For its part, the Jewish Agency preferred dealing with Webb rather than French. Yet the Jewish Agency was careful not to alienate French totally since he was the person who ultimately determined the validity of claims. The Jewish Agency did protest to French about what it believed to be a manifest inflation of claims. Arlosoroff warned French that in the fellaheen's current desperate economic state, the swelling of expectations would end in disillusionment and become a threat to security, life, and property. Arlosoroff went further and asserted that public opinion among the Arabs would blame the Jews for obstructing their expectations.[49]

Despite his initial reservations concerning Jewish Agency participation in the investigation of claims, French acceded to Webb's advice to allow Jewish Agency involvement. Neither the Jewish Agency nor the Arab Executive appointed an adviser as originally planned. Detailed information regarding individual claims, *mukhtars'* lists, and questionnaires were not made known to the Arab Executive. 'Awni 'Abd al-Hadi approached Dr. Eliash of the Jewish Agency Executive in early September 1931 and confirmed the receipt of general information from the Development Department, but he requested that the Jewish Agency provide the Arabs with the detailed material supplied to it by the adminis-tration.[50]

In defining the guidelines for Jewish Agency participation, French de-cided from the outset to have Webb reject any claim that was evidently baseless without asking the Jewish Agency to scrutinize such claims. But in order to avoid delay in processing the claims, Webb, nevertheless, sent the Jewish Agency all the files he received without first scrutinizing them and gave it the option to decide whether there was prima facie evidence in any particular case. After all applications were evaluated and opinions rendered by the Jewish Agency Legal Committee, Webb made his deci-sion for or against a claim's inclusion on the register of displaced Arabs. Then Webb submitted the list to French. After several months, it became more expeditious for Webb to rule first on a claim and then submit it to the Jewish Agency for its comment. If there were sufficient question whether a claimant should be included on Webb's register, an inquiry was held and the claimant's remarks heard. When Webb's inquiry into a claim was completed, the case was then referred back to the Jewish Agency for comment. In the great majority of cases, there was little controversy between the claimants and the evidence of the Jewish Agency regarding matters of fact.[51] The supporting data for most claims of previous ownership and tenancy status were either tithe records sup-plied to Webb by district officers or the claimants' own estimate of land that they had once owned. Neither evidence was considered reliable in itself when carefully investigated. Tithe payments did not reflect land ownership. Often a tenant would sublease part of his land to an agricul-tural laborer who paid the tithe and had his name entered into the tax register; such a record, if taken at face value for tenancy and ownership purposes, would have ascribed to the agricultural laborer ownership rights, thereby discounting the rights of the title-deed holder to the land. At other times, one tenant would make the tithe payment for himself and several others collectively with only the name of the actual tenant who paid the money entered into the tax register. Those tenants who did not actually make the payment therefore had no proof that they were tenants. As for self-estimate of land in one's possession, Webb believed that the fellaheen had not deliberately exaggerated "their" land areas but rather that the concept of a dunam had very little meaning to a fellah.[52] Thus, the supportive evidence of claimants was not a complete or true representation of their former holdings or tenancy status.

Webb, therefore, relied heavily upon Jewish Agency documentation and opinion. The method of ascertaining the credibility of claims be-came an exclusive question of Webb's personal disposition. Nevertheless, he retained his judicial impartiality, restricting himself only to a narrow definition of what constituted a landless Arab. On claims that appeared valid, Webb made every effort to clarify and strengthen that opinion. He was quite favorably impressed with the evidence that Arabs presented on their own behalf. He often relied upon the comments of a particular *mukhtar*, but he found that when personally confronted the *mukhtar* would admit that such and such a person was not a cultivator as claimed in writing.[53]

The Landless Arab Inquiry: Results of Enumeration

The majority of the landless Arab claims were submitted for inclusion in the legal assessor's register by early January 1932. Originally the deadline for submission of claims was set for the previous September, but because of the time required for the Jewish Agency to compile information on each claimant, the time period was extended. Claims continued to be submitted through 1935. Some 3,737 claims were received by December 1931–January 1932, including 1,074 applications made by *mukhtars* on behalf of individuals considered by them to be eligible claimants. The remaining 2,663 claims came from individuals and appear in Table 9. According to statistics prepared by the Development Department, 80 percent of the claims supplied by *mukhtars*, or approximately 860 claims, came on behalf of independent owners of land and not tenants. Most of these claims involved the transfer of 1 to 5 dunams to Jewish ownership, which the legal assessor ruled did not qualify for inclusion in the landless Arab register. Of the individual claims received, about 20 percent came from former owners, while the remainder, or approximately 2,128 claims, came from former tenants. Of all the claims submitted by December 1931–January 1932, a quarter came from those who claimed to be previous owners, while the majority of the total claims, approximately 2,800, came from those who considered themselves former tenants.[54] It is not clear whether the Jewish Agency's trepidations concerning the filing of applications by seasonal laborers were hollow fears or not. No distinction was made between the tenant and the agricultural laborer in official enumerative terms. That tenants made up the bulk of claims suggests that their economic situation was more precarious at this time than individual owners who might have continued to maintain some land of their own. The past aversion of some tenants to associate with any administration was lessened by the expectation that the British would provide them with land.

The fact that more tenants did not file claims for resettlement was explained by the chief secretary of the Palestine administration. He said that many had found more profitable occupations and were, therefore,

TABLE 9
*Claims for Inclusion in the Landless Arab Register, December 1931–
January 1932*

Region	Number of Claims Submitted
Tulkarm	646
Nazareth	281
Safed	170
Haifa	565
Beisan	126
Jenin	57
Jerusalem	71
Jaffa-Ramle	537
Gaza-Beersheba	119
Tiberias	91
Total	2,663

Source: The data in Table 9 are derived from the correspondence of Arlosoroff to Horowitz, 1 January 1932, Central Zionist Archives, S25/7620.

reluctant even to consider giving up better-paying urban jobs for a return to agricultural life.[55] Tenants' names did not appear prominently on *mukhtar*'s lists, as the *mukhtar* was more familiar with those in his locality who had a certain degree of landed permanency. Moreover, he was more personally concerned with claims of individual owners from whom he derived support for his own position in the village community. For differing reasons, the Arab Executive and the Jewish Agency wished to keep the submission of all claims to a minimum. The former wished to protect its members by keeping complicity in land sales hidden from public view; the latter wished to limit the number of claims so that the number classified as landless would also be kept to a minimum.[56] Certainly, the number of claims submitted was neither representative nor reflective of the number of Arabs displaced by Arab land sales or Jewish land purchases; nor was the final tally of 899 demonstrative of anything except a Jewish Agency political victory.

Some grazers, herdsmen, shepherds, and agricultural laborers of the Wadi Hawarith tribe were classified as landless. There was a pressing need to make their resettlement a showcase for the Arab population. Almost all other claimants in these categories were not classified as landless. In some cases, this was accurate since the claimants had been neither actual owners of land nor displaced because of Jewish land purchase. Nevertheless, the definition that Webb used *excluded* the following categories of former cultivators:

1. Persons who owned land other than that which they cultivated as tenants
2. Persons who had found land other than that from which they were displaced and were now cultivating it as tenants
3. Persons who, subsequent to the sale of the land from which they were displaced, obtained other land, but, on account of poverty or other reasons, had since ceased to cultivate it
4. Persons who, at the time of sale, were not cultivators such as laborers and plowmen
5. Persons who had themselves sold land to Jews
6. Persons who, although landless, had obtained equally satisfactory occupation.[57]

Further diluting the true representative meaning of the inquiry was the policy adopted concerning persons in category 5. Those who sold their own lands and thereafter remained on that land as tenants were only admitted to the list of landless Arabs if the Development Department believed that the tenant (once an owner) could not receive protection under the existing Protection of Cultivators Ordinance.[58] But that protection, in existence since June 1929, provided only for payment of compensation and not for provision of land, a primary objective of the landless Arab inquiry from the outset.

The Landless Arab Inquiry: Efforts at Resettlement

The data in Table 10 give a partial representation of the claims accepted for consideration. They include those claims that were accepted into or rejected from the register of landless Arabs and those claims that remained pending. Despite the instruction by district officers in Nablus and Hebron to contact those Arabs who considered themselves landless, no claims were recorded from these subdistricts. Claims from the Bethlehem subdistrict were submitted through the Jerusalem district office. More of the claims accepted came from the Tulkarm subdistrict, which represented in a large measure the condition of the Wadi Hawarith Arabs. With the exception of 229 claims, all the claims that remained pending after 31 January 1933 were eventually rejected by the director of development or his assistant.

By May 1933, with no large development loan available, the Development Department concentrated on resettling the fewer than 900 families it deemed landless. Projected estimates were made for the amount of money required for resettlement. Allocation was made for 899 families (an additional 10 families were later provided for). These included 584 families already on the legal assessor's register; 237 families consisting of Arab agriculturists who were at that time cultivating land for Jewish owners and for whom provision was deemed to be necessary when their tenancy period elapsed; and 68 families of the Zubeid Bedouin tribe in the Safed subdistrict. It was proposed to settle all the families by 1936, or approximately 300 per year. That timetable was not maintained because of reluctance among most landless Arabs to take up residence in localities distant from their village or origin and in areas unfamiliar in climate, topography, and geography. Costs for resettlement of a landless Arab and his family were set at £P500 for dry farming, and £P650 to £P800 for citrus growing. A base allotment of 40 dunams was adjudged necessary for each landless Arab family, but that area size varied according to locality, quality of the soil, and access to water sources. The administration had intended to purchase 36,000 dunams, but in fact less than 20,000 dunams were actually purchased at a cost of £P72,240.[59]

During the initial discussions involved in specifying the tasks of the Development Department, the Colonial Office and the high commissioner in Jerusalem believed it would be necessary to pay exorbitant prices for land acquisition in its landless resettlement program. While land speculation and land prices surged upward in the period from 1933 to 1935,[60] compulsory acquisition of land by the administration was not affected as anticipated by HMG. Alternatively, four methods were considered by the Development Department for obtaining land for landless Arab resettlement. They included (1) inducing landless Arabs to absorb themselves into existing villages; (2) persuading landowners through monetary grants to employ more Arabs on their lands; (3) leasing land from private Arab landowners; or (4) purchasing land outright and placing landless Arabs on administration land as its tenant. There was a growing absence of space and accommodation for newcomers in villages. Moreover, there was a strong disinclination on the part of landed proprietors to enter into proposed contracts of service with the administration.[61] A landowner was financially wiser to keep his land available for possible sale on the free market than to encumber it to the administration. In productively poor agricultural years it was not profitable to hire landless Arabs as the administration suggested. The second option involved the issuance of long-term loans to Arab landowners in an effort to induce them to employ landless Arabs and thereby provide land for them. Some £P16,000 for loans to landowners was budgeted, but only three landowners from Maliha village in the Jerusalem subdistrict applied for these loans. The acting director of development believed that these three landlord applicants were themselves either in land-sale negotiations with Jews or willing to "bind themselves to anything to get

TABLE 10

Landless Arab Inquiry—Claims Accepted, Rejected, and Pending

Subdistrict	1 January 1932				30 June 1932		
	C	A	R	P	C	A	R
Tulkarm	646	—	—	—	671	198	129
Nazareth	281	—	—	—	281	21	37
Safed	170	—	—	—	102	—	4
Haifa	565	—	—	—	403	—	19
Beisan	126	—	—	—	127	22	72
Jenin	57	—	—	—	5	—	—
Jerusalem	71	—	—	—	71	—	67
Jaffa-Ramle	537	—	—	—	913	6	562
Gaza-Beersheba	119	—	—	—	149	—	131
Tiberias	91	—	—	—	NI	NI	NI
Totals	2,663	—	—	—	2,722	247	1,021

Source: The data in Table 10 are derived from the following correspondences: Arlosoroff to Horowitz, 1 January 1932, Central Zionist Archives, S25/7620; Wauchope to Cunliffe-Lister, 14 July 1932, Colonial Office 733/214/97049; Wauchope to Cunliffe-Lister, 4 February 1933, Colonial Office 733/230/17490, Part 1.

Note: C = Claims, A = Accepted, R = Rejected, P = Pending. No claims were accepted, rejected, or classified as pending as of 1 January 1932. No information (NI) was available

money."[62] It was also found impossible to lease lands from Arab landowners. Arab landowners were reluctant to volunteer land for landless Arab resettlement because the passage of the Protection of Cultivators Ordinance in 1933 guaranteed land to a statutory tenant as compensation for eviction. A tenant could claim land if the landowner decided to sell his property in the future. Only the fourth option of land purchase became viable for acquisition of land.

By the process of geographical elimination, the Beisan area was chosen as the most suitable for settlement. An economic survey carried out by the Development Department indicated that areas in the coastal plain were not capable of absorbing an appreciable number of Arabs.[63] The Development Department stayed within the guidelines of its operational procedures to restrict resettlement only to the hill areas, save in exceptional cases. But because the hill areas suffered from a steady demographic increase, Beisan was chosen. The administration refrained from seeking Arab resettlement in the Huleh region because Jewish purchasers were in the last stages of negotiation for land. HMG refused to purchase lands in Transjordan for landless Arab resettlement because it

31 January 1933			
⊃	A	R	P
18	239	478	—
)4	69	229	—
)2	16	17	69
)3	107	297	2
28	22	106	—
6	—	6	—
71	—	68	3
18	109	789	10
49	4	144	1
78	4	374	—
77	570	2,508	85

a the Tiberias district for 30 June 1932. As of 31 January 1933, 570 claims were
pted, 2,508 were rejected, and 85 were still pending. These statistics should not be
l as a geographical barometer for Jewish land-purchase concentration since a claimant
have moved from his original locality and filed his claim in another.

was feared that such action would provoke serious opposition from Palestinian Arabs and be tantamount to expulsion of the existing inhabitants of the country whose rights had been secured by the Mandate.[64]

Some landed Arabs did not pass up the opportunity to sell land to the
Development Department for the resettlement process. Not atypical of
the personal involvement in land sales, on the one hand, and espousal of
Palestinian nationalism, on the other, was the situation found in segments of the 'Abd al-Hadi family. Present in the Jenin area since at least
the seventeenth century, the 'Abd al-Hadis had acquired large areas of
land in the Beisan, Affula, and Jenin areas as well as large tracts in the
Jezreel Valley. Five members of the 'Abd al-Hadi family had previously
sold portions of Zirin village to the Jewish National Fund. Notwithstanding his own involvement in the Wadi Hawarith sale to the Jewish
National Fund in 1929, 'Awni 'Abd al-Hadi called upon his fellow Arabs
three years later to refrain from all land sales to Jews.[65] Yet despite these
injunctions against the alienation of Arab land, Tahseen (the mayor of
Jenin), Nazim, Rushdi, and Amin 'Abd al-Hadi (the latter a member of
the Supreme Muslim Council) sold over 7,000 of the 18,200 dunams

purchased by the Development Department while enriching themselves to the tune of £P23,000 from these sales.[66] While much of the land of 'Abd al-Hadi Ashrafiyat in the Beisan subdistrict was purchased by the Development Department, this Beisan alternative was rejected by the Wadi Hawarith Arabs in favor of their former lands in the Tulkarm subdistrict. This land was left unused for a lengthy period of time.

Prior to the Wadi Hawarith rejection of lands at Beisan in May 1933, the Development Department made very extensive preparations for their eventual resettlement. Every effort was made to induce them to go to Beisan including the payment of monetary advances. The administration had a train readied for their transfer as well as space arranged for their animals and tents. Ten truckloads of fodder were prepared for their immediate usage. In expectation of their transfer to Beisan, the administration planted millet and durra to be harvested by the Bedouin upon arrival. The administration also provided each family with 60 dunams of irrigable land, 30 more than other landless Arabs were to be allotted when resettled at Beisan, and 20 more than the projected base allocation for each landless Arab and his family. The administration also promised possible rent remission or the return of 25 percent of the crop yield for the first two years, deep plowing of the land, canalization of the irrigation ditches, and storage facilities for the duration of the initial months of transfer.[67]

The Wadi Hawarith Arabs rejected the administration's offer of land at Beisan for three major reasons: some refused to give up their employment as carriers, vegetable growers, milkmen, and day laborers in the neighboring Jewish village of Hadera; others were coerced by political "agitators" and "provocateurs" to boycott any solution presented by the administration; while still others perceived that if the administration were going to be so generous in offering them land and other benefits at Beisan, then it might also make an effort to have them stay at Wadi Hawarith. There seems little doubt that the administration pampered the Wadi Hawarith Arabs. This paternalistic policy raised unrealistic expectations among other displaced Arabs. The Palestine administration failed at making the Wadi Hawarith Arab resettlement a showcase. The Development Department was categorically unsuccessful in its first major effort at landless Arab settlement.

The hopes raised by the landless Arab inquiry, the subsequent activity of the Development Department, and the passage of a stronger Protection of Cultivators Ordinance in 1933 combined to create an illusory perception among some of the Arab rural population that land and rights to land would be restored to those who had lost them. The notion of an anticipated dole on the part of the administration was further strengthened by the passage of the Land Disputes Possession Ordinance in 1932. This ordinance put the owner of a title deed in a defensive posture in legal proceedings and placed the individual or individuals in actual possession of the land in the position of plaintiff.[68] There is strong evidence that the Arab agriculturist believed that the administration was duty bound to look after his welfare, especially after the initiation of the landless Arab inquiry and the commencement of the Development Department's activity.[69] For example, in the village of Muqeibila in the Beisan subdistrict, despite the distaste for village life by their womenfolk, resettled Arabs considered their relocation as a country estate to be resided in as long as the administration made it easy for them to enjoy an enviable existence. In contrast, when the administration was firm in its demand for repayment of loans and less inclined to truckle to inflated demands and expectations, resettled landless Arabs attended to their cultivation, had a tendency to remain in their new environs for a longer period of time, and repaid administration loans.[70]

But only seventy-four Arab families were actually resettled. In seeking to resettle landless Arabs within the framework of the Development Department, HMG clearly sought public visibility in its attention to this class of agriculturists. Although it made only limited amounts of money available, HMG wanted the most political mileage it could get from the resettlement process. HMG's Middle Eastern policymakers believed that they were being generous in their attitude to the needs of Palestine's rural population.[71] But paternalism in the Mandate's context was no substitute for genuine commitment; it merely bought time and then only temporarily until 1936.

The French Reports

By appointing individuals or investigative panels, HMG was able to let political passions cool while evaluating the available options. In linking its policy decisions about development to the publication of the director of development's reports,[72] HMG remained consistent with the methods used in policy determination. It had linked the 1930 Passfield White Paper to the Hope-Simpson Report and linked its policy formulation in May 1939 to the findings if not the conclusions of the Peel Report (1937) and the Woodhead Partition Report (1938). In the case of the French Reports, HMG argued to the Arab population that means were being considered to aid the Arab agriculturist. Yet after the submission of the French Reports, the British Cabinet decided that there would not be any new development scheme for Palestine.[73]

Though the administration had accrued a large revenue surplus, the issue had turned from capital availability to one of priority and commitment.

On 16 October 1931, the director of development reluctantly agreed to the Jewish Agency's demand that they be allowed to review each landless Arab claim. Lewis French, thereafter, left it to Webb to use whatever material necessary to prove or disprove claims. French did not believe that the Jewish Agency should have been made a partner in these investigations; he believed this to be a matter between the administration and the individual Arab claimant.[74] But French's preoccupation with the writing of his report due in December 1931 forced him to leave procedural questions to Webb's determination. French would liked to have taken a more forceful anti-Jewish settlement position in the writing of his first report, but he was constrained by HMG's policy commitment to duality or coequal Arab and Jewish settlement.

French, like Hope-Simpson, intimated in his first report that Jewish settlement activity was not in the best interests of the Arab population of Palestine. Whereas Hope-Simpson had forcefully advocated the need to introduce methods of intensive cultivation, French was more cautious. He did advocate improving Arab agricultural methods and consolidation of landholdings, but he reasoned that total conversion to intensive agriculture by the rural Arab population would upset the economic balance in Palestine. He noted, correctly, that there would not be sufficient markets available for those who had to dispose of their produce domestically. He correctly feared the artificial creation of more citrus farms, banana plantations, and dairy, poultry, and egg producers, more than the Palestine market could absorb. Recommendations for development were in fact secondary to French.

The central theme dominating French's first report was the question of landless Arabs, their resettlement, and the prevention of further landlessness. His approach was to recommend long-term solutions whose indirect benefits would create durability in land tenure and thereby prevent more landlessness. By concentrating the contents of his first report on protracted solutions, the value of his remarks lost considerable meaning to both Colonial Office and Palestine administration officials who wanted an immediate interim solution.[75] The Colonial Office received in his first report a restatement of needs for the land regime in Palestine already presented by individuals and investigatory bodies who had been sent out to Palestine.[76] The overriding concern for landless Arabs in this report lost its credibility after the Jewish Agency had successfully exploded the notion of large Arab landlessness because of Jewish land purchase. The Colonial Office was not terribly dismayed by French's concentration on the landless Arab problem, for when it was shown to be of vastly smaller proportions than was initially believed, HMG had a convenient means of withdrawing funds from a project it never genuinely intended to fund fully.

In emphasizing the landless Arab problem and its prevention in the future, French advocated five conditions before development activity could take place. What French suggested presaged serious constraint for future Jewish purchases and consequently for settlement activity in general. The prerequisites he suggested were: (1) acceleration of survey and settlement operations; (2) acceleration of partition of village land (*musha'*) held in common; (3) establishment of a land administration agency; (4) government control of lands in areas coming under development; and (5) government control of water in similar areas.[77] These recommendations, if implemented, would have had a commendable impact upon HMG's record keeping in the land sphere. But the absolute devotion to administrative intervention and peculiar faith in bureaucratic engineering would not achieve immediate improvement of the rural Arab population's worsening economic condition.

French, like his predecessors, failed to grasp the rural population's reluctance to have contacts with any government or administration. Perceptions remained strong in rural areas that taxes would be increased, boundaries reduced, and village anonymity disturbed by government intervention. Local landlords and landowners were not willing to give up their protracted local political and social dominance in unpartitioned *musha'* villages. When partition proceedings began, large holders of *musha'* shares were absent.[78] Furthermore, landowners who wished to dispose of land were not enamored of any of the previous proposals of the administration for the institution of land-transfer controls. When rumor spread that French was going to recommend institution of a "lot viable," many landowners rushed to the Land Registry offices to see how many tenants they might be responsible for and what excess land still remained for disposal at high prices.[79]

French's prerequisites were unacceptable in the sense that the local Arab community for one reason or another was not going to support such drastic changes in the land regime. The Arabs found these conditions politically damaging. They perceived the French demands as an attempt to intensify Arab agriculture so that more land could be made available for Jewish settlement activity, a claim made previously by the Arabs.[80]

In his first report, before he was asked to amend it, French demonstrated unhidden disdain for Jewish settlement practices. He considered the Jewish National Fund to be extraterritorializing land contrary to Article 6 of the Mandate. He viewed the process of displacing Arabs in Beisan and the acquisition of water rights there as the first stage in making these tracts unirrigable and leading finally to the starvation of the cultivators. He pointed to the need for protection of the small proprietor against plentiful Jewish financial resources,[81] a myth in its own right. Although Hope-Simpson had also defined the existence of these aspects of Jewish settlement activity, French was not as silent as Hope-Simpson had been on the matter of Arab involvement in land sales. While assigning responsibility to Jewish land acquisition for Arab landlessness in the coastal plain, he observed the "absorption, gradual but inevitable, of the Arab peasant proprietor by the Arab *effendi* or capitalist landlord" in the hill districts and commented that "in some leading Arab quarters such disposal of surplus lands are viewed with no disfavor."[82]

After being forced to make changes in his draft, French's first report was ready for HMG in December 1931. The contents of the report caused Wauchope, even after the corrections, to inform Arlosoroff that the report was not in acceptable form. The high commissioner, therefore, decided not to make it public. Wauchope believed that no benefit would be derived from subjecting the proposals to public criticism.[83] At a time when the Jewish Agency was mediating between the Palestine administration and the Jewish National Fund in seeking a temporary lease for the displaced Arabs of Wadi Hawarith, Wauchope wished to avoid souring his initial rapport with the Jewish Agency. French was asked, therefore, to write a second report in which precise solutions for the prevention of further landlessness were to be emphasized. He was also directed to make recommendations for the institution of immediate development procedures.

Not surprisingly, French's second report foresaw little value in corrective measures through financial credit cooperatives. He too viewed the Arab peasant as notoriously improvident.[84] Instead of recommending the infusion of capital from either the monetarily tight Colonial Office or solvent Palestine administration, French wished HMG to introduce legislation that would guarantee the small cultivator some portion of his land. The three draft ordinances that he suggested were (1) a Transfer of Land Ordinance; (2) a Homestead Protection Ordinance; and (3) a Tenants Occupancy Ordinance.[85] These ordinances were similar in spirit and sometimes identical in phraseology to Chancellor's recommendations of January–March 1930.

In advocating restrictions on the free disposition of land, French's goal ran counter to those Arab and Jewish interests desirous of a laissez-faire land market. French was unsure in his own mind as to what should be the extent of geographic land-transfer controls. In his first report, devoid of specific legislative recommendations, he advocated administration control over areas coming under development, changing that later to administration control of the entire country under the purview of the high commissioner, and finally administration control for just the coastal plain.[86] Inexplicably, French did not call for land-transfer restrictions or controls in the hill regions where he explicitly faulted Arab landlords and Arab merchant capitalists. His inconsistencies on the extent of land-transfer controls suggest he was uncomfortable in advocating them or did not support de facto geographic partition. Like his predecessors who investigated the land situation in Palestine, he had to work between the hammer of what he perceived the situation to be and the anvil of Colonial Office restraint. French was asked to write his second report from a more positive viewpoint, one that was less antagonistic to Jewish enterprise and more conciliatory toward the encouragement of Jewish settlement. There is little doubt that he was strongly urged to deemphasize land-transfer controls and was asked instead to generate legislative suggestions that would not be as adverse to Jewish settlement activity. The compromise legislative solution was achieved by underscoring protection of the tenants. Yet, in spite of his pragmatic refusal to propose land-transfer controls, French believed that land-transfer controls were really the *only* answer.

In addition to his call for protection of the tenants, French recommended small-landowner protection through the Homestead Protection Ordinance. He saw this ordinance as a legislative instrument to implement the "lot viable" concept set forth by Hope-Simpson. In defending the need for retention of minimum areas, French pointed to the precepts of land inalienability already present and active in Palestine embodied in the handling of *waqf* property and Jewish National Fund lands. A district commissioner was to be the ultimate determining authority under this proposed ordinance. He would decide whether a disposition could be made, and prescribed minimum areas were to be varied according to the different agricultural zones in Palestine.[87] In conjunction with the Homestead Protection Ordinance, the Tenants Occupancy Ordinance was suggested as a means to keep the Arab tenant cultivator on the land and prevent further Arab landlessness. Such an ordinance, if implemented, would have curtailed the flexibility of an Arab landlord to sell his tenanted land and would have given those classified as tenants unprecedented legal protection vis-à-vis a landlord in matters of eviction and rental payment. But his Tenants Occupancy Ordinance offered an intricate number of exceptions concerning a tenant's ability to sell his tenancy rights. This proposed legislation came close to being the epitome of administrative obfuscation.[88] Yet the notion of giving the tenant legal right against his landlord found expression in the 1933 Protection of Cultivators Ordinance described below.

French's predisposition against further Jewish settlement activity was predicated on the assumption that there was limited unoccupied cultivable land in Palestine. The Cabinet said that such a finding did not make his second report a hopeful document.[89] French was accurate in his assessment, despite public Jewish Agency protestations to the contrary. After successfully exploding publicly the myth of Arab landlessness because of Jewish land purchase and fully aware that unoccupied cultivable land did not exist in great quantities, the Jewish Agency saw the French Reports as nothing less than a perilous reappearance of Hope-Simpson's ghost. Fortunately for the Jewish Agency, the throttles of the Palestine administration and the Colonial Office were this time neither in the hands of a high commissioner nor of a secretary of state strongly opposed to Zionist activity in Palestine. As a consequence and because of the requisite for Jewish capital inflow, French's recommendations did not become, nor were they allowed to become, the focus of controversy that Hope-Simpson's findings generated.

The French Reports: Jewish Agency and Arab Executive Reaction

Still obliging Jewish Agency attention, even prior to the official receipt of French's first report, was the potential imposition of land-transfer controls through a newly constituted Development Department. Having gained access to the first report prior to its official release, the Jewish Agency had its worst fears confirmed. The implications of an assiduous defense of Arabs who had been found landless were not lost thereafter on Jewish Agency activity. Arlosoroff wanted all aspects of the Development Department and development loan thoroughly diluted, or in some way allocated to foster Zionist interests. He threatened the nonappointment of a Jewish adviser to the Development Department until some assurances were given that no land-transfer proposals would be instituted. Furthermore, he wanted parity applied in the expenditures for Arabs and Jews.[90] Because the Jewish National Fund Directorate feared that its own unsettled land might be expropriated for landless Arab resettlement, Arlosoroff was forced to compromise with the high commissioner. He told Wauchope that the Jewish Agency would be willing to support land-transfer controls in particular areas that might be set aside for the development scheme, such as Beisan, on the condition that the concept of land-transfer controls for all of Palestine be dismissed entirely. Wauchope and Phillip Cunliffe-Lister, then the colonial secretary, agreed to such a proposal in theory, rejecting any thought of total land-transfer restrictions. They awaited designation of those areas that were to come under control in French's second report.[91] The Jewish

National Fund, interested in land purchases in the Lake Huleh region and in Beisan, was not keen to Arlosoroff's conditional compromise.[92] For the time being the Jewish Agency had succeeded in gaining HMG concurrence to talk about the land-transfer restrictions only after the second report was submitted. In the meantime, Wauchope assured Arlosoroff that prevalent rumors of land-transfer controls in the coastal plain were incorrect and that the 50,000 to 60,000 dunams of unsettled Jewish National Fund land would not be used for landless Arab resettlement.[93]

Jewish Agency officialdom's concern for French's remarks did not stop just at his suggestion for land-transfer controls. Not surprisingly, Ussishkin of the Jewish National Fund believed the five proposed remedies suggested by French would be detrimental to free maneuver in the land-purchase sphere. Ruppin, more inclined to compromise with the Arab population than was Ussishkin, was also skeptical of any active administration land policy that might curtail Jewish land purchase. Of particular concern to Ruppin were the areas of Beisan, the Huleh Valley, and the Beersheba plain, where French had intimated a desire to resettle landless Arabs. Ruppin distinguished between stillborn administration land policy and active development policy, and he preferred the latter. He wanted the administration to provide the financial means for coastal plain Arab landowners to build irrigation facilities, develop potential plantation land, and make surplus lands available to prospective Jewish buyers.[94]

The reaction of the London Jewish Agency Executive to the first French report was even more hostile than it had been to the Passfield White Paper. Colonial Office officials assured the London Jewish Agency Executive that French's first report would be neither considered nor officially endorsed, as the Shaw and Hope-Simpson reports had been. The question of timing in the publication of French's first report became an issue for the Jewish Agency.[95] Both Jewish Agency Executives in London and Palestine had seen the report, despite it not being officially communicated to them. The Jewish Agency Executive understood that the Arab Executive had not seen the report. The Jewish Agency wanted to keep the report from the Arab Executive as long as possible because its publication would only have rekindled the undeniable assertion repeated by French that Jewish land purchase was *the* cause for Arab landlessness. For fund-raising reasons, the Jewish Agency considered it wiser not to antagonize the non-Zionist Jews in South America and South Africa by release of another controversial indictment of Jewish settlement in Palestine.[96] In an attempt to soften the political impact and uproar that was expected from the release of French's first report, Arlosoroff tried but failed to obtain an explanatory letter from the Colonial Office similar to the MacDonald Letter.[97] Both Wauchope and Cunliffe-Lister were otherwise attentive to Jewish Agency political sensitivities. The high commissioner said he would await the Jewish Agency's and Arab Executive's comments before publishing French's first report. The secretary of state for the colonies chose not to offer an explanatory letter lest it elicit further antagonism from the Arab community. Instead he offered to set up a committee of inquiry composed of Arabs and Jews that would determine the cultivable land area in Palestine as outlined in Paragraph 10 of the MacDonald Letter. Because of the nonavailability or unwillingness of either a Jewish or Arab representative to participate in such an inquiry, the idea was stillborn.

French's second report was completed on 20 April 1932, and together with his first report, it was officially communicated to the Arab Executive and to the Jewish Agency in mid-June. The contents of his reports were considered by HMG to be of a delicate nature because both Jew and Arab would be antagonized. HMG wished to keep the reports private as long as possible. But in May, French, for reasons of his own, prepared a summary of his two reports for the *New York Times* correspondent stationed in the Near East. When Wauchope found out that French indiscreetly leaked classified information, he asked the Colonial Office to relieve the director of development of his duties. The Colonial Office in turn put pressure on the London office of the *New York Times* not to publish the summary while French returned to London after having been "given a leave of absence." French's departure from the Development Department was not made public until November 1932, when he resigned from his position and Lewis Andrews was appointed as his replacement. At that time, the Arab press claimed that he had been forced to resign because of Arab opposition to the entire development scheme, while the Jewish press said he quit because funds were not made available for the development scheme he had advocated.[98]

French's dismissal did not harm Jewish Agency attempts to discredit his recommendations, because the Colonial Office was predisposed to be less than enthusiastic toward a large development scheme. The Jewish Agency in its dealings with the Development Department, after French's departure, was able to woo his successor to at least a neutral position on the question of continued Jewish settlement activity. But French's departure did not remove the effect of his reports from Palestine's political climate. The psychological impact of his reports left the impression among Arabs that Jews were a world financial force that both urban and rural Arabs could not resist.[99] French's reports were the third in a series, including the Shaw and Hope-Simpson reports, which claimed that Arab landlessness was directly caused by Jewish settlement.

It is difficult to assess how well the illiterate or semiliterate fellaheen understood the content of the French Reports, but the Arab Executive during the last days of October 1932 rejected the contents of the reports. Their bases for rejection were threefold: (1) HMG's refusal to disavow the contents of the MacDonald Letter, (2) HMG's refusal to implement countrywide land-transfer restrictions, and (3) HMG's intent to have a development scheme *merely* to increase Jewish presence in Palestine. In its official reply, the Arab Executive focused its attention on the labor practices of Jewish landowners, who were accused of hiring Jewish laborers only; the nonexistence of unoccupied cultivable land; and the need for a minimum "lot viable" subsistence area for each cultivator. Although there was some mild condemnation of Arab landowner and land-broker affiliation in land sales to Jews, there was no denial of French's assertion that Arab landlords and capitalists were buying out the fellaheen. Aimed at the protection of the Arab agriculturist in virtually all its aspects, the official reply noticeably failed to mention the need to partition *musha'*-held areas in a compulsory manner.[100] The Arab Executive, for whatever reason, cosmetic or otherwise, decided in private to investigate the passages of French's reports that alluded to its members' participation in land sales. A committee whose purpose was to investigate such allegations was to have its report ready in February or March 1933. That report, if written at all, was not available to me.[101]

Lewis Andrews as French's successor was not as politic or imprecise as his predecessor. He noted in a covering letter to the Arab Executive's official reply that 'Omar al-Baytar, Shukri al-Taji, Salim 'Abdul Raouf al-Baytar, and Dimitri Tadrus had sold land or acted as agents in land sales to Jewish organizations.[102]

Both the Jewish Agency's and Arab Executive's replies to the French Reports were communicated to the high commissioner on the same day, 10 March 1933. Whereas the Arab Executive criticized both reports for failing to stop Jewish growth in Palestine, the Jewish Agency blamed French for neglecting to emphasize the beneficial aspects of Jewish settlement upon the Palestine economy in general and the Arab population in particular. By August 1932, the Jewish Agency had discredited French for advocating the beginning of the end of Jewish settlement activity. Arlosoroff believed that the Jewish Agency could not afford to let the results of French's and Webb's inquiries "go down to Hades without a first-class political funeral."[103] Granovsky wanted to dispense with the displaced Arab inquiry, while Hexter thought it wiser not to comment at all so as to minimize the displaced Arab issue.[104] Yet the Jewish Agency held to past policy and made an official response. Signed by Arlosoroff, the Jewish Agency reply focused on the sterility of French's reports, a point with which Wauchope agreed, and the inconsistencies of the French Report with the MacDonald Letter. Like past official reports to the high commissioner, this Jewish Agency missive was extremely detailed. Arlosoroff's reply was more than a hundred typed pages, almost as long as both of French's reports combined, causing H. F. Downie of the Colonial Office to note that while the Jewish Agency's reply was penetrating in parts, it was appalling in length.[105]

The results of French's reports and the landless Arab inquiry did not immediately jeopardize Jewish settlement activity. The Arab Executive was embarrassed by the implication of Arab collusion in land sales. French's own indiscretions, coupled with Jewish Agency activity in refuting the idea of Jewish responsibility for Arab landlessness, forced HMG and the Colonial Office to postpone once again land-transfer controls even on a restricted basis. The time was propitious neither economically nor politically for HMG to reinterpret or abridge Article 6 of the Mandate. That time was to come following the 1936–39 disturbances and with the cloud of World War II on the horizon. HMG rejected the Homestead Protection Ordinance and the Tenants Occupancy Ordinance as too drastic, but once again there was renewed awareness that the saturation point in land availability and in population was being reached in Palestine.[106] However, the Jewish Agency's dedicated efforts, unremitting attention to detail, and careful use of its prerogative as consultant to Judge Webb helped to sustain the perception that only political reasons prevented the establishment of a Jewish national home.[107] HMG much preferred to accept this reasoning, especially after it had decided not to deliver the proposed development loan. And although many fellaheen remained destitute, HMG did little to alleviate their suffering.

The British government had made a political commitment to resettle landless Arabs. Keeping their number to a minimum was not at all contrary to HMG's interest in reducing expenditures. Reducing the prospects of future landlessness meant financial expenditure for resettlement and more for the maintenance of a large gendarmerie.[108] French's clouded departure from Palestine, the Jewish Agency refutation of his reports, and the Jewish Agency's surgical success in the landless Arab inquiry freed the Jewish settlement effort from the otherwise potentially dangerous political aftermath of the status reports on land availability. Jewish nation-building institutions used that freedom wisely and effectively to create a Jewish geographic and demographic presence during the remainder of the decade.

Chapter 6
Jewish Land Purchase, 1933–1939

Progress toward establishing a Jewish state and fulfilling the Zionist goal was dramatically advanced from 1933 to 1939. Politically and pragmatically the drive to establish the national home proceeded with renewed commitment. By blunting the anti-Zionist pronouncements of the Shaw commissioners, the Hope-Simpson Report, the Passfield White Paper, Sir John Chancellor, and Lewis French, the Jewish Agency won critical political victories. Indeed, the Jewish Agency avoided being judged responsible for or in compliance with either the creation of a landless Arab class or the dispossession of Arabs from their lands. For the Jewish Agency and Jewish purchasers, the absolution was gratifying. These hard-won successes derived from a combination of factors: the Jewish Agency had secured detailed information and data on the land regime in Palestine that no one else possessed; its leadership utilized sophisticated understanding of bureaucratic procedures and personnel that discredited its ideological opponents; and its excellent legal counsel anticipated and neutralized the potential barriers to land acquisition. The Jewish Agency and its affiliated land-settlement institutions avoided both debilitating land-transfer controls and unsavory political incriminations.

While efforts to impede development of the Jewish national home were avoided, other problems confronted the Zionists. The enormous competition for decreasing amounts of unoccupied land drove up prices. The increase in small-landowner and land-broker involvement in land sales complicated the land-sale process. Additional British laws and regulations in Palestine forced the development of creative means to circumvent the legal intent such as those for the protection of tenants' rights.[1] Land and demographic pressures required the purchase of new land areas geographically distant from previous concentrations. Negotiations for the purchase of land in Transjordan, Syria, the Galilee, and in the central range were advanced beyond the fertile coastal and valley regions. Within Palestine, areas with higher demographic densities of Palestinian Arabs were not offered and considered for purchase. Palestinian Arab opposition and vocal antagonism to Jewish presence and land purchase intensified noticeably. The political climate heated up as the number of disturbances over limited land use was increased.

Finally, the outbreak of protracted violence in Palestine from 1936 to 1939 affected the pace of Jewish development, but land purchases continued despite civil unrest. The suggestion by the Peel Report in 1937 to partition Palestine into a Jewish and an Arab state gave added inspiration to Zionist leaders. The relative ease by which land was acquired unofficially and the Jewish Agency's ability to fulfill specific geopolitical purchases contributed to the drive to establish not just a Jewish national home but a Jewish state.

Influences on Jewish Land Purchase

Numerous factors influenced a change in the geographic direction of Jewish land purchase after the 1929 disturbances. Those disturbances demonstrated to the Jewish Agency that isolated areas distant from Jewish enclaves of settlement were difficult to defend. Acquiring lands coterminous with existing Jewish settlements became a key priority in the acquisition of new land. Serious negotiations for the Wadi Hawarith lands had begun two years prior to the 1929 disturbances, suggesting a clear attempt to connect Jewish settlements on the coastal plain. In 1934, when Jewish land-purchase attempts had already begun in the foothills of the central range, the Jewish National Fund turned down an offer to purchase 5,000 dunams in the environs of Ramallah specifically because of its isolation from other existing Jewish settlements.[2] The political aftermath of the 1929 disturbances, with the threats to truncate or limit the physical development of the Jewish national home, brought sobering realizations to leaders of the Jewish Agency and affiliated land-settlement organs. Not knowing whether land-purchase restrictions would be imposed forced the Jewish Agency to establish wholly Jewish-owned areas. Even HMG, in hopes of maintaining peace between the communities, noted quite specifically the areas of Jewish-population concentrations and sought the resettlement of landless Arabs away from Jewish areas. The first policy formulation that pertained to the creation of distinctly Jewish areas was a result of the controversy involving the resettlement of the Wadi Hawarith Bedouin and the fellaheen after their eviction in 1930.

Two days before the issuance of the MacDonald Letter in February 1931, Kisch circulated a letter to several land-purchasing organizations and individuals associated with the land-purchase process. The head of the Jewish Agency asked for suggestions regarding future Jewish Agency policy toward Arab tenants and agricultural laborers displaced because of Jewish purchase. A fortnight later, Kisch sent a follow-up letter, urging the need for policy suggestions on this point.[3] Only Moshe Smilansky, who had strong political attachments to the concept of binational-ism, opposed the acquisition of land for tenants in Transjordan. He viewed such an option as the same as dispossessing the Arab tenant.[4] Smilansky was in the minority in suggesting the resettlement of Arabs in the vicinity of existing Jewish settlements. The prevailing point of view suggested protecting areas that might come into Jewish ownership from resettlement of Arab tenants and agricultural laborers. Victor Cohn of the Palestine Colonization Association noted that it would be "impracti-cable to proceed to consolidate the fellaheen in our midst so long as we have any hope of acquiring their land in the distant future."[5] He af-firmed the aim "to unite our lands so far as possible into continuous blocks."[6] Zvi Botkovsky, in the employ of the Jewish Agency and famil-iar with Jewish Agency–fellaheen relations, emphasized that on "no ac-count should enclaves separated by strips of (Arab) tenant colonies be agreed to."[7] Cohn, Botkovsky, and Jacob Thon of the Palestine Land Development Company advocated obtaining land from Emir 'Abdullah of Transjordan in a quiet manner so that former Arab tenants could be settled there. Thon and his colleagues recognized the sensitive nature of acquiring land in Transjordan for Palestinian Arab resettlement. They concurred that private and discreet contacts with Transjordanian leaders would eventually prove fruitful.[8] The prospects for legal protection of Arab small landowners stimulated dialogue that included serious discus-sion about the resettlement of Palestinian fellaheen either in particular non-Jewish areas or in Transjordan.[9]

The concept of creating a distinct geographic nucleus for a Jewish state took concrete form in late 1930. Specific boundaries for a Jewish state, as far as it is possible to ascertain, were not delimited on a map, but land-purchase discussions within the Jewish Agency were dominated by the need to create "national" property.[10] Curiously, three Palestinian Arab newspapers ran articles in December 1933 suggesting that either a Jewish government would be established in the Sharon plain or that Palestine would be divided into two independent districts.[11] Not until after the 1936 disturbances, but before the publication of the Peel Re-port's recommendations for partition, was there explicit discussion re-garding the purchase of land for defensive protection of existing Jewish settlements in the coastal plain.[12] In September 1936, plans were formu-lated by the Jewish National Fund for settlement in the hill areas, par-ticularly in the Galilee. Geopolitical priorities and strategic conclusions dominated all land-purchase discussions immediately prior to, during, and after the outbreak of the 1936 Arab revolt. The Jewish Agency and the Jewish National Fund did not feel morally bound to confine land purchases within the proposed demarcation lines for the Jewish state as proposed by the Peel Report. Again, the ominous shadow of land-transfer restrictions or prohibitions after the withdrawal of the partition notion in 1938 only advanced Jewish land-purchase efforts farther into the hill regions and the Galilee. Considerable efforts, some successful, were made to acquire land north of Nahariyah on the Mediterranean coast, on the Lebanese border, and from Acre to Safed.[13] Responding to the perceived threat of land-transfer prohibitions, the Jewish National Fund pursued a policy of tidying up existing agreements, as it had in June 1930 when a similar threat presented itself. It restricted purchase to areas where the transfer of title deeds to Jewish ownership could be expedited with the least amount of effort, time, and money.

Filling in the geographic gaps between existing Jewish settlements and purchasing land for Jewish national and strategic considerations occurred in the 1930s. Soaring land prices and the involvement of small landowners in the land-sale process influenced the pace and nature of Jewish land acquisition. With limited resources, but with virtually unlimited opportunities to purchase land, speculation and a land-price spiral greatly affected Jewish land acquisition.[14] Land values tended to rise on Arab-owned land in proximity to existing Jewish settlements. Arab owners, aware of the keen desire of Jewish settlements to increase their geographic size, held out for higher prices. The phenomenon of high prices in areas close to Jewish settlements was first present after World War I. Then, in land areas of similar quality far from Jewish settlements, the cost per dunam was 20 to 40 francs. Near to Jewish settlements, the cost of the same kind of land was 60 to 70 francs per dunam.[15] Land of similar location and kind that cost the Palestine Land Development Company and the Jewish National Fund £P3 to £P4 per dunam in 1931 ranged from £P15 to £P45 in 1933.[16] In May 1933, according to Yehoshua Hankin, there were many areas available to purchase in the coastal plain, the Jezreel Valley, around Tiberias, and in the south (Beersheba-Negev), but high prices in the coastal plain caused him at least to suggest that lands be acquired elsewhere.[17]

In the same year, Joseph Weitz of the Jewish National Fund noted, "Before us stands principally the question of speculation. Speculators are moving about the villages and Arabs mock them. They [the Arabs] sell their lands three and four times and in the end don't hand over their land at all. . . . The Arab waits for a further rise in prices."[18] An already strained budget due in part to the general worldwide economic crisis in the early 1930s retarded speculation, and price rises crippled Jewish land purchase. Speculation and accompanying increases in land values reached threatening proportions. Thon of the Palestine Land Development Company, not one to be cowed easily by any obstacle, thought of asking the Palestine administration to expropriate land simultaneously for the Palestine Land Development Company and the Development Department, which were then seeking land for resettlement of landless Arabs. Some members of the Jewish Agency, remembering that in September 1931 they had effectively diluted the threat of administration intervention in land matters, dismissed Thon's suggestion. Further reflecting the crippling effects that land speculation might have upon future Jewish land purchase, Granovsky, also one never to compromise when the well-being of Jewish land purchase was at stake, advocated postponing new Jewish purchases until the rampant speculation had subsided.[19] As Thon's approach to the administration was dismissed as impolitic, so also was Granovsky's self-imposed purchase interregnum considered untimely. The Jewish National Fund decided that even with its limited financial resources, it was better to move ahead steadily with land purchases as best as possible and suffer through the high prices being asked.

Speculation and the rise of land prices had other effects upon Jewish land acquisition. The influence of these two factors caused Jewish land purchasers to seek out areas other than those exclusively situated in the coastal plain and the Jezreel Valley. Never was the idea discarded of creating contiguous settlements for reasons of security or of concentrating purchase efforts in areas adjacent to those already settled by Jews. But land speculation forced a turn toward preliminary acquisition attempts in areas less costly, e.g., in the foothills of the central range, in the central range itself, in the Gaza and Beersheba subdistricts, in the environs of Tiberias and Beisan, and around the Lake Huleh region. Land speculation pushed Jewish land purchase in a north and south direction. The impetus for seeking land in the foothills of the central range and the central range itself was not determined by the existence of a few large landowners: speculation elsewhere and the precarious economic condition of the central range Arab population who sought financial relief through land sales were the influencing factors. It was precisely negotiation attempts in these areas, where there were not large, if any, previous Jewish population concentrations, that heightened fears among Palestinian Arabs about the wide extent and ultimate purposes of Jewish land acquisition. Palestinian Arab anxieties generated by wider Jewish purchase efforts contributed in part to the frustrations vented in the 1936 Arab general strike and revolt.

In the early 1930s, greater care and attention had to be paid by Jewish purchasers to the prices and contractual conditions of land transfers. A policy, however informal, was formulated for acquiring land necessary to build a strategically defensible geographical nucleus for a state, but this policy took land costs into account.

A third important feature altering the nature of Jewish land purchase was the acquisition of smaller parcels of land from a larger number of landowners. During the 1920s and early 1930s, the overwhelming majority of Arab land transferred by legal purchase and sale into Jewish ownership came from several hundred or so Palestinian and non-Palestinian Arabs who owned large tracts of land. Dealing with fewer sellers meant minimal acquisition of *musha'* shares with all the complications related thereto; it meant simpler, faster, and more circumspect negotiations. But by the early 1930s, there were few Arab owners who owned between 5,000 and 10,000 dunams or more.

According to statistics gathered by the Palestine Lands Department in March 1932, there were fifty-nine absentee (Palestinian and non-Palestinian) landlords residing outside of Palestine in possession of only 117,869 dunams. (See Table 11.) This area did not include the 57,000 dunams of the Huleh Concession (discussed below) transferred to the Palestine Land Development Company by Beirut merchants in December 1934. After 1932 but before 1945, Jews acquired 338,133 dunams, which were legally registered with the Palestine Lands Department.[20] If we assume that Jews purchased all of the Arab absentee-owned land, and there is no confirmation of this fact, then no less than 65 percent of the land sold legally to Jews in Palestine between 1932 and 1945 came from nonabsentee landlords, or exclusively from landlords and owner-occupants living in Palestine. To perpetuate the myth that land sold to Jews during the Mandate, and above all after 1932, came from predominantly absentee landlords is a contradiction of historical fact.

The lands in absentee-landlord possession in March 1932 were concentrated primarily in the north of Palestine in the Acre, Tiberias, and Safed subdistricts and totaled 81,663 dunams. There were no recorded absentee landlords for the subdistricts of Bethlehem, Gaza, Haifa, Hebron, Jaffa, Jericho, Jerusalem, Nablus, Ramallah, and Ramle. With the exception of the Haifa and Gaza areas, no statistical information is presently available about either the hill regions of the central range, where absentee ownership had been traditionally minimal, or the regions where cultivable land was not in quality or quantity sufficient to entice absentee-landlord participation.

The source for Jewish land acquisition in the early 1930s was generally a small owner-occupier or *musha'* shareholder, usually in financial debt to a moneylender or merchant, who had been buffeted by a series of successive meager crop yields and who found retention of small plots of land increasingly untenable. In addition, these owners were lured from traditional agricultural activity to sometimes more lucrative per diem labor. Jewish purchasing organizations still preferred to deal with a single owner or with few owners. This desire, spurred by the intent to keep negotiations as simple and uncomplicated as possible, enhanced the development of land brokerage and intermediary activity. Sometimes

TABLE 11
Absentee Landlords Owning Land in Palestine as of March 1932

Number of Absentee Landlords	Subdistrict	Total Area Held
		(in Dunams)
6	Acre	22,500
3	Beisan	2,703
2	Jenin	7,400
1	Nazareth	3,000
31	Safed	36,170
7	Tiberias	22,993
6	Tulkarm	15,562
3	Beersheba	7,541
Totals 59		117,869

Source: Israel State Archives, Box 3340/file 4.

brokers, because of their pivotal importance in the land-sale process, were able to charge double and triple the amount they had paid per dunam while acting as intermediaries.

Obviously, there were political ramifications associated with an upsurge of small landowner and Palestinian peasant involvement in land sales. No longer restricted to just several hundred sellers, Palestinian Arabs were clearly aware of the objective(s) of the Zionist enterprise. Recognizing that the Palestinian Arab economic, political, and even physical future was at stake, the British tried in vain to conjure up legislation that would halt the land-alienation process. Many in the Palestinian Arab community were faced with the knowledge that the British were unable to protect them, some of their own leadership was inadequate or deceitful, and the agricultural environment continued to be inhospitable. Sudden disillusionment was transformed into burgeoning frustrations. Expressions of disenchantment were more public, vocal, and frequent in the early 1930s.

Yet there is little evidence to suggest that the Jewish Agency or Jewish National Fund appreciated the magnitude of anxiety fostered by the obvious increase in land sales by small landowners. If anything, the Jewish leadership realized just how insincere and inconsistent Arab nationalist sentiment was. Both private Jewish purchasers and public organizations were able to capitalize on Palestinian Arab willingness to sell land to build their national home. But social and economic ramifications incurred by the change of profile of former owners now selling land had little effect upon the Jewish Agency's coordination of a national land policy with geostrategic objectives. That is, the implications of buying land from small landowners and their eventual social dislocation caused little if any conscious attention among Jewish buyers.

Lastly, the change to small Arab landowner sales did not result in a major alteration in style and method of transfer. It did present a clear deterrent to land transfers. Shrewdness, ability to improvise, and knowledge of the land market enabled Jewish land purchase to continue unabated. Jewish land acquisition clearly capitalized on the inherent political, economic, and social weaknesses of the Palestinian Arab community.

Sales statistics provide evidence for the increase in smaller area sales. In the twenty-seven months from 1 June 1934 to 31 August 1936, Jews purchased from Arabs no less than 121,207 registered dunams. (See Table 12.) An average sale in this period amounted to 51.8 dunams. Of the 2,781 individual sale transactions registered with the Lands Department, at least 2,134 of them, or 75 percent, were sales of 100 dunams in size, and the average sale amounted to 15.5 dunams. The overwhelming predominance of small-land transactions can be seen in Table 13. Yet in terms of the total land area transferred, almost 75 percent, or 87,982 metric dunams, was sold in units of 100 metric dunams or more. What does not appear in Land Registry or Lands Department statistics is the effect and impact that land brokers, agents, and intermediaries had upon the sales. There is conclusive evidence at the Jewish National Fund archives and from the Palestine Lands Department statistics to indicate that land brokers were accumulating areas smaller than 100 dunams and selling areas larger than 100 dunams to the Palestine Land Development Company as early as 1931.[21] The Palestine Arab press criticized the activities of the landowners, land brokers, and intermediaries. Its vivid and strong denunciation of their practices also showed a profound understanding of the social and political implications associated with these activities.

Clearly, many Palestinian Arabs had knowledge of the land-sale process, its magnitude, and its ultimate impact upon Palestinian Arab society. Several examples from the Palestine Arab press in the early 1930s illustrate the character of the criticism:

> *al-Hayat*, 17 December 1930—The Jaffa correspondent wrote, "Land brokers who took some 13 Bedouin of Wadi Hawarith to Mr. Hankin recently to drop their occupancy rights are paid 10 pounds for each Bedouin brought before him. This is done on the condition that they will receive the money after at least 30 Bedouin have signed the agreement."

> *al-Hayat*, 23 January 1931—"The Tulkarm Arabs are busy selling their lands to Jews through the mediation of certain brokers."

TABLE I2

Sale of Lands by Arabs to Jews, 1 June 1934–31 August 1936, by Number and Size of Sales in Dunams

Date of Sales	Number of Sales (up to 100 Dunams)	Total Area	Number of Sales (between 100 and 500 Dunams)	Total Area	Number of Sales (over 500 Dunams)	Total Area
June 1934	90	997	2	503	1	571
July	101	3,789	4	1,111	1	1,218
August	141	1,808	7	1,138	4	7,816
September	84	1,102	2	284	1	501
October	85	1,150	3	411	1	526
November	137	2,330	1	348	1	1,378
December	147	2,232	4	814	—	—
January 1935	118	1,303	19	3,652	1	628
February	191	2,578	6	1,370	1	1,661
March	169	3,820	3	365	2	4,387
April	39	845	4	1,289	4	3,559
May	105	1,114	7	1,409	1	624
June	94	1,101	17	4,244	7	8,119
July	90	1,814	12	2,671	5	9,025
August	58	954	9	2,168	1	781
September	54	878	9	1,897	2	1,244
October	44	704	13	2,180	1	798
November	64	899	7	1,304	1	599
December	61	956	5	1,434	1	1,149
January 1936	75	791	6	1,323	—	—
February	56	771	4	892	1	1,000
March	64	833	14	3,100	3	6,572
April	11	327	3	401	1	1,024
May	20	221	1	184	—	—
June	7	7	—	—	—	—
July	19	276	1	167	—	—
August	10	35	1	143	—	—
Totals	2,134	33,635	164	34,802	41	53,180

Source: Schedule of Jewish land purchase, Israel State Archives, Box 3874/file 7.

182 · The Land Question in Palestine

TABLE 13
*Registered Sales Involving the Sale of Land from Arabs to Jews,
1933–1942*

Year	All Sales	Sales Less Than 100 Dunams	Percentage of Less Than 100 Dunams
1933	673	606	90.04
1934	1,178	1,116	94.73
1935	1,225	1,087	88.73
1936	343	306	89.21
1937	423	382	90.30
1938	330	273	82.72
1939	221	172	77.82
1940	416	408	98.07
1941	685	673	98.24
1942	713	690	96.77

Source: The statistics for 1933 and 1934 are taken from the correspondence of Wauchope to Cunliffe-Lister, 6 March 1935, CO 733/75072, and for the years 1935 to 1942, from Israel State Archives, Box 3874/file 7. Both were culled from Palestine Lands Department statistics and should be considered reasonably accurate.

al-Jami'ah al-'Arabiyyah, 29 October 1931—"One Abu Khadra stated that his financial condition was so bad at the beginning of 1929 that he decided to sell his land. Before doing so, he saw al-Hajj Amin and Jamal al-Husayni, but they were ultimately unable to help the man. In the meantime Abu Khadra was declared bankrupt in Jaffa, and he accepted the price for his land by the Jewish Ahuza Company. . . . Abu Khadra said, 'All my efforts with Arab bodies whom I requested to buy the land in question had failed. This convinced me that the activities of our national organizations are confined to writing articles and to uttering boastful words.'"

Filastin, 7 January 1932—"At the Fourth Session of the Arab Youth's Conference held in January 1932, the following resolution among others was passed. 'The whole of Palestine is holy Arab land and whoever endeavors, allows, or helps to sell all or any part of these lands to the Jews will be considered as one who committed high treason.'"

al-Jami'ah al-Islamiyyah, 21 August 1932—". . . because the Jews are alert, and our leaders are asleep, the Jews are buying the lands."

al-Jami‘ah al-Islamiyyah, 2 September 1932—"The Arab will never regard these sales as legal although the Jews possess the titles to these lands; and when political conditions change, the Arabs will demand that their lands be given back to them because they were sold in very extraordinary [circumstances]."

al-Jami‘ah al-‘Arabiyyah, 16 September 1932—"There is no doubt that the question of the sale of land is about one of the greatest dangers that threatens the future of the country."

Filastin, 5 August 1933—"If the government seriously cared for the interest of the masses, it would prohibit land transactions which prejudice the fellaheen and cause them more harm than any number of successive bad seasons."

al-Jami‘ah al-‘Arabiyyah, 24 May 1934—This newspaper severely criticized land brokers and asked that a list be published containing the names of the brokers, including small and large ones. "The situation is unbearable and our lands are now falling on easy prey into the hands of the raiders. The brokers are increasing every day among various classes of rich and poor people who have been dazzled by the Zionist gold."

al-Jami‘ah al-‘Arabiyyah, 7 September 1934—A lead article condemned land brokers and landowners who sell their land to Jews. It claimed, "By selling land, they sell the blood and remains of their fathers."

al-Jami‘ah al-‘Arabiyyah, 10 October 1934—This newspaper criticized the Arabs for assisting the establishment of the Jewish national home by accepting a transfer of their lands to Jews.

al-Difa‘, 5 November 1934—This newspaper attacked land brokers and noted that "those who adopted this profession [land brokers] aim at becoming rich and at collecting money even if they take it from the lives of the country. . . . Is it human that the covetous should store capital to evict the peasant from his land and make him homeless or even sometimes a criminal? The frightened Arab who fears for his future today melts from fear when he imagines his offspring as homeless and as criminals who cannot look at the lands of their fathers."

al-Jami‘ah al-‘Arabiyyah, 16 January 1935—This newspaper attacked illegal brokerage of land and those doctors and lawyers who looked for profit and disregarded every national cause.

Filastin, 14 February 1935—This newspaper reported that the areas bought by Jews "are much more than the government reports and that the unregistered areas of land bought by Jews exceed very much the registered areas."

al-Difa', 25 March 1935—An article reported, "If you sellers of land and brokers try to give back their money to the Jews, will they give back our land? They will never do it because land lasts forever and God created it, while money does not last and Satan created it."[22]

The repeated references to intermediary activity confirm the widespread nature of such practices. After the outbreak of the Arab general strike in April 1936, which eventually grew into a rebellion, the land broker's usefulness increased. Arab vendors wishing to sell their lands, and also wishing to retain anonymity from hostile Arab bands, found it easier and safer to make unregistered transfers through an intermediary or broker. Because of the heightened agitation against land sales and the threats made to persons and property who cooperated with the Zionists, the land broker's trade became both more lucrative and more dangerous.[23]

The Impact of Owner-Occupier Sales

The predominant increase and impact of small-land sales to Jews from 1933 on did not go unnoticed by the Palestinian administration, the Jewish purchasers, or the Arab population affected by such transfers. High Commissioner Wauchope wavered between fearing and not fearing disturbance and violence as a result of these small-land sales, their presence in the hill districts, and the continued influx of Jewish immigrants.[24] His evenhandedness was viewed at least as indecision on the part of the Arab community that wanted ironclad protection from Jewish demographic and physical growth. Jewish Agency and Jewish National Fund officials had as early as 1931 and 1932 acknowledged that there was not sufficient empty land for their acquisition.[25] Official Jewish purchasing organizations and private purchasers continued to acquire land from the Arab population. The ultimate result of Jewish purchase was what concerned Jewish Agency and Jewish National Fund officials, not the interim consequences of Arab "landlessness" or the sociodemographic changes in the Arab population's geographic and occupational distribution.

From the perspective of the Jewish Agency and the Jewish National Fund, it was the Palestinian Arab who was alienating himself. He took money and gave away his claim to his land instead. By relinquishing land to Jews, more than £P4,370,976 for registered land sales changed hands from 1 January 1933 to 31 December 1936, most of which went to Palestinians from Jews.[26]

Some tentative conclusions can be drawn about the impact that land sales had upon the population movements of Palestinian Arabs affected by the land transfers. As far as can be ascertained, two parallel though not necessarily numerically equivalent migratory patterns seem to have evolved after the reestablishment of Jewish land purchase in the 1920s. Some Palestinians moved to the periphery of existing Jewish settlements in the coastal plain and the Jezreel Valley.[27] Others moved toward the hill regions of the Galilee and the central range, close to relatives and existing Arab villages. Those Arabs who moved to the coastal plain or the Jezreel Valley sometimes found work in other Arab villages or worked for the Jews in citrus groves or did other labor.

The growth of the building trades lured more than a few Jewish agricultural workers from their settlements to the towns, enabling hired Arab labor to replace them in the rural environment.[28] By October 1933, there were at least five thousand Arab laborers employed by Jews in orange-growing districts alone.[29] Arab laborers, who may have once been small landowners, tenants, or agricultural laborers were easily attracted to work in Jewish settlements for a predictable wage.[30] Others found positions in the urban building trades. When that industry slumped at the end of 1935 and early 1936, some Jews returned to their former agricultural settlements, and the hired Arab labor was not needed. Some of the surplus Arab manpower was immediately absorbed by the need to harvest the citrus crop from October 1935 to March–April 1936, but that employment was temporary. After the general strike developed in April 1936, many Jews returned or initially came to Jewish plantation areas such as Hadera, Petah Tikva, Rishon LeTzion, Nes Tziona, and Rehovoth. Many Arabs who had found temporary per diem labor either left voluntarily or were forced from their jobs by Jewish workers.[31]

As early as June 1934, the Palestine Department of Agriculture noted that there was a shortage of unskilled labor, especially in the villages of the central coastal plain and in the foothills.[32] Jenin landowners reported to the high commissioner in June–July 1935 that they could scarcely find enough laborers to work their lands.[33] The shortage of labor in the hill regions around Jenin is partially explained by the migration of these laborers to the coastal plain and urban areas. Lack of economic viability in agriculture pushed many Arab workers from the foothills and from the central range to seek more remunerative urban employment elsewhere.

A second group of migrating Palestinians tended to find work in neighboring Arab villages. Failing that, they migrated to the hill regions where there had been a longer continuity of Arab settlement. There is evidence to suggest that the families of former agricultural laborers and tenants remained in the hill regions while the workers of these families went to the coastal plain, the Jezreel Valley, or the urban areas to find employment.[34] This process was not unlike that existing after the June 1967 war that saw hired Arab labor come from the West Bank and Gaza areas to work inside the prewar borders of Israel.

Population density increased 25 percent in the central range from 1922 to 1931. In comparison, the coastal plain's population density increased 50 percent in the same period. Good soil quality and cultivable land were less available in the central range than in the coastal plain. But the density increase in the hill regions and the pressures on the soil were not appreciably felt during the 1922–31 period because people from the hill country were attracted to work in the coastal plain. In 1931, there was already a noticeable increase of males migrating from the central range to the coastal plain. The 1931 census report remarked that "development attracts productive labor from areas where development is not anticipated or where livelihood is stationary."[35]

Lewis French accurately noted in his *First Report on Agricultural Development and Land Settlement in Palestine* that there was congestion in the hill districts.[36] This congestion seems to have increased from 1931 through at least 1935 in great measure because of the migration of Arabs who formerly had worked lands in the coastal and valley areas now owned by Jews. The Palestine administration noted that former Arab tenants who had received monetary compensation during the land-purchase process engaged in agricultural pursuits among their own people or migrated, though unappreciably, eastward away from Jewish settlements.[37] The Palestine Lands Department, in preparing answers to questions submitted by the Shaw Commission, stated that tenants reluctantly retained land in the district in which they worked because they feared that they would be surrounded by Jewish settlements and thus isolated from their fellow Arabs.[38]

Even sustaining a stagnant population in the central range was precarious. Exacerbating the poor agricultural situation in this region were the seasonal misfortunes that befell the local population in the four years prior to 1934–35. Furthermore, during the period 1931–35, there was a precipitous decline in the cultivable land available per family in the central range.[39] The Johnson-Crosbie Report, which investigated the economic condition of agriculturalists in 1930, considered 75 dunams necessary to maintain an owner-cultivator and 130 dunams to provide for a tenant.[40] Hope-Simpson suggested that an area not less than 130 dunams in unirrigated land was necessary as a "lot viable," or as a subsistence area for a cultivator.[41] The Johnson-Crosbie estimate was an average for all of Palestine. Given the meager cultivable area in the central range, it would seem that a large area would have been necessary to sustain a family in the central range assuming a constancy of crop and yield produced. Both Johnson-Crosbie and Hope-Simpson estimates for subsistence areas were greater than the 1931 census-report estimate of 88 dunams as the land area held by an average household in the central range.[42] By the middle of 1935, Jewish Agency and Jewish National Fund officials figured that each Arab family in the hill districts could only count on between 45 and 56 dunams for their use.[43] In the Jenin areas in August 1934, 90 percent of the Arab owners were holding areas less than what was believed to be a subsistence area.[44] In early 1935 in the village of Qubab in the foothills of the Ramle subdistrict, ninety-five owners of limited holdings sold 1,036 dunams among them; the result was that of these ninety-five, three families were landless, sixty-four possessed under 60 dunams, and eighteen were left with less than 100 dunams.[45] The Arab landowners in Qubab were also holding areas well below what were believed to be necessary subsistence plots for owner-occupiers and tenants. One cannot generalize for the entire central range, as conditions varied from village to village, but it is clear from the data that cultivable land per capita in this region was severely reduced in the early 1930s. The natural increase of the population does not alone explain the reduction in the availability of land per capita; migration from the coastal and valley regions and from Syria, and the settlement of Arab females and many nonlaboring males, is accountable for a portion of the population increase in the central range. Simultaneous with the decrease in subsistence areas for a family in the central range, more than 155,000 dunams of land (stretching from northwest of Ramallah to Surif and Jaba near Kefar Etzion on the Hebron-Bethlehem road in the south, and from Rammun in the northeast near Ramallah to Silwan and Abu Dir east of Jerusalem) were in early stages of sales negotiations between Arab villagers, intermediaries, brokers, and Jewish purchasers.[46]

The Protection of Cultivators Ordinances

If land were being sold readily by artful ruses, the rights of agricultural tenants were being circumvented with equal alacrity and finesse. The Palestine administration tried but failed to legislate against the flourishing Jewish purchaser–Arab seller symbiotic relationship. HMG believed that keeping the Arab on the land would militate against restlessness, vagrancy, and disturbance. In both the resettlement of landless Arabs and in providing legal protection for tenant cultivators, HMG sought to prolong the fellaheen's attachment to land. Both efforts failed miserably, especially since tenants comprised less than 10 percent of the total Arab rural population in the early 1930s. Nevertheless, the Palestine administration made an effort, however hopeless ultimately, to strengthen the legal rights of agricultural tenants.

The Protection of Cultivators Amendment Ordinance of May 1931 gave protection for the first time to persons who had used land for grazing for a period of five consecutive years. These persons could not be evicted by a court or judge, as the fellaheen and Bedouin had been at Wadi Hawarith in 1930. No provision for land as compensation was offered to those qualifying for tenancy under this amendment.[47] In May 1932, an additional amendment was made in an effort to respond to evasions used by Arab landlords. Section 2 of this amending ordinance provided "that where a tenant [had] been moved by the landlord from one plot to another such plots [would] together constitute a holding."[48] Arab landlords had successfully evaded the provisions of the 1929 ordinance by avoiding commitments of two-year leases that would have made a tenant eligible for compensatory privileges. Landlords had moved their tenants around annually or between summer and winter crops.[49] This amendment broadened the definition of a tenant to include subtenants. According to Wauchope, it had become the practice for a large landowner to lease his land to a tenant middleman or agent who in turn contracted to pay the landlord a quarter of the produce. The tenant middleman then sublet the land to the actual working tenant who agreed to pay a third of the produce. As previously noted, Raja Ra'is in Shatta village had used both these circumventions to avoid payment of tenants' compensation prior to his collection of parcels and their subsequent sale to the Jewish National Fund in 1930–31.

The Protection of Cultivators Ordinance of August 1933 replaced all previous legislation regarding a tenant's protection. For the first time, limitations on a landlord's prerogative to increase rents were established by legislative ordinance. The tenant was entitled to compensation for improvements on the holding he had worked, guaranteed a specific amount of advance notice prior to an eviction, and, most important of all, assured a subsistence area if he proved to be a statutory tenant.[50]

The purpose of this ordinance was to prevent landlords from selling their tenanted land without first making efforts either to relocate or to assure their tenants of relocation. The Palestine administration was not purposely seeking to alienate landowners. In fact, the administration did not wish to disturb the moderate political attitudes of the landowners, who sometimes reluctantly but pragmatically acquiesced to its rule in Palestine. However, the administration also wished to place the financial burden of tenant resettlement upon the Arab landlord and not upon the administration or the British taxpayer, just as it preferred to maintain Jewish capital inflow through Jewish land purchase and immigration.

As previously, the spirit and intent of the ordinance were successfully circumvented. Although the ordinance sought to keep the tenant on some land, landlords in the Southern District refused to permit their tenants to begin plowing in preparation for the upcoming agricultural season. Although tenants were not evicted, this policy had the unwelcome effect of making an already-precarious economic condition all the more tenuous. Since some tenants were at a financial breaking point if they continued their agricultural pursuits, they were likely to take monetary compensation without hesitation when it was offered. Landlords in the coastal plain often left all their lands fallow rather than run the risk of tenancy claims.[51]

The overwhelming reaction to this ordinance was negative. Arabs in Palestine interested in the immediate total prohibition of land sales believed that such an ordinance only partially fulfilled their demands. Relationships between a landowner and his tenants became strained and tense, especially in cases where a tenant asked to be classified as a statutory tenant but failed in his claim because of contrary testimony from his landlord or his agent. The more moderate and less compromising political leaders in the Arab community acknowledged that such an ordinance was at least a positive, although not a sufficient, step in protecting tenant rights.[52]

Because almost all of the claims for statutory tenancy were made by Arabs against Arab landlords, Jewish owners were only marginally affected by the ordinance. The ordinance did have the effect of making larger purchases more complicated because purchasing land free of tenant encumbrances became more difficult. As a consequence, land brokers, intermediaries, and agents were increasingly employed to purchase smaller but contiguous parcels that could eventually be sold to Jewish buyers free of tenants in occupation. The intermediary protected the landlord's anonymity to some degree. The Arab landlord who was in need of capital and wished to obtain it through the sale of his land found it more difficult to rid his land of tenants.[53] But even with the restrictions imposed upon a landlord with tenants, the landlord could sell tenanted land if it were necessary to upgrade or improve the agricultural worth of his holding. The problem for the landlord was that if he wished to resume or take control of his land from occupying tenants, he had to apply to, and receive sanction from, the administration. But by making such a request public, a landlord became susceptible to criticism from politically more extreme segments of the Arab community. In one case, an Arab landlord and a high-ranking official in the Education Department, Abdul Latif Tabawi, claimed that if he did not evict his tenants in his Tulkarm subdistrict lands, he would suffer material loss. In a letter to the assistant district commissioner in Nablus, he claimed that he had to "maintain a high standard of living which would not be fair to compare to that of tenants."[54] The landlord in this case was able to evict his three tenants according to the provisions of Section 15 of this ordinance.

Decisions about the validity of a tenant's claim were made by a board composed of administration district officials. Some tenants failed to make claims because of their traditional fear of dealing with any government. Other tenants were reluctant to make claims because the land they had been working had never been registered or the boundaries delimited. Tenants who may have been statutory tenants feared that submission of claims would somehow increase their tax payments and circumscribe their otherwise unrestrained use of the land. Where claims were made on previously unregistered land, ownership rights had to be determined first, which resulted in increased tax assessments. In some cases, tenants admitted to administration officials that they had cultivated land without the consent of the owner, but such statements were sometimes given *after* the tenant had received £P25 from the owner.[55] Tenants who perceived the intent of the ordinance as absolute legal protection against eviction and an administration guarantee of a tenant's rights took the liberty of not paying either the rent or the required tithe.[56] Although some landlords did testify on behalf of their tenants, in most cases where tenants offered only an oral claim to tenancy without written documentation, such as a credible tithe receipt, statutory tenancy was not granted.

At the time of its implementation, members of the Palestine Secretariat and the Colonial Office in London believed that this ordinance was effectively protecting tenants and keeping them on the land.[57] Yet reality was very different. Between August 1933 and May 1936, landlords moved tenants from summer to winter croplands thereby making them ineligible for statutory tenancy privileges. This periodic alternation contributed to unsettled and despondent feelings among tenants. Although they had worked a "holding," or area, they were not statutory tenants because they were prevented from working a plot or plots of land for a year on a continuous basis. In an effort to plug this loophole, an amending ordinance was passed in May 1936 that redefined a "holding." In addition, tenants on *musha'* land, which was redistributed periodically, were allowed to claim entitlement to a holding. Even with a tightening of definitions within the ordinance, circumventions continued. In 1941, an investigatory committee comprised of Palestine administration officials labeled the Protection of Cultivators Ordinances and their amendments as "contentious, uniformly unsatisfactory, consistently evaded, and an obstacle to [economic] development."[58] Like the landless Arab inquiry, HMG's and Palestine administration's unlimited faith in bureaucratic and legislative solutions proved insufficient, unworkable, and impracticable. But perception of increased British paternalism for the Palestinian Arab was enhanced.

Small-Landowner Protection: A Mirage

When the Protection of Cultivators Ordinance was passed in August 1933, careful consideration was given to the necessity of protecting owner-occupiers as well. Although a year later small owner-occupiers were the predominant sellers to Jewish purchasers, Wauchope still considered it unnecessary to protect small landowners. Members of the Colonial Office insisted that, before they granted legal protection to owner-occupiers, they be shown that this segment of the population was in grave economic straits.[59] While Sydney Moody told the League of Nations in June 1935 that small landowners were not considered dispossessed because they sold their own lands, Wauchope's view was changing, and he was becoming increasingly concerned with the effect small-landowner sales would ultimately have upon social stability in Palestine. He believed that if, in the future, these former landowners lost their alternative work in urban areas or in seasonal employment, then the administration would be faced with a disenchanted and restive population. By the summer of 1935, Wauchope had two committees considering means by which to prevent a landowner from selling the minimum area necessary for himself and his family's livelihood. By February 1936, the committees recommended that no landowner be permitted to sell any land required as a "lot viable" for himself and his family. The secretary of state consented to the recommendation, and land that was deserted or uncultivated for any reason was to revert to the government. This legislation was not to apply to the Beersheba subdistrict, where land was considered plentiful, to urban areas, or to lands already planted with citrus.[60]

Even without the demands made by Palestinians in November 1935 for the cessation of Jewish immigration and land sales, and for the establishment of self-government, Wauchope would have initiated protection for the small landowner. Like Chancellor, Wauchope believed that he had to protect all segments of the population in Palestine, notwithstanding the negative response expected from the Jewish Agency or the image of paternalism HMG was cultivating.

As anticipated, the Jewish Agency argued that such possible prohibitions would contravene Article 6 of the Mandate and Paragraphs 12 and

13 of the MacDonald Letter. The Jewish Agency worried that the imposition of a "lot viable" concept would result in withholding from the free market a very considerable portion of agricultural land in Arab ownership.[61] Once again, the Jewish Agency saw the unwelcome possibility of land-transfer controls coming under the direct purview of the high commissioner, because he alone was to approve the sale of each "lot viable." In addition, the Jewish Agency tried to demonstrate in a private memorandum that there was no cause for the administration to protect the position of the fellaheen population. In spite of Jewish Agency claims to the contrary, the average "lot viable" needed for a rural Arab family (taking into consideration the wide varieties of land quality) was determined to be 75 dunams. Yet the existing average "lot viable" was only 44 dunams.[62] HMG replied to the Jewish Agency that it had to give attention *in equal measure* to both parts of Article 6.

Had not the April 1936 Arab general strike or revolt erupted to the point of "requiring" another investigatory commission, the draft of the Lot Viable Ordinance might have been passed. The Colonial Office delayed its consent to such legislation because it wanted "to make time" to give the Peel Commission the opportunity to take up the matter of small landowner protection.[63] The only protection small landowners received was granted by the general 1940 Land Transfer Restrictions.

Further exacerbating the sense of uneasiness and the erosion of control over one's future for many in the Palestinian Arab community were the Jewish Agency and Jewish National Fund efforts to acquire land outside of Palestine and in the Galilee. Certainly, the cultivable portions of western Palestine remained the primary foci for Jewish land acquisition, but the real prospects for acquisition of land in Transjordan and in Syria in the 1930s increased anxiety and hardened anti-Zionist and anti-British feeling among Palestinians.

The Transjordan Option

There were several reasons why areas of land distant from the cultivable and defensible centers were considered by Jewish purchasers. First, some areas were still owned by relatively few persons, which simplified the land-transfer process; second, these areas, if acquired, would become physical territorial buffers for the Jewish-population concentrations; third, Arab landowners, who were also social and political notables in Transjordan and Syria, could have their anti-Zionist sentiments diluted via land sales and monetary payments; and fourth, areas distant from Jewish settlements could be utilized, if desired, to resettle Palestinian Arabs previously displaced by Arab land sales and Jewish purchases.

Purchasing land in Transjordan was not a novel idea for Jewish immigrants. As far back as the nineteenth century, the concept of Jewish colonization and settlement in Transjordan had been suggested.[64] In a letter of February 1919, Chaim Weizmann expressed the wish that the eastern boundary of Palestine run along the Hijaz Railway, east of the Jordan River.[65] An indication of deep Jewish interest in settlement in Transjordan was reflected by the willingness of one Zionist official to surrender equal Jewish representation (with the Arabs) on the twelve-member Jerusalem Municipal Council "if that were the price for Jewish entry into Transjordan."[66]

But from the outset of the Mandate, HMG expressed very strong reservations about Jewish settlement there. High Commissioner Samuel made it clear that the lack of security and insufficient military presence meant that the Zionists could not be assured of the protection that they might require.[67] Similar arguments against Jewish settlement in Transjordan were offered again by Wauchope to the Jewish Agency in 1932 and 1933.

Yet the political sensitivities that were bared in 1920 and 1921 had become less visible and constraining by the early 1930s. By that time, HMG's presence in Transjordan was solidified; its client, Emir 'Abdullah, enjoyed a restricted degree of political autonomy. In 1920, HMG was reluctant to make any provision for Transjordan aside from the scope of HMG's authority. Although some argued otherwise, HMG took the position that Palestine was outside of the areas promised to Sharif Husayn by Henry MacMahon in October 1915. The areas lying to the east of the Jordan were, however, considered to be wholly Arab areas. Hence, because of the displeasure voiced by the Arabs in Damascus after Faysal's removal from the self-proclaimed Arab state in July 1920, and unsure about the future of another of Husayn's sons, 'Abdullah, HMG was wary of generating further communal antagonisms in the early 1920s. The British refrained from granting the Zionists permission to purchase land and settle in Transjordan.

At least since the 1929 disturbances, the perception was held by some Palestinians that the Jews aspired to enter Transjordan.[68] During the Anglo-Zionist debate about land availability in 1930, Zionist officials reintroduced the notion of acquiring land in Transjordan, both among themselves and to Hope-Simpson.[69] But in a strictly confidential memorandum prepared prior to the arrival of Hope-Simpson, and for internal Jewish Agency consumption only, no mention was made of acquiring land for settlement in Transjordan or for Arab tenant resettlement.[70]

When Hope-Simpson was in Palestine, the Jewish Agency made substantive contacts with 'Abdullah and with other Transjordanian Bedouin leaders regarding the acquisition of lands.[71] British officials in both Palestine and Transjordan believed that the respective indigenous Arab population would strongly oppose Jewish settlement there.[72]

The British, consumed by their preoccupation for the maintenance of civil order and stability, were either naive to the reality or purposely ignored the fact that Arabs and Jews were negotiating with each other for the mutual benefit of both parties. The British Foreign Office feared Zionist settlement in Transjordan because of the possibility that Ibn Saud might use it as a pretext to make a thrust northward, threatening Britain's stable presence in Transjordan. Opposition to Zionist land purchase in Transjordan seems to have been greater among Palestinians who were not involved in these negotiations than among those landowners and tribal leaders in Transjordan who sought Jewish capital to relieve their abysmal financial status and economic woes. Some wanted the money for private needs; others looked for outside capital to upgrade other holdings.

It was the very poor agricultural situation in Transjordan between 1929 and 1934 that influenced many Bedouin tribal leaders to seek monetary assistance through the Zionists.[73] Arlosoroff, the head of the Jewish Agency, knew that 'Abdullah and the other tribal *shaykhs* could easily acquire property rights to large tracts of state lands by paying nominal transfer fees to the Transjordanian government. Obtaining access to state lands was another means of avoiding the purchase of privately held lands and the associated political rancor. It was no doubt reasoned that recent procurement of state lands under the revised Beisan Agreement gave added impetus to state-land acquisition in Transjordan.

Moreover, the Jewish Agency was keen on doing business with those who simultaneously held physical power, political influence, and social prestige. The Jewish Agency believed that if it entered into a lease or sale agreement with Mithkal al-Fayiz, the leader of the Beni-Sakr tribe, fifteen hundred rifles would be neutralized and a respected Transjordanian leader would have come out openly against the mufti.[74] Arlosoroff had a similar ulterior motive in striking a deal with the al-Majali tribe of Kerak (formerly of the Hebron area) and its leader. When the 1936 Arab revolt broke out, 'Abdullah sought to prevent the rebel bands from using Transjordan as an operation base.

When several tribal leaders visited Palestine for the Pan-Islamic Congress in December 1931, direct contact with the Jewish Agency was already a year and a half old. The head of the al-Majali tribe did not wish to sell land directly to the Jewish Agency. Rather, he wanted to use Jewish capital investment on his land. But Arlosoroff was not enthusiastic about such a proposal. If there were to be a financial outlay, land and a title deed were the minimum requirements in return. In 1932, several Jewish Agency employees with agricultural expertise went to Transjordan to set up small orange groves for local leaders. As a result, the head of the al-Majali tribe received several threatening letters suggesting that he was monopolizing the benefit expected from Jewish settlement.[75]

Arlosoroff wanted to pursue the amiable relationships that had been started with the Bedouin tribal leaders, but he realized that the key to any success in Transjordan lay with 'Abdullah. The only constraint on the Jewish Agency and the Jewish National Fund was insufficient capital at their disposal for entering into fresh lease and sale agreements.

'Abdullah was not wrong to assume that the Zionists were intent upon acquiring land in Transjordan. 'Abdullah needed capital for personal reasons and because it would give him greater independence from British control. Furthermore, he was motivated to create a better relationship between the Palestinian Arabs and the Zionists so that he, and not al-Hajj Amin al-Husayni, could lead a reunified Palestine-Transjordan.[76]

After 'Abdullah's initial contact with the Jewish Agency, very few people were privy to the discussions and negotiations that followed. In November 1932, 'Abdullah met two representatives of the Jewish Agency at a house near the Allenby Bridge, which spanned the Jordan River. The question was not whether 'Abdullah would make his land available to the Jewish Agency but rather whether the Jewish Agency could be assured of physical protection if it wished to settle large numbers of Jews in Transjordan. 'Abdullah and his spokesmen at this meeting took issue with raising the question of security guarantees with British officials. The land that the emir wished to make available to the Jewish Agency had been granted to him as a gift by the British government in June 1931. Thus, the land belonged to him, and he was not obliged to obtain the sanction of the Legislative Council of Transjordan for any transactions. He wanted to demonstrate the freedom to dispose of his land as he wished. Yet, in order to conclude the agreement, 'Abdullah promised his full protection for potential Jewish settlement.[77]

In mid-January 1933, agreements were drawn up between the Jewish Agency and 'Abdullah. 'Abdullah offered 17,500 acres, or 70,000 dunams, or something just less than thirty square miles on a six-month option to lease. The lease, if made operative, was to run for a thirty-three-year period and then was renewable for two more similar periods at an annual rental of £P2,000 (equivalent at that time to $6,700). The area to be leased was located along the Jordan River from the Allenby Bridge in the south, northward to the town of Shuneh, which was to be its central point; it was to be bound by the Jabok River in the north, by the Moab Mountains and the town of Salt in the east, and by the Jordan

River in the west. With the Jewish capital he acquired, 'Abdullah wished to erect a large sugar refinery on part of his land. In addition to the growth of sugar cane, which was to supply the refinery, citrus fruits, bananas, dates, and silk were also produced. The lease option stipulated that 'Abdullah was to receive 5 percent of the net income from the agricultural products and 20 percent from any mineral products discovered by Jewish settlers.

Despite the shortage of capital in the hands of the Jewish Agency, the Palestine Land Development Company, and the Jewish National Fund, each of these organizations paid equal amounts of the total £P500 to 'Abdullah for the option to lease in the future.[78] According to the lease agreement (not the option), the Jewish Agency was entitled to credit the amount received by the emir to the rental amount due the entire first year, an amount of £P2,000. Then 'Abdullah would have received nothing for the first year, and he could demonstrate to nationalists at home that he was not receiving any money from the Zionists. However, it was the Jewish Agency's intention to spread the payments over a two- or three-year period so that the emir would receive at least £P1,000 for each of the first two years and £P2,000 for each of the following years. From the Jewish Agency's perspective, this agreement would make the emir financially beholden to it. Further tying 'Abdullah to the Jewish Agency was a clause in the lease option, which, when renewed, would prohibit 'Abdullah from transferring his land to anyone else for forty years.[79]

During a dinner conversation with Wauchope in January 1933, Arlosoroff informed the high commissioner on an "informal" basis of the details of the Jewish Agency lease option signed with 'Abdullah. Wauchope cautioned silence on this agreement, lest it cause an uproar among Arabs in Palestine. Even though he saw the advance of Jewish economic interests into Transjordan as an inevitable process, Wauchope nevertheless considered their contact with 'Abdullah as inopportune and very ill-advised. Arlosoroff strongly argued against the high commissioner's claim that the security situation in Transjordan warranted discontinuing Jewish Agency settlement there.[80] Concerned with the political stability in Palestine, Wauchope and Cunliffe-Lister viewed the Jewish Agency thrust into Transjordan as possible grounds for extremist behavior by moderate Arabs in Palestine, because such movement by the Jews would confirm the Arabs' worst fears.[81] Wauchope disagreed with Arlosoroff's information that opposition to the lease-option transaction was confined to the hill areas on the West Bank of the Jordan. The high commissioner felt that influential "quarters" in Transjordan were hostile.[82] Yet the evidence of documents and events suggests that Wauchope was not entirely correct in his assessment.

If by influential "quarters" Wauchope was referring to the chief British representative in Amman in the person of Colonel Charles Henry Cox, then the high commissioner's judgment was accurate. Cox had in fact approached Emir 'Abdullah and threatened him with the withdrawal of British support if he did not renounce the lease option.[83] But the Bedouin leadership on the East Bank, exercising authority in Transjordan's Legislative Council in April 1933, defeated a move to ban the sale of all land to non-Transjordanians. The bill lost by a decisive vote of thirteen to three, suggesting the legislator's desire not to close off the option of Jewish purchase. When the Fifth Transjordanian National Congress met in Amman in June 1933, a call was again made for legislation to prevent land sales to Jews. The committee established to implement that decision admitted readily that covert contacts had been made for the introduction of Jews into Transjordan by means of long leases, land brokers, and mortgages.[84] One mechanism of Jewish land acquisition in Transjordan was mentioned by Paul Knabenshue, the American consul general in Jerusalem, in a letter of August 1932 to former High Commissioner Chancellor: "What they [the Jews] are really doing is to furnish money for certain Arab friends to purchase land in Transjordan in their names [that is, in the names of Arabs], and then to let it to the Jews on leases of ten years or more."[85] Some segments of the Transjordanian political leadership, particularly members of the Istiqlal party, agitated publicly against 'Abdullah's arrangement with the Jewish Agency. Other Arab nationalist groups in Palestine, Iraq, and Syria tried but failed to apply political pressure on HMG in Jerusalem and on 'Abdullah to cancel the lease option. While the dominant political voices in Transjordan were divided over Jewish entry there, Wauchope reiterated to 'Abdullah the scope of security problems presented by Jewish settlement.[86]

The most forceful representations to 'Abdullah against the lease option came from the Arabs of Palestine. Particular pressure came from the Istiqlal party there, the Young Men's Muslim Association, Musa Kazim al-Husayni of the Arab Executive, and al-Hajj Amin al-Husayni. Akram Zu'aytar of the Istiqlal party was able to generate opinion against the lease option during Friday prayers in Nablus in January and February 1933 within three weeks after the lease option was signed.[87] While 'Abdullah publicly announced that he was withdrawing the offer to the Jewish Agency, those sympathetic to the interests of Ibn Saud expressed doubts about the emir's sincerity.[88] Some Palestinian Arabs had grave fears about Jewish settlement in Transjordan, which was considered to be the bulwark of Arab nationalism. Some Palestinian politicians emphasized that Transjordan should be kept as a place of refuge for Palestinian Arabs.[89] Such an emphasis is particularly revealing. Not only does such a perception suggest an apparent distinction of geography between Palestine and Transjordan, but it also suggests a very strong fear that a refuge for Palestinians might be required.

'Abdullah's public disavowal of the lease option did not allay Arab fears about Zionist aspirations for land purchase and settlement in Transjordan. Yet the lease option was not canceled, and it was renewed in December 1933.[90] Despite the agitation to the contrary, Transjordanian *shaykhs* continued to pay visits to Tel Aviv, where they obtained monetary advances on account for lands to be sold. Like some Arab landowners in Palestine, they were not concerned whether HMG sanctioned the sales.[91] By late spring and early summer 1933, Arab protests against land sales turned from exclusive attention to the emir's lease option to the second eviction of the Wadi Hawarith Arabs then taking place. In Nablus in June, Akram Zu'aytar and Salim 'Abd al-Rahman al-Hajj Ibrahim, members of the Istiqlal party, centered their protests against the eviction, using local mosques as the centers of their activity. But even while public attention concentrated on the plight of the evicted Arabs at Wadi Hawarith, Transjordanian landowners continued to approach the Jewish Agency with offers to sell. Several Transjordanian politicians who wished to retain their anonymity sought to barter their lands for money. Some wished to use the money in election campaigns for positions on the Transjordanian Legislative Council in early 1934.[92]

In December 1933, another attempt was made to prevent land sales to Jews in Transjordan. Introduced in the Legislative Council, this legislation was supposed to give the emir's Executive Council the right to approve all transactions involving foreign nationals. The bill was shelved in the Executive Council because of Wauchope's pressures on the Transjordanian administration.[93] On the other hand, in Palestine Wauchope favored continued Jewish settlement and unrestricted land purchase. There it was vital to the capital inflow in an otherwise depressed agricultural economy. Even if disturbances could be avoided, Jewish settlement and land purchase in Transjordan was not strenuously encouraged. In 1934, the high commissioner told Jewish Agency officials that he would do everything possible to prevent restrictive land-transfer legislation from coming into effect in Transjordan. Such legislation in Transjordan would be an ominous precedent for the Jewish enterprise in Palestine. Wauchope suggested protecting 'Abdullah from embarrassment. In fact, the high commissioner wanted to approach other *shaykhs* who were not in such a politically sensitive and exposed position.[94] The British, though not giving 'Abdullah the degree of independence he wanted, still protected him as their political interest in the administration of Transjordan.

Demonstrating its intent to protect 'Abdullah, in March 1935 HMG said it could not encourage Jewish settlement in Transjordan under existing circumstances.[95] Although HMG did not expressly forbid Jewish settlement, it frowned upon it. HMG certainly did not wish to exacerbate anti-British sentiments in either Palestine or Transjordan. But in advocating minimal encouragement of Jewish settlement in Transjordan, the British nevertheless fostered the perception among Palestinian Arabs that Transjordan would be used by the Jews to settle Arabs from Palestine who were dislocated by Jewish land purchase.[96]

An environment of anxiety and fear was mounting among Palestinian Arabs. Their patrimony and destiny were slipping away because their leadership was impotent. During the 1929 disturbances, Palestinians had heard rumors that the Jews had intended to take over the Muslims' holy places. The fellaheen were frustrated and disappointed because they were not being resettled on land once owned or tenanted. Neither tenants nor small landowners were being protected against Jewish land purchase; land sales and Jewish immigration were at all-time high levels in 1934 and 1935; Jews were seeking land in Transjordan from Emir 'Abdullah, a leading Arab political figure; and now lands in Syria were about to be sold to the Zionists as well.

Purchase Attempts in Syria
and Success at Lake Huleh

Zionists had for a long period of time wished to purchase the area and environs of Lake Huleh situated north of Lake Tiberias. Impediments to the purchase of this land area of some 52,000 to 57,000 dunams were insufficient capital to make the purchase and uncertainty about security in the areas to the north and east of the lake. Since much of the land lying to the north and to the east was owned by large landowners in Syria and in Beirut, the Jewish Agency first had to gain the confidence of these landowners. Very detailed feasibility studies were readied by the Jewish National Fund for the potential acquisition of these lands;[97] its concern about the Arab control of the (Golan) heights to the east of the lake had been eased somewhat when Yehoshua Hankin entered into negotiations for 300,000 dunams of land in Buteiha and in Golan in 1933. But as Arab anxiety manifested itself in Transjordan and Palestine over 'Abdullah's lease option, so also did Arabs in Syria and French authorities in Damascus view Jewish land acquisition there with extreme apprehension. Yet, as in the case of Transjordan, influential tribal and political leaders readily engaged in negotiations with the Jewish purchasing organizations for the sale of their lands.

Exactly when the first contacts with prospective Syrian vendors took place is unclear,[98] but the reason for their contacts with the Jewish Agency—the need for money—was similar to that of the Palestinian and Transjordanian landowners. The economic condition of landowners in southern Syria was poor as a result of several marginal crop yields. By July 1933, Hankin's preliminary initialed contract for the 300,000 dunams set the price at 500 mils per dunam. When Hankin offered an additional £P10,000 to the vendors to remove the tenants from the land, the vendors refused, offering instead a reduction in the purchase price on the understanding that Hankin would deal with the tenants in occupation.[99] Hankin paid £P70,000 at once to the vendors in the form of a mortgage, followed by a quarter of the purchase price on the transfer of the land, and the balance to be paid over the next five years. The tenant-cultivators, according to clauses within the sale agreement, were to receive a total of £P20,000 from the vendor and £P10,000 from the purchaser, with the vendor required to lease an area of land elsewhere for the tenants. But before all stipulations in the contract could be met, opposition was raised by Syrian Arabs over the prospective purchase. A deputation of Arab inhabitants from the Hauran area went to Damascus to protest against the sale.[100]

Despite the signing of the contract by one 'Abd al-Rahman al-Yusuf and Hankin, the high commissioner of Syria issued two administrative orders for governmental control over land transfers to foreigners. These two orders of 18 January 1934 pertained to the purchase by foreigners of land on the frontiers between Syria, on the one hand, and Lebanon, Palestine, and Transjordan, on the other. According to the estimate of the British consulate in Damascus, the French authorities in Syria believed that if land were purchased by Palestinian residents or a registered Palestinian corporation—in this case the Palestine Land Development Company—then Great Britain would ultimately ask for boundary rectifications in order to include the Jewish-purchased land within the territory and purview of the Palestine Mandate.[101] The Palestine administration did not want Jewish land purchases in Syria to be used for the relocation of displaced Palestinian Arabs. Hankin "assured" the high commissioner that this area was to be used for Jewish settlement only. Hankin's assurances appear to have been quite credible, because the Palestine Land Development Company and the Jewish National Fund both wished to "protect" the environs of the Lake Huleh region with Jewish-owned land and settled areas for geostrategic reasons.

According to the Jewish Agency, the intent was to purchase not less than 2,000,000 dunams of land in Syria.[102] The Arab intermediary in the negotiations between the Syrian landowners and politicians and the Palestine Land Development Company in Syria was one Emir Rihal. In

July 1934, Rihal told the Palestine Land Development Company that it had erred in failing to establish cordial contacts with those landowners neighboring on the borders of Buteiha, particularly Fa'ur al-Fa'ur, of the al-Fadl tribe in the Golan. Further, Emir Rihal reported to Dr. Thon that while Shakib Arslan, an ardent nationalist, was against Zionist entry into Syria, Jamil Mardam, then a leader of the Syrian nationalist bloc, tacitly consented to the Zionist land purchase in Syria. Mardam's acquiescence was, however, provisional. If Emir Rihal did not take care to prevent fears arising among the Syrian population, then Mardam made it abundantly clear that he would lead the opposition to such sales.[103] Ultimately, the Palestine Land Development Company was not successful in acquiring and retaining land in southern Syria. How much of Hankin's initial payment was returned is not clear; but despite being thwarted in the attempt to secure areas to the east of Lake Huleh in the Golan, the Jewish National Fund and the Palestine Land Development Company were successful in purchasing the Lake Huleh area itself in 1934.

The Lake Huleh lands, comprised mostly of marshes, were situated to the north of the lake itself. The area around the lake was considered state land;[104] therefore anyone interested in draining the marshes or making them into productive farmlands had to negotiate with the administration. But the Palestine administration had not always possessed the ownership rights to this land. Before the British occupation, the Ottoman government granted the concession to drain the marshes to two Beirut merchants.[105] With the occupation of Palestine by the British and of southern Syria by the French, the territory of the concession at the close of World War I fell partly under French and partly under British purview. The concessionnaires paid the rent demanded by the Syrian authorities for the years 1918 and 1919, but defaulted on payment in 1920 and 1921. In 1919, the concessionnaires applied to the British military administration for official recognition of the Ottoman concession. No immediate action was taken by the military administration, but the Colonial Office revised the concession in 1923. The Palestine administration refused the Ottoman concessionnaire's offer to purchase the rights to the concession.[106]

In 1933, the Syrian concessionnaires began work by building a dam north of the Bnot Ya'akov Bridge on the Jordan, allowing a deepening of the riverbed to proceed. In December 1934, the Palestine administration approved the transfer of the concession to the Palestine Land Development Company, which paid £P191,794 to the concessionnaires. The transfer was approved on the condition that an area of 15,000 dunams be held in reserve for the use of the local cultivators. Immediately after the Palestine Land Development Company gained the concession, a Palestinian Arab delegation protested to Wauchope. Guarding his remarks by saying that he could blame no one for failing to cure the drainage problems in the previous twenty-year period, the high commissioner intimated that it was necessary to increase agricultural productivity in Palestine and that the previous concessionnaires had had their chance but failed.[107] In permitting the Palestine Land Development Company to acquire the concession, Wauchope and the Palestine administration minimized criticism from Jewish quarters about the administration's prior failure to provide state lands for Jewish settlement as outlined in Article 6 of the Mandate.

Land Acquisition during the 1936–1939 Disturbances

The northward thrust for Jewish land acquisition continued after the purchase of the Huleh area. It proceeded in spite of internal disturbances, British policy reviews, and financial limitations. By 1937, Palestinian and non-Palestinian Arabs had sold enough land to Jewish purchasers so that the Peel Commission was able to recommend the partition of Palestine. The commission proposed to create separate Jewish and Arab states, but the British withdrew this proposal in 1938. Nevertheless, the boundaries outlined for the Jewish state by the Peel Commission, which had investigated the general strike and disturbances of 1936, mirrored almost precisely the parameters of Jewish land purchase up to that time.

For the Zionists, the period from 1936 through 1939 was a time of land acquisition motivated by specific geopolitical and geostrategic interests. Neither the British investigations nor the disturbances deterred the Zionists' intent to buy more land. Their ability to do so was certainly constrained. But privately leading Zionists continually reevaluated the political climate for the purpose of building the Jewish national home. Zionists like David Ben-Gurion, Moshe Shertok, Menachem Ussishkin, Joseph Weitz, Yehoshua Hankin, Arthur Ruppin, Jacob Thon, Yitzhak Vilkansky, Abraham Granovsky, Berl Katznelson, Maurice Hexter, and others made decisions about the Jewish state's dimensions. They were energized by the knowledge that Palestinian Arabs were selling land, which added to their drive to create a Jewish state. Epitomizing that intent was David Ben-Gurion, then the head of the Jewish Agency.

Ben-Gurion, like his contemporaries, was deeply committed to the creation of a Jewish state. But his forcefulness, his pragmatic understanding of politics, his comprehension of which issues could be negotiated, and his unwillingness either to be intimidated by Arab violence or

10. Arab Higher Committee, 1936 (pictured from left to right, first row) Raghib al-Nashashibi, Hajj Amin al-Husayni, Ahmad Hilmi, Abd al-Latif al-Salah, Alfred Rok; (back row) Jamal al-Husayni, Dr. Husayn Fahkri al-Khalidi, Yaqub al-Ghusayn, and Fu'ad Saba
Courtesy of the National Library, Jerusalem

deterred by British policies made him an equal above equals. His presence lent Jewish National Fund land-purchase policy the additional vigor, historical perspective, shrewd analysis, and long-term planning necessary for consolidating gains and making new ones in land acquisition. At the 6 December 1937 meeting of the Jewish National Fund he noted, "There will not be any absolute security until a Jewish state is established in Eretz-Yisrael."[108]

By the end of 1937, between 200,000 and 300,000 dunams were tendered to the Jewish National Fund for purchase. These offers ranged from 100 to 5,000 dunams, but most of them were less than 500 dunams in size.[109] The disturbances, the British suggestion for the creation of a Jewish state, and ultimately the 1940 Land Transfer Regulations forced careful and thoughtful decision making and a more concentrated awareness of what offers should be accepted in an unstable political climate.

Arab violence and British temporizing stimulated Zionist action, and both had enormous impacts upon the pace, nature, and scope of Jewish

11. Dr. Joseph Weitz, 1946
Courtesy of Central Zionist Archives, Jerusalem

12. David Ben-Gurion, 1946
Courtesy of Central Zionist Archives, Jerusalem

purchases. First, the disturbances raised tensions and increased insecurity. People were attacked, fields were pillaged, crops were destroyed, trees were uprooted, and shops were looted. Whether the motivation to engage in these civil disruptions emerged from frustrated nationalist aspirations, local political conflicts, economic causes, simple desires to plunder, or any combination of these, the resulting uncertainty drove private Jewish capital away from the land-purchase process. The small-capital purchasers had fewer reserves, and their potential margins for error were narrower. They could not sustain as many losses caused by default as could the large-capital purchasers. For private buyers, negotiating for land was both financially hazardous and bodily perilous. The decline in public security made the accumulation of *musha'* shares much more difficult; preliminary contract negotiations were carried out with high risks; and compensatory payments to tenants often could not be delivered. For example, smaller private companies like the Hanotiya Land Company, which had previously bought and sold enormous areas of land, found itself during the disturbances either without capital or without personnel to fulfill prior obligations. Unexpectedly, the impact of the disturbances was that the Jewish National Fund eventually became the only organization that continued to buy land for Jewish settlement.[110] The Jewish National Fund, however, was now capable of not only making land-purchase decisions based upon geostrategic needs, but it was also able to play the central role in land-purchase strategy because of reduced competition.

Second, the instability and disruption of the market caused by the disturbances affected the manner in which the Jewish National Fund purchased and registered land. Greater secrecy and clandestine procedures had to be used if potential sellers and land brokers were to sell land and live to benefit from the money they received. In one case, the Jewish National Fund was able to effect a transfer by bringing the Arab owners to Tel Aviv in European dress, lodging them in private homes, and having the Land Registry officials record the transaction in a private home.[111] Terrorism and brigandage forced some Arab landowners to flee Palestine, leaving the negotiations for land sales to their agents. Brokers' fees inevitably increased. Although land was often offered at a reasonable price and on convenient terms, the Jewish National Fund found it difficult to take possession of the land it purchased because tenants in occupation were often protected by rebel bands. In other instances, Arab gangs extorted a monthly sum from an owner in exchange for protecting the land. Because rents were difficult to collect during the disturbances, some Palestinian Arab landowners preferred to sell portions of their property or to liquidate their holdings entirely. Others, not in immediate need of money, refused to sell at depressed prices; they hoped for a rise in market values when the violence subsided.[112] The level of periodic violence was sufficient to close the Land Registry offices in Beisan and Tiberias, to suspend eleven of the twenty-two district courts, to curtail land-settlement procedures, and to prevent access to many Land Registry offices.[113] Without total access to the government registries, the Jewish National Fund established procedures for acquiring land through regular purchase channels, but it did not officially register the transfers. From 1936 to 1940, while Jews legally purchased and registered more than 100,000 dunams, the Jewish National Fund bought an additional 60,000 dunams that were not registered.[114] The procedures and methods adopted for buying land from Palestinians, but not registering it with the government, continued to a much larger extent after the institution of the 1940 Land Transfer Regulations.

Third, the Peel Report's conclusions stimulated a Zionist geopolitical reply. Apparently, the British just simply failed to anticipate the impact the report would have upon Zionist planning. The Jewish Agency and the Jewish National Fund dispassionately and systematically evaluated future purchases based upon actual and contingent strategic consequences. This meant identifying those land areas necessary for the consolidation of Jewish-held regions, for the creation of territorial depth, and for geopolitical requirements. By the end of 1937, the Jewish National Fund factored into its land-acquisition calculus the possibility of the imposition of land-transfer prohibitions. Debate at Jewish National Fund meetings never suffered from unanimity. The decisions and discussions of which land to purchase, when, and for how much during the period 1936 to 1940 amply support that observation. Deliberations were heated, lengthy, and sometimes rancorous, but the principals never lost sight of the final goal or the political necessity for coordinated action. They expressed regret continually about the very meager funds available to the Jewish National Fund. A consensus of priorities emerged in spite of the uncontrollable political impediments. Properties in the already heavily populated Jewish areas of the coastal plain and the valley regions were to be increased. In addition, a definite thrust into the hill regions of northern Palestine was contemplated. In the coastal and valley regions, the attempt was made to acquire rural land before urban land because rural property could be bought at a lower price.[115]

Land in the Upper Galilee near the Lebanese border and land in the Beisan plain were the priority areas for Jewish land acquisition. The Negev area and the south were not yet given preeminence. Even though the Upper Galilee was outside of the Peel Report's proposed boundaries for the Jewish state, the Jewish National Fund reasoned that holdings along the northern frontier would increase security for the existing settlements and would prevent the segregation of these areas in any land-transfer prohibition scheme. Before the outbreak of the disturbances in 1936, Hankin entered into negotiations for land in Lebanon, but bargaining for the acquisition of 100,000 dunams was broken off for a variety of financial and political reasons.[116] By late 1939, however, the Jewish National Fund had entered into contractual agreements with several Lebanese Christians for land near the Lake Huleh basin. Negotiations for 408,000 dunams of land in the northeast corner of the Sea of Galilee wholly in Syria and on the Yarmuk River partially in Palestine and partially in Syria were being concluded when capital that was to come from Poland failed to arrive, thus preventing the sale.[117] In spite of such failures, the focus of land acquisition remained in the Beisan, Safed, and Acre subdistricts. Most of the land in these northern regions was purchased from Syrian, Lebanese, and Palestinian landlords residing outside of Palestine.[118]

Before the outbreak of the disturbances, the Jewish National Fund owned only 103 dunams of land in the Galilee region in the Acre, Safed, and Beisan subdistricts. By April 1940, it owned 54,873 dunams in the Galilee area alone. Between 1936 and 1940, it added 25,180 dunams to the 39,424 it already held in the Jordan Valley near Beisan.[119] Almost half of its registered and unregistered land acquired during those four years was located in northern Palestine. It also established forty-four *kibbutzim* or *moshavim* between 1937 and 1939, more than half of them north of the Haifa-Beisan town line.[120] Thus, Jewish National Fund land-purchase policy objectives were at least partially fulfilled between 1936 and 1940 because there was no dearth of land for sale and no reluctance to sell it to Jews.

A third priority area for Jewish land acquisition in the 1936 to 1940 period included land near the Tel Aviv–Jerusalem road. For example, land in Abu-Gosh, even with its high price of £P7 to £P8 per dunam, was purchased because of its strategic importance.[121] Ben-Gurion believed that the Haifa region was a fourth critical area. He reasoned correctly that the port of Haifa was an increasingly important key to Great Britain's strategic presence in the Middle East because Britain was in the advanced state of granting independence to Egypt. A Jewish demographic majority at the Iraqi oil-pipeline terminus ultimately gave the Zionists an important influence over Haifa's future disposition.[122] No such specific discussion of what to buy and for what strategic purposes had existed in 1930; at that time, the discussions merely emphasized the need to acquire contiguous areas and to settle Arabs far from the Jewish settlements. With the May 1939 White Paper, the effort to achieve Jewish territorial depth was evident, paramount, and urgent. The nature of the considerations for particular purchases, though dominated by geopolitics, was also guided by other factors. These included the pace at

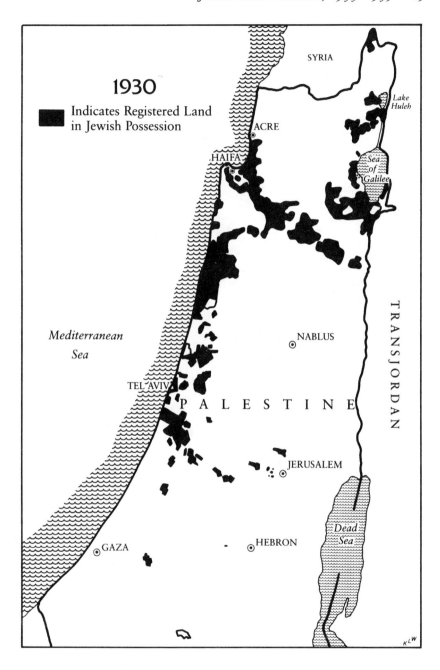

4. *Registered Land in Jewish Possession, 1930*

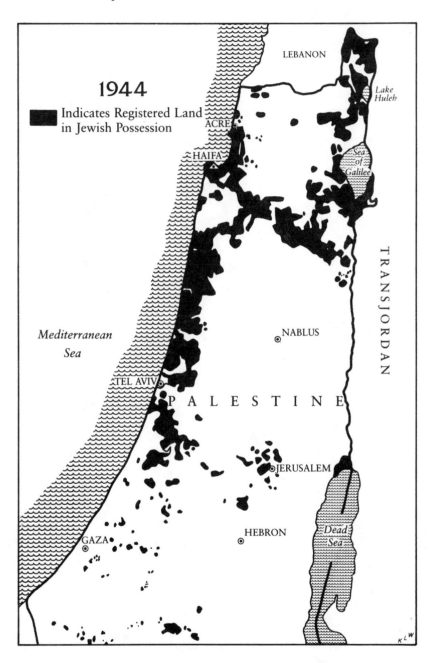

5. Registered Land in Jewish Possession, 1944

which a transfer could be effected, the presence of tenants on the land, the problems in removing any tenants, the feasibility of actual Jewish physical occupation of the land, and the cost of the land. Land areas that could be improved were still preferred by the Jewish National Fund, although strategic demands placed political requirements above exclusive settlement needs. The inclusion of geostrategic factors in Jewish land-purchase policy reflected the advanced stage of the Jewish state's evolution perhaps more than any other change in settlement philosophy. By 1939, and before events in Europe focused the world's attention on the Jewish condition, a geographic nucleus for a Jewish state was present in Palestine.

Chapter 7

Conclusions

A variety of reasons coalesced in the 1940s to create the state of Israel. These included British withdrawal from the Mandate and from Palestine, the United Nations partition resolution on Palestine in November 1947, American diplomatic and financial support for Israel, profound differences within the Arab world about the future of Palestine, a fragmented Palestinian Arab community, a stubborn Zionist leadership and dedicated cadre of Jewish nationalists, and a moral imperative to take positive actions after the holocaust in Europe. But these reasons could not have enabled a community to declare statehood in 1948 without the acquisition and establishment of Jewish national territory upon which a state could function and in which a population could survive.

Accumulating land for the Jewish state was an arduous task. It spanned more than six decades and overcame numerous administrative and political obstacles. Jewish land purchase succeeded for essentially five reasons. First, the inherited Ottoman land regime was vulnerable to manipulation; second, Palestinian Arab society was divided socially and politically, thus allowing the Zionists to move into the land sphere without real opposition; third, Palestine's rural economy remained weak prior to, during, and after World War I and was therefore susceptible to Zionist land-purchase overtures; fourth, the British acted only as an umpire in Palestine and did little to strengthen the condition of the Palestinian fellah; and fifth, the Zionists were able to use their special status under the Mandate to organize themselves in the effort to reach their goal.

Ottoman attempts at land reform did not help the economic condition of the fellaheen population in Palestine. Instead, the *musha'* and taxation systems remained, and the continuing usurious rates of interest and the process of land registration combined to tighten the grip that the notable and the *effendi* classes had over the Palestinian peasantry. Changes in the Ottoman administration of Palestine generated anxiety among the fellaheen about increased taxation and military conscription. When the British established their mandate, the fellaheen continued to shun government policy, though numerous allowances were made to accommodate customary practice. The fellaheen were terrified of Land Registry offices and the courts, and they were not cognizant of their legal rights and status before the law.[1] Fellaheen skepticism of British intent, compounded by British unwillingness to aid a destitute fellaheen population, contributed to increasing political dislike for the British as they supported the development of the Jewish national home.

Meanwhile, the Ottoman administrative legacy bequeathed to the notable, merchant, and *effendi* classes access to information and privilege that had permitted land accumulation. Ottoman administrative reform did little to influence change in the nature of local politics, which was based upon kinship, close family structure, village identity, and personal connections. These parochial affinities hindered the emergence of national integration and organization of the Palestinian Arab political leadership. By establishing more efficient and enforceable bureaucratic directives, the British administration blocked unrestrained land accumulation by the more powerful classes. At the same time, the residue of previously acquired social prestige and political power remained with those who had large landowning interests.

Jewish land purchase benefited from the loss of land-accumulation prerogatives once enjoyed by notables who had been local Ottoman administrators. Jewish land purchase also benefited from the personal nature of Arab politics, which transcended the Ottoman administration. No longer possessing financial means or bureaucratic access to bid on available or vacant land, Arab notables during the Mandate increasingly sold land for capital. They did so to maintain their local political status and accustomed standards of living. At the same time, the Zionists exploited the special status they enjoyed under the Mandate—a trusteeship that protected Jewish interests while rejecting any clear form of Palestinian (Arab) majority self-government.

Palestine was administered by a high commissioner who possessed absolute executive, judicial, and legislative authority and who was guided by a policy that included an obligation to both Arab and Jew. The dual-obligation policy and the absolute power that the high commissioner wielded determined the nature of Jewish-Arab interaction with the British authorities. Both the Balfour Declaration and the articles of the Mandate defined the concept of political duality. Great Britain reaffirmed its dual obligation in somewhat different policy statements in 1922, 1930, and 1939. Ultimately, the politics of duality failed because the obligation to establish a Jewish national home was not equivalent to protecting the civil and religious rights of the non-Jewish communities. One was a statement of right; the other was a statement of sufferance.

Cognizant of this reality, the Palestinian Arab political leadership refused to accept the Mandate's legality. It chose instead to boycott official participation in the Mandate. The leadership itself was elitist, narrowly based, and interested in protecting its dwindling prerogatives and prestige, remnants from Ottoman times. It, like the Palestinian fellaheen population, distrusted British intentions. It possessed a growing fear of being overwhelmed, and it resorted to civil disturbance to demonstrate its frustrations with British policy and Zionist development. The Palestinian Arab political leadership lacked the diplomatic sophistication and willingness to make pragmatic compromises with the British.

The Jewish leadership, on the other hand, with its diverse and pluralistic origins, used the articles of the Mandate to enhance its special status. The land sphere was just one area in which the Zionists utilized their consultative prerogative, which they were given in Article 4 of the Mandate. Zionists influenced the appointments of key officials, wrote documents, and drafted the terminology used in the Balfour Declaration, the articles of the Mandate, the 1920 Land Transfer Ordinance, the 1926 Correction of Land Registers Ordinance, successive pieces of legislation for the protection of cultivators, the MacDonald Letter, and the definition of a landless Arab. Each time a major British statement on land or policy was issued in Palestine—including the Shaw Report, the Hope-Simpson Report, the French Reports, and the Peel Report—the Zionists issued their own verbal reply. Zionist input into policy concerning land began with Chaim Weizmann's opposition to loans for the fellaheen in 1918 and continued beyond the Jewish Agency's scrutiny of landless Arab claims in the 1930s. The appointment of Norman Bentwich as attorney general, which was a position of influence in the Land Registry Department in the 1920s, as well as Judge A. H. Webb's appointment to evaluate landless Arabs, aided Zionist fortunes in the land sphere. Although some Zionists did not like Sir Herbert Samuel's public policy of political neutrality from 1920 to 1925, the fact that a Jew and a Zionist was the first high commissioner in Palestine meant that the growth and development of the Jewish national home was not inhibited during the Mandate's formative years.

The Zionists' successes and the Palestinian Arab inability to thwart Jewish land purchase were indicative of the differences in background and experience between the two groups. First, the Zionists brought with them immigrant baggage that included survival against nefarious regimes and bureaucracies of eastern and western Europe. Many Zionists were accustomed to using wily, manipulative, innovative, and calculating methods to survive. The Arabs' primary experience was of survival against nature, and they had little experience in confronting the bureaucratic and legislative machinery introduced by the Ottomans and the British. They were used to working through traditional hierarchical channels. Second, most Zionists were accustomed to verbal negotiations and written evidence in defending and expanding their communal status in Palestine, and the Arabs lacked verbal and writing skills. Third, high literacy levels helped the Jews use their knowledge of the Arab community for their own purposes. In 1931, though Jews constituted only 18 percent of the total population, there were more literate Jews in Palestine than literate Muslims and Christians combined.[2] Equally noteworthy was the fact that in 1931 there were 2,216 Jews who read and used Arabic while only 21 Muslims and Christians in all of Palestine knew Hebrew.[3] This linguistic ability assisted all aspects of Zionist land purchase and helped Jews to evaluate the composition, strengths, and weaknesses of the diverse Palestinian Arab community.

In a highly competitive and aggressive style, the Zionists continuously strove for increased authority and autonomy in Palestine; they repeatedly diluted policies and laws that threatened the development of the Jewish national home. The Zionists did not have vast resources at their command, but they were skilled, schooled, and able to purchase a nucleus for a state. The Palestinian Arabs, in contrast, suffered from severe deprivation, a lack of capital, and less clear-cut goals.

Jewish land purchase continued despite obstacles thrown in its path by Ottoman prohibitions, exorbitant prices, and a steady increase of British restrictions. The British myopically believed that the passage of legislation and regulations would physically and economically assist the poor Palestinian Arab fellah. What was needed was an agrarian policy that provided credit facilities, agricultural tax reform, modernization of agricultural methods, and more efficient land use. The British had neither the trained personnel nor the political and financial commitment to implement such policies. Instead, solutions through administrative directives and ordinances were considered sufficient. When ordinances dealing with land were decreed in Palestine, they inevitably incorporated Zionist opinion. For example, the Land Transfer Ordinance in 1920 and its amendments did not prevent land speculation, and the Zionists had helped draft them. Under the Beisan Agreement in 1921, the fellaheen in the region could not retain the lands guaranteed to them by the British even when they were available at incredibly low prices, and the Zionists helped rewrite the Beisan Agreement in 1928 in order to gain legal access to these lands. In 1929 and 1933, Arab tenants were not protected by the various editions of the Protection of Cultivators Ordinances that Zionist lawyers had helped to write; and from 1931 to 1936, the landless Arab inquiry did not enumerate property or resettle Palestinian fellaheen on alternative land because of Zionist access to the process. Finally, because small-landowner protection never evolved, the British ultimately imposed legislative restrictions on land purchase through the 1940 land-transfer prohibitions. But, like the previous legislative attempts, they proved incapable of stopping the transfer of land because of economic forces.

There is little doubt that Arabs sold land to the Jews primarily because they needed money.[4] Both British administrators and Jewish land purchasers knew about the perennial economic distress of the Palestinian fellaheen. Prior to World War I, the economic viability of the Palestinian fellaheen was precarious at best, and the war severely damaged Palestine's rural economy. Successive crop failures followed in the 1930s. The continued retention of small and unproductive parcels of land became untenable. Factors such as insufficient plow animals, plagues, locusts, drought, usurious interest rates—all totally unrelated to Zionist policies—helped create a landless Arab population. Furthermore, economically solvent Palestinian Arabs sold land enthusiastically, voluntarily, and collusively. For many reasons, Jewish purchase and Arab land sales created changes in the life-style of many Palestinian Arabs.

Economic factors, Jewish land purchase, and a British policy unresponsive to the needs of a rural population had dramatic effects upon social relationships within the Palestinian Arab community. The dominant and domineering position that the notable-*effendi* classes enjoyed over many fellaheen in the villages of Palestine began to erode severely in the early 1930s when the inflow of Jewish capital into Palestine reached all-time highs. Land once inviolable became a fair-market item. Entire Palestinian Arab villages disappeared because of land sales. The slow decline in the *musha'* system eroded further the meager control a fellah had over the land he worked. Urban jobs and per diem labor on public-works projects or in Jewish settlements were the employment alternatives for former agricultural laborers, tenants, and owner-occupiers. Once in the urban environment, the former fellah was susceptible to different economic vicissitudes such as inflation and unemployment.[5] For moneylenders, merchants, lawyers, landowners, and others with investment in agricultural land, the process of rural-urban migration upset traditional relationships between the suppliers of seeds, agricultural equipment, and financial loans, on the one hand, and the fellaheen on the other. With fewer workers on poorly cultivated land, yields were lower, rents were less, and the retention of these parcels became increasingly less economical for the landowners. In the early 1930s, Arab social bonds frayed at a time when the political leadership of the Palestine Arab Executive was again fragmented by kinship, family, and local rivalries.

Between 1931 and 1935 many small owner-occupiers became aware of the potential monetary benefit of selling their small parcels of land directly or indirectly to Jewish purchasers. At the time of the disturbances in 1936, the landlord who lost some of his field hands to urban migration realized that he could prevent severe economic losses and gain access to capital by selling land to Jewish purchasers.[6] The agricultural laborer, not in possession of any land and gradually estranged from his customary seasonal sources of occupation (such as plowing or harvesting), was already dependent upon a subsidiary income in a new urban environment that he found unfamiliar and inhospitable.

By 1936, Palestinian Arab society was undergoing fundamental social changes. The Westernization of norms and modernization of values challenged the traditional patterns and lines of authority. The meager Ottoman reforms, the paternalistic British administration, and the committed Jewish presence collectively impressed changes upon Palestinian Arab society. Mores, customs, habits, beliefs, and manners were slowly transformed. Change meant that the prestige of the past and the disciplined structure of Arab society were altered. The magnitude of change was too much for the Palestinian Arab community to absorb. Norms of informality were replaced by a formal bureaucratic structure and a more efficient administration. The issuance of title deeds to the fellaheen in Beisan in the 1920s was revolutionary. It gave them physical proof of ownership and made it possible for each fellah to sell land, and not necessarily through an intermediary.

Tensions rose as traditional social ties were strained and broken. Lack of steady employment of a class disenfranchised over time heightened its despair. Urbanization in the late 1930s stimulated an awareness of goods that only money could purchase. Property was exchanged for capital. The peasant was caught in the transition from a barter to a market economy without possessing the means to attain economic solvency or the education or experience to manage and protect his own destiny. Many fellaheen and landowners were disillusioned and frustrated. Many expressed their anger by participating in social unrest, land disputes, and the disturbances that lasted from 1936 to 1939.

In the 1930s, Palestinian Arabs from all segments of society were aware of the dangers that increased Jewish immigration and land purchase posed for them. Palestinian Arabs clearly and unambiguously knew that the Zionists wanted a state in Palestine. Yet there was little that a generally poor, unorganized, uneducated, unsophisticated, and splintered Arab community could do to defend itself. The Arab community in Palestine just could not compete. Precisely at the time in the 1930s when land sales from Palestinians proliferated, Arab Muslim leaders sought to invoke Islamic symbolism against the Jewish interloper. But the resort to primordial instincts failed, although anti-British and anti-Zionist feeling was high. The use of religious injunctions in 1934 and 1935, which labeled land brokers and sellers of land as infidels who were not to be accorded the rights of burial in Muslim cemeteries, proved ineffective.[7] The effort to create an Arab National Fund in 1931 and the Tulkarm-based Society for the Preservation of Arab Lands in 1932 failed to attract public commitment to protect and defend Palestinian land. Later efforts in the 1940s by Palestinian Arabs to stop land sales to Jews, already prohibited in most cases by the Land Transfer Regulations, were ineffective also.

The separation of Palestinian Arabs from lands they had habitually owned and worked began with the Ottoman land-registration system of the late nineteenth century. This process favored large-landowning interests ultimately at the expense of many Palestinian fellaheen. Economic factors, Jewish land purchases, and Arab land sales further displaced the fellaheen. The climax was reached by the population shifts prior to, during, and after the 1947–49 war. The creation of the Palestinian refugee problem in 1948–49 was a culmination of social, economic, and political processes that had begun a century earlier.

The turning point for the creation of the Jewish state and the acquisition of land for it came in 1930, before which time a "land issue" had not existed. In 1930, the Zionists successfully repudiated the British challenge. The British had forced a coherent and comprehensive Zionist response, which stimulated thinking, organization, communication, and political planning that saw the evolution of coordination and geostrategic implementation.

Why had there not been a land issue in the 1920s? There were at least six major reasons. First, a severe shortage of Jewish capital necessitated the acquisition of only large parcels of land from relatively few landowners, whose tenants and agricultural laborers could be easily compensated. Jewish purchasers made contact with a minimum of Arab sellers, certainly less than several hundred. Second, the absence of a coordinated, enunciated, and well-planned Jewish land-purchase policy gave the Palestine Arab political leadership little to berate. On the other hand, Jewish immigration was easily detected. Certificates for Jewish immigrants had to be issued, but land sales took place in an impersonal Land Registry office unseen by the majority of the Palestinian Arab population. Third, during the 1920s, more than 60 percent of the land purchased by Jews was bought from Arab absentee landlords residing outside of Palestine. However, political rancor about absentee sales in the 1920s was not as great as the attention paid to domestic sales in the 1930s. Fourth, Palestinian Arab landowners had no reason to be angry with the Palestine administration, once it removed area limitations on land sales in the 1921 Land Transfer Amendment Ordinance. That law stayed in force until the 1940 Land Transfer Regulations placed restrictions on the areas in which a person could sell land. Fifth, most of the Palestinian Arab political complaints and petitions to the high commissioner focused on the illegality of the Balfour Declaration, the Mandate system, and Jewish immigration, but not on land purchase. And sixth, the magnitude of land sales was neither understood nor discussed by some in the Palestinian Arab leadership. The absence of a Palestine-wide network to monitor Jewish land sales and the reluctance of some leaders to raise an issue that would betray their own involvement kept the land issue quiet in the 1920s.

The land issue emerged as a political question in 1930 first and foremost because the British raised it; it emerged because of steadily increasing Arab population pressures upon a decreasing amount of cultivable land. Many fellaheen were living below a subsistence existence and were landless; they became increasingly despondent over their economic plight and lacked corrective recourse. Their plight and British inaction were much more frequently discussed by the Palestine Arab press in articles and editorials in the early 1930s than at any time in the 1920s. And, finally, the land issue emerged because the Zionists were forced to react publicly to the imposition of land-transfer prohibitions threatened by the British.

The findings of the Shaw Report and Hope-Simpson Report and the issuance of the Passfield White Paper in 1930 convinced the Zionists that High Commissioner Chancellor's anti-Zionist philosophy had to be neutralized. The defeat of the White Paper by the MacDonald Letter, the postponement of land-transfer controls for a decade, and their successful intervention in the landless Arab inquiry gave the Zionists a needed breathing space to expand on previous purchases and to create contiguous land areas. Though successful at winning several important bureaucratic and political victories in the early 1930s, the Zionists found that their successes were not without subsequent problems. Chancellor's leadership motivated the British to adopt a clearly paternalistic policy toward the Palestinian Arabs. It was a policy that developed slowly in the 1930s and was given meaning in the 1939 White Paper. After the application of the Land Transfer Regulations in 1940, Sir John Shuckburgh of the Colonial Office remarked that "the Arab landowner [needed] to be protected against himself."[8]

The British had already exhibited a taste for legal palliatives instead of for financial expenditures to ameliorate a worsening economic situation. British intervention in the land sphere evolved into a paternalistic protection of the Arab community. The adoption of such an attitude increasingly put the onus of responsibility for the unsettled situation in Palestine upon the Zionists instead of upon British frugality and Arab collusion in land sales to Jews.

The Zionists were the beneficiaries of a hierarchical Arab social structure in Palestine. Zionists did not have to compete with an Arab middle class; instead, they negotiated with relatively few notables and with a poor uneducated peasantry. When the traditional community leaders proved incapable of providing protection and defending Palestine from an intrusion of demographic and social change, many Palestine fellaheen hoped that the British would return the land to them. Expectations were high, but they repeatedly went unfulfilled. Despite the Protection of Cultivators Ordinances and the Land Disputes Possession Ordinance, small-landowner protection and the eventual partition of *musha'* land did not materialize.

The Zionist success in defeating what was essentially Chancellor's intent to "protect" the Arabs had a profound impact upon Zionist motivation and policymaking. The Jewish Agency had confronted and beaten back a steady series of very grave political and physical threats. The defeat of Chancellor's intentions catalyzed the Zionist drive to keep building a national home. A sense of self-confidence, resilience, and autonomous existence evolved from the Zionist struggle with the British about land between 1929 and 1933. While the Zionists were creating an opportunity to develop and streamline a collective land policy with a sighted goal, the Palestinian Arab community was floundering and divided. The Zionists manipulated the British bureaucracy in Palestine. They were enormously successful at nullifying attempts to curtail the development of the national home. When necessary, they made compromises, but they did so only very reluctantly. Specific committees on colonization, Arab tenants' resettlement, and land availability were established. The Zionists were constantly nurtured by the knowledge that there were more Arab offers to sell land than Jewish ability to purchase them. Zionists were aware of the inconsistencies in the Palestinian Arab leadership between its anti-Zionist public statements and its private involvement in land sales. These inconsistencies were to be found all over Palestine—not just in one family, one class, or one region. This factor unquestionably fueled Zionist efforts to establish a national home.

In the early 1930s, three unrelated factors combined to bring about the physical division of Palestine into distinct Jewish and Arab zones. First, the Zionists decided that Arab tenants should not be resettled between existing Jewish settlements, and they expressed a clear intention after the 1929 disturbances to create contiguous Jewish areas. Second, the British perceived that the coastal and valley regions were becoming more and more Jewish, and thus the 1931 directive for the resettlement of landless Arabs indicated that, save for exceptional instances, Arabs were to be resettled in the hill regions. The Peel Commission Report and Land Transfer Regulations made similar suggestions for the geographic division of Palestine into Jewish and Arab sectors. And third, natural migratory patterns brought many Arabs to the hill regions around Nablus, Tulkarm, Jenin, Bethlehem, Hebron, and the Galilee, and away from Jewish settlements. Individual Arab laborers still worked in urban areas and on Jewish settlements, but their families were settled far from Jewish concentrations. It is not surprising, therefore, that the Peel commissioners suggested the first partition of Palestine in 1937.

In February 1936, six years after Arthur Ruppin had expressed the fear that there was insufficient cultivable land in Palestine, Menachem Ussishkin of the Jewish National Fund sounded a similar warning.[9] Yet in those six years, Jewish land purchase had abounded. The rate of purchase and the amount of land acquired had confirmed that the Zionists had succeeded in creating a nucleus for a state. That areas in Transjordan, Syria, and Lebanon were eagerly sought by Zionist land-purchase agents also indicated a recognition that land in Palestine could not long sustain its population under the existing methods of agriculture. When Jewish land-purchase efforts were rebuffed in these areas, the focus of land acquisition was redirected at areas, such as the Galilee, within Palestine.

The suggestion in 1937 that Palestine be partitioned into separate Jewish and Arab states expanded Zionist land-purchase objectives. Discussions at Jewish Agency and Jewish National Fund meetings thereafter centered on how land could be procured to derive the utmost political benefit. Unlike the 1929–31 period, the interval between 1936 and 1940 was marked by an unmistakable Zionist conviction that a Jewish state would ultimately be established. In the earlier period, the Zionists were openly committed to the goal of a Jewish national home, but after 1936 they felt a greater overt self-confidence in the feasibility of the objective. It is therefore not surprising that the imposition of the 1940 Land Transfer Regulations did little to impede Zionist efforts to buy more land. The events of the 1940s, which greatly affected the Jewish condition, the weakening British presence in the Middle East, and the varied Arab and Great Power responses certainly contributed to the establishment of Israel in 1948. But an analysis of Jewish land acquisition and Arab land sales makes it seem quite evident that a formidable Jewish national territory was necessary and was already present in Palestine in 1939.

Appendixes

Appendix 1

Large Estates in Palestine, 1919[1]

Name and Location of Estate[2]	Name and Residence of Proprietor	Area in Dunams[3]
In the District of Tiberias		
Kefar-Saba, Shaareh, Madir, Olem	Emir Ali Pasha, Damascus	30,000
Ghweir (near Mejdal)	Ali Aga Kurdi, Acre	12,000
Manaar, Tiberias land	Said Tabari, Tiberias	10,000
Bteiha	Abdel Rahman Pasha, Damascus	15,000
		67,000 Total
In the District of Tyre and Acre		
Nakura (Tyre)	Fuad Saad, Haifa	30,000
Shif'amir	Salekh Mohammad, Acre	10,000
Shif'amir in Acre District	Fuad Saad, Haifa	20,000
Menshieh	Ahmad Pasha Shami, Damascus	15,000
Jidrah, Kufreitah, Mejdal, Tel Shemen	Tweini and Alfred Sursock, Beirut	82,000
		157,000 Total
In the District of Haifa		
Hartieh, Harbadj, Sheikh Brek	Alexander Sursock, Alexandria	28,000
Kuskus Tabun	Heirs of Hafar, Beirut	10,000
al-Yajur	Yusuf Khoury, Haifa	7,000
Abou Shousha	Beddun, Acre	8,000
Daliah-im-Tfuf	Jemal Bey and brothers, Haifa, and Tweini and Sursock, Beirut	13,000
Rihanieh	Mustafa Pasha heirs, Haifa	10,000
Kirikimon	Joseph Khoury, Haifa, and Tweini and Sursock, Beirut	20,000
Kafar Lam	Heirs of Mustafa Pasha, Haifa	7,000
Sarafend	Salekh Bey, Haifa	8,000
Wadi-Ara	Abd al-Hadi, Jenin	10,000
Kafer-Kara	Habib, Haifa	8,000
Worakany	Haddad, Haifa	12,000
		141,000 Total

Large Estates in Palestine, 1919[1] (continued)

Name and Location of Estate[2]	Name and Residence of Proprietor	Area in Dunams[3]
In the District of Nazareth		
Malul, Gingar, Samony, Rubb-en-Nassra	Yusuf Sursock, Beirut, and Najib Sursock, Alexandria	40,000
Tel-Adas	George Lutfallah Sursock, Alexandria	24,000
Affula	Michael Sursock, Beirut	16,000
Solem	Sursock and Hanna Bshara, Jenin	6,000
Kneifes, Jibbata	Sursock, Beirut	10,000
Dabourieh Um al Ghanam	Fahum, Nazareth, and Fuad Saad, Haifa	15,000
		111,000 Total
In the District of Jenin		
Nuris	Yusuf Sursock, Beirut, and Negib Sursock, Alexandria	30,000
Shatta	Anis Abyad and Salim Ra'is, Haifa	14,000
Zabubeh	Mutran, Beirut	20,000
Zerin, Arraba, Muqeibila, Taibeh	Abd al-Hadi, Nablus	50,000
		114,000 Total
In the District of Tulkarm		
Wadi Hawarith	Tayan, Alexandria	40,000
Wadi Hawarith	Ibrahim Samara, Jaffa	6,000
Arab al-Aujeh Jelil	Umri Effendi, Damascus	45,000
Muhaleth	Hajj Abdul Rahman, Tulkarm	10,000
		101,000 Total
In the District of Nablus		
Sebastiah, Nakurah, Jelsieh, Nisf-al-Jebeil	Fares Massoud, Nablus	20,000
		20,000 Total
In the District of Jaffa		
Bir Adas	Qassab, Haifa and Jaffa	6,000
Ared al-Aujeh	Abu Kishk	10,000
Bnei-Brak, Rentieh, Shueireh, Kuleh, Muzaarah	Bitar family, Jaffa	8,000
Shakhmeh	Husni Bey, Jaffa	5,000
Kheimeh, Gaza	Abou Gosh, Jaffa	8,000
Hulda, Mansourah, Zernoukah	Tagi, Ramle	20,000
		57,000 Total

Large Estates in Palestine, 1919[1] (continued)

Name and Location of Estate[2]	Name and Residence of Proprietor	Area in Dunams[3]
In the District of Jerusalem		
Rafat, Saraa	Najib Abou Suwan, Jerusalem	16,000
Various places in the district of Jaffa and Jerusalem	Osman Nashashibi, Jerusalem	15,000
Bnibbeh and other places in the districts of Jerusalem, Gaza, and Transjordan	al-Husseini family, Jerusalem	50,000
		81,000 Total
In the District of Gaza		
Various villages	Abu Khadra, Jaffa	55,000
Khan Yunes and other places	Hajj Said Shawa	45,000
		100,000 Total
All land held in large estates with the owners outside of the geographic boundaries of Palestine		405,000 Total
All land held in large estates with the owners resident within the geographic boundaries of Palestine		455,000 Total
All land held in large estates with some of the owners resident in and outside of the boundaries of Palestine		89,000 Total
		949,000 Total

1. Names of persons and places have been reproduced exactly as they appeared on the document in the CZA, Z4/771/1.

2. A large estate in this listing is 5,000 dunams or more. No listing is given for the Beersheba subdistrict.

3. Measurement given is in Turkish dunams.

Appendix 2

Absolute Increase of *Registered* Jewish Land Purchase Excluding Government Concessions, 1882–1945

Year(s)	Dunam Increase	Cumulative Increase	Year(s)	Dunam Increase	Cumulative Increase
To 1882	22,530		1930	19,366	987,600
1883–90	82,100	104,630	1931	18,586	1,006,186
1891–1900	113,540	218,170	1932	18,893	1,025,079
1901–14	199,930	418,100	1933[4]	36,992	1,062,071
1915–20	36,760[1]	454,860[2]	1934	62,115	1,124,186
1920	1,143	456,003	1935	72,905	1,197,091
1921	90,785	546,788	1936	18,145	1,215,237
1922	39,359	586,147	1937	29,367	1,244,604
1923	17,493	603,640	1938	27,280	1,271,884
1924	44,765	648,405	1939	27,974	1,299,857
1925	176,124[3]	824,529	1940	22,481	1,322,338
1926	38,978	863,507	1941	14,531	1,336,869
1927	18,995	882,502	1942	18,810	1,355,679
1928	21,215	903,717	1943	18,035	1,373,714
1929	64,517	968,234	1944	8,311	1,382,025
			1945	11,506	1,393,531[5]

Sources: Data for this table are from "Land Ownership in Palestine," CZA, KKL5/1878. The statistics were prepared by the Palestine Lands Department for the Anglo-American Committee of Inquiry, 1945, ISA, Box 3874/file 1. See also Gurevich and Gertz, *Jewish Agricultural Settlement in Palestine*, p. 35. Area sizes are in standard dunams with totals given to the last day of each year.

1. Much of the 36,760 dunams acquired during this period of administrative turmoil and during the period of land-disposition prohibition changed ownership via various legal circumventions.

2. It has been generally assumed that the total area in Jewish possession or ownership prior to 1920 was approximately 650,000 Turkish dunams. The equivalent metric dunam sum is 597,350. Included in this first total were 74,900 metric dunams, mostly in the Hauran region, which later fell under Syrian jurisdiction. Thus, between the remaining assumed amount of 522,450 metric dunams and the 454,760 metric dunams of land acquired by title deeds to 1920 for which we have records, there remain 67,690 metric dunams. These lands were probably under some form of mortgage, sale, or rental agreement at the time of estimation and were therefore considered to be in Jewish possession or ownership. Some of these 67,690 dunams may also have been unregistered transfers that later received legal status under the Correction of Land Registers Ordinance of 1926. Yehoshua Hankin of the Palestine Land Development Company confirms this 450,000 figure in his letter to the Jewish Agency of 17 January 1937. See CZA, S25/6563.

3. Government statistics detailing Jewish land purchase during the Mandate give an annual figure of 101,131 for the year 1925. The Department of Statistics of the Jewish Agency, however, gives the statistic of either 103,584 or 176,124 dunams. The Palestine government figures give a higher amount for 1924 but less for 1925 than the Jewish Agency statistics, which gives the opposite. A large portion of the 1924 and 1925 sales were the so called Sursock purchases that took place in 1924 and 1925. The discrepancy is explained because some of the village sales were listed in different years by Jewish Agency and Palestine government statisticians. See Gurevich to Jewish Agency Political Department, 31 March 1938, CZA, S25/6563.

4. For the period beginning 1 January 1933 and ending 31 March 1936, Jewish Agency statistics (Gurevich and Gertz, p. 35) show that Jews acquired 224,336 dunams by transfer of title deeds while Lands Department documents record the amount for the same period as 187,294 dunams. The discrepancy of 37,042 dunams may be explained by unregistered transfers, an explanation supported by the Arab Executive in December 1934. See al-Kayyali, *Watha'iq al-Muqawama al-Filastiniyyah al-'Arabiyyah*, p. 358.

5. This amount does not represent total Jewish land-purchase acquisition to 15 May 1948. By 31 March 1936, Jews had acquired 161,806 dunams by concession from the Palestine administration. No information is currently available regarding concessionary allotments made after that date and before 15 May 1948. This amount does not include areas where lease options were written but not exercised, areas transferred and unregistered in the 1918–20 period or during the 1936–39 Arab revolt, or areas illegally transferred and unregistered from February 1940 to the end of the Mandate when the Land Transfer Regulations were in effect. It may be assumed that total Jewish land purchase to 15 May 1948 closely approximated 2,000,000 dunams, including concessionary areas, unregistered transfers, and legal transfers made after 1945.

Appendix 3

Partial List of Palestinian Arab Politicians and Notables Involved in Land Transfers to Jews, 1918–45

Name	Administrative, Social, Religious, or Political Position or Status	Available Comments Regarding Land Transfers
ABU-HANTASH, 'Abd al-Latif	Village *shaykh* at Qaqun; participated in attacks on Jews at Hadera in 1921; helped to organize "Farmers party" in 1924; organized opposition to JNF purchase of Wadi Qabbani in the 1930s.	Sold 821 dunams at Qaqun in 1925 for £P2,564 in the Tulkarm subdistrict. (11)
ABU-HANTASH, 'Abdul	Member of the Palestine Arab party.	Sold lands in Attil and Qaqun in Tulkarm subdistrict. (2, 6)
ABU-HANTASH, Muhammad	Member of the Palestine Arab party.	Sold lands in Attil and Qaqun in Tulkarm subdistrict; in Qaqun his was a portion of 143.457 dunams. (2, 3, 6)
ABU-KHADRA, Hashim	Notable of Jaffa.	Sold 4,600 dunams to the "Ahuza" Company at a rate of 350 piastres per dunam (*al-Hayat*, 8 July 1931). (2, 6)
ABYAD, Anis, Jemal, Yusuf, Adlin	Notable family from Haifa and environs.	Sold at least 4,500 dunams to Raja Ra'is in Shatta village in the Beisan subdistrict with the knowledge that Ra'is was about to sell the land to the JNF (Hankin to PLDC, 2 July 1930, CZA, KKL 5/Box 532)
al-ALAMI, Musa	Government advocate; private secretary to High Commissioner Wauchope; member of the Palestine Arab delegation to London Conference of 1939; brother-in-law of Jamal al-Husayni; in 1946 was a member of the Arab Executive Committee.	Sold 900 dunams of land in Beisan (Minutes of the Eighth Meeting of St. James Palace Conference, London, 20 February 1939, CZA, S25/7333). (2)

Partial List of Palestinian Arab Politicians and Notables Involved in
Land Transfers to Jews, 1918–45 *(continued)*

Name	Administrative, Social, Religious, or Political Position or Status	Available Comments Regarding Land Transfers
al - B A Y T A R, 'Abdul Raouf	Member of the National Defense party; brother of 'Omar al-Baytar.	Sold an unspecified amount of land at Bnei Brak. (2, 6, 8)
al - B A Y T A R, 'Omar	Representative from Jaffa to 4th, 5th, 6th, and 7th Arab congresses; former chairman of the Muslim-Christian Association of Jaffa; member of the Arab Executive, 1921–34; several tenures as mayor of Jaffa, the last one in 1941–45.	Sold lands at Yahudiya in the Jaffa subdistrict; sold 3,276 dunams for £P40,879 in Kheirieh in the Jaffa subdistrict in conjunction with fellaheen; sold an unspecified amount of land in Miska in the Tulkarm subdistrict. This amount included compensation to tenants as well as key money for other purposes (Criminal Investigation Division Reports, 10 March 1933, FO/371/16926). (2, 6, 8, 10, 12)
B A S I S O, Khalil Yusuf	Member of the Arab Executive, elected to 7th Congress for Gaza.	In April 1942, sold 471 dunams to the JNF in Gaza for £P1,200 (ISA, Box 3874/file 7, Schedule for April 1942). (6)
B A S I S O, Shaykh Salim	Mufti of Beersheba and Gaza.	Sold an unspecified amount of land near Gaza town. (2, 6)
B U S H N A K, 'Abdul	Teacher at Jerusalem College.	Sold 41 dunams in the Tulkarm subdistrict. (3)
B U S H N A K, Ahmad, Ali		Shared in the sale at Baqa al-Gharbiyah in the Tulkarm subdistrict of 21,300 dunams transferred between 1920 and 1929; shared in the sale price of £P70,000. (9, 10)
B U S H N A K, Mahmud Amin	Notable from Tulkarm.	Shared in the sale at Baqa al-Gharbiyah; sold an additional 134 dunams at Shuweikah and 318 dunams at Qaqun, both in the Tulkarm subdistrict. (3, 9)
B U S H N A K, Dr. Mustafa	Representative to the 4th Arab Congress from Nablus.	Shared in the sale at Baqa al-Gharbiyah; lands that he sold later became the Jewish settlement of Kafar Yonah. (9, 10)

Partial List of Palestinian Arab Politicians and Notables Involved in
Land Transfers to Jews, 1918–45 *(continued)*

Name	Administrative, Social, Religious, or Political Position or Status	Available Comments Regarding Land Transfers
CANNAN, Dr. Tawfiq	Exponent of Palestine Arab cause in articles and pamphlets.	Sold an unspecified amount of land at Beisan along with Musa al-Alami. (2)
al-DAJANI, 'Abdullah	Notable from Jaffa and member of the Supreme Muslim Council from 1922–26.	Sold an unspecified amount of land at Beit Dajan in the Jaffa subdistrict. (1, 2, 6)
DALLAL, Yaqub	Notable from Jaffa.	Acted as a broker intermediary in transfer of 8,000 dunams in Beersheba; sold an unspecified amount of land at Kafr Saba; sold 1,700 dunams for approximately £P5,500 at Biyar 'Adas in the Jaffa subdistrict between 1922 and 1929 (Weitz, *Yomani,* 1:101–5). (3, 5, 12)
al-DA'UDI, Shaykh Mahmud	Close associate of the Mufti, al-Hajj Amin al-Husayni.	Sold an unspecified amount of land at Najd and Dier Suneid in the Gaza subdistrict. (2)
al-FAHUM, Ibrahim	Lawyer from Nazareth.	Sold 80 dunams to the JNF in Nazareth area in 1944–45 (Letter dated 19 December 1945, CZA, KKL 5/1797).
al-FAHUM, Yusuf and Tawfiq and children	Notable family from Nazareth; Yusuf was the mayor in Nazareth.	Sold an unspecified amount of land in the environs of Nazareth (CZA, KKL 5/1438, notation for 27 August 1942). (6, 9)
al-GHUSAYN, Yaqub	Citrus grower from Ramle; organizer of the Arab National Fund; member of the Arab Higher Committee; participated in London Conference, 1939; leader of the Arab Executive Youth organization.	Sold an unspecified amount of land at Nes Tsiyona in the Jaffa subdistrict. Together with Muhammad Tawfiq al-Ghusayn he sold 306 dunams in 1942 at Beit Hanun in the Gaza subdistrict for £P4,000+ and received a loan of £P5,000 from the JNF (CZA, KKL 5/1433). (2)

Partial List of Palestinian Arab Politicians and Notables Involved in
Land Transfers to Jews, 1918–45 *(continued)*

Name	Administrative, Social, Religious, or Political Position or Status	Available Comments Regarding Land Transfers
'Abd al-HADI, Afif	Brother of 'Awni 'Abd al-Hadi.	Mortgaged and sold portions of their respective parcels
'Abd al-HADI, Fuad Kassem	Jenin representative to the 7th Arab Congress; member of the Arab Executive.	and shares of Zirin village in the Jenin subdistrict directly to the Jewish National Fund from 1929 to 1933 (ISA, Box 3511/file 1).
'Abd al-HADI, Wajih 'Abdul Karim	Resided in Nablus.	
'Abd al-HADI, Yusuf 'Abdul Karim		
'Abd al-HADI, Amin	Member of the Supreme Muslim Council, 1930–37; a Palestinian representative to the Political Committee of the Bludan Arab National Congress, 1937.	Sold an unspecified amount of land in Muqeibila village near Jenin (CZA, S25/7443).
'Abd al-HADI, 'Awni	Member of the Syrian Arab Congress; served with Emir Faysal; legal adviser to the Supreme Muslim Council; representative from Jenin to the 5th and 6th Arab congresses; representative from Beisan to the 7th Arab Congress; member of the Palestine Arab delegation to London, 1930; leader of the Istiqlal party, 1932 and 1933; member of the Palestine Arab delegation to London, 1939.	Acted as legal advocate to the PLDC and JNF in the sale of 30,000 dunams at Wadi Hawarith in April 1929; received £2,700 as his fee (Hankin to PLDC, 3 December 1929, CZA, Z4/3444/3); exchange of correspondence between Tulkarm District Officer and Assistant Director of Development (7 and 12 January 1933, ISA, Box 3372). (2, 6)
'Abd al-HADI, Hajj Na'im	District officer in Jenin.	Sold an unspecified amount of land in Wadi Ara in the Haifa subdistrict in 1926. (2, 3, 6, 11)
al-HAJJ IBRAHIM, Shaykh 'Abdul Latif	Representative to 3rd and 5th Arab congresses from Tulkarm.	Sold 484 dunams at Taiyibah and 300 dunams at Kafr Zibad in the Tulkarm subdistrict in 1928 and 1929. (3)

Partial List of Palestinian Arab Politicians and Notables Involved in
Land Transfers to Jews, 1918–45 *(continued)*

Name	Administrative, Social, Religious, or Political Position or Status	Available Comments Regarding Land Transfers
al-HAJJ IBRAHIM, 'Abdul Rahman	Mayor of Tulkarm; a Muslim religious judge.	Sold an unspecified amount of land at Kafar Saba, 430 dunams at al-Haram (Jaffa subdistrict), 165 dunams at Kafr Abbush, and 300 dunams at Kafr Zibad, all in the Tulkarm subdistrict (Hankin to JNF, 19 December 1932, CZA, A238/file 17). (2, 3, 6)
al-HAJJ IBRAHIM, Rashid	Istiqlal party leader; manager of the Arab Bank in Haifa; leader of the Young Men's Muslim Association; president of the Arab Chamber of Commerce at Haifa; Palestinian representative to the Economic Committee of the Bludan Arab National Congress, 1937.	Sold an unspecified amount of land in the Haifa subdistrict. (2, 6)
al-HAJJ IBRAHIM, Salim 'Abdul	Representative to 4th and 6th Arab congresses from Tulkarm; member of the Arab Executive; spokesman for the Wadi Hawarith inhabitants in the early 1930s.	Sold unspecified amounts of land at Tira, Kafr Zur, and Kafar Saba, all in the Tulkarm subdistrict (*al-Hayat*, 30 July 1931). (2, 6, 8)
HAMDAN, Hajj Ahmad	Notable from Tulkarm; member of the Palestine Arab party.	Sold an unspecified amount of land at Karkur in the Haifa subdistrict. (2, 6)
HANUN, 'Abdul Rahman	Notable from Tulkarm.	Sold an unspecified amount of land near Natanya in the Tulkarm subdistrict. (2, 6)
HANUN, Tahar	Notable from Tulkarm.	Sold 3,988 dunams for £P9,383 at Kafr Zur in the Tulkarm subdistrict in 1929. (2, 6, 9)
HANUN (unidentified sons of)	Notable family from Tulkarm.	Sold 1,030 dunams to the JNF in September 1937 for £P15,461 at Shufa and 1,163 dunams for £P17,454 in November 1937 (ISA, Box 3874, schedules for September and November 1937).

Partial List of Palestinian Arab Politicians and Notables Involved in
Land Transfers to Jews, 1918–45 *(continued)*

Name	Administrative, Social, Religious, or Political Position or Status	Available Comments Regarding Land Transfers
HARTABIL, Hajj Khalil	Notable from Tiberias.	Sold an unspecified amount of land. (6)
HEYKAL, Khalil		Sold 8,760 dunams between 1922 and 1929 for £P42,364 at Jalil in the Jaffa subdistrict; the sale was made with Mahmud Salim al-Omari, 'Abdul Latif al-Omari, Ibrahim al-'Asi, Mustafa Salah al-'Asi, Sa'ida al-Aswad, and Salha Mahmud al-Karim. (3)
al-HUSAYNI, Fahmi	Mayor of Gaza from May 1928 through 1936.	Sold an unspecified amount of land near Gaza town (CO 733/248/17693). (2, 6)
al-HUSAYNI, Ismail Bey	Member of the Advisory Council, 1920–22; cousin of al-Hajj Amin al-Husayni.	Sold an unspecified amount of land at Nazlat Abu Nar in the Tulkarm subdistrict. (2, 6)
al-HUSAYNI, Jamil	Organizer of the Arab youth organization Nadi al-'Arabi.	Sold an unspecified amount of land at Deir 'Amr in the Jerusalem subdistrict. (2, 6)
al-HUSAYNI, Muhammad Tahir	Father of al-Hajj Amin al-Husayni.	Sold an unspecified amount of land in and around Jerusalem probably before World War I. (1)
al-HUSAYNI, Musa Kazim	*Qaimmaqam* at Jaffa under Ottoman regime; mayor of Jerusalem, 1918–April 1920; president of the Muslim-Christian Association of Jerusalem; president of the Arab Executive December, 1920–34; headed Palestine Arab delegation to London, 1921; member of the Palestine Arab delegation to Lausanne conference 1922; member of the Palestine Arab delegation to London, 1923.	Sold an unspecified amount of land at Dilb and Motza in the Jerusalem subdistrict before 1918 (*al-Sirat al-Mustaqim*, 22 May 1930); also received monetary subventions from the Arab Bureau of the Palestine Zionist Executive in 1922 and 1923 (CZA, Z4/1392/2B). (2, 6)

Partial List of Palestinian Arab Politicians and Notables Involved in
Land Transfers to Jews, 1918–45 (continued)

Name	Administrative, Social, Religious, or Political Position or Status	Available Comments Regarding Land Transfers
al-HUSAYNI, Tawfiq	Official of the Immigration Department of the Palestine administration; member of the Palestine Arab party; brother of Jamal al-Husayni.	Sold an unspecified amount of citrus groves at Wadi Hanin in the Ramle subdistrict. (6)
al-IMAM, Raghib	Notable from Jaffa.	Sold an unspecified amount of land near Tel Aviv. (2, 6)
al-IZZEH, Isma'il	Notable from Gaza.	Served as a land broker in early 1935 in the sale of 4,048 dunams in Huj in the Gaza subdistrict (ISA, Box 3548/2/67). (2)
al-IZZEH, Khalil	Notable from Gaza.	Sold an unspecified amount of land at Bureir in the Gaza subdistrict. (2)
al-JAMAL, Shibli	Member of the Palestine Arab delegation to London, 1921; member of the Palestine Arab delegation to Lausanne Conference, 1922; representative to 5th Arab Congress from Jaffa.	Sold an unspecified amount of land at Beisan. (2)
al-JAYUSI, Rashid	Member of the Palestine Arab party.	Sold an unspecified amount of land at Qalansuwa in the Tulkarm subdistrict. (2, 6)
al-KHADRA, Subhi	Member of the Arab Executive Committee from Safed; involved in disseminating information against land sales during the 1936 disturbances.	Sold an unspecified amount of land in the Safed region. (2)
al-KHALIL, Ibrahim, Saleh, Salim, Yusuf	Notables from Haifa.	Sold areas of land to PICA in the Tulkarm and Haifa subdistricts. (2, 3, 6)
al-KHALIL, Tawfiq	Magistrate from Haifa.	Sold 1,287 dunams in July 1937 to PICA for £P4,552 and 462 dunams in February 1938 to the JNF for £P1,725 in the Haifa subdistrict (ISA, Box 3874, Schedules for July 1937 and February 1938). (2, 6)

Partial List of Palestinian Arab Politicians and Notables Involved in
Land Transfers to Jews, 1918–45 *(continued)*

Name	Administrative, Social, Religious, or Political Position or Status	Available Comments Regarding Land Transfers
KITTANA, Al-fred Anton		Served as intermediary in the sale of 4,048 dunams at Huj in the Gaza subdistrict in 1935 (ISA, Box 3548/2/67).
al-MADI, Mu'in	Head of Intelligence for Faysal in Damascus in January 1920; member of the Palestine Arab delegation to London, 1921; Haifa representative to 3rd and 7th Arab congresses; member of the Istiqlal party; emissary of the Arab Higher Committee to Iraq, Syria, and Saudi Arabia; Palestinian representative to the Political Committee of the Bludan Arab National Congress, 1937.	Sold an unspecified amount of land near Atlit in the Haifa subdistrict. (2, 6)
MUGHANNAM, Mughannam	Protestant lawyer from Jerusalem; leader of the al-Husayni opposition in the 1920s; representative to 7th Arab Congress.	Acted as an intermediary for Jewish purchases in the sale of 8,000 dunams at Wadi Qabbani in Tulkarm subdistrict *(al-Jami'ah al-'Arabiyyah,* 20 May 1931, 10 July 1931, 12 July 1931).
al-NASHASHIBI, Fahkri	Secretary of the National Defense party; organizer of boatmen's strike in Jaffa in 1936; cousin of Raghib.	Served as intermediary in land sale at Wadi Qabbani for which he received £P200 (CZA, KKL 5/Box 363/file 500).
al-NASHASHIBI, Raghib	Mayor of Jerusalem, 1920–34; member of the Palestine Arab delegation to London 1930 and 1939; president of the National Defense party.	Sold an unspecified amount of lands in the Jaffa subdistrict in addition to the 1,200 dunams sold in conjunction with 'Omar al-Baytar and 'Asim Bey al-Said near Jaffa in the late summer of 1924; land he sold in Jerusalem was later used to build a portion of the Hebrew University of Jerusalem on Mt. Scopus (Bericht zum Mitglieder im Ausland, 1 September 1924, CZA, KKL 5/file 1203). (2, 3)

Partial List of Palestinian Arab Politicians and Notables Involved in
Land Transfers to Jews, 1918–45 *(continued)*

Name	Administrative, Social, Religious, or Political Position or Status	Available Comments Regarding Land Transfers
R O K, Alfred	Former mayor of Jaffa; vice-president of the Palestine Arab party; member of the Arab Higher Committee; member of the Palestine Arab delegation to London, 1930 and 1939.	Sold unspecified amounts of land at Rantiya, Beit Dejan, and Fajja in the Jaffa subdistrict and at Jabalya in the Gaza subdistrict; in 1942 and 1943 he sold 700 dunams to the JNF in Kikar Hamoshavot (in the immediate proximity of the Tel Aviv central bus station) receiving £P45,000 + (Minutes of JNF meeting, 29 July 1943, CZA, KKL 10). (1, 2, 6)
R O K family members		Sold 600 dunams on the Jerusalem–Tel Aviv road in 1939 and 1940 and additional lands in Beit Dejan in 1945–46 (Minutes of the JNF meeting 30 May 1940, CZA, KKL 5/1730).
S A ' D, Fu'ad	Leader of the Greek Catholic community of Haifa; member of the Arab Executive Committee.	Between 1903 and 1929 sold 7,838 dunams at £P2 per dunam at Marah in the Haifa subdistrict. (9)
S A H Y U N, Ibrahim	Member of the Arab Strike Committee from Haifa.	Sold an unspecified amount of lands at Carmel in the Haifa subdistrict. (2, 6)
al - S A I D, 'Asim Bey	Mayor of Jaffa from 1927; member of the National Defense party; active in the local Muslim-Christian Association.	Sold 5,000 dunams at Qubeiba in conjunction with Shukri al-Taji and 'Abdul Rahman al-Taji and an unspecified amount of land at Eqron, both in the Jaffa subdistrict (Bericht zum Mitglieder im Ausland, 1 September 1924, CZA, KKL 5/file 1203). (1, 2, 6)
S A M A R A, 'Abdul Fattah	Notable from Tulkarm.	In May–June 1925 sold an unspecified amount of land near Hadera; involved in a case of land registration fraud with Haifa District Court Judge Strumza (ISA, Box 3889/file 4, and CO 733/158/57421).

Partial List of Palestinian Arab Politicians and Notables Involved in
Land Transfers to Jews, 1918–45 *(continued)*

Name	Administrative, Social, Religious, or Political Position or Status	Available Comments Regarding Land Transfers
SAMARA, 'Abdullah	Notable from Tulkarm; active supporter of al-Husaynis in the Arab Executive; agitated on behalf of Wadi Hawarith Arabs.	Sold an unspecified amount of land to the JNF in 1940 (Aharon Gerts, *'Emek Hefer-Toldot VeSikumim* [Wadi Hawarith—history and conclusions], [Jerusalem, 1948], p. 16).
SAYEGH, George		Served as a land broker in early 1935 in the sale of 4,048 dunams in Huj in the Gaza subdistrict; received with Isma'il al-Izzeh an amount of more than £P4,000 (ISA, Box 3548/file 2/folio 7). (2, 6)
al-SHAWA, 'Abdul Said	Notable from Gaza.	Sold 153 dunams for £P382 in April 1942 in the Gaza subdistrict (ISA, Box 3874/file 7, Schedule for April 1942).
al-SHAWA, 'Adil, Rashad, Rushdi, Saadi	Members of notable family from Gaza; Rushdi was a mayor of Gaza and a member of the Palestine Arab party and Rashad was a member of the National Defense party.	Sold unspecified amounts of land in the Gaza subdistrict. (2, 6)
al-SHAWA, Sabri	Notable from Gaza.	Sold 63 dunams to the JNF in Beit Hanun in April 1942 for £P660 in the Gaza subdistrict (ISA, Box 3874/file 7, Schedule for April 1942).
SHIBL (unidentified sons of Salah Muhammad)	Notable family from Haifa.	Sold 3,019 dunams in 1934 to the Hanotiah Co. and H. Goldberg for £P38,225 in Shafa 'Amr in the Haifa subdistrict (ISA, Box 3390/file 3, "Land Purchased by Jews from non-Jews for 1934"). (6)
SHUQAYRI, Shaykh Assad	Mufti of Acre; member of the National Defense party; prominent Muslim scholar.	Sold an unspecified amount of land at Neve Shaanan near Haifa. (2, 6)
al-SURANI, Musa	Member of the Palestine Arab party from Gaza.	Sold an unspecified amount of land at Yibna in the Gaza subdistrict. (2, 6)

Partial List of Palestinian Arab Politicians and Notables Involved in
Land Transfers to Jews, 1918–45 *(continued)*

Name	Administrative, Social, Religious, or Political Position or Status	Available Comments Regarding Land Transfers
al-TABARI, 'Abdul Salah	Mufti from Tiberias.	Sold an unspecified amount of land in the environs of Tiberias. (6)
al-TABARI, Sa'id	Former mayor of Tiberias.	Sold an unspecified amount of land in the environs of Tiberias. (6)
al-TABARI, Sidki	Representative to 7th Arab Congress from Tiberias; managed Tiberias branch of the Arab National Bank.	Sold an unspecified amount of land in the environs of Tiberias. (2, 6)
al-TAJI, 'Abdul Rahman	Member of the Supreme Muslim Council 1926–37; member of the National Defense party.	Sold 5,000 dunams at Qubeiba in 1922 in conjunction with 'Asim Bey al-Sa'id and Shukri al-Taji and an unspecified amount of land at Nes Tsiyona, both in the Jaffa subdistrict; for his involvement as a broker in land sales to Jews, see CO 733/222/97208, Part 2; interview between the High Commissioner and the Mufti of Jerusalem. (2, 8)
al-TAJI, Shukri	Representative to 7th Arab Congress from Ramle; member of the National Defense party.	Sold 5,000 dunams at Qubeiba in the Ramle subdistrict in 1922 in conjunction with 'Asim Bey al-Said and 'Abdul Rahman al-Taji; sold 2,600 dunams at Zarnuqa in 1926 and an unspecified amount of land at Nes Tsiyona all in the Jaffa subdistrict (Criminal Investigation Division Reports, 10 March 1933 and 7 July 1933, FO 371/16926). (2)
TUMA, Mikhail	Member of the Arab Strike Committee at Haifa.	Sold an unspecified amount of land at Carmel in the Haifa subdistrict. (2, 6)

Key to Sources:

1. CZA, S25/3366.
2. List of Palestinian Arabs, Personal Positions, and Location of Land sold to Jews, 1937, CZA, S25/3472.
3. List of Lands Purchased in the Sharon Plain after 1920, CZA, S25/7615.
4. CZA, S25/7620.
5. CZA, S25/7622.
6. List of Notable Palestinians Who Sold Land to Jews, 1937, CZA, S25/9783.
7. CZA, ISA, Box 3874/file 7.
8. Letter from the Acting Director of the Development Department to Chief Secretary, 24 March 1933, CO 733/230/17249.
9. List of Lands Purchased by PICA from Absentee Landlords and Owner Occupiers, CZA, S25/7615.
10. List of Lands Purchased by Jews and Submitted by Mr. Farrah of the Arab Executive to the Shaw Commissioners, ISA, Box 3542/G 612.
11. Land and Agricultural Development in Palestine Submitted by the Jewish Agency to Sir John Hope-Simpson, CZA, May 1930, p. 52.
12. CZA, S25/7621.

Note: The individuals mentioned in this list sold lands prior to, during, or after their involvement in the Palestinian national movement. Where possible, details concerning place, sum, and date are provided.

Appendix 4

Die Pächterfrage in Palästina—Das Verhältnis der Grossgrund besitzer
zu den Fellachen [The Tenants' Question in Palestine—Fellaheen and
Landlord Relationships]

1. Die gegenwärtigen Erhebungen beschränken sich (wenigstens soweit man die
Juden in Kenntnis gesetzt hat) auf die Frage: ob Pächter, d.h. Besitzlose oder
zumindest kushanlose Fellachen vom Boden vertrieben wurden und ob sie eine
Abfindung dafür erhielten.
2. "Vertreibung"—das Wort klingt sehr gruselig. Aber es verliert sofort diesen
Klang, wenn man sich vor Augen hält, dass hier ein zugrundeliegender ökono-
mischer Vorgang, nämlich die Aufforderung an einen Fellachen, künftig einen
anderen Boden zu bearbeiten, einen selbstverständlichen Bestandteil der arabischen Feudal- und Fellachen- Wirtschaft bildet, ohne jeglichen Zusammenhang
mit dem Zionismus und ohne dass man eine exzeptionelle Härte darin erblickt:
den auch der bestfundierte schuldenfreie Fellach-Bodenbesitzer erhält, sofern
sein Kushan ein Musha-Kushan ist, genau die gleiche Aufforderung alle zwei
Jahre und alle zwei Jahre, wird er durch Dorfbeschluss transplantiert nach einem
Boden, den er sich nicht aussuchen kann.
3. Vergleicht man das Los des Pächters, der durch jüdische Käufer mit Geld
abgefunden wird (nach der P.L.D.C.—Liste mit Beträgen bis zu £100.—mit dem-
jenigen des Musha-Fellachen, so ist es sehr leicht nachzuweisen, dass der Pächter
sich in der weitaus besseren Lage befindet. Da er gänzlich besitzlos ist, keinen
Boden, keinen Kushan besitzt, ist das Bargeld, dass er bekommt, ein gänzlich
unverhofftes Geschenk, ein Vermögenszuwachs, auf den er normalerweise nie-
mals hätte hoffen können und, bezogen auf seine Besitzlosigkeit ist ein Betrag
vor £50.–110. bereits ein sehr respektables Kapital. Im Gegensatz zum Musha-
Fellachen, der einen neuen Boden zugeteilt bekommt, ohne dass er Einfluss auf
die Auswahl hat und ohne dass er Bargeld investieren kann, kann sich der so
Beschenkte den Boden aussuchen und sein Geld hineinstecken.
4. Wenn die ganze Diskussion tatsächlich beschränkt bleiben würde auf die
Pächterfrage, so würde die Exekutive bei geschichter Argumentierung sicherlich
keinen schweren Stand haben. Aber es hiess erneut den Kopf in den Sand
stecken, wollte man annehmen, dass die Regierung sich damit zufrieden geben
würde. Es liegt ihr nicht daran, gerade den Pächtern zu helfen, sondern es liegt
ihr daran, den "Vertreibungsprozess" zu treffen, soweit er mit dem Zionismus in
Verbindung steht. Tatsache ist nun, dass dieser Vertreibungsprozess vorhanden
ist, weit über den Kreis der Pächter hinaus und wenn die Regierung durch die
Diskussion über die Pächterfrage nicht zu ihrem Ziel gelangt, so wird sie nicht
auf das Ziel verzichten, sondern die Fragestellung erweitern.
5. Nicht der Pächter ist das schutzbedürftige Opfer der Bodenkäufe, sondern der

Musha-Fellach und gerade über ihn wird bisher nicht gesprochen. Dadurch wird die Diskussion so unklar. Der Effendi und Bodenspekulant schwindelt dem Musha-Fellachen seinen Boden-Anspruch ab zu Preisen, die einen lächerlichen Bruchteil darstellen desjenigen Preises, zu dem er den Boden weiterverkäuft. Hier findet neben der Transplantierung, die, wie dargelegt, keine Härte ist, eine tatsächliche Exproprierung statt—genau das Gegenteil zu dem Fall des Pächters, der aus der Besitzlosigkeit zu Geldvermögen kommt. Und während der Pächter zum Gegenstand öffentlicher Fürsorge gemacht wird, muss der Musha-Fellach schweigen, weil er ja "freiwillig" verkauft hat und noch dazu an Araber.

6. Sowohl die Effendis wie die Exekutive wünschen nicht, dass man darüber spricht. Die Effendis fürchten, dass das ganze Fellach contra Effendi aufgerollt werden könnte, denn sie sind es ja, die die Kushane räubern, und sie können es nur kraft der schrankenlosen Versklavung, in der die Fellache der Feudalwirtschaft leben; und die Exekutive hofft, in der Pächterfrage einen halbwegs leichten Stand zu haben, den sie nicht gefährden will durch die Ausweitung der Diskussion auf Gebiete, wo wirkliche wirtschaftliche Härten unbestreitbar sind.

7. Zu dieser Befürchtung ist zunächst zu sagen, dass die Bauernlegerei und Kushanräuberei seitens der Effendis von jeher existiert hat und existiert ohne jeden Zusammenhang mit dem Zionismus. Nur so sind die Effendis zu Grossbesitz gekommen und Grossbesitz bedeutet in Palästina die einzige Basis für die wirtschaftliche und politische Machtposition der herrschenden Klassen. (Industriemacht und Kapitalmacht als Basis gibt es nicht.) Aber der Zionismus hat diese Entwicklung zumindest sehr gefördert, und wissentlich oder unwissentlich hat ihr Vorschub geleistet.

8. Es kommt jedoch nich darauf an, ob die Effendis oder die Exekutive zu einem stillschweigenden Übergehen dieser Frage tendieren, sondern darauf, was die Regierung tun wird. Es ist deutlich erkennbar, dass sie sich in Palästina auf die herrschenden Klassen stützen und seine Effendipolitik treiben will. Dass Passfield sich dazu hergab, diese Effendipolitik nicht nur zu stützen, sondern sie mit Ettikett Fellachenschutz zu popularisieren, zeigt nur, dass die konservativen Drahtzieher gut verstanden, ihn in eine Sache hineinzumanövrieren, die er nicht übersah, oder aber dass die imperialen Interessen, denen der Frieden mit den herrschenden Klassen heute unentbehrlich ist, stark genug waren, um sogar die Labour Party in ihren Dienst zu zwingen. Jedenfalls besteht kein Zweifel, dass alles was geschehen ist, nur im Interesse der Effendis geschah und wenn das schon hinter einem Labour-Kabinett geschehen konnte, so wird es unter dem neuen Tory Kabinett noch viel mehr der Fall sein.

9. Es ist also nicht ausgeschlossen, dass die Regierung im Einvernehmen mit den Effendis die Musha-Fellachen-Frage ausschalten wollte, und dass sie sich mit der relativen harmlosen Pächterfrage den Anschein eines Schutzaktes geben will die sie ernstlich gar nicht beabsichtigt. Und es ist ferner möglich, dass das neue Kabinett die ganze Aktion zu liquidieren wünscht.

Source: Heinrich Margulies of the Anglo-Palestine Bank to the Palestine Jewish Agency, 9 November 1931, CZA, S25/7619.

Notes

Abbreviations Used in the Notes

AE   Arab Executive
CAB   Cabinet
CID   Criminal Investigation Department of the Palestine Administration
CO   Colonial Office
CP   John Chancellor Papers
CS   Chief Secretariat of the Palestine Administration
CZA   Central Zionist Archives
FO   Foreign Office
HMG   His Majesty's Government
ISA   Israel State Archives
JA   Jewish Agency
JNF   Jewish National Fund
KH   Keren Hayesod (Jewish Foundation Fund)
KKL   Keren Kayment LeYisrael (Jewish National Fund)
LT   *Times* (London)
LTAO   Land Transfer Amendment Ordinance (1921)
LTO   Land Transfer Ordinance (1920)
NYT   *New York Times*
PICA   Palestine Colonization Association
PLDC   Palestine Land Development Company
POCAB   Protection of Cultivators Amendment Bill (proposed 1930)
POCO   Protection of Cultivators Ordinance (1929 and 1933)
PZE   Palestine Zionist Executive
SMC   Supreme Muslim Council
TALB   Transfer of Agricultural Land Bill (proposed 1930)
WA   Weizmann Archives

Chapter 1

1. Wingate, "Agriculture and Supplies in Palestine" (1917), FO; Endres, *Die wirtschaftliche Bedeutung Palästinas als Teiles der Turkei*, p. 14; U.S. Department of Commerce, *Palestine*, p. 14; Sawer, "A Review of the Agricultural Situation" (1923), CO; James N. Stubbs to Maurice Bennett of the Department of Lands, 21 June 1930, ISA, Box 3768/file 4; Bonne, *Palästina Land und Wirtschaft*, pp. 28–29; and Samuel, *A Lifetime in Jerusalem*, p. 65.

2. One metric dunam equals 1,000 square meters or one-quarter of an acre. A Turkish dunam was refined by the British Palestine administration on 15 Febru-

ary 1928 from its previous measure of 919.3 square meters to equal a metric or standard dunam. In actual practice before that date a dunam in Palestine ranged from 900 to 1,000 square meters. Hereafter dunam refers to one metric dunam unless otherwise noted.

3. Palestine Government, Department of Agriculture and Fisheries, *Review of the Agricultural Situation in Palestine* (1921), p. 7.

4. Ibid.

5. Oliphant, *Haifa, or Life in Modern Palestine*, pp. 59–60; Granott, *The Land System in Palestine*, p. 170; Hadawi, *Palestine*, p. 60; Cohen, *Palestine in the 18th Century*, p. 203; and Amiran, "The Pattern of Settlement," pp. 195–98.

6. Palestine Government, *Census for Palestine, 1931*, 2:282, table 16.

7. Ma'oz, *Ottoman Reform in Syria and Palestine*, pp. 4, 20.

8. Some of those families whose local prestige transcended the *tanzimat* in Palestine were the Abu-Gosh, al-Nashashibi, al-Husayni, and al-Alami families from the Jerusalem area; the al-Nimr, Tuqan, 'Abd al-Hadi, and al-Jayusi from the Nablus, Jenin, and Tulkarm areas; the al-Madi and al-Sa'adi families from the Haifa region; the al-Fahum family from Nazareth; the al-Tabari family from Tiberias; and the al-Khadra family from Safed. At unspecified times during the nineteenth century, the al-Baytar, al-Said, and al-Taji al-Faruqi families held local sway in the Jaffa region, and the al-Shawa family was dominant in the Gaza area. See Report of the Committee on Village Administration, pp. 5, 9, CO; Shimoni, *'Arave Eretz Yisrael*, pp. 213–20, 225–26, 228–31, 233, and 237. See also Hoexter, "The Role of Qays," pp. 249–312; Rustum, *The Royal Archives of Egypt*, pp. 13, 21–24, 73; and al-Barguthy, "Traces of the Feudal System," pp. 70–79.

9. For a list of Arab Executive representatives elected at these Palestinian congresses, see Porath, *The Emergence*, pp. 383–87. No comparative information was available for the *sanjaq* of Jerusalem, nor was any comparison made to identify those individuals who may have served in the Ottoman regime but who did not continue under the British administration. For data on administrative service under the Ottoman regime, see the Ottoman Government, *Salnahmah Vilayet Beirut* (1893, 1900, 1908). Palestinian-elite continuity is confirmed in a recent study by al-Hout, "The Palestinian Political Elite," pp. 85–111.

10. See Palestine Government, *Report on the Palestine Administration July 1920–December 1921*, p. 21; Davison, *Reform in the Ottoman Empire*, p. 148; Hoexter, "The Role of Qays," p. 285; and Porath, *The Emergence*, pp. 9–10.

11. Ma'oz, *Ottoman Reform in Syria and Palestine*, pp. 92–93.

12. A few examples will serve to illustrate but not conclusively prove that a few local families in comparison to the large rural population had a powerful hold on local administrative functions. Some individuals held more than one administrative position at the same time. Dr. Ibrahim Khouri in 1893 sat on the Municipal Council of Haifa, on the Chamber of Commerce for the *qaza* of Acre, and on the Judicial Committee of Nablus; Hafiz Tuqan from Nablus was a member of the local Agricultural Bank and the Finance Commission at the same time in 1893; 'Abd al-Rahman al-Hajj Ibrahim served on the local Education Committee of the *Beni Sha'b* (Tulkarm) *qaza* in 1900 and was an elected member of the local *majlis idara* in the same *qaza* in 1908; Joseph Samara from the

Tulkarm area was a *tabu* (land registry) official in 1893; 'Abdullah Samara served in the same post in 1900; and Ibrahim Samara was a member of the Court of the First Instance in 1908. In Jenin in 1893 Sa'id Mansur was a member of the Chamber of Commerce and the Land Commission; in 1900 he served on the local Education Committee and was president of the Chamber of Commerce, while in 1908 Hajj Mahmud Mansur was an elected member of the *majlis idara* of Nablus while also serving on the Commission for Procurement of Military Transportation; and Ali Mansur was an official on the Court of the First Instance at Nablus. Grouped according to subdistrict in the period from 1893 to 1908, the recurring family names in administrative positions were Dallal, al-Sa'adi Nuri, Sa'd, and 'Adlabi from Acre; al-Madi, Murad Salah, Khatib, Qatran, Abyad, and Khalil from Haifa; al-Fahum from Nazareth; Mustafa, Khalil, and al-Tabari from Tiberias; Qaddurah from Safed; al-Nimr, al-Tamimi, 'Abd al-Hadi, and al-Tahir from Nablus; Barkani from Nablus-Beni Sha'b; al-Nashif, 'Abd al-Rahman al-Hajj Ibrahim, Hamdan, Hanun, and al-Jayusi from *Beni-Sha'b* (Tulkarm); and 'Abd al-Hadi, 'Abushi, Taqqi al-Din, and Jarrar from Jenin. See Ottoman Government, *Salnahmah Vilayet Beirut*, 1311–1312 (1893), pp. 180, 187, 189–91; *Salnahmah Vilayet Beirut*, 1318 (1900), p. 221; and Ottoman Government, *Salnahmah Vilayet Beirut*, 1326 (1908), p. 356. This list should not be considered exhaustive, rather only representative of particular familial dominance in 1893, 1900, and 1908 for the *sanjaqs* of Acre and Nablus.

13. Lewis, *The Emergence of Modern Turkey*, p. 119; Karpat, "Land Regime," p. 86; Ma'oz, *Ottoman Reform in Syria and Palestine*, p. 162.

14. Stubbs to Bennett, 21 June 1930, ISA, Box 3768/file 4; League of Nations, *Permanent Mandates Commission: Minutes*, Fifth Session, Remarks by High Commissioner Samuel, 29 October 1924, p. 80.

15. Darwaza, *Hawla al-Harakah*, p. 70; Post, "Essays on Sects," p. 106.

16. Stubbs to Bennett, 21 June 1930, ISA Box 3768/file 4.

17. Commission of Inquiry—1929, Schedule F—State Domain, ISA, Box 3542/file G 612.

18. Stubbs, "Memorandum on Land in Palestine" (1930), ISA.

19. Palestine Government, *Annual Report for the Commissioner of Lands and Surveys for 1936*, p. 5, ISA.

20. See Lewis Y. Andrews to J. M. Martin, secretary of the Royal Commission, 6 March 1937, CO 733/345/75550/33/; 'Abd al-Hadi, "Official Reply to the French Reports," p. 34, CO; Layish, "The Muslim Waqf," p. 53; and Dowson, "Preliminary Study of Land Tenure in Palestine" (1924), p. 19, ISA.

21. Darwaza, *Hawla al-Harakah*, p. 74.

22. For an excellent and well-researched study on the Supreme Muslim Council, see Kupferschmidt, "The Supreme Muslim Council, 1921–1937"; see also Porath, *The Emergence*, pp. 194–207. Cf. Barron, *Mohammadan Wakfs*, esp. pp. 46–73.

23. Moghannam, "Palestine Legislation," p. 51; High Commissioner Arthur Wauchope to Phillip Cunliffe-Lister, 15 April 1932, CO 733/230/17249, Part 1; Land Settlement Commission Report (1921), p. 5, CO.

24. Land Settlement Commission Report (1921), p. 1, CO. A previous figure

established during the tenure of the Land Settlement Commission but not considered to be accurate estimated *mahlul* land at 116,789 Turkish dunams with 101,969 considered cultivable. See also Dowson, "Preliminary Study of Land Tenure" (1924), p. 26, ISA.

25. League of Nations, *Permanent Mandates Commission: Minutes*, Twentieth Session, Remarks by Mr. Young of the Palestine Administration, 10 June 1931, p. 88.

26. Dowson, "Preliminary Study of Land Tenure" (1924), p. 22, ISA. See also Alhassid, "Observations by a Land Officer" (1941), p. 8, CZA.

27. The political factors surrounding the assignment of these 302,000 dunams to Arab cultivators is discussed below in Chapter 2. Altogether there were a total of thirty-eight *jiftlik* villages in Palestine, of which twenty-two fell under the Beisan Agreement; five were in the Gaza subdistrict and the remaining eleven were scattered throughout the rest of the country. See note on an interview by Colonel Kisch with Mr. Stubbs, 14 March 1924, CZA, KKL5/1875. See Protection of Cultivators Ordinance, *Palestine Gazette*, 31 August 1933, Section 21.

28. Tannous, "The Arab Village Community," p. 532; Tannous, "Land Tenure," p. 177; Bonne, *Palästina Land und Wirtschaft*, p. 150; and Jaussen, *Coutumes des Arabes*, pp. 237–38. For a recent comprehensive assessment of the *musha'* village in late Ottoman Palestine, see Held, "The Effects of the Ottoman Land Laws."

29. Schulman, *Zur türkischen Agrarfrage*, pp. 64–66; Sir John Chancellor's Dispatch of 17 January 1930, CP Box 20/MF20/folio 50; and Dowson, "Preliminary Study of Land Tenure" (1924), pp. 35–37, ISA.

30. High Commissioner Wauchope to Cunliffe-Lister, Secretary of State for the Colonies, 15 April 1933, CO 733/230/17249, Part 1.

31. Land Settlement Commission Report (1921), p. 22, CO; Dowson, "Preliminary Study of Land Tenure" (1924), p. 37, ISA; Hilmi Husayni, Inspector of Lands of the Northern District, to Director of Lands, 14 July 1923, ISA, Box 3317/file 6. Cf. Klat, "Musha' Holdings," p. 18.

32. Notes by Sir John Chancellor on land legislation, n.d., CP, Box 20/MF 20, folio 22.

33. Great Britain, Cmd. 5479, *Palestine Royal Commission Report* (hereafter cited as Peel Report), p. 219.

34. Dr. Jacob Thon of Palestine Land Development Company to the General Secretary of the Zionist Executive, 15 January 1930, CZA, S25/10396.

35. Palestine Government, *Report by Mr C. F. Strickland* (hereafter cited as Strickland Report), p. 11; Dowson, "Preliminary Study of Land Tenure" (1924), p. 35, ISA; and Granott, *The Land System*, p. 218.

36. Palestine Government, *Report on the Palestine Administration July 1920–December 1921*, 1922, p. 9; Ashkenazi, *Tribus Semi-Nomades*, pp. 53–55; Wilson, *Peasant Life*, pp. 292–93; and al-Barguthy, "Traces of the Feudal System," p. 78.

37. League of Nations, *Permanent Mandates Commission: Minutes*, Ninth Session, Remarks by Colonel Symes of the Palestine Chief Secretariat, 29 June 1926, p. 164; Grant, *The People of Palestine*, p. 226; Oliphant, *Land of Gilead*,

pp. 127–29; Stracey, "Palestine," pp. 241–42; and Gerber, "HaMinhal Ha'Oto-mani," pp. 29–31.

38. See Money, "A History of Agricultural Loans" (1919), CO; Downie, "Memorandum on an Agricultural Bank" (1933), CO; and Ruppin, *Syrien als Wirtschaftsgebiet*, p. 113. The Agricultural Bank was first established by Imperial Decree in August 1888. See Quataert, "Dilemma of Development," pp. 210–27.

39. Post, "Essays on Sects," pp. 106–7; Oliphant, *Land of Gilead*, p. 320. Said al-Shawa's land in Gaza was estimated in 1919 to be approximately 50,000 Turkish dunams. He collected the tax from more than one village with it sometimes reaching 50 percent of the yield. See Gerber, "HaMinhal Ha'Otomani," p. 28.

40. Certificates of *mukhtars* and notables in communication in Moses Douk-han, Acting Director of Lands, to Chief Secretary, 30 October 1931, ISA, Box 3428/file 15; Land Registry Office, Hebron, to Director of Lands, 28 September 1921, ISA, Box 3314/file 16; and League of Nations, *Permanent Mandates Commission: Minutes*, Seventh Session, 18 September 1925, p. 174. For a fine evaluation of the *mukhtar*, see Baer, "The Office and Function," pp. 103–23.

41. Oliphant, *Haifa, or Life in Modern Palestine*, pp. 194–95.

42. Director of Agriculture to Civil Secretary, 7 August 1922, ISA, Box 3852/file 492; Palestine Government, *Report on the Palestine Administration July 1920–December 1921* (1922), p. 10.

43. Moshe Shertok of the Jewish Agency's Political Department to A. H. Webb, Legal Adviser to the Development Department, 13 March 1932, CZA, S25/7620.

44. League of Nations, *Permanent Mandates Commission: Minutes*, Fifteenth Session, Remarks by Mr. De Caix, 13 July 1929, p. 194.

45. Great Britain, Colonial no. 40, *Report by His Majesty's Government to the Council of the League of Nations for 1928* (1929), pp. 76–77; Note by Acting Treasurer W. J. Johnson to Lord Passfield, Secretary of State for the Colonies, 19 April 1929, CO 733/171/67275; and Commissioner of Lands to Acting Chief Secretary, 11 May 1931, CO 733/207/87275.

46. Minutes of an interview with High Commissioner Wauchope by Moshe Shertok, 16 June 1935, CZA Z4/4100; Wauchope to Malcolm MacDonald, Secretary of State for the Colonies, 6 July 1935, CO 733/290/75072. The Rural Property Tax Ordinance was not applicable to the Beersheba subdistrict or to the Huleh Concession area where the Commuted Tithe Ordinance continued in force. Special arrangements were made for villages that had detached lands and for those lands held in *musha'* ownership.

47. Peel Report, p. 1; Poliak, *Feudalism in Egypt*, p. 69; and Volney, *Voyage en Syrie*, 2:373–79.

48. Oliphant, *Haifa, or Life in Modern Palestine*, p. 181; Grant, *The People of Palestine*, p. 149; and Bonne, *Palästina Land und Wirtschaft*, p. 153. For a synopsis of all taxes paid or due in Palestine under the late Ottoman regime, see Auhagen, *Beiträge zur Kenntnis*, pp. 31–35.

49. See CO 733/70; Keith-Roach, Acting Northern District Commissioner, to

Chief Secretary, 5 February 1932, ISA Box 3891/file 2. For a summary of the deteriorating economic condition of the fellaheen population from 1931 to 1935, see Chapter 5 and Strickland, "Summary Relief" (1933), ISA.

50. Nawratzki, *Die Jüdische*, p. 74. For claims submitted under the Protection of Cultivators Ordinance of 1933, see ISA, Boxes 3922 and 2887–94. For evidence of the proletarianization process occurring simultaneously in areas of Syria, see Dabbagh, "Agrarian Reform in Syria," p. 2; for areas of Iraq, see Dowson, *An Inquiry into Land Tenure*, p. 20.

51. Palestine Government, *Census for Palestine, 1931*, 1:291–92.

52. Ibid., 2:282, table 14.

53. Ibid., 2:444–545 and 1:291.

54. Rizk, "Remarks on a Note" (1923), p. 1, ISA; "Land Tenure," p. 126. See also Granott, *The Land System*, pp. 73–75.

55. Mutris Hanna, Assistant Inspector of Lands, to Director of Land Registries, 15 April 1921, ISA, Box 3314/file 16; Interview with Reuven Alcalay, an official in the Press Bureau of the Palestine Secretariat, 3 September 1972; and Rizk, "Remarks on a Note" (1923), p. 1, ISA.

56. Harry Sacher of the Anglo-Palestine Bank to Norman Bentwich, Attorney General, 17 March 1925, CZA, Z4/771/file 11.

57. Stubbs to Director, Development Department, 10 February 1922, ISA, Box 3390/file 3.

58. Wyndham Deedes, Chief Secretary for the High Commissioner, to Winston Churchill, Secretary of State for the Colonies, 10 February 1922, CO 733/18/7979; Palestine Government, *Report on the Palestine Administration July 1920–December 1921* (1922), p. 10. At the bottom of every *kushan* issued by the Palestine administration it was clearly stated that the title was not guaranteed. See *NYT*, 13 December 1936.

59. Weulersse, *Paysan de Syrie*, p. 95; Klat, "The Origins," pp. 60–61; McDonnell, *Law Reports of Palestine, 1920–1933*, p. 13; and Frumkin, *Derech Shofet BeYerushalaim*, p. 305. Cf. League of Nations, *Permanent Mandates Commission: Minutes*, Fifth Session, 31 October 1924, p. 109.

60. Tibawi, *A Modern History*, p. 176. Tibawi could have been more accurate by stating that this process was carried out with "later" Zionists as well. Cf. Nawratzki, *Die Jüdische*, p. 74.

61. Dowson, "Notes on Abolition" (1928), p. 13, CO; "Land Tenure," p. 126.

62. Turkish Registers, ISA, Box 3527/files 8–14, Box 3546/files 39–41; Land Settlement Commission Report (1921), p. 27, CO; Memorandum on Lands of Uncertain Ownership Prepared for the Zionist Commission (July 1919), CZA, L18/125/file 31; Smilansky, *Prakim BeToldot*, 6:136; Memorandum on Points Arising (1936), CO; Protocols of the JNF Directorate Meeting, 12 November 1942, CZA, KKL 10; and Bentwich to Director of Revenues et al., 7 February 1922, CO 814/24.

63. See Dowson, "Notes on Land Tax" (n.d.), p. 10, ISA, and Lees, "Land Settlement" (1937), CO.

64. See Lowick, "Note on the Drayton Memorandum" (n.d.), ISA; "Problem of Ascertainment of Land Titles," prepared by Department of Lands for Edwin

Samuel's unpublished "The Administration of Palestine under British Mandate, 1920–1948"; and Alhassid, "Observations by a Land Officer" (1941), p. 31, CZA.

65. Land Department General, ISA, Box 3334/file 14/folio L/1703; Maps and Turkish Documents, ISA, Box 3542/G44/1; Zionist Commission to Major William Ormsby-Gore, 1 May 1918, CZA, S25/7432; League of Nations, *Permanent Mandates Commission: Minutes*, Fifth Session, Remarks by Mr. De Caix, 31 October 1924, p. 109; and Turkish Registers, ISA, Box 3527/files 8–14.

66. Chaim Weizmann to Herbert Samuel, 22 November 1919, WA; Political Report for November 1922, CO 733/28/63733; Political Report for January 1923, Minutes, by Sydney Moody of the Palestine Secretariat, CO 733/42/8933; Palestine Government, Department of Agriculture and Fisheries, *Review of the Agricultural Situation in Palestine* (1921), p. 7; Caplan, *Palestine Jewry*, p. 104; and Graves, *Land of Three Faiths*, p. 174. When Chaim Weizmann visited Arab merchants in Nablus in 1919, they asked him to see to it that a bank be established there to provide long-term credit for mortgages. Weizmann to Lord Curzon, Secretary of State for Foreign Affairs, 2 February 1920, WA.

67. Political Report for October 1922, CO 733/27/57552; Political Report for November 1922, CO 733/28/63733; and Director of Agriculture to Chief Secretary, 7 August 1922, ISA, Box 3852/file 492.

68. Commissioner of Lands to Acting Chief Secretary, 12 May 1931, CO 733/207/87275.

69. Klein, "Fellaheen of Palestine," p. 112. See also Arlosoroff, *Yoman Yerushalaim*, p. 29; Jarvis, "Southern Palestine," p. 206.

70. Political Report for January 1923, Minute Sheet, Note by Sydney Moody, 23 February 1923, CO 733/42/8933.

71. Tannous, "The Village Teacher," p. 236.

72. See Ettinger, "Land Ownership in Palestine" (1924), CZA; Shimoni, *'Arave Eretz Yisrael*, p. 52.

73. Ruppin, *Three Decades of Palestine*, p. 256.

74. Smilansky, "Jewish Colonization," p. 7; Ruppin to Moshe Kaplansky, 16 February 1930, CZA, S25/7453; Granott, *The Land System*, p. 39. Again, extreme caution must be exercised with the word "owned," which in certain areas of Beersheba subdistrict meant customary grazing rights without actual title or deed. The absence of reliable detailed landownership statistics from either Arab sources or from the Palestine Lands Department necessitates some dependence upon Jewish sources.

75. For this partial list of large landowners in 1919, see Appendix 1. It is our estimate that 500,000 metric dunams of land were held in Palestine by absentee (nonresident Palestinian) Arab landlords as of 1920.

76. Palestine Government, *Report of a Committee on the Economic Condition* (hereafter cited as Johnson-Crosbie Report), p. 1.

77. For various descriptions of the different types of lease agreements, see the Johnson-Crosbie Report, pp. 10–11; Bonne, *Palästina Land und Wirtschaft*, pp. 117–18; Firestone, "Production and Trade," pp. 185–209; and Firestone, "Crop-Sharing Economics," pp. 3–23.

78. Johnson-Crosbie Report, p. 11; Post, "Essays on Sects," p. 109; Chancel-

lor to Passfield, 27 December 1930, CO 733/199/87072. See also Land Tax Committee Report for 1932, ISA.

79. Stubbs to W. J. Miller, Gaza District Officer, 9 January 1931, ISA, Box 3921/file 1/folio 73; Ruppin, *Syrien als Wirtschaftsgebiet*, p. 64; and Johnson-Crosbie Report, p. 11. See also Note of an Interview with A. H. Webb by S. Horowitz of the Jewish Agency, 19 or 24 April 1932, CZA, S25/7620.

80. Stubbs to Bennett, 21 June 1930, ISA, Box 3728/file 4; Kisch to London Jewish Agency Executive, 1 May 1931, CZA, KKL 5/Box 536.

81. Kisch to Palestine Land Development Company, 12 September 1928, CZA, S25/7456; Moshe Shertok to Legal Assessor Development Department, 15 September 1932, CZA, S25/5799.

82. Marlowe, *Rebellion in Palestine*, pp. 106–8. Cf. Hourani, "Ottoman Reform," pp. 41–68.

83. Village Ghaffirs Ordinance, *Official Gazette*, no. 49, July 1921; Supreme Muslim Council and Awqaf Regulations, *Official Gazette*, January 1922; Palestine, Palestine Land Registries Instructions (1920–21), p. 7, ISA; Acting District Governor to Director of Land Registries, 26 September 1921; and A. Abramson, Chairman of the Land Commission, to Civil Secretary, 3 October 1921, ISA, Box 3705/file 2.

84. Great Britain, Colonial no. 12, *Report of His Majesty's Government on the Administration under Mandate of Palestine and Transjordan for the Year 1924* (1925), p. 8.

85. Goadby and Doukhan, *The Land Law of Palestine*, p. 206; *Official Gazette*, no. 171, 16 September 1926, p. 487.

86. Darwaza, *Hawla al-Harakah*, p. 74; Report for the 1936 Peel Commission by the Jewish Agency (1936), CZA; League of Nations, *Permanent Mandates Commission: Minutes*, Ninth Session, Remarks by Marquis Theodoli, Chairman, 22 June 1926, p. 101; and Hooper, *The Civil Law*, pp. 73–74.

87. S. G. Kermack, Assistant Director of Lands, to Attorney General, 21 March 1923, ISA, AG Box 755/file LS 79/23.

88. The Arab Executive also recognized that land transfers were not being registered. See its memorandum to the High Commissioner regarding the problems surrounding Jewish land and immigration, 1 December 1934, in al-Kayyali, ed., *Watha'iq al-Muqawama al-Filastiniyyah*, pp. 357–58. For some mention of unregistered Jewish National Fund purchases after 1940, see Lehn, "Zionist Land," pp. 90–91.

89. R. F. Jardine to Chief Secretary, 14 December 1947, ISA, Box 3541/file 14/folio 11.

90. An die Mitglieder des Directoriums des Keren Kayemet im Ausland, Bericht no. 4, 8 March 1923, CZA, KKL 5/file 1202; Hankin to Thon, 22 August 1913, CZA, L18/245/4; Mandel, "Turks, Arabs, and Jewish Immigration," p. 82; and Mandel, "Ottoman Practice," p. 35.

91. Harry Sacher to the Director of Lands, 23 May 1924, CZA, S25/631.

92. McDonnell, *Law Reports of Palestine, 1920–1933*, p. 36.

93. Correction of Land Registers Ordinance, 1926, *Official Gazette*, no. 151,

16 November 1925, Section 4. See also comments made by Mr. Sacher in comparison with the ordinance as issued, CZA, Z4/771/file II.

94. Cf. Ashbee, "The Palestine Problem," p. 530; Bonne, *Palästina Land und Wirtschaft*, pp. 15–16.

Chapter 2

1. Interview with Sherif Husayn at the British Residency, Jeddah, 18 July 1918, FO 686/10.

2. Kimche, *There Could Have Been Peace*, p. 180; see also Weizmann to David Eder, 4 December 1918, WA. Cf. Potter, "Origin of the System of Mandates," pp. 563–83. For a varied discussion of the historical controversy surrounding Palestine's place in the Husayn-McMahon correspondence, see Antonius, *The Arab Awakening*; Friedman, *The Question of Palestine*; Kedourie, *In the Anglo-Arab Labyrinth*; Tibawi, *Anglo-Arab Relations*; and Zeine, *The Struggle for Arab Independence*.

3. Gilbert F. Clayton, Chief Political Officer, Egyptian Expeditionary Force, to the Secretary of State for Foreign Affairs, 16 March 1918, FO 307/3405/3292. See also Wasserstein, *The British in Palestine*, pp. 34–58; Samuel, *Unholy Memories of the Holy Land*, pp. 27, 36, 54, 59–60.

4. Ro'i, "Nisyonotaihem Shel HaMosadot HaTziyoniyim," pp. 200–227; Yehoshua, "*Al-Munadi* Ha'Iton HaMuslami HaRishon," p. 212; Mandel, "Turks, Arabs, and Jewish Immigration," pp. 85–86; and *LT*, 21 September 1911.

5. Mandel, "Turks, Arabs, and Jewish Immigration," pp. 90, 95, 96; Alsberg, "HaShe'elah Ha'Aravit BeMediniyut," p. 168.

6. Ormsby-Gore, Political Officer in Charge of the Zionist Commission, to A. J. Balfour, Secretary of State for Foreign Affairs, 21 April 1918, FO 371/3395/86912; Clayton to Balfour, 16 March 1918, FO 307/3405/3292.

7. Weizmann to Lord Curzon, 2 February 1920, WA.

8. Weizmann's Interview with Faysal, 11 December 1918, in a letter from Weizmann to Sir Eyre Crowe, Under Secretary of State for Foreign Affairs, 16 December 1918, FO 371/3420.

9. Mandel, "Ottoman Policy and Restrictions," pp. 312–32; Mandel, "Ottoman Practice as Regards Jewish Settlement," pp. 33–46.

10. Weizmann to Lord Curzon, 2 February 1920, ISA, CS/file 6.

11. List of Lands Belonging to Palestine Colonization Association (1929–30), CZA. For a discussion of Jewish land purchase and agricultural settlement from 1908 to 1920, see Ruppin, *Pirke Hayay*, 2:114–39.

12. Gurevich and Gertz, *Jewish Agricultural Settlement in Palestine*, p. 35. For a complete summary of Jewish land purchases prior to World War I, see Doukhan-Landau, *HaHevrot HaTziyoniot Lerchishat*.

13. Memorandum on the Land Question in Palestine (1919), CZA.

14. Mandel, "Ottoman Practice as Regards Jewish Settlement," p. 42.

15. Ruppin, *Three Decades in Palestine*, pp. 35–65.

16. [Zionist] Proposals to the British Government for the Solution of the Land Question (1919), CZA. The notion of close settlement seems to have been first suggested by Herbert Samuel in early 1919. See Herbert Samuel Archives, ISA, file 5, esp. Samuel to Balfour, 6 May 1919. See also Weizmann to his wife Vera, 31 January 1919, WA.

17. Memorandum on Land to be Acquired in Palestine (1919), CZA.

18. Boustany, *The Palestine Mandate*, pp. 86–87.

19. League of Nations, *Permanent Mandates Commission: Minutes*, Remarks by Mr. Ormsby-Gore, Secretary of State for the Colonies, 13 August 1937, Twenty-second Meeting, p. 78.

20. Ormsby-Gore to Balfour, 7 April 1918, FO 371/3394/83691.

21. Israel Sieff, Secretary of the Zionist Commission, to Ormsby-Gore, 1 May 1918, CZA, S25/7432; Ormsby-Gore to Sir Gilbert Clayton, 20 May 1918, FO 371/33995/99964; and Thon to Zionist Commission, 6 May 1918, CZA, Z4/737.

22. Palestine Land Department, Memorandum on the Reopening of the Land Registries (1919–20), ISA. Palestine Government, *Proclamations, Ordinances, and Notices*, p. 12.

23. Transfer of Land Ordinance no. 2, 1921, *Official Gazette*, 15 April 1921.

24. Samuel to J. H. Thomas, Secretary of State for the Colonies, 8 February 1924, CO 733/64.

25. S. S. Davis, Treasurer of Palestine, to Thomas, 3 July 1924, CO 733/70; Symes, "Political Report on the Northern District" (1923), CO.

26. Weizmann to Samuel, 6 November 1918, WA; Thon to the Zionist Commission, 6 May 1918, CZA, Z4/737; Sieff to Ormsby-Gore, 1 May 1918, CZA, S25/7432; and Granovsky, *Land Policy in Palestine*, pp. 17–85.

27. Felix Frankfurter, member of the Zionist delegation to the Peace Conference, to Harry Friedenwald, Acting Chairman of the Zionist Commission, 25 April 1919, CZA, S25/7432.

28. Weizmann to Sir Ronald Graham, Assistant Under Secretary of State for Foreign Affairs, 13 July 1919, FO 371/4225/73497 or WA.

29. Weizmann to Nahum Sokolow, head of the Zionist delegation to the Peace Conference, 11 July 1919, WA.

30. Ibid.; Graves, *Land of Three Faiths*, p. 174.

31. Chief Administrator of O.E.T.A. South to Chairman of the Zionist Commission, 1 September 1919, CZA, S25/7432.

32. Weizmann to Gerald Spicer of the Foreign Office, 6 September 1919, CZA, S25/3472.

33. Weizmann to Louis Brandeis, 29 October 1918, WA. See also FO 371/4171/98705 and FO 371/4214/37389; and Friedenwald to Money, 20 May 1919, CZA, S25/7432.

34. Great Britain, *Parliamentary Debates*, House of Lords, Remarks by Lord Curzon, 29 June 1920, 5th Series, vol. 40; General Bols, Chief Administrator of O.E.T.A. South, to the Secretary of State for Foreign Affairs, 2 June 1920, FO 371/5114/6914.

35. Moghannam, "Palestine Legislation," pp. 47–54.

36. Minute by O. A. Scott of the Foreign Office, 8 August 1919, FO 371/

4226/73497. See also Land Department General, ISA, Box 3314/file 14.

37. Bentwich, "Memorandum on Land Transfer for the Military Governors" (1919), ISA.

38. Minute by O. A. Scott, 2 February 1920, FO 371/4226/73497. See also FO 371/5032/E 18/6.

39. Curzon to the War Office, 6 March 1920, FO 371/5032/E 18/6.

40. Land Transfer Ordinance, *Official Gazette*, 1 October 1920.

41. See ISA, Box 3314/file 16 for monthly statistics for 1920–21. See also Minute Sheet, 24 November 1921, CO 733/7/58411.

42. *Al-Karmil*, ? November 1920, vol. 7, no. 673.

43. Eder to Bentwich, 16 July 1920, CZA, Z4/1260/V.

44. Ibid.

45. *Al-Karmil*, ? November 1920, vol. 7, no. 673. See also ISA, Box 3744/file R525.

46. *Al-Karmil*, ? November 1920, vol. 7, no. 673.

47. Samuel to Secretary of State for the Colonies, 22 November 1921, CO 733/7/58411.

48. Stubbs to Chief Secretary, 23 November 1922, ISA, Box 3314/file 16.

49. Rizk, "Memorandum on the Land Transfer Ordinance" (1921), ISA. See also Stubbs to the Chief British Representative in Amman, 24 September 1924, ISA, Box 3314/file 16.

50. Minutes of the Land Commission Meeting, 9 November 1920, ISA, CS/G57.

51. Minute by Mr. Mills, n.d., CO 733/7/58411.

52. Great Britain, Cmd. 1540, *Palestine Disturbances in May 1921*, p. 51.

53. Memorandum for the Cabinet by the Secretary of State, June 1921, CO 733/13/29675; Peel Report, pp. 34–37; Wasserstein, *The British in Palestine*, p. 102.

54. See Samuel, *Unholy Memories of the Holy Land*, p. 87; and Caplan, *Palestine Jewry*, pp. 104–5.

55. Churchill to Samuel, 2 December 1921, CO 733/7/58411; PZE to Adolf Böhm, 3 July 1922, CZA, Z4/736.

56. Samuel to Churchill, 9 December 1921, CO 733/8/62654; League of Nations, *Permanent Mandates Commission: Minutes*, Fourth Session, Remarks by Mr. Keith-Roach, 20 June 1924, p. 89; Downie, "Note on the Palestine Land Problem" (1935), CO; and Summary of a discussion by the *Vaad Leumi* (National Council) Executive with Sir John Hope-Simpson, 5 June 1930, CZA, S25/412.

57. Transfer of Land Amendment Ordinance, no. 2, 1921, *Official Gazette*, 15 December 1921, p. 8.

58. Minute Sheet, 24 November 1921, CO 733/7/58411.

59. C. F. Cox to Chief Secretary, 8 November 1922, ISA, Box 3334/file 10.

60. Some agricultural laborers who also cultivated their own holdings were entitled to receive monetary compensation under the ordinance's definition of tenant. See Protection of Cultivators Ordinance, 1929, *Official Gazette*, 16 June 1929, pp. 710–14.

61. A feddan varied from time to time and from place to place in Palestine

from 100 to sometimes more than 250 dunams. For compensatory amounts paid at Wadi Hawarith, see CZA, S25/7620.

62. Palestine Land Development Company to Palestine Zionist Executive, 5 May 1925, S25/685; Great Britain, Cmd. 3530, *Report of the Commission on the Palestine Disturbances of August 1929* (hereafter cited as Shaw Report), 1930, p. 115.

63. Shaw Report, p. 115. See also Previous Arab Occupiers of Land Acquired by Jews (1929), CZA. For a full discussion of the intricacies involved in the Jewish National Fund/Palestine Land Development Company purchase of land at Malul from the Sursocks, see *A Survey of Palestine*, 1:299–308.

64. Political Report for December 1921, CO 733/8/1677; Political Report for January 1922, CO 733/18/6937.

65. See Political Report for March 1921, CO 733/2/21698/folio 77; McDonnell, *Law Reports of Palestine, 1920–1923*, p. 458.

66. Zionist Commission to Ormsby-Gore, 1 May 1918, CZA, S25/7432. See also Instructions to the Land Commission, 1920, ISA.

67. Land Settlement Commission Report (1921), CO.

68. C. H. Cox to Assistant Civil Secretary, 23 February 1921, ISA, Box 3599/file G41.

69. Political Report for February 1921, CO 733/1/13449; Political Report for March 1921, CO 733/2/21698; and Dinier et al., eds., *Sefer Toldot Hahaganah*, vol. B, pt. 1, p. 64.

70. Samuel to Churchill, 23 July 1921, CO 733/4/38832.

71. For the text of the Beisan Agreement, see French, *First Report*, Appendix III B, pp. 40–43.

72. ISA, Box 3548/file 1.

73. For detailed information on size of transfers and some of the transferees, see CO 733/155/517312 and CO 733/345/75550/33F. See also Samuel, *Unholy Memories of the Holy Land*, p. 87.

74. ISA, Box 3542/G419/file 3.

75. Ibid.

76. Report of the Ghor Mudawara Demarcation Commission (1932), ISA.

77. Report by the Committee on State Domain on the Ghor Mudawara Agreement (1940), ISA.

78. Max Nurock of the Palestine Secretariat to the Commissioner of Lands, 8 April 1930, ISA, Box 3555/file 1.

79. Galilee District Commissioner's Office to Director of Land Registration, 8 July 1940, ISA, Box 3548/file 4.

80. Minutes of an interview with the High Commissioner by the Palestine Zionist Executive, 20 November 1922, 4 December 1922, and 11 December 1922, CZA, S25/610; Political Report for November 1922, CO 733/28/63733.

81. Mr. Bawley of the Palestine Zionist Executive's Colonization Department to Sacher, 10 January 1929, CZA, Z4/3450/III. Although Lehn, in "Zionist Land: The Jewish National Fund," p. 40, paraphrased Granott, *Agrarian Reform*, pp. 34–35, there is no evidence to suggest that the enunciation and then pursuit of land-purchase policy was coincidental to national objectives. Confirmation of this point was made through a systematic investigation of the minutes

of the Jewish National Fund Directorate and the files of the Political Department of the Palestine Zionist Executive.

82. Granovsky, *Land Policy in Palestine*, p. 31.

83. Bein, *The Return to the Soil*, p. 333.

84. Kisch to the Palestine Zionist Executive, 16 December 1928, CZA, Z4/3450/III.

85. See Schedules B, C, and D prepared for Hope-Simpson in ISA, Box 3542/G 612.

86. The listings made here and in Appendix 3 should not be considered exhaustive or complete. For further information regarding the participation of the individuals mentioned above in Palestinian Arab politics, see Porath, *The Emergence*.

87. *Al-Sirat al-Mustaqim*, 22 May 1930.

88. McDonnell, *Law Reports of Palestine 1920–1933*, p. 69.

89. List of Palestinian Arabs, Personal Positions, and Location of Land Sold to Jews, 1937, CZA, S25/3472; List of Notable Palestinians Who Sold Land to Jews, 1937, CZA, S25/9783.

90. Ibid.

91. Bericht zum Mitglieder im Ausland, 1 September 1924, CZA, KKL 5/file 1203.

92. It is presumed that the amount here is in Turkish dunams. See Smilansky, *Prakim BeToldot HaYishuv*, 6:145. See also CZA, S25/3472 and S25/9783.

93. Hankin to Palestine Land Development Company, 3 December 1929, CZA, Z4/344/III; Dinier et al., eds., *Sefer Toldot Hahaganah*, vol. B, pt. 3, p. 1174; and Exchange of Correspondence between the Tulkarm District Officer and Assistant Director of Development, 7 and 12 January 1933, ISA, Box 3372. In a gesture of communal concern, Mrs. 'Awni 'Abd al-Hadi took clothes to the Bedouin at Wadi Hawarith in December 1930 (*Filastin*, 16 December 1930).

94. See Hankin's remarks to Hope-Simpson, 17 June 1930, CZA, KKL 5/Box 536; Committee Report to Chief Secretary on Means to Prohibit Land Purchase, 10 September 1937, CO 733/329/75072/folio 16.

95. Great Britain, Colonial no. 15, *Palestine: Report of the High Commissioner on the Administration of Palestine, 1920–1925* (1925), p. 32; Land Acquisition (1934), CZA; and Epstein, "The Political Significance of Land Purchase" (1937), CZA.

96. Yehoshua Hankin turned down a "small" offer of 800 dunams in October 1922 that was tendered by Isa al-Isa, the editor of *Filastin*. See letter from Hankin to Palestine Land Development Company, 18 October 1922, CZA, A238/file 14.

97. Epstein, "The Political Significance of Land Purchase" (1937), CZA; Minutes of the Jewish National Fund Directorate Meeting, 12 December 1940, CZA, KKL 10.

98. See CO 733/16/24124 and Appendix 3.

99. See Remarks by 'Awni 'Abd al-Hadi, 10 March 1933, CZA, S25/7597.

100. See Appendix 3.

101. See *al-Liwa*, 5 January 1936.

102. See Appendix 3.

103. *Al-Liwa*, 14 May 1936.
104. See Notes on Land Sales, CZA, KKL 5/1433.
105. See, for example, Report for the 1936 Peel Commission by the Jewish Agency (1936), p. 4, CZA; Minutes of the Jewish National Fund Directorate Meeting, 14 December 1938, CZA, KKL 5/Box 1048; Gaza Land Settlement Officer to Director of Land Settlement, 11 July 1942, ISA, Box 3548/file 2/folio 67.
106. L. Ussishkin, "Notes on the Protection of Cultivators Ordinance, 1933–36" (1936), CZA.
107. See Stein, "Legal Protection and Circumvention of Rights," pp. 231–60.
108. Kisch to Palestine Zionist Executive, 2 February 1931, CZA, S25/6552.
109. S. Tolkovsky of the Palestine Land Development Company to Kisch, 22 January 1930; Kisch to Zionist Office London, 24 January 1930, CZA, S25/5789; Extract of a letter from Heinrich Margulies to Felix Rosenblueth, 5 February 1930, CZA Z4/3450/V; and Interview with Heinrich Margulies, 11 May 1973, Jerusalem, Israel.
110. For just a few examples confirming the *mukhtars*' or *shaykhs*' receipt of money in the land-sale process to Jews, see ISA, Box 2637/G536; ISA, Box 3568/file 5; CZA, S25/9581 and Officer Administering the Government to Ormsby-Gore, 24 June 1937, CO 733/327/75049.
111. Minutes of an interview with the Director of Development by Chaim Arlosoroff, 8 January 1932, CZA, A202/119.
112. Interview at the Palestine Land Development Company with Sir John Hope-Simpson, 17 June 1930, CZA, KKL 5/Box 536; Executive Council Decisions for 24 December 1934, CO 814/30, and March 1936, CO 814/32; and Minutes of the Jewish National Fund Directorate Meeting, 25 December 1940, CZA, KKL 10.
113. Bein, *The Return to the Soil*, p. 404; Ashbel, *Shishim Shnot Haksharat HaYishuv*, pp. 81–88; Contract de Ventre entre les sous signées Tayan et Hankin, CZA, KKL 5/Box 363/file 500.
114. Hankin to Palestine Land Development Company, 11 March 1932, and Moshe Shertok, Secretary of the Political Department of the Jewish Agency, to A. H. Webb, Legal Adviser to the Development Department, 13 March 1932, CZA, S25/7620.
115. Judgment of the Court, 11 June 1930, CO 733/190/77182; McDonnell, *Law Reports of Palestine, 1920–1933*, pp. 471–73.
116. Minutes of the Executive Council of the Palestine Government, 17 January 1930 and 7 February 1930, CO 814/26.
117. Max Nurock to the Jewish National Fund, 29 December 1933; Lease Agreement between the Government and the Wadi Hawarith Arabs, ISA, Box 3372/jacket 2/folio 17.
118. Tulkarm Assistant District Commissioner to Samaria District Commissioner, 28 October 1939, Box 3372/jacket 4/folio 45.

Chapter 3

1. Great Britain, Colonial no. 146, *Report by His Majesty's Government to the Council of the League of Nations for the Year 1936* (1937), p. 236.
2. Porath, *The Palestinian Arab National Movement, 1929–1939*, pp. 20–79.
3. Very convincing evidence for this assumption is offered by Ofer, "The Role of the High Commissioner."
4. John Chancellor to Lord Passfield, Secretary of State for the Colonies, 17 January 1930, CO 733/183/77050, Part 1.
5. Sheffer, "Policy Making and British Policies," p. viii. See also typescript memoirs of Sir John Chancellor, CP, Box 18/218.
6. League of Nations, *Permanent Mandates Commission: Minutes*, Fifteenth Session, Remarks by Sir John Chancellor, 5 July 1929, p. 79.
7. Chancellor to his son, Christopher, 12 October 1929, 3 November 1929, and 11 November 1929, CP, Box 16/3; Arlosoroff, *Yoman Yerushalaim*, p. 21.
8. Chancellor to Christopher, 12 February 1930, CP, Box 16/3.
9. Chancellor to Christopher, 12 October 1929, CP, Box 16/3.
10. Chancellor to Christopher, 11 November 1929, CP, Box 16/3; Mossek, *Palestine Immigration Policy*, pp. 17–31.
11. Mossek, *Palestine Immigration Policy*, pp. 17–31; Chancellor to Christopher, 21 February 1930, CP, Box 16/3.
12. Chancellor to Passfield, 17 January 1930, CO 733/183/77050, Part 1.
13. Chancellor to Christopher, 15 January 1930, CP, Box 16/3.
14. Ibid.
15. Transfer of Agricultural Land Bill, 29 March 1930, p. 2, CO 733/182/77050, Part 1.
16. Typescript memoirs of Sir John Chancellor, CP, Box 18/170.
17. The only existing provision required that a landlord give his tenant written notice of a rent increase. If the tenant refused, then the landlord only had to give one year's notice for the tenant to quit the land he was working. Protection of Cultivators Ordinance of 1929, Section 4, *Official Gazette*, 6 June 1929. The notion of setting the tenant up against his landlord was given an additional airing by Lewis French and in the Protection of Cultivators Ordinance of 1933.
18. Shuckburgh to Chancellor, 24 January 1930, CP, Box 16/4; see Sheffer, "Intentions and Results," p. 45.
19. Memorandum by the Attorney General on the Transfer of Agricultural Land Bill and Protection of Cultivators Amendment Bill, 1930, p. 2, CO 733/182/77050, Part 1.
20. Memorandum by the Attorney General on the Transfer of Agricultural Land Bill, 1930, p. 4, CO 733/182/77050, Part 1.
21. Observations by the Acting Chief Secretary on the Transfer of Agricultural Land Bill, 1930, p. 3, CO 733/182/77050, Part 1.
22. Abramson to Chief Secretary, 21 February 1930, ISA, Box 3380/file 2.
23. Minute by Mr. Bennett, 3 February 1930, ISA, Box 3380/file 2.
24. Hoofien, "Immigration and Prosperity," pp. 30–31; Great Britain, *Parliamentary Debates*, Commons, 17 November 1930, Remarks by Lloyd George, 5th Series, vol. 245; and *Manchester Guardian*, 3 April 1930.

25. League of Nations, *Permanent Mandates Commission: Minutes*, Twenty-ninth Session, 8 June 1936, p. 140.

26. *LT*, 2 September 1929, 4 September 1929, 2 April 1930; *NYT*, 2 April 1930.

27. Shaw Report, p. 158. In his minority report, Mr. Snell, the Labour M.P. on the Shaw Commission, attributed a greater share of the responsibilities for the disturbances to the mufti.

28. *LT*, 2 April 1930.

29. Shaw Report, p. 161.

30. Ibid., pp. 124, 162.

31. *LT*, 4 April 1930; *LT*, 15 May 1930.

32. *LT*, 15 May 1930.

33. Great Britain, *Parliamentary Debates*, Commons, 3 April 1930, 5th Series, vol. 238.

34. Great Britain, Cmd. 3582, *Palestine Statement with regard to British Policy*, p. 889.

35. See Rose, *The Gentile Zionists*.

36. Conclusions of the Cabinet Meeting, 2 April 1930, CAB 23/63-1883; Chancellor to Lord Southborough, 12 April 1930, CP, Box 16/5; and Shuckburgh to Chancellor, 30 April 1930, CO 733/191/722/11.

37. Rose, *The Gentile Zionists*, p. 8.

38. Kisch, *Palestine Diary*, p. 295.

39. Passfield to Hope-Simpson, 4 April 1930, CO 733/191/77211.

40. Extracts for notes of a meeting of the Secretary of State with the Arab Delegation, 6 May 1930, CP, Box 15/3.

41. Minute Sheets, Memorandum 42, n.d., CO 733/185/77072.

42. Arabic Press Summary, CO 733/185/77072, Part 2.

43. Kisch to Weizmann, 20 May 1930, CZA, S25/5791; Passfield to Chancellor, 31 May 1930, CP, Box 13/4; and Hankin to Hope-Simpson, 14 July 1930, CZA, KKL 5/Box 536. A prime Zionist advocate of Transjordan settlement of Palestine Arabs was Pinhas Ruthenberg, the recipient of the Palestine Electric Company Concession. See CO 733/185/77072. See also *LT*, 6 May 1930.

44. Note by Mr. Campbell, Colonial Office official, 8 April 1930, CO 733/191/77211. See also Rose, *The Gentile Zionists*, pp. 8–9.

45. *LT*, 5 May 1930.

46. Rose, *The Gentile Zionists*, p. 9; see Minute by Shuckburgh, 6 May 1930, CO 733/191/77221.

47. Rose implies that Chancellor instigated the immigration suspension, but Chancellor's letter to Passfield of 7 May 1930 suggests otherwise. There is little doubt that Chancellor was the philosophical parent of this notion. See CP, Box 13/4. See also extract from Note of Proceedings of Meeting of the Prime Minister and Secretary of State with the Arab Delegation, 1 May 1930, CP, Box 15/3.

48. Chancellor to Passfield, 2 May 1930, CP, Box 13/4.

49. Passfield to Chancellor, 27 May 1930, CP, Box 13/4.

50. Chancellor to Passfield, 2 June 1930, CP, Box 13/4.

51. Passfield to Hope-Simpson, 17 April 1930, CO 733/191/77211; Passfield to Chancellor, 31 May 1930, CP, Box 13/4.

52. League of Nations, *Permanent Mandates Commission: Minutes*, Twentieth Session, Remarks by Dr. Drummond Shiels, accredited representative of HMG, 16 June 1931, p. 91.

53. Hope-Simpson recommended himself to be head of the Development Department, a department whose formation was suggested in his report. Hope-Simpson wanted the Director of the Development Department to succeed Chancellor as High Commissioner. See Hope-Simpson to Chancellor, 29 September 1930, CP, Box 16/6.

54. Land and Agricultural Development in Palestine (1930), CZA.

55. Second Meeting of the Colonization and Immigration Committee, 26 May 1930, CZA, KKL 5/Box 536.

56. Revised Text of the Document Handed to the Colonial Office by the Jewish Agency, 26 May 1930, CZA, S25/1. For further details regarding overtures made by Zionists for temporary self-imposed land-purchase restraints, see CO 733/185/77072, Part 1.

57. Bodenpolitik im Zusammenhang mit den eventuellen Beschränkungen der Bodensaktionen seitens der Regierung (Land policy in relation to the eventual limitation of land activities by the administration), 18 June 1930, CZA, S25/1946; Memorandum by Dr. Granovsky on Hope-Simpson's Visit, 7 July 1930, CZA, KKL 5/Box 536.

58. Land and Agricultural Development in Palestine (1930), CZA; Memorandum on Land Purchase (1930), CZA.

59. Kisch to JA Executive, 28 February 1930, and 6 June 1930, CZA, S25/5791. See also Bloom, "Yahasim shel 'Arave Eretz-Yisrael," pp. 141–46; Passfield to Chancellor, 31 May 1930, CP, Box 13/4; and *NYT*, 23 November 1930.

60. Bonne, *Palästina Land und Wirtschaft*, p. 117.

61. Alsberg, "HaShe'elah Ha'Aravit BeMediniyut," p. 177; Weizmann to Samuel, 6 November 1918, WA.

62. Report of the Committee to Advise on the Protection of Agricultural Tenants (1927), p. 9, ISA.

63. Memorandum on a Proposal Laid before the Royal Commission (1937), CO.

64. Land Settlement Policy (Continued) Protection of Cultivators (1929–30), CZA. Farago, *Palestine at the Crossroads*, pp. 123, 171–72.

65. Great Britain, *Parliamentary Debates*, House of Lords, 20 May 1925, 5th Series, vol. 61.

66. Ruppin to Weizmann, 30 January 1930, CZA, Z4/3450: "I fear that the result of such an investigation will in the end show that there is generally only a little unoccupied and unworked cultivable land in Palestine." Heinrich Margulies confirmed Ruppin's estimate and fear that another inquiry would find only a small amount of unowned and unworked land. Margulies was a former employee of the Anglo-Palestine Bank involved in the late 1920s in land purchase and land settlement. Interview with Heinrich Margulies, 11 May 1973, Beit Hakerem, Jerusalem, Israel. See also Protocol of First Meeting of Committee Preparing Material for the Development Scheme, Remarks by Yehoshua Hankin, 27 October 1931, CZA, KKL 5/Box 688.

67. In 1914, Dr. Ruppin suggested that land be purchased in the environs of

Homs and Alleppo for the transfer of Palestinian fellaheen from whom land was purchased. See Alsberg, "HaShe'elah Ha'Aravit BeMediniyut," p. 177.

68. Memorandum by Dr. Granovsky, 7 July 1930, CZA, KKL 5/Box 536. See also CO 733/185/77072, Part 2; Hope-Simpson to Secretary of State, 2 June 1930, CP, Box 13/4.

69. Minutes of the Second Meeting of the Colonization and Immigration Committee, 26 May 1930, CZA, KKL 5/Box 536; Kisch to Dr. Frankel, 20 May 1930, CZA, S25/5791; and Hankin to Hope-Simpson, 14 July 1930, CZA, KKL 5/Box 536.

70. Arlosoroff to Selig Brodetsky, member of the JA in London, 15 September 1931, CZA, S25/5796; Arlosoroff, *Yoman Yerushalaim*, p. 49.

71. Kisch to Hoofien, 29 May 1930, CZA, S25/5791.

72. Minutes of the Meeting of the Colonization and Immigration Committee, 19 June 1930, CZA, KKL 5/Box 536. The reference to land sales by villagers refers to the sale of *musha'*-held shares, which by 1930 were of considerable import to Jewish land acquisition. See also Kisch, *Palestine Diary*, p. 308.

73. Hope-Simpson's visit to the Jewish National Fund, 17 June 1930, CZA, S25/4112.

74. Hope-Simpson to Chancellor, 30 June 1930, CP, Box 16/6.

75. Hope-Simpson's visit to the Jewish National Fund, 17 June 1930, CZA, S25/4112.

76. Hope-Simpson to Lord Passfield, 18 August 1930, CAB 24/215.

77. Great Britain, Cmd. 3686, *Palestine: Report on Immigration, Land, Settlement and Development* (hereafter cited as Hope-Simpson Report), pp. 21–22.

78. Only four of the five plains regions had been partially surveyed. Percentages of the total land areas surveyed were: coastal plain, 88 percent; Acre plain, 30 percent; plain of Esdraelon, 71 percent; Huleh plain, zero percent; and plain of Jordan, 75 percent. No survey existed for the uninhabited hills, uninhabited hill wilderness, Beersheba area, or southern desert. More than three-quarters of Mandatory Palestine was not as yet surveyed. See Hope-Simpson Report, Appendix 3, p. 159.

79. Chancellor to Passfield, 17 January 1930, CO 733/182/77050.

80. Hope-Simpson Report, p. 22.

81. Ibid., p. 23.

82. Kisch, *Palestine Diary*, p. 373; Sykes, *Crossroads to Israel*, pp. 144–45; and Laqueur, *A History of Zionism*, p. 492.

83. Great Britain, *Parliamentary Debates*, Commons, Remarks by Sir George Jones, 17 November 1930, 5th Series, vol. 245; Ruppin, *Three Decades in Palestine*, p. 206; and Interview with David Ben-Gurion, then a labor leader in Palestine, *NYT*, 30 November 1930.

84. League of Nations, *Permanent Mandates Commission: Minutes*, Twentieth Session, Remarks by Dr. Drummond Shiels, HMG-accredited representative to the Permanent Mandates Commission, 15 June 1931, p. 75.

85. Great Britain, Colonial no. 104, *Report by His Majesty's Government to the Council of the League of Nations for the Year 1934* (1935), pp. 51–53; League of Nations, *Permanent Mandates Commission: Minutes*, Twenty-seventh Session, 5 June 1935, p. 51.

86. Peel Report, p. 238.

87. Sami Hadawi, *Village Statistics—1945*, p. 79.

88. Appendix 12 of the Hope-Simpson Report was taken directly from the sheet entitled "State Domain," which appears in the Commission of Inquiry of 1929, ISA, Box 3542/file G 612. Both sets of statistics carefully stated that the "areas shown are as registered but are only approximately correct as they have not been surveyed."

89. In 1936, the Palestine administration estimated state land as 1,036,000 metric dunams (Peel Report, p. 244). The increase in the area considered to be state land from 1930 to 1936 is attributable to the ongoing cadastral survey in Palestine that showed areas larger than previously registered under the Ottoman regime. By the end of 1945, the area considered state land was believed to be 1,542,680 dunams. See High Commissioner MacMichael to G. H. Hall, Secretary of State for the Colonies, 30 November 1945, CO 733/75072/9/1945.

90. Hope-Simpson Report, pp. 56–60.

91. Ibid., p. 59.

92. Shaw Report, pp. 120–21; Hope-Simpson Report, p. 142.

93. Hope-Simpson Report, p. 142.

94. Ibid., p. 143.

95. Shaw Report, p. 162.

96. League of Nations, *Permanent Mandates Commission: Minutes*, Seventeenth Session, Remarks by M. Orts, Permanent Mandates Commission Member, 9 June 1930, p. 78.

97. Hope-Simpson to the Secretary of State for the Colonies, 2 June 1930, CP, Box 13/4; Interview of Dr. Ruppin with the Chief Secretary, 13 November 1930, CZA, S25/9843.

98. Johnson-Crosbie Report, pp. 20–21.

99. Hope-Simpson Report, p. 142.

100. Using the multiplier of 5.7 persons per family, as indicated by the Johnson-Crosbie Report statistic, and a total Arab rural population of 478,390, as suggested by Hope-Simpson, no less than 30 percent of the total rural Arab population was therefore landless, according to Hope-Simpson. See Hope-Simpson Report, pp. 25, 158.

101. Ruppin to Jewish Agency Executive, 15 July 1930, CZA, S25/7577.

102. For evidence of Arab landowner rotation of tenant cultivators, see Kisch to Jewish Agency Executive, London, 1 May 1931, CZA, S25/5795. For the definition of tenant and regulations for compensatory payments, see Protection of Cultivators Ordinance, 1929, *Official Gazette*, 16 June 1929, pp. 710–12.

103. See Chapter 5, where the landless Arab issue is discussed.

104. Shaw Report, p. 167.

105. Hope-Simpson Report, p. 141; Great Britain, Cmd. 3692, *Palestine: A Statement of Policy by His Majesty's Government in the United Kingdom* (hereafter cited as Passfield White Paper), paragraph 15.

106. Passfield White Paper, paragraph 25.

107. Hope-Simpson Report, p. 143.

108. Hope-Simpson to Chancellor, 5 August 1930 and 29 September 1930, CP, Box 16/6.

109. HMG estimated Jewish land reserves at 125,000 acres or 500,000 dunams. Total Jewish land purchase from October 1920 to December 31, 1930 was only 532,740 dunams. Not less than sixty Jewish settlements were established in the same period. The absurdity of HMG's estimate seems all the more intentional because Hope-Simpson was told by Ussishkin, when Hope-Simpson visited the JNF, that the Jewish unoccupied land totaled only 83,974 dunams, 30,000 of which had been purchased only a year earlier at Wadi Hawarith. For HMG's estimate, see Great Britain, Cabinet Committee on Policy in Palestine, Second Report, 23 September 1930, paragraph 8, CAB 24/215 2009. For Ussishkin's remarks to Hope-Simpson, see CZA, KKL 5/Box 536; Hope-Simpson Report, p. 39.

110. Hope-Simpson Report, pp. 143–44.

111. Hope-Simpson to Passfield, 18 August 1930, CAB 24/215 2116.

112. Chancellor to Passfield, 6 June 1930, CP, Box 13/4.

113. Passfield to Chancellor, 26 June 1930, CP, Box 13/4; Memorandum 36 by Sir John Shuckburgh, 18 June 1930, CO 733/185/77072, Part 2.

114. Chancellor to Christopher, 21 February 1930, CP, Box 16/3.

115. Hope-Simpson to Chancellor, 29 September 1930, CP, Box 16/6.

116. Passfield to Chancellor, 17 October 1930, and Chancellor to Passfield, 20 October 1930, CP, Box 13/4.

117. Hope-Simpson to Passfield, 24 October 1930, CO 733/194/77402.

118. Hope-Simpson to Chancellor, 24 October 1930, CP, Box 16/6.

119. Statement Regarding Question of Appointment of Sir John Hope-Simpson as Director of Development in Palestine, 29 October 1930, CO 733/194/77402. It is interesting to note that one of the only closed files on land in the Colonial Office Record Group 733 housed at the Public Record Office in London is CO 733/199. This file details the Hope-Simpson Report.

120. For examples, see Petition of Emir Shakib Arslan, 6 October 1934, League of Nations, *Permanent Mandates Commission: Minutes*, Twenty-seventh Session, pp. 200–203; Document #152 in *Milaff al-Witha'iq al-Filastini*, pp. 560–61; 'Abd al-Hadi, "Official Reply of the Arab Executive to the French Reports" (1933), p. 9, CO.

Chapter 4

1. See Arnon-Ohana, *Destruction from Within*, esp. 35–141.

2. Hope-Simpson to Passfield, 18 August 1930, CAB 24/215 2009.

3. Passfield White Paper, paragraph 23.

4. See CAB 24/215 2009; CP, 301 (30), Appendix 1.

5. Great Britain, Cabinet Committee on Policy in Palestine, Second Report, 23 September 1930, CAB 24/215 2009. Hope-Simpson's presence on the Cabinet Committee gave Chancellor another spokesman for his political viewpoint in addition to Passfield.

6. Great Britain, Cabinet Committee on Policy in Palestine, Second Report, 23 September 1930, CAB 24/215 2009.

7. Great Britain, Minutes of the Cabinet Meeting, 24 September 1930, CAB 23/65 1939.
8. Passfield White Paper, paragraph 3.
9. Ibid., paragraph 15.
10. Ibid., paragraph 21.
11. *NYT*, 23 and 24 October 1930; *LT*, 22 October 1930.
12. *LT*, 19 November 1930.
13. *NYT*, 12 January 1931; *LT*, 15 January 1931.
14. Zvi Botkowsky of PICA to Kisch, 3 March 1931, CZA, S25/9836; *NYT*, 23 October and 9 November 1930. The *New York Times* editorially praised the White Paper, noting that it was a blow to Zionist aspirations and at least recognition of the Arab people's aspirations. See *NYT*, 22 October 1930.
15. Minutes of the Jewish National Fund Directorate Meeting, 17 November 1930, CZA, S25/1946; *NYT*, 4 January 1931.
16. *LT*, 22 October 1930. See also Weizmann to Felix Green, 19 October 1930, CZA, S25/7586; Rose, *The Gentile Zionists*, pp. 16–17; and Sheffer, "Intentions and Results of British Policy," p. 51.
17. See *LT*, 22 October 1930; *NYT*, 23 and 24 October 1930.
18. *LT*, 4 October 1930; Chancellor to Christopher, 24 October 1930, CP, Box 16/3.
19. *LT*, 4 November 1930. The importance of the Simon-Hailsham letter upon Henderson is noted by Sheffer, "Intentions and Results," p. 54.
20. *LT*, 15 November 1930.
21. Chancellor to Christopher, 22 October 1930, CP, Box 16/3; Palestine Executive Council Decision, 24 October 1930, CO 814/26. The other four proposed bills were the Registration of Agriculturist Bill (1930), the Law of Execution (Amendment) Bill (1930), the Land Courts Bill (1921–30), and the Land Settlement Bills (1929–30).
22. Memorandum on the Proposed Land Transfer Restrictions to the London Jewish Agency Executive (1930), CZA.
23. Stubbs to the Chief Secretariat, 5 September 1930, ISA, Box 3511/file 1.
24. M. Eliash and S. Horowitz, Legal Advisers of the Jewish Agency, to Ruppin, 20 November 1930, CZA, KKL 5/Box 536; Memorandum on Proposed Land Transfer Restrictions (1930), CZA.
25. Yaqub Farrah, for President of the Arab Executive, to the Chief Secretary, 30 December 1930; 'Awni 'Abd al-Hadi to the Chief Secretary, 30 January 1931, CO 733/199/87072, Part 1.
26. *Al-Jami'ah al-'Arabiyyah*, 20 May 1931, 10 July 1931, and 12 July 1931. Fahkri al-Nashashibi received £P200 from the Jewish National Fund in the name of Shafiq Zantat on 14 December 1929. See KKL 5/Box 363/file 500.
27. Kisch to London Jewish Agency Executive, 19 April 1931, CZA, KKL 5/Box 532; Kisch to London Jewish Agency Executive, 1 May 1931, CZA, S25/7595. Ra'is's tenants were subtenants and therefore not entitled to protection under the prevailing Protection of Cultivators Ordinance. Moreover Ra'is was moving his tenants from one plot to another to avoid their accruing continued tenancy. The Protection of Cultivators (Amendment) Ordinance (No. 1) of 27

May 1932 specifically plugged these loopholes. See *Official Gazette*, 27 May 1932.

28. Note of a Conversation with the High Commissioner by Col. Kisch, 1 December 1930, CZA, S25/13.

29. Weizmann, *Trial and Error*, pp. 33–34.

30. Hope-Simpson to Chancellor, 7 February 1931, CP, Box 16/6. See also Lewis Namier to Kisch, 27 November 1930, CZA, S25/7587; Note by Dr. Hexter, 9 January 1931, CZA, S25/7586; and Rose, *The Gentile Zionists*, pp. 22–25.

31. Sheffer, "Policy Making and British Policies," p. 72, fn. 2 and 3.

32. Hope-Simpson to Chancellor, 7 February 1931, CP, Box 16/6.

33. Ibid.; Rose, *The Gentile Zionists*, pp. 37–40. See Great Britain, *Parliamentary Debates*, Commons, 17 November 1930, 5th Series, vol. 245.

34. See Bentwich, *England in Palestine*; *NYT*, 4 January 1931. Kisch said of Drayton, "I only know that the Jew haters and the Jew baiters in the administration regard Mr. Drayton as their friend, and it is well known that they consult with him and that he prompts them with suggestions." Kisch to London Jewish Agency Executive, 20 January 1930, CZA, S25/5789.

35. Shuckburgh to Bentwich, 14 January 1931, CO 733/199/87082, Part 1. Chancellor noted that there was an absence of Jewish protests against Bentwich's retirement from his Attorney General's post. Chancellor believed that this was due to the Jewish Agency belief that "he was more valuable to the (Jewish) cause at the Colonial Office than in Palestine." Chancellor to Christopher, 27 January 1931, CP, Box 16/3.

36. Report of the Committee to Advise on the Protection of Agricultural Tenants (1927), p. 9, ISA.

37. Hope-Simpson to Chancellor, 26 February 1931, CP, Box 16/3. Other Zionist representatives who took part in these discussions were Harry Sacher, Harold Laski, Professor Selig Brodetsky, and James de Rothschild. Besides Henderson, Passfield, and Malcolm MacDonald, A. V. Alexander represented HMG. See Brodetsky, *Memoirs from Ghetto to Israel*, pp. 142–43.

38. Namier to Kisch, 9 January 1931, CZA, S25/7587.

39. Great Britain, *Parliamentary Debates*, Commons, 13 February 1931, 5th Series, vol. 248, cols. 751–57 (hereafter cited as MacDonald Letter), paragraph 9.

40. Correspondence between Weizmann and Henderson, 9 December and 12 December 1930, CO 733/185/77072, Part 4; Passfield to Chancellor, 21 November 1930, CO 733/185/77072, Part 4.

41. Great Britain, Minutes of the Cabinet Meeting, 4 and 11 February 1931, CAB 23/66 2013.

42. MacDonald Letter, paragraph 7.

43. Passfield White Paper, paragraphs 20, 27, and 28; MacDonald Letter, paragraph 17; *NYT*, 4 March 1931.

44. Chancellor to Passfield, 5 March 1931, CO 733/210/87042, Part 1; Arlosoroff, *Yoman Yerushalaim*, p. 20.

45. *NYT*, 4 March 1931; *LT*, 14 March 1931. In March 1931 the moderates

in the Arab Executive who were not willing to cut their British connection entirely carried a proposal to participate in the legislative council election suggested by the White Paper. That moderate voices were prominent on the Arab Executive at this time reflected in some measure the decision not to be extreme in reacting to the MacDonald Letter's contents.

46. Great Britain, Colonial no. 75, *Report by His Majesty's Government to the Council of the League of Nations for the Year 1931* (1932), pp. 30–31. In March 1931, when the land-sale boycott was called for by the Arab Executive, more land was transferred into Jewish ownership than in any other month that year. See table 10 in this volume.

47. This was in keeping with HMG's concern for the Jewish settlements to possess sealed armories for their self-protection. Such a decision was an outgrowth of recommendations made by Herbert Dowbiggin to reorganize the Palestine police force after the disturbances of 1929. For an evaluation of his report, see Dinier et al., eds., *Sefer Toldot Hahaganah*, vol. B, pt. 1, pp. 407–14.

48. Thon to Kisch, 12 June 1931, CZA, KKL 5/Box 536.

49. Kisch, *Palestine Diary*, p. 405. Kisch to Granovsky, 1 May 1931, CZA, KKL 5/Box 536.

50. For one Zionist official's thoughts on Arab, British, and Jewish silence in regard to Arab participation in land sales to Jews, see Appendix 4, esp. paragraphs 6 and 8.

51. London Jewish Agency Executive to Kisch, 19 April 1931, CZA, KKL 5/Box 535; Kisch to Granovsky, 1 May 1931, CZA, KKL 5/Box 536.

52. Great Britain, Minutes of the Cabinet Meeting, 15 April 1931, A.M.; 15 April 1931, P.M.; and 22 April 1931, CAB 23/66 2013; Note of a Conversation with Sir John Shuckburgh and Mr. Williams of the Colonial Office by the London Jewish Agency Executive, 4 April 1931; and London Jewish Agency Executive to Kisch, 16 April 1931, CZA, S25/9968.

53. *LT*, 16 April 1931. Chancellor went so far as to offer financial assistance to the Arab Executive to defray their transportation costs to London. Hexter to Kisch, 12 April 1931, CZA, S25/7595.

54. High Commissioner to Secretary of State, 22 April 1931, CP, Box 13/5; *NYT*, 24 May 1931.

55. *Al-Karmil*, 25 July 1931. See also *NYT*, 26 July 1931.

56. Arlosoroff to Brodetsky, 11 September 1931, CZA, S25/5796.

57. French, *First Report on Agricultural Development and Land Settlement in Palestine* (hereafter cited as French Report), paragraph 70.

58. Mr. Beckett to Mr. Waterfield, Colonial Office officials, 17 April 1931, CO 733/199/87072, Part 2.

59. Legal cases brought by agriculturalists seeking statutory tenancy status under the Protection of Cultivators Ordinance of 1933 confirm that some Arab landlords sought to sell their land in anticipation of the proposed land-transfer controls of August 1931. See ISA, Box 3893/file TR 70/33.

60. Great Britain, *Parliamentary Debates*, Commons, 2 June 1931, 5th Series, vol. 253; League of Nations, *Permanent Mandates Commission: Minutes*, Twentieth Session, 15 June 1931, pp. 75–76.

61. Secretary of State to High Commissioner, 8 July 1931; High Commissioner to Secretary of State, 8 July 1931, CP, Box 13/5.

62. Taylor, *English History, 1914–1945*, p. 372.

63. Lewis Namier of the London Jewish Agency played an instrumental role in fashioning this demographic division. See Namier to Mrs. Dugdale, 11 January 1931, CZA, S25/7587. See also Great Britain, *Parliamentary Debates*, Commons, 20 July 1931, 5th Series, vol. 225.

64. London Jewish Agency Executive to Palestine Jewish Agency Executive, 4 December 1931, CZA, S25/7596; *NYT*, 26 July 1931.

65. For the complete correspondence between the Colonial Office and the Jewish Agency on this subject, see CO 733/199/87082/1, Part 1.

66. Minutes of an Interview with the High Commissioner, 19 August 1931, CZA, S25/15; Arlosoroff, *Yoman Yerushalaim*, p. 18. See also Notes on Land Transfer Ordinance by Leonard Stein, 14 August 1931, CZA, S25/459; Arlosoroff to Brodetsky, 15 September 1931, CZA, S25/7596.

67. Brodetsky to the Colonial Office, 31 August 1931, CO 733/211/87040/3; J. H. Thomas to Sir Mark Aitchison Young, 11 September 1930; and Note on the Palestine Land Question, no author and no date, CO 733/199/87072/1, Part 2.

68. Note of a Conversation with O. G. R. Williams by Selig Brodetsky, 30 August 1931, CZA, A202/119. See also CO 733/199/87082/1, Part 2.

Chapter 5

1. Palestine Government, *Census for Palestine, 1931*, 2:282.

2. Mr. Pevsner, an aide to Yehoshua Hankin, to Dr. Ruppin, 1 June 1930, CZA, S25/7448.

3. Ibid.

4. Johnson-Crosbie Report, p. 44. These figures should be considered representative only of the 104 villages surveyed by the investigators and not representative of all of Palestine.

5. Ibid., p. 45.

6. Great Britain, Colonial no. 40, *Report by His Majesty's Government to the League of Nations for the Year 1928* (1929), p. 5; Colonial no. 59, *Report for 1930* (1931), p. 15; Colonial no. 75, *Report for 1931* (1932), p. 6; Dinier et al., eds., *Sefer Toldot Hahaganah*, vol. B, pt. 1, 303; and *LT*, 24 December 1932.

7. Palestine Government, *Annual Report of the Department of Agriculture and Forests from 1927 to 1930*, pp. 7, 130; Report of the Agricultural Settlement Department (1931), CZA.

8. Brown, "Agriculture," in Himadeh's *Economic Organization of Palestine*, p. 128. In 1937, for example, the citrus crop accounted for 25 percent of the value of all crops.

9. Palestine Government Executive Council Minutes, 5 February 1935, CO 814/31.

10. Palestine Government, *Annual Report of the Department of Agriculture and Forests for 1927 to 1930*; *Report for 1931*; and *Report for 1932*.

11. Chancellor to Secretary of State, 29 June 1930, CP, Box 13/4.

12. Ibid., 10 November 1930, CP, Box 13/4; Great Britain, Colonial no. 59, *Report by His Majesty's Government to the League of Nations for the Year 1930* (1931), pp. 15–16; Colonial no. 75, *Report for 1931* (1932), p. 7; and Colonial no. 82, *Report for 1933* (1934), p. 23.

13. Chancellor to Passfield, 21 June 1930, CP, Box 13/6; Bonne, *Palästina Land und Wirtschaft*, p. 124.

14. Strickland, "The Struggle for Land in Palestine," p. 47.

15. Remarks by Moshe Smilansky, Minutes of the Meeting of the French Report, 22 June 1932, CZA, S25/7599.

16. Commissioner of Lands to Chief Secretary, 12 May 1931, ISA, Box 3280/ file 2.

17. High Commissioner to Secretary of State for the Colonies, 10 August 1932, CO 733/224/97270; *LT*, 24 December 1932.

18. Palestine Government, *Official Communiqué*, no. 23/33, 14 July 1933; Palestine Government, *Official Communiqué*, no. 31/33, 3 September 1933.

19. High Commissioner to Cunliffe-Lister, 14 August 1933, CO 733/245/ 17493.

20. Palestine Government, *Official Communiqué*, no. 11/34, 25 March 1934; Palestine Government, *Official Communiqué*, no. 8/34, 8 March 1934.

21. Great Britain, Colonial no. 129, *Report by His Majesty's Government to the League of Nations for the Year 1936* (1937), p. 35.

22. Wauchope to Cunliffe-Lister, Situation in Palestine, 2 January 1934, CAB 24/247 2033.

23. *NYT*, 3 February 1935.

24. League of Nations, *Permanent Mandates Commission: Minutes*, Thirtieth Session, Remarks by Mr. Trusted of the Palestine administration, 1 June 1936, p. 61.

25. Great Britain, Colonial no. 112, *Report by His Majesty's Government to the Council of the League of Nations for the Year 1935* (1936), p. 166; Great Britain, *Parliamentary Debates*, Commons, 25 July 1935, 5th Series, vol. 304. Before the outbreak of the 1936 disturbances the Palestine administration's surplus revenue reached £P6,000,000.

26. Great Britain, Colonial no. 112, *Report by His Majesty's Government to the Council of the League of Nations for the Year 1935* (1936), p. 166; *LT*, 13 June 1933.

27. Conversation with O. G. R. Williams by Selig Brodetsky, 6 October 1931, CZA, S25/7596; Wauchope to Cunliffe-Lister, 23 March 1932, CO 733/214/ 97049, Part 2; and Cunliffe-Lister to Wauchope, 6 January 1933, CO 733/217/ 97072.

28. Wauchope to Cunliffe-Lister, 6 May 1935, CO 733/270/75049/1; L. Andrews to J. M. Martin, 4 March 1937, CO 733/345/75550/33; and High Commissioner MacMichael to Malcolm MacDonald, 24 May 1939, CO 733/405/ 75720. While the Peel Report of 1937 stated that more than 332 proven displaced Arabs had land provided for them, the fact remained that only 74 families were actually resettled. See Peel Report, p. 240.

29. Heinrich Margulies to the Palestine Jewish Agency Executive, 9 November

1931, CZA, S25/7619. See Appendix 4, paragraphs 5 and 6.

30. Arlosoroff to Brodetsky, 15 September 1931, CZA, S25/7596.

31. Ibid., 13 November 1931, CZA, S25/7596. See also Extract of a Conversation between Arlosoroff and the High Commissioner, 8 January 1932, CO 733/217/97072, Part 1; Minutes of a Meeting on the Suggestions of the Director of Development, 2 February 1932, CZA, S25/7599; and Arlosoroff, *Yoman Yerushalaim*, p. 194.

32. Arlosoroff to Brodetsky, 15 September 1931, CZA, S25/7596; Arlosoroff, *Yoman Yerushalaim*, p. 49.

33. Arlosoroff to Brodetsky, 11 September 1931 and 13 November 1931, CZA, S25/7596; Arlosoroff, *Yoman Yerushalaim*, pp. 77, 226.

34. Minute by O. G. R. Williams, 14 January 1932, CO 733/214/97049, Part 1. French could have claimed that because he did not know of the budgetary cut in the proposed Development Loan, he was forced merely to reword Hope-Simpson's relatively imprecise suggestions for development. That excuse is not valid. French had clear knowledge that the Development Loan was very problematical. See French Report, p. 7, paragraph 11.

35. High Commissioner to Secretary of State, 10 August 1931, CP, Box 13/5.

36. Arlosoroff to Brodetsky, 14 December 1931, CZA, S25/7620. See also Arlosoroff to Brodetsky, 11 September 1930, CZA, S25/7596; Arlosoroff to London Jewish Agency Executive, 13 December 1931, CZA, S25/7620; and Arlosoroff, *Yoman Yerushalaim*, p. 35. Sir John Shuckburgh of the Colonial Office wrote, "The incident [Tute's intended appointment] illustrates the embarrassing position in which we are placed in respect to all our dealings in Palestine. We are under no sort of obligation to consult the Jews about this appointment. The plain fact is that by exploiting their backstairs influence to the utmost, the Jews have acquired what amounts in practice to a veto over all our activities in Palestine." 8 September 1931, CO 733/211/87402/1, Part 2.

37. Besides Arlosoroff, Abraham Granovsky of the Jewish National Fund and Shabtai Levi of the Palestine Colonization Association had served on the Colonization and Immigration Committee. The Legal Committee also included S. Horowitz, E. Eliash, and later A. Ben-Shemesh (legal advisers to the Jewish National Fund), and Hankin, Thon, and Joseph Nehemey of the Palestine Land Development Company.

38. Minutes of the First Meeting of the Jewish Agency Legal Committee with Regard to the Development Scheme, 15 September 1931, CZA, A202/119; Second Meeting of the Jewish Agency Legal Committee with Regard to the Development Scheme, 14 October 1931, CZA, A202/119; and Joseph Nehemey to the Palestine Jewish Agency Executive, 23 September 1931, CZA, S25/7614.

39. Minutes of the Second Meeting of the Jewish Agency Legal Committee with Regard to the Development Scheme, 14 October 1931, CZA, A202/119.

40. Wauchope to Cunliffe-Lister, 22 December 1932, CO 733/217/97072; Arlosoroff, *Yoman Yerushalaim*, pp. 49–50.

41. Minutes of the Second Meeting of the Jewish Agency Legal Committee with Regard to the Development Scheme, 14 October 1931, CZA, A202/119.

42. Minutes of an Interview with Officer Administering the Government by C. Arlosoroff, 30 October 1931, CZA, KKL 5/Box 688.

43. Arlosoroff to Brodetsky, 14 December 1931, CZA, S25/7620; Peel Report, p. 240.

44. Minutes of an Interview with Officer Administering the Government by C. Arlosoroff, 30 October 1931, CZA, KKL 5/Box 688.

45. Arlosoroff to Brodetsky, 15 September 1931, CZA, S25/7596; *Filastin*, 22 September 1931.

46. Extract of Confidential Letter of the Registration Proceedings in the Northern District, 16 October 1931, CZA, A202/119; Minutes of the Second Meeting of the Jewish Agency Legal Committee with Regard to the Development Scheme, 19 October 1931, CZA, A202/119.

47. In the Beisan Agreement, the amount of 150 dunams suggests not only that a "lot viable" was to be made available to former owners but that former owners would be supplied with the identical amount of land provided for cultivators in the Beisan area by the administration.

48. Arlosoroff to Brodetsky, 14 December 1931, CZA, S25/7620.

49. Minutes of an Interview with Officer Administering the Government by C. Arlosoroff, 30 October 1931, CZA, KKL 5/Box 688; Arlosoroff to Director of Development, 30 October 1931, CZA, A202/119; and Arlosoroff, *Yoman Yerushalaim*, pp. 61–62, 79.

50. Minutes of the First Meeting of the Jewish Agency Legal Committee with Regard to the Development Scheme, 15 September 1931, CZA, A202/119; Arlosoroff to Brodetsky, 4 October 1931, CZA, S25/7596. When he wrote the Arab Executive's official reply to the French Reports in March 1933, he stridently reproached the *government* in the name of the Arab Executive for sharing information with the Jewish Agency. See 'Awni 'Abd al-Hadi to High Commissioner, 10 March 1933, paragraph 5, CO 733/230/17249.

51. Arlosoroff to Brodetsky, 14 December 1931, and Arlosoroff to Horowitz, 1 January 1932, CZA, S25/7629; L. Andrews, Acting Director of Development to Chief Secretary, 24 March 1933, CO 733/230/17249.

52. Note of an Interview with Mr. Justice Webb by S. Horowitz, 24 April 1932, CZA, S25/7620.

53. Ibid.

54. A. H. Webb to Director of Development, 12 December 1931, CZA, KKL 5/Box 688.

55. League of Nations, *Permanent Mandates Commission: Minutes*, Thirty-second Session, Remarks by J. H. Hall, 9 August 1937, p. 114.

56. Arlosoroff to Director of Development, 9 November 1931, CZA, KKL 5/Box 688; Arlosoroff, *Yoman Yerushalaim*, p. 119.

57. Officer Administering the Government to Secretary of State for the Colonies, 17 November 1932, CO 733/214/97049, Part 4; Peel Report, pp. 239–40.

58. Wauchope to Cunliffe-Lister, quoting Lewis Andrews, Acting Director of Development, 22 December 1932, CO 733/217/97072.

59. H. H. Trusted, Officer Administering the Government, to Cunliffe-Lister, 25 May 1933, CO 733/231/17249/1; Annual Progress Report on Arab Resettlement, 12 May 1934, in a dispatch from Wauchope to Cunliffe-Lister, 2 June 1934, CO 733/251/37249/1; and Annual Report of the Development Department 1934/1935, CO 733/270/75049/1.

60. The average cost per dunam of rural land was £P7.42 in the 1930–32 period, whereas in the subsequent three-year period it was £P24.32 per rural dunam. These costs excluded compensatory amounts needed to effect a land purchase.

61. Annual Report of the Palestine Government for 1933, CO 733/278/75156, Part 1, folio 75.

62. Andrews to Chief Secretary, 16 September 1933, in a letter from Wauchope to Cunliffe-Lister, 18 November 1933, CO 733/230/17249, Part 3, folios 15–18. The landowners mentioned by Andrews were 'Isa Joha, Said Darwish, and 'Abdul Fattah Darwish. 'Abdul Fattah Darwish was accused of acting as a land broker for Jewish acquisition of land at Nebi Samuel, just outside of Jerusalem. See al-Difa', 28 December 1934.

63. Wauchope to Cunliffe-Lister, 15 April 1933, CO 733/230/17249, Part 1.

64. Wauchope to Cunliffe-Lister, 22 July 1933, CO 733/231/17249, Part 1.

65. Remarks by 'Awni 'Abd al-Hadi to the High Commissioner, 24 February 1933, CO 733/234/17272; Filastin, 24 September 1932. See Shimoni, 'Arave Eretz Yisrael, pp. 229–30.

66. For a summary of the land areas purchased and the amounts paid by the Development Department, see CO 733/218/97082; CO 733/231/17249, Part 1, folio 43; Annual Progress Report of Arab Resettlement, 12 May 1934, in a dispatch from Wauchope to Cunliffe-Lister, 2 June 1934, CO 733/251/37248, Part 1; and Beisan District Office files, ISA, Box 2606/file 36/folio 1.

67. Palestine Government, Official Communiqué, no. 32/33, 4 September 1933, and Annual Report of the Department of Development 1934/1935, CO 733/270/74059, Part 1.

68. NYT, 20 March 1932. This ordinance generated a new wave of trespass on Jewish National Fund-owned land in expectation of restoration of land previously owned and worked.

69. Financial Adviser to the Director of Development to the Colonial Office, 20 April 1932, p. 3, CO 733/214/97049; Minutes by H. F. Downie, 22 May 1935, CO 733/270/75049, Part 1; and Memorandum on a Proposal Laid before the Royal Commission (1937), CO.

70. Assistant District Commissioner, Jenin, to Nazareth District Commissioner, 10 August 1939, ISA, Box 2629/file G 312/folio 54.

71. Statement by the Secretary of State before Parliament, 14 July 1933, CO 733/230/17249, Part 1.

72. League of Nations, Permanent Mandates Commission: Minutes, Twenty-third Session, Remarks by Mr. Young, 27 June 1933, p. 101.

73. Great Britain, Minutes of the Cabinet Meeting, 8 February 1933, CAB 23/75 2037.

74. Arlosoroff to Brodetsky, 4 October 1931; Arlosoroff to French, 12 October 1931; French to Arlosoroff, 16 October 1931; and Arlosoroff to French, 23 October 1931, CZA, S25/7596.

75. Wauchope to Cunliffe-Lister, 2 January 1932, CO 733/214/97049, Part 1; Brodetsky to Arlosoroff, 14 December 1932, CZA, S25/7597.

76. What French suggested had been previously advocated by the Land Settlement Commission Report of 1921, the Dowson Report on the Land System in

Palestine of 1925, the Land Settlement Ordinance of 1928, and the Johnson-Crosbie and Hope-Simpson reports of 1930.

77. French Report, paragraph 22.

78. Commissioner of Lands to Chief Secretary, 10 May 1932, ISA, Box 3317/file 7.

79. Minutes of the Jewish Agency Meeting on the suggestions of the Director of Development, 2 February 1932, CZA, S25/7599.

80. *Filastin*, 29 October 1932; *LT*, 31 October 1932.

81. Minute by O. G. R. Williams, 14 January 1932, CO 733/214/97049, Part 1.

82. French Report, paragraphs 70 and 73.

83. Arlosoroff, *Yoman Yerushalaim*, p. 171. See Minute by O. G. R. Williams, 14 January 1932, CO 733/214/97049, Part 1.

84. French, *Supplementary Report on Agriculture Development and Land Settlement in Palestine* (hereafter cited as French Supplementary Report), paragraph 70. Cf. Extract of a Note from the Secretary of State's discussion with Dr. Weizmann, 30 November 1932, CO 733/223/97248.

85. For the next of these three ordinances, see French Supplementary Report, pp. 98–111.

86. French Report; cf. paragraphs 22, 60, 72, and 74.

87. French Supplementary Report. The proposed ordinance's Section 7, which dealt with selling of one's occupancy right, had no less than five subsections and twelve subtitles under one part of the section.

88. Distinctly uncharacteristic of French's own personal predisposition was Clause 5 in the Homestead Protection Ordinance, which gave the High Commissioner the right to waive the homestead area to individuals who had found other permanent occupations. Just as in the landless Arab inquiry, neither French nor Webb wished to provide for absolute tenant protection.

89. Great Britain, Minutes of the Cabinet Meeting, 11 May 1932, CAB 23/71 2013.

90. Arlosoroff, *Yoman Yerushalaim*, p. 194; Minute of an Interview with His Excellency the High Commissioner by Chaim Arlosoroff, 27 January 1932, CZA, S25/15; Remarks by C. Arlosoroff, Minutes of the Jewish Agency Meeting on the Suggestions of the Director of Development, 2 February 1932, CZA, S25/7599.

91. Extract of a Conversation between Dr. Arlosoroff and the High Commissioner, 8 January 1932, CO 733/217/97072, Part 1; Arlosoroff, *Yoman Yerushalaim*, pp. 172–73; Cunliffe-Lister to the High Commissioner, 17 February 1932, CO 733/217/97072, Part 1.

92. See remarks by Arthur Ruppin, Minutes of the Jewish Agency Meeting on the Suggestions of the Director of Development, 2 February 1932, CZA, S25/7599.

93. Minute of an Interview with His Excellency the High Commissioner by C. Arlosoroff, 25 February 1932, CZA, Z4/3904.

94. Minutes of the Jewish Agency Meeting on the Suggestions of the Director of Development, 2 February 1932, CZA, S25/7599.

95. London Jewish Agency Executive to Arlosoroff, 25 March 1932; Inter-

view with Cunliffe-Lister and A. C. C. Parkinson, Head of the Middle East Department of Colonial Office, by Selig Brodetsky, 26 April and 25 April 1932 respectively, CZA, S25/7594.

96. Malcolm MacDonald to Cunliffe-Lister, 22 April 1932, CO 733/214/97049, Part 2, folios 16 and 17; Secretary of State for the Colonies to the High Commissioner, 9 March 1932, CO 733/214/97049, Part 3.

97. Minutes of an Interview with His Excellency the High Commissioner by C. Arlosoroff, 17 May 1932, CZA, Z4/3904; Arlosoroff, *Yoman Yerushalaim,* pp. 272, 273.

98. Great Britain, Minutes of the Cabinet Meeting, 1 June 1932, CAB 23/71 2013; Minute by O. G. R. Williams, 1 June 1932, CO 733/214/97049, Part 3; S. Moody of the Palestine Chief Secretariat to Chancellor, 28 November 1932, CP, Box 17/4; and *NYT,* 17 November 1932.

99. Arlosoroff to Dr. Robert Weltsch, 19 June 1932, CZA, S25/7598; 'Abd al-Hadi, Official Reply of the Arab Executive to the French Reports (1933), p. 1, CO.

100. The reference to Arab collusion in land sales was made with regard to the employment by Jews of "mean Arabs" who induce "the simple *fellah,* through devilish means, to sell his land to the Jews." 'Abd al-Hadi, Official Reply of the Arab Executive to the French Reports (1933), p. 17, CO.

101. Speculation might lead us to believe that one of the reasons for the Arab Executive's failure to convene a meeting for a year after October 1932 was due to its embarrassment over French's allusions to Arab (Executive) landowner collusion in land sales.

102. Lewis Andrews to Chief Secretary, 24 March 1933, p. 4, CO 733/230/17249. The phrase "and many others" was typed below this list but crossed out by hand.

103. Arlosoroff to Brodetsky, 14 December 1932, CZA, S25/7597. See also Resolution on the French Reports Prepared by the Jewish Agency, 8 August 1932, CO 733/223/97213.

104. Remarks on the Reports by Mr. Lewis French by A. Granovsky, 5 July 1932, CZA, S25/7602; Arlosoroff to London Jewish Agency Executive, 22 February 1933, CZA, S25/7597.

105. H. F. Downie to R. A. Grieve of HMG's Treasury, 27 May 1933, CO 733/230/17249, Part 1.

106. Brodetsky to Arlosoroff, 7 July 1932, CZA, S25/7597.

107. Ibid., 14 December 1932, CZA, S25/7597.

108. See Secret Draft Memorandum for the Cabinet, Land Policy in Palestine, 1932, CO 733/217/97072, folios 108–13.

Chapter 6

1. See Stein, "Legal Protection and Circumvention," pp. 233–61.

2. Minutes of the Jewish National Fund Directorate Meeting for 20 September 1934 and 26 November 1934, CZA, KKL 5/Box 698; Gurevich, "Land Acquisition" (1934), CZA.

3. Kisch to *Vaad HaPoel* (Committee of Workers) of the Histadrut and Messrs. Botkovsky, Smilansky, Wilkansky, Thon, and Palestine Colonization Association, 11 February 1931; Kisch to *Vaad HaPoel* of the Histadrut, Palestine Colonization Association, and Messrs. Smilansky, Botkovsky, Wilkansky, Thon, Chilik, Weizmann, Baruch, Raab, and Passman, 24 February 1931, CZA, S25/9836.

4. Moshe Smilansky to Colonel Kisch, 1 March 1931, CZA, S25/9836.

5. Victor Cohn to Kisch, 4 March 1931, CZA, S25/9836.

6. Ibid.

7. Zvi Botkovsky to Kisch, 3 March 1931, CZA, S25/9836.

8. Thon to Kisch, 2 June 1931, CZA, S25/9836.

9. Meeting of the Jewish Agency and Jewish National Fund Directorate, 19 February 1936, CZA, S25/6538.

10. See, for example, remarks by Dr. Ruppin, Minutes of Jewish Agency Meeting with Regard to Land, 19 May 1933, CZA, S25/6542; Minutes of the Jewish National Fund Directorate Meeting, 6 December 1937, KKL 10.

11. *Al-Jami'ah al-'Arabiyyah*, 24 and 25 December 1935; *al-Jami'ah al-Islamiyyah*, 25 December 1933; and *Filastin*, 27 December 1933.

12. Shertok to Ben-Gurion, 5 November 1936, CZA, S25/9839. See also Epstein, "The Political Significance of Land Purchase" (1937), CZA.

13. Minutes of the Jewish National Fund Directorate Meeting, 14 December 1938, CZA, KKL 5/Box 1048. See also CZA, S25/10250; Weitz, *Yomani*, 1:327, 373, 377; 2:4–5.

14. For a detailed account of this problem as it affected Jewish land purchase, see Granovsky, *Land Policy in Palestine*, pp. 17–85; and *LT*, 13 June 1933.

15. Audiovitz, "Der Landkauf in Palästina" (1918), CZA.

16. Minutes of Jewish Agency Meeting with Regard to Land, 19 May 1933, CZA, S25/6542; Minutes of the Jewish National Fund Directorate Meeting, 20 September 1934, CZA, KKL 5/Box 698; and *NYT*, 25 November 1934.

17. Minutes of Jewish Agency Meeting with Regard to Land, Remarks by Yehoshua Hankin, 19 May 1933, CZA, S25/6542.

18. Minutes of Jewish Agency Meeting with Regard to Land, 19 May 1933, CZA, S25/6542.

19. Minutes of Jewish Agency Meeting on Negotiations with the Government with Regard to Land Speculation, 19 November 1933, CZA, S25/6542; and Weitz, *Yomani*, 1:67.

20. Anglo-American Committee of Inquiry, *A Survey of Palestine*, 1:224, table 1. The total arrived at here is the sum for the years 1933 to 1944 inclusive.

21. Heinrich Margulies to Palestine Jewish Agency Executive, 9 November 1931, CZA, S25/7619.

22. These press articles may be found in the newspaper archives housed at the National Library on the Hebrew University campus in Jerusalem.

23. Palestine Government, *Department of Lands Annual Report*, 1936, ISA, Box M3420/file 2.

24. Wauchope to Cunliffe-Lister, 11 February 1935, CO 733/278/75156, Part 1; Great Britain, Minutes of the Cabinet Meeting, January 1936, CAB 24/259 2116.

25. Yehoshua Hankin, Protocol of First Meeting of the Committee for Preparing Materials for the Development Scheme, 27 October 1931, CZA, KKL 5/Box 688; Remarks by Arthur Ruppin and Moshe Smilansky, Meeting of the Committee on the French Report, 22 June 1932, CZA, S25/7599.

26. Some of this money was used for payments that were due from land acquired in previous years, payments that had been stretched over a certain fixed period of time. See file marked Palestine Land Department, ISA, Box 3574/file 3.

27. Ruppin, "Jewish Land Purchase and Its Effect" (1929), p. 7.

28. Great Britain, *Parliamentary Debates*, Commons, 25 July 1935, 5th Series, vol. 304.

29. See Situation in Palestine, Wauchope to Cunliffe-Lister, 2 January 1934, CAB 24/247-2033.

30. Gurevich and Gertz, *Jewish Agricultural Settlement in Palestine.* See esp. table 66, "Employment of Jewish and Arab Workers in 5 Principal Plantation Villages during 1933–1938," p. 83.

31. Ibid. It may be conjectured that the unrest in 1936 and after had the effect of increasing the population size of some rural Jewish settlements, which might not have otherwise benefited from a manpower injection.

32. Great Britain, *Parliamentary Debates*, Commons, 18 July 1934, 5th Series, vol. 292.

33. *Filastin*, 12 July 1935.

34. D. Horowitz notes this conclusion in his report on the 1940 Land Transfer Regulations, 1 April 1940, CZA, S25/6938.

35. Palestine Government, *Census for Palestine, 1931*, 1:51. The central range ran from the hills of the Galilee in the north through the environs of Nablus, Ramallah, Jerusalem, and Bethlehem, to Hebron in the south.

36. French Report, paragraphs 69 and 70. French referred to them as "hill tracts." For the Galilee, it would be most difficult to determine what percentage of the increase, if any, in population density was due to factors other than natural increase and immigration from Syria.

37. League of Nations, *Permanent Mandates Commission: Minutes*, Remarks by Colonel Symes, Chief Secretary of the Palestine Administration, Ninth Session, 22 June 1926, p. 116; Report of the Committee to Advise on the Protection (1927), pp. 2 and 9, ISA. For further evidence of this, see Arlosoroff, "The Economic Background," in Sereni and Ashery, eds., *Jews and Arabs in Palestine*, pp. 15–16.

38. Questionnaire for the 1929 Commission of Inquiry (1929–30), p. 6, ISA.

39. League of Nations, *Permanent Mandates Commission: Minutes*, Twenty-fifth Session, 31 May 1934, p. 14; Remarks by Mr. Moody of the Palestine administration, 2 June 1935, Twenty-seventh session, p. 39.

40. Johnson-Crosbie Report, p. 22.

41. Hope-Simpson Report, p. 64.

42. Palestine Government, *Census for Palestine, 1931*, 1:22.

43. Land Policy in Palestine (1936), p. 48, CZA; CZA, S25/6916; Weitz, *Yomani*, 1:119.

44. Wauchope to Cunliffe-Lister, 23 August 1934, CO 733/252/37272, Part 1.

45. Wauchope to Cunliffe-Lister, 6 March 1935, CO 733/272/75072.

46. Ibid.

47. Protection of Cultivators (Amendment) Ordinance no. 3 of 1931, *Official Gazette*, 29 May 1931, pp. 414–16.

48. Protection of Cultivators (Amendment) Ordinance no. 1 of 1932, *Official Gazette*, 22 April 1932, p. 312.

49. Wauchope to Cunliffe-Lister, 26 March 1932, CO 733/224/97284.

50. Protection of Cultivators Ordinance of 1933, *Official Gazette*, 31 August 1933, pp. 1170–80.

51. J. Hathorn Hall for the High Commissioner to Cunliffe-Lister, 27 April 1934, CO 733/252/37272/1, folios 17 to 30, or ISA, Box 3262/file G195.

52. Cf. *al-Jami'ah al-Islamiyyah*, 3 August 1933, and *Filastin*, 27 July 1933.

53. A. Ben Shemesh to the Jewish Agency, 19 October 1933, CZA, S25/6930.

54. Abdul Latif Tabawi to Assistant District Commissioner, Nablus, 16 November 1934, ISA, Box 3922/file TR 114/33.

55. ISA, Box 3922/file TR 61/33.

56. ISA, Box 3890/file TR 94/33.

57. League of Nations, *Permanent Mandates Commission: Minutes*, Remarks by Mr. Moody, Twenty-seventh Session, 5 June 1935, p. 50.

58. Report of the Committee on State Domains on the Proposal to Exempt State Domain from the Provisions of the Cultivators (Protection) Ordinance, 28 June 1941, CO 733/447/76117. The inefficacy of the Protection of Cultivators Ordinance was noted quite explicitly by the Supreme Muslim Council in 1934. See Supreme Muslim Council to Wauchope, 27 December 1934, CO 733/272/75072.

59. Minutes by O. G. R. Williams, 9 May 1933, CO 733/234/17242.

60. Extract from the Cabinet Papers 3 (36), January 1936, CO 733/290/75072.

61. "Land Politics, 1935–1937," CZA, KKL 5/Box 1037. For the official Jewish Agency reply to the proposed small-owner protection, see CZA, S25/10088.

62. "Scheme for Restricting Land Transfers," probably by Dr. Thon, CZA, S25/9970.

63. Telegrams from the Secretary of State to Wauchope, 22 May 1936, and Wauchope to the Secretary of State, 26 May 1936, CO 733/290/75072, Part 2.

64. Alsberg, "HaShe'elah Ha'Aravit BeMediniyut," p. 177; Sykes, *Crossroads to Israel*, p. 61. Sykes's asssertion that the Zionists neither attempted nor planned any settlement in Transjordan is not correct. Cf. Sykes, *Crossroads to Israel*, p. 366.

65. Chaim Weizmann to Sir Henry Wilson, 4 February 1919, CZA, Z4/16024.

66. Minute of an Interview with His Excellency the High Commissioner by Moshe Shertok, Political Secretary of the Jewish Agency, 8 February 1934, CZA, S25/18.

67. Interview with the High Commissioner by Menachem Ussishkin, later head of the Jewish National Fund, 19 October 1920, CZA, S25/18.

68. Dinier et al., eds., *Sefer Toldot Hahaganah*, vol. B, pt. 1, p. 438.

69. Land and Agricultural Development in Palestine (1930), CZA.

70. Memorandum on Land Purchase and Agricultural Colonization (1930), CZA.

71. Note of a Meeting Held at Beisan between 'Abdullah and Beisan Area *shaykhs,* 2 June 1930, CZA, S25/5791; Arlosoroff to Justice Louis Brandeis, 8 May 1932, CZA, S25/3489. For a thorough, informative, and detailed analysis of Jewish Agency land-purchase efforts in Transjordan in the 1930s, see Shapira, "The Option of Emir 'Abdullah's Lands," pp. 239–84.

72. C. H. F. Cox, British Resident in Transjordan to Chancellor, 22 April 1931, CO 733/199/87082, Part 2; Wauchope to Cunliffe-Lister, 22 July 1933, CO 733/231/17249 Part 1.

73. League of Nations, *Permanent Mandates Commission: Minutes,* Twenty-fifth Session, 1 June 1934, p. 36; Dinier et al., eds., *Sefer Toldot Hahaganah,* vol. B, pt. 1, p. 456.

74. The Beni-Sakr tribe had control of land in the Beisan area east and west of the Jordan River and had in the past employed Palestinian fellaheen in working their lands. Oppenheim, *Die Beduinen,* 2:237; Arlosoroff to Brodetsky, 1 February 1932, CZA, S25/5797.

75. Arlosoroff to Brandeis, 8 May 1932 and 19 May 1932, CZA, S25/3489.

76. See Shapira, "The Option of Emir 'Abdullah's Lands," p. 249.

77. Minutes of a Conference between Messrs. Neumann and Farbstein and the Emir of Transjordan, 27 November 1932, CZA, S25/3487.

78. Minutes of the Jewish National Fund Directorate Meeting, 10 January 1933, CZA, KKL 5/Box 543; *NYT,* 18 January 1933.

79. Minutes of the Jewish National Fund Directorate Meeting, 14 February 1935, CZA, KKL 5/Box 698.

80. Note of a Conversation with His Excellency the High Commissioner by C. Arlosoroff, 20 January 1933, CZA, S25/16; Arlosoroff, *Yoman Yerushalaim,* p. 303.

81. Extract from Note of Conversation between the Secretary of State and the High Commissioner, 22 April 1933, CO 733/243/17456.

82. Note of a Conversation with His Excellency the High Commissioner, 2 February 1933, CZA, S25/16.

83. Arlosoroff, *Yoman Yerushalaim,* p. 308.

84. Musa and Madi, *Tarikh al-Urdun fi al-Qarn al-'Ashrin,* pp. 339, 350, 351.

85. American Consul General Knabenshue to High Commissioner Chancellor, August 1932, CP, Box 17/4.

86. Arlosoroff, *Yoman Yerushalaim,* pp. 310–11; Note of an Interview with His Excellency the High Commissioner, 20 February 1933, CZA, S25/16. See also *NYT,* 24 January 1933.

87. CID Reports, 28 January 1933 and 10 March 1933, FO 371/16926.

88. CID Report, 18 January 1933, FO 371/16926.

89. CID Report, 18 February 1933, FO 371/16926.

90. Minutes of the Jewish National Fund Directorate Meeting, 25 December 1933, CZA, KKL 5/Box 698.

91. CID Reports, 20 June 1933, FO 371/16926. Colonel Cox acknowledged the readiness of Arab landowners to sell land east of the Jordan River to Jews.

The opposition to such sales in Transjordan emanated from some notables in Kerak and Salt, who were reportedly influenced by some Syrian nationalists to demonstrate against the Emir. See Cox to Wauchope, 9 May 1933, CO 733/243/17456.

92. Shertok to Ben-Gurion, 7 December 1933, CZA, S25/3827.

93. Minute of an Interview by Moshe Shertok with His Excellency the High Commissioner, 10 December 1933, CZA, S25/18. See also CO 831/221/1773 for Wauchope's spring 1933 opposition to Jewish settlement in the Transjordan.

94. Minute of a Conversation with His Excellency the High Commissioner by David Ben-Gurion, 15 August 1934, CZA, S25/18; Minute of an Interview with His Excellency the High Commissioner by Moshe Shertok, 10 December 1934, CZA, S25/18.

95. Great Britain, *Parliamentary Debates*, Commons, 26 March 1935, 5th Series, vol. 229; League of Nations, *Permanent Mandates Commission: Minutes*, Twenty-seventh Session, 4 June 1935, p. 202.

96. League of Nations, *Permanent Mandates Commission: Minutes*, Twenty-seventh Session, Petition by Emir Shakib Arslan and Ishan al-Jabri to the League of Nations, 6 October 1934, pp. 200–203.

97. Weitz, *Yomani*, 1:124, 131, 132.

98. Members of Palestine Colonization Association in 1924 were keenly aware of French suspicions regarding Jewish land purchase in the Hauran region south of Damascus. It was considered more judicious not to irritate the French, who feared the creation of an irredenta and the possible inclusion of the Hauran lands in Palestine under the British Mandate. Kisch to Joseph Sprinzak, member of the Palestine Zionist Executive, 8 September 1924, CZA, S25/689.

99. Lewis Andrews, Acting Director of Development, to the Chief Secretary, 17 July 1933, CO 733/243/17456; Wauchope to Cunliffe-Lister, 10 March 1934, CO 733/263/37456, Part 1.

100. Dispatch from British Consul MacKereth to Sir John Simon, Principal Secretary of State, 1 May 1934, CO 733/263/37456. Cf. League of Nations, *Permanent Mandates Commission: Minutes*, Twenty-fifth Session, 5 June 1934, p. 76.

101. British Consulate to Sir John Simon, 24 March 1934, CO 733/263/37456.

102. Suggestions for Acquisition of Land in Syria (1934), CZA.

103. Ibid. Through the mufti of Jerusalem's brother, Fahkri al-Husayni, some Palestinians seem to have been aware and concerned over Zionist land purchases in Syria.

104. Great Britain, Colonial no. 59, *Report by His Majesty's Government to the League of Nations for the Year 1930* (1931), Appendix 6, pp. 249–50; Hope-Simpson Report, p. 172.

105. This account of the history and purchase of the Huleh area is an abbreviated attempt to point out the highlights that led to the sale. The documentary material in Jerusalem alone is so vast that a thorough history of the Huleh Concession warrants at least a short monograph. For further details of the history and the purchase, see ISA, CS 230/file 1, CS 230/file 2, and Attorney Gen-

eral file 757; Minutes of the Jewish National Fund Directorate Meetings for 16 January 1935, 25 April 1935, 6 November 1935, 6 July 1936, and 2 December 1936, CZA; and Weitz's *Yomani*, index entry "Zichayon HaHuleh (Huleh Concession)," 5:336.

106. Great Britain, Colonial no. 5, *Palestine: Report on the Palestine Administration, 1923* (1924), p. 42; Great Britain, Colonial no. 104, *Report by His Majesty's Government to the Council of the League of Nations for the Year 1934* (1935), p. 75.

107. Great Britain, Colonial no. 104, *Report by His Majesty's Government to the Council of the League of Nations for the Year 1934* (1935), p. 75.

108. Minutes of the Jewish National Fund Directorate Meeting, 6 December 1937, CZA, KKL 10.

109. Remarks by Joseph Weitz, Minutes of the Jewish National Fund Directorate Meeting, 6 December 1937, CZA, KKL 10; Minutes of the Jewish National Fund Directorate Meetings, 6 July 1938 and 8 August 1938, CZA, KKL 10.

110. "Current Problems of the Jewish National Fund," an Address by Joseph Weitz in Reply to Questions of Jewish National Fund Delegates, October 1937, CZA, S25/10250; *Report of the Executives of the Zionist Organization and of the Jewish Agency for Palestine*, submitted to the Twenty-first Zionist Congress, August 1939, p. 187, JA; Smilansky, *Prakim BeToldot HaYishuv*, 6:71.

111. Granovsky, *Geulat HaAretz*.

112. Ibid.; "Current Problems of the Jewish National Fund," October 1937, CZA, S25/10250.

113. Palestine Government, *Palestine Estimates, 1939–1940* (Revenue and Expenditure), Jerusalem, 1940, paragraph 45.

114. See Appendix 2; D. Gurevich to Joseph Weitz, 11 May 1941, CZA, KKL 5/1351.

115. Remarks by David Ben-Gurion, Minutes of the Jewish National Fund Directorate Meeting, 6 December 1937, CZA, KKL 10.

116. Shertok to Weizmann, 1 June 1936, CZA, S25/6566.

117. High Commissioner Sir Harold MacMichael to Malcolm MacDonald, Secretary of State for the Colonies, 4 February 1939, CO 733/392/75072; see also Minutes of the Jewish National Fund Directorate Meeting, 28 December 1938, CZA, KKL 5/Box 1048.

118. League of Nations, *Permanent Mandates Commission: Minutes*, Thirty-sixth Session, Remarks by Mr. Moody, 13 June 1939, p. 64.

119. See Jewish Telegraphic Agency Bulletin, 30 May 1940, in CO 733/418/75072, Part 9.

120. See Smilansky, *Prakim Betoldot HaYishuv*, 6:30–31.

121. Minutes of the Jewish National Fund Directorate Meeting, 3 March 1937, CZA, KKL 5/Box 855.

122. Minutes of the Jewish National Fund Directorate Meeting, 14 December 1938, CZA, KKL 5/Box 1048.

Chapter 7

1. Kisch, *Palestine Diary*, p. 418; Interview with Dr. Farhad J. Ziadeh, Former Magistrate in the Safed-Tiberias area, Ramallah, August 28, 1972.

2. Palestine Government, *Census of Palestine, 1931*, 2:110, table 9 (A). There were 969,268 persons in Palestine in 1931. Literacy broken down by religious group was as follows: Muslims, 693,159 (75,659 literate); Jews, 174,610 (126,092 literate); Christians, 91,398 (43,659 literate); others, 10,101 (1,870 literate).

3. Ibid., 2:147, table 10.

4. League of Nations, *Permanent Mandates Commission: Minutes*, Thirty-fourth Session, Remarks by Sir John Shuckburgh, 10 June 1938, p. 56; Protocols of the Jewish National Fund Directorate Meeting, 25 April 1938, CZA, KKL 10.

5. Taqqu, "Peasants into Workmen," pp. 261–85.

6. Montribloux, "Palestine 1938," p. 191.

7. CID Reports, 30 August 1933 and 7 October 1933, FO 371/16926, and 19 December 1933, FO 371/17878; *al-Hayat*, 21 January 1931; *Filastin*, 2 June 1932; *al-Jami'ah al-'Arabiyyah*, 16 September 1932; *al-Jami'ah al-Islamiyyah*, 7 September 1934; and *al-Difa'*, 5 November 1934.

8. Remarks by Sir John Shuckburgh, 14 June 1940, CO 733/425/75872, Part 2.

9. Protocol of a Joint Jewish Agency and Jewish National Fund Meeting on Land, Remarks by Menachem Ussishkin, 19 February 1936, CZA, S25/6538.

Glossary

ALIYA. Going up (lit.); refers to the "waves" of Jewish immigration to Palestine.

DAIMI. Perpetual (lit.); refers to land registers for those persons who held old titles usually before 1839.

EFFENDI. A landowner with considerable holdings, usually possessing some political influence as well.

FELLAHEEN (fellah, sing.). Peasants.

GHOR MUDAWARA. Refers to the Beisan Agreement of 1921.

HAGANAH. Defense (lit.); the Jewish self-defense force in Palestine.

HAJJ. Pilgrimage to Mecca.

HAMULA. Clan.

HATTI SHERIF OF GULHANE. Rescript of the Rose Chamber (lit.); first of the reforming edicts of the Ottoman Empire issued in 1839.

HISTADRUT. Jewish labor organization.

IFRAZ. Partition of *musha'* shares.

ISTIQLAL. Independence.

JIFTLIK. A term used also to designate *mudawara* lands.

KIBBUTZIM. Jewish collective settlements, mainly agricultural in which there is no private wealth, only collective ownership and enterprise.

MAHLUL. *Miri* lands left uncultivated for some reason.

MAJLIS IDARA. A district administrative council in the Ottoman Empire.

MATRUKA. Lands for general public use, such as communal pastures, threshing floors, and places of worship.

MAWAT. Lands classified as unoccupied, hilly, scrub, and grazing grounds not held by title deed.

MIRI. Lands in which the owner held the usufruct, but not title, and considered "state" lands.

MOSHAVIM. Jewish settlements combining features of both cooperative and private enterprise.

MUDAWARA. Lands originally held privately and then in the possession of the sultan.

MUFTI. A Muslim jurisconsul who issues authoritative opinions.

MUKHTAR. A village administrator with functions that may have included security and tax collection, distribution of government aid, and notarian duties for personal status and landownership.

MULK. Lands held in complete freehold.

MULTAZIM. Tax farmers.

MUSHA'. A type of land ownership or land use by which a group of people, usually a village, held shares or parcels, with those shares or parcels redistributed periodically.

MUTASARRIF. A district governor usually of a *sanjaq*.

QADI. A judge in a *Shar'ia* (canonical law) court.

QAIMMAQAM. Administrative head of a *qaza*.

QAZA. A local jurisdiction in the Ottoman Empire.

SANJAQ. A district in the Ottoman Empire.

SHAYKH. An elder, chief of a tribe or village.

SIPAHIS. In the Ottoman Empire a cavalryman rewarded with the grant of a fief.

TABU. Title (lit.).

TANZIMAT. Arrangements (lit.); reformed institutions of the Ottoman Empire beginning in 1839.

WALI. Governor of a *wilayat*, or an area comprising several *sanjaqs*.

WAQF (AWAQF, pl.). Unalienable property in Islamic law usually established for pious purposes for the benefit of the donor's family.

WAQF GHAR SAHIH. Untrue *waqf* constituted from *miri* lands.

WAQF SAHIH. True *waqf* constituted from *mulk* lands.

WILAYET. An Ottoman administrative area usually composed of several *sanjaqs* and usually headed by a *wali*.

YOKLAMA. Census (lit.); refers to land registers for those persons without previous title deeds.

Bibliography

Manuscript Sources

Central Zionist Archives (CZA), Jerusalem, Israel.

Record Groups
A202 = Personal file, Abraham Granott (Granovsky).
A238 = Personal file, Yehoshua Chankin (Hankin).
KKL = Jewish National Fund, Jerusalem, 1922–48.
L18 = Palestine Land Development Company, 1908–24.
S15 = Agricultural Settlement Department, 1918–40.
S25 = Political Department, Palestine Zionist Executive/Jewish Agency.
Z4 = Zionist Organization, Central Office, London, 1917–55.

CZA-housed memoranda and internal reports were written by the Palestine
Office, Zionist Commission, the Palestine Zionist Executive, the Jewish
Agency, and other Zionist institutions and officials. The author is cited where
known. Where a record group and file number are not given, the entry is
found in the archive's library.

Agricultural Development and Land Settlement in Palestine: Observations by
    the Jewish Agency on Mr. Lewis French's Reports, 1933. CZA, library.
Alhassid, M. C. "Observations by a Land Officer—Some Notes on Land
    Matters in Palestine" (1941). CZA, library.
Audiovitz, Abraham. "Der Landkauf in Palästina" (1918). CZA, L18/13/8.
Bodenpolitik im Zusammenhang mit den eventuellen Beschränkungen der
    Bodensaktionen seitens der Regierung, 1930. CZA, S25/1946.
Epstein, E. "The Political Significance of Land Purchase" (1937). CZA, S25/
    10250.
Ettinger, Akiva. "Land Ownership in Palestine and Its Division According to
    Kind of Ownership: Public and Private" (10 June 1924). CZA, KKL 5/
    1878.
Gurevich, D. "Land Acquisition" (September 1934). CZA, S25/6563.
Land Acquisition, 1934. CZA, S25/6563.
Land and Agricultural Development in Palestine Submitted to Sir John Hope-
    Simpson, July 1930. CZA, Z4/3450/file 6.
Land Policy in Palestine, 1936. CZA, S25/6918.
Land Settlement Policy (Continued) Protection of Cultivators, 1929–30.
    CZA, S25/7453.
List of Lands Belonging to Palestine Colonization Association (with) Respec-
    tive Areas Purchased from Absentee Landlords and Owner-Occupiers,
    1929–30. CZA, KKL 5/Box 536.

Memorandum by Dr. Granovsky on Hope-Simpson's Visit, July 1930. CZA, KKL 5/Box 536.
Memorandum on Land to Be Acquired in Palestine, 1919. CZA, z4/1260/file 1.
Memorandum on the Land Question in Palestine, 1919. CZA, z4/771/file 1.
Memorandum on Lands of Uncertain Ownership, 1919. CZA, L18/125/file 31.
Memorandum on Land Purchase and Agricultural Colonization, March 1930. CZA, z4/4106.
Memorandum on Proposed Land Transfer Restrictions (1930), November 1930. CZA, KKL 5/Box 536.
Previous Arab Occupiers of Land Acquired by Jews in the Plains of Esdraelon and Acre, 1929. CZA, s25/7620.
Proposals to the British Government for the Solution of the Land Question in Palestine, 1919. CZA, z4/1260/file 2.
Report for the 1936 Peel Commission by the Jewish Agency, 1936. CZA, s25/4687.
Report of the Agricultural Settlement Department, 1931. CZA, z4/3450/file 5.
Ruppin, Arthur. "Jewish Land Purchase and Its Effect on the Condition of the Farmer and Arab Cultivator" (November 1929). CZA, s25/4207.
Suggestion for Acquisition of Land in Syria, 1934. CZA, s25/6560.
Ussishkin, L. "Notes on the Protection of Cultivators Ordinance, 1933–36" (1936). CZA, s25/4678.

Israel State Archives (ISA), Jerusalem, Israel

Record Groups
Arab Executive Committee
Chief Secretariat, ADM, 1918–25; CS, 1918–25; POL, 1918–25.
Department of Agriculture and Fisheries.
Department of Land Registry.
Department of Lands.
Department of Land Settlement.
District Commissioner's Office, Beisan.
District Commissioner's Office, Galilee.
District Commissioner's Office, Haifa.
District Commissioner's Office, Jenin.

ISA-housed memoranda and reports were written by officials and departments of the Palestine Administration. The author is cited where known. Where a record group and file number are not given, the entry is found in the ISA library.

Bentwich, Norman. "Memorandum on Land Transfer for the Military Governors" (1919). ISA, Box 3314/file 14.
Department of Lands Annual Reports, 1922, 1923, 1924, 1926, 1928, 1929, 1931, and 1936. ISA, library.

Dowson, Ernest. "Notes on Land Tax, Cadastral Survey and Settlement" (n.d.). ISA, 065/file 02059.
———. "Preliminary Study of Land Tenure in Palestine" (1924). ISA, Box 3571/file 1.
Instructions to the Land Commission, 19 July 1920. ISA, CS/G57.
Land Policy in Palestine, 1932. ISA, Box 3552/file 3.
Land Tax Committee Report for 1932. ISA, Box 3372/file 18/33.
Lowick, F. G. "Memorandum on Land Settlement in Palestine" (1926).
———. "Note on the Drayton (Land Registration) Memorandum" (n.d.). ISA, LS 274/file 2.
Mills, Eric. "An Inquiry into Municipal Government in Palestine" (1926). ISA, Box M10.
Palestine. Palestine Land Registries Instructions, 1920–21. ISA, AG Box 755/LS/79/23.
Palestine Land Department. Memorandum on the Reopening of the Land Registries, 1919–20. ISA, Box 3314/file 14.
———. Questionnaire for the 1929 Commission of Inquiry on Land Matters, 1929–30. ISA, Box 3542/file G12.
Report by the Committee on State Domain on the Ghor Mudawara Agreement, 2 December 1940. ISA, Box 3548/file 4.
Report of the Committee to Advise on the Protection of Agricultural Tenants, 1927. ISA, Box 3548/file G 612.
Rizk, Amin. "Memorandum on the Land Transfer Ordinance to the Director of Land Registry" (1921). ISA, Box 3314/file 16.
———. "Remarks on a Note of the Governor of Samaria on Werko and Land Registry" (February 1923). ISA, AG Box 755/L3/79/23.
Strickland, C. F. "Summary Relief of Indebted Cultivators" (1933). ISA, Box 3891/file 2.
Stubbs, J. N. "Memorandum on Sursock Lands" (1921). ISA, Box 3544/file 21.
———. "Memorandum on Land in Palestine" (January 1930). ISA, Box 3542/file G.

Public Record Office, London, England

Record Groups
Cabinet Papers: 23; 24.
Colonial Office: CO 733; CO 814.
Foreign Office: FO 371; FO 686.

Public Record Office-housed memoranda and reports were written by officials and departments of the Arab Executive, the Colonial Office, the Foreign Office, and the Palestine Administration.

'Abd al-Hadi, 'Awni. "Official Reply of the Arab Executive to the French Reports" (March 1933). CO 733/230/17249.
Downie, H. F. "Memorandum on an Agricultural Bank" (1933). CO 733/233/97248.

———. "Note on the Palestine Land Problem" (1935). CO 733/272/75072.

Dowson, Ernest. "Notes on Abolition of the Tithe and Establishment of a Land Tax in Palestine" (April 1928). CO 733/152/59195.

Land Settlement Commission Report, May 1921. CO 733/18/9614.

Lees, A. T. O. "Land Settlement" (1937). CO 733/329/75072/11.

Memorandum by the Attorney General on the Transfer of Agricultural Land Bill, 1930. CO 733/182/77050, Part 1.

Memorandum by the Solicitor General on the Transfer of Agricultural Land Bill and the Protection of Cultivators Amendments Bill, 1930. CO 733/182/77050, Part 1.

Memorandum on Points Arising out of Submission of the Executive of the Jewish Agency to the Royal Commission to the Effect That Government Should Facilitate Jewish Settlement and Development in the Beersheba Area, 1936. CO 733/345/75550/335.

Memorandum on a Proposal Laid before the Royal Commission for the Creation of Public Utility Companies to Undertake Large-Scale Irrigation Development Schemes, 1937. CO 733/345/75550/33E.

Money, Major General A. "A History of Agricultural Loans" (May 1919). CO 733/48/40600.

Observations by the Acting Chief Secretary on the Transfer of Agricultural Land Bill, 1930. CO 733/182/77050, Part 1.

Report of the Committee on Village Administration and Responsibility (1941). CO 733/182/77050, Part 1.

Sawer, E. R. "A Review of the Agricultural Situation" (1923). CO 733/46/31959.

Symes, G. S. "Political Report on the Northern District" (December 1923). CO 733/63.

Wingate, Reginald. "Agriculture and Supplies in Palestine, 1917" (1918). CZA s25/4678.

Private Papers

Oxford University, Oxford, England
Sir John Chancellor Papers, Rhodes House.
Hugh Granville Le Ray Papers, St. Antony's College.
Sir Harold MacMichael Papers, St. Antony's College.
Sydney Moody Papers, Rhodes House.

Chaim Weizmann Archives, Rehovoth, Israel
Chaim Weizmann Papers. The papers and letters are arranged chronologically; dates reviewed, 1917–37.

Unpublished Manuscripts and Theses

Angst, Doris. "Nichtzionisten in Palästina Die Rolle der Jewish Colonization Association 1900–1924." Master's thesis, University of Zurich, September 1977.

Arnon, Yuval. "Fellahim BaMered Ha'Aravi BeEretz Yisrael 1936–1939" (Fellaheen in the Arab revolt in Palestine, 1936–1939). Master's thesis, Hebrew University of Jerusalem, 1971.

Bloom, Sasson. "Yahasam shel 'Arave Eretz-Yisrael al HaYehudi VeMif'al HaTziyoni Ben Meor'ot AV Tarpat leben Prots Meora'ot Tarzav-tarzat" (The relations of the Arabs of Palestine toward Jewish settlement and Zionist enterprise between the riots of AV [August 1929] and the outbreak of the riots of 1936–1939). Master's thesis, Tel Aviv University, 1971.

Held, Joanne Dee. "The Effects of the Ottoman Land Laws on the Marginal Population and Musha' Village of Palestine, 1858–1914." Master's thesis, University of Texas at Austin, 1979.

Kupferschmidt, Uri M. "The Supreme Muslim Council, 1921–1937: Islam under the British Mandate for Palestine." Ph.D. dissertation, Hebrew University of Jerusalem, 1978.

Lesch, Ann Mosely. "The Frustration of a Nationalist Movement: Palestine Arab Politics, 1917–1939." Ph.D. dissertation, Columbia University, 1973.

Miller, Ylana. "Government and Society in Rural Palestine, 1920–1948." Ph.D. dissertation, University of California, Berkeley, 1975.

Ofer, Pinhas. "The Role of the High Commissioner in British Policy in Palestine: Sir John Chancellor, 1928–1931." Ph.D. dissertation, University of London, 1971.

Saliba, Najib Elias. "Wilayat Suriya, 1876–1909." Ph.D. dissertation, University of Michigan, 1971.

Samuel, Edwin. "The Administration of Palestine under British Mandate, 1920–1948." Manuscript, Israeli State Archives, 1950.

Sheffer, Gabriel. "Policy Making and British Policies toward Palestine, 1929–1939." D. Phil., Oxford University, 1971.

Interviews

Reuven Alcalay, Jerusalem, Israel, 3 September 1972.
Lord Caradon (Hugh Foot), London, England, 20 June 1973.
Heinrich Margulies, Jerusalem, Israel, 11 May 1973.
Edwin Samuel, Jerusalem, Israel, 11 February 1973.
Aharon Ben Shemesh, Tel Aviv, Israel, 3 May 1973.
Farhad J. Ziadeh, Ramallah, West Bank, Israel, 28 August 1972.

Published Sources

Official Publications

Great Britain
  Colonial Office Reports
    Colonial no. 5. *Palestine: Report on Palestine Administration 1923.* London, 1924.
    Colonial no. 12. *Report of His Majesty's Government on the Administra-*

tion under Mandate of Palestine and Transjordan for the Year 1924. London, 1925.
Colonial no. 15. Palestine: Report of the High Commissioner on the Administration of Palestine 1920–1925. London, 1925.
Colonial nos. 20, 26, and 31. Report by His Britannic Majesty's Government to the Council of the League of Nations on the Administration of Palestine and Transjordan for the Years 1925, 1926, and 1927. London, 1926, 1927, 1928.
Colonial nos. 40, 47, 59, 75, 82, 94, 104, 112, 129, 146, 166. Report by His Majesty's Government in the United Kingdom of Great Britain and Northern Ireland to the Council of the League of Nations on the Administration of Palestine and Transjordan for the Years 1928, 1929, 1930, 1931, 1932, 1933, 1934, 1935, 1936. London, 1929, 1930, 1931, 1932, 1933, 1934, 1935, 1936, and 1937.

Parliament, Command Papers
Cmd. 1176. Draft Mandates for Mesopotamia and Palestine for the Approval of the League of Nations. London, 1921.
Cmd. 1499. An Interim Report on the Civil Administration of Palestine during the Period 1st July 1920 to 30th June 1921. London, 1921.
Cmd. 1500. Final Drafts of the Mandates for Mesopotamia and Palestine for the Approval of the Council of the League of Nations. London, 1921.
Cmd. 1540. Palestine Disturbances in May 1921: Reports of the Commission of Inquiry with Correspondence in Relation Thereto. London, October 1921.
Cmd. 1700. Correspondence with the Palestine Arab Delegation and the Zionist Organization. London, 1922.
Cmd. 1708. Mandate for Palestine. London, 1922.
Cmd. 1785. Mandate for Palestine with a Note on Its Application to Transjordan. London, 1923.
Cmd. 1889. Papers Relating to the Elections for the Palestine Legislative Council, 1923. London, 1923.
Cmd. 1989. Proposed Formation of an Arab Agency: Correspondence with the High Commissioner for Palestine. London, 1923.
Cmd. 2919. Agreement between Palestine and Syria and the Lebanon to Facilitate Neighborly Relations in Connection with Frontier Questions. London, 1927.
Cmd. 3229. The Western or Wailing Wall in Jerusalem. London, November 1928.
Cmd. 3530. Report of the Commission on the Palestine Disturbances of August 1929 [Shaw Report]. London, 1930.
Cmd. 3582. Palestine: Statement with regard to British Policy in Palestine. London, 1930.
Cmd. 3686. Palestine: Report on Immigration, Land, Settlement and Development [Hope-Simpson Report]. London, 1930.
Cmd. 3692. Palestine: A Statement of Policy by His Majesty's Government

in the United Kingdom [Passfield White Paper]. London, 1930.
Cmd. 5479. *Palestine Royal Commission Report* [Peel Report]. London, 1937.
Cmd. 5854. *Palestine Partition Commission Report.* London, 1938.
Cmd. 6019. *Palestine: A Statement of Policy by His Majesty's Government in the United Kingdom.* London, 1939.
Parliamentary Debates (Commons), 1914–48.
Parliamentary Debates (Lords), 1914–48.

Jewish Agency
  Reports, Addresses, and Resolutions of the Zionist Congresses
    Eleventh (1913); Twelfth (1921); Thirteenth (1923); Fourteenth (1925); Fifteenth (1927); Sixteenth (1929); Seventeenth (1931); Eighteenth (1933); Nineteenth (1935); Twentieth (1937); Twenty-first (1939); and Twenty-second (1946). Jerusalem. Each report was published in same year during which the congress met.

League of Nations
  Permanent Mandates Commission: Minutes
    Fourth Session, 1924; Fifth Session, 1924; Seventh Session, 1925; Ninth Session, 1926; Eleventh Session, 1927; Thirteenth Session, 1928; Fifteenth Session, 1929; Seventeenth Session, 1930; Twentieth Session, 1931; Twenty-second Session, 1932; Twenty-third Session, 1933; Twenty-fifth Session, 1934; Twenty-seventh Session, 1935; Twenty-ninth Session, 1936; Thirty-second Session, 1937; Thirty-fourth Session, 1938; Thirty-sixth Session, 1939.

Ottoman Government
  Salnahmah Vilayet Beirut, 1311–1312 (1893).
  Salnahmah Vilayet Beirut, 1318 (1900).
  Salnahmah Vilayet Beirut, 1326 (1908).

Palestine Government Military and Civil Administration, ISA.
  Annual Report for the Commissioner of Lands and Surveys for 1936. ISA, Box 3532/file 2.
  Annual Reports of the Department of Agriculture and Forests for 1927 to 1930; Report for 1931; Report for 1932. Palestine, 1931, 1932, 1933.
  Barron, J. B. *Report and General Abstracts of the Census of 1922.* Jerusalem, 1923.
  Census for Palestine, 1931. Vols. 1 and 2. Palestine, 1931.
  Civil Service Lists, 1931, 1933, 1937, 1939.
  Department of Agriculture and Fisheries. *Review of the Agricultural Situation in Palestine.* Palestine, 1921.
  Department of Lands. *Annual Reports.*
  Department of Surveys. *Report of the Years 1940–1946.* Palestine, 1947.
  French, Lewis. *First Report on Agricultural Development and Land Settlement in Palestine* [French Report]. Palestine, 1931.
  ———. *Supplementary Report on Agricultural Development and Land Set-*

tlement in Palestine [French Supplementary Report]. Palestine, 1932.
Official Communiqués.
Official (Palestine) Gazette. 1920–48.
Palestine Estimates, 1939–40. Jerusalem, 1940.
Palestine Gazette—Proclamations, Regulations, Rules, Orders, and Notices. 1930–38.
Palestine Royal Commission—Rural Indebtedness. Palestine, 1936.
Proclamations, Ordinances, and Notices Issued by O.E.T.A. South to August 1919. Cairo, 1920.
Report by Mr. C. F. Strickland of the Indian Civil Service on the Possibility of Introducing a System of Agricultural Cooperation in Palestine [Strickland Report]. 1930.
Report of a Committee on the Economic Conditions of Agriculturists in Palestine and Fiscal Measures of Government in Relation Thereto [Johnson-Crosbie Report]. July 1930.
Report on the Palestine Administration July 1920–December 1921. 1922.
United States
Department of Commerce. *Palestine: Its Commercial Resources with Particular Reference to American Trade.* Washington, D.C., 1922.

Newspapers

Arabic
al-Difaʿ.　　　　　　　　　　*al-Jamiʿah al-Islamiyyah.*
Filastin.　　　　　　　　　　*al-Karmil.*
al-Jamiʿah al-ʿArabiyyah.　　*al-Sirat al Mustaqim.*

English
Manchester Guardian.
New York Times.
The Times (London).

Books

English
Anglo-American Committee of Inquiry. *A Survey of Palestine.* Vols. 1 and 2. Palestine, 1946.
Antonius, George. *The Arab Awakening.* New York, 1965.
Ashbee, Charles. *A Palestine Notebook, 1918–1923.* Garden City, N.Y., 1923.
Baer, Gabriel. *A History of Land Ownership in Modern Egypt, 1800–1950.* London, 1962.
Barron, J. B. *Mohammadan Wakfs in Palestine.* Jerusalem, 1923.
Bein, Alex. *The Return to the Soil.* Jerusalem, 1952.
Ben-Gurion, David. *My Talks with Arab Leaders.* Tel Aviv, 1967.
Bentwich, Norman. *England in Palestine.* London, 1932.
―――. *Mandate Memoirs.* London, 1932.

_____. *The Mandate System*. New York, 1930.
_____. *Palestine*. London, 1934.
Bertram, A., and Luke, Henry C. *Report of the Commission to Enquire into the Affairs of the Orthodox Patriarchate of Jerusalem*. London, 1921.
Bertram, A., and Young, I. W. A. *Report of the Commission Appointed by the Government of Palestine to Enquire into and Report upon Certain Controversies between the Orthodox Patriarchate of Jerusalem and the Arab Orthodox Community*. London, 1926.
Boustany, W. F. *The Palestine Mandate: Invalid and Impracticable*. Beirut, 1936.
Bowle, John. *Viscount Samuel*. London, 1957.
Brodetsky, Selig. *Memoirs from Ghetto to Israel*. London, 1960.
Caplan, Neil. *Palestine Jewry and the Arab Question, 1918–1925*. London, 1978.
Cohen, Amnon. *Palestine in the 18th Century: Patterns of Government and Administration*. Jerusalem, 1973.
Cutileiro, José. *A Portuguese Rural Society*. Oxford, 1971.
Davison, Roderic H. *Reform in the Ottoman Empire, 1856–1876*. Princeton, 1963.
Doukhan, Moses, ed. *Laws on Palestine, 1926–1931*, Vol. 4. Tel Aviv, 1933.
Dowson, Sir Ernest. *An Inquiry into Land Tenure and Related Questions* (in Iraq). London, 1932.
Erskine, Beatrice. *Palestine of the Arabs*. London, 1937.
Ettinger, Jacob. *Emek Jezreel, a Flourishing District*. Jerusalem, 1926.
Fargo, Ladislas. *Palestine at the Crossroads*. New York, 1937.
Fisher, Stanley. *Ottoman Land Laws*. Oxford, 1919.
Friedman, Isaiah. *The Question of Palestine, 1914–1918: British-Jewish-Arab Relations*. New York, 1973.
Friedman, Max D., ed. *Collection of Judgements of the Courts of Palestine, 1919–1933*. 6 vols. Tel Aviv, 1937.
Furlonge, Sir Geoffrey. *Palestine Is My Country: The Story of Musa Alami*. New York, 1969.
Gibb, H. A. R., and Bowen, Harold. *Islamic Society and the West*. 2 vols. Oxford, 1967.
Goadby, Frederic M., and Doukhan, Moses I. *The Land Law of Palestine*. Tel Aviv, 1935.
Granott (Granovsky), Abraham. *Agrarian Reform and the Record of Israel*. London, 1956.
_____. *Land and the Jewish Reconstruction in Palestine*. Jerusalem, 1931.
_____. *The Land Issue in Palestine*. Jerusalem, 1936.
_____. *Land Policy in Palestine*. New York, 1940.
_____. *The Land System in Palestine: History and Structures*. London, 1952.
_____. *Towards an Economic Jewish Agriculture in Palestine*. Tel Aviv, 1927.
Grant, Elihu. *The Peasantry of Palestine*. Boston, 1907.
_____. *The People of Palestine*. London, 1921.

Graves, Phillip. *Land of Three Faiths.* London, 1923.
Gurevich, D., and Gertz, A. *Jewish Agricultural Settlement in Palestine.* Jerusalem, 1938.
Hadawi, Sami. *Palestine: Loss of a Heritage.* Austin, Texas, 1963.
———. *Village Statistics, 1945.* Beirut, 1970.
Halpern, Ben. *The Idea of the Jewish State.* Cambridge, Mass., 1969.
Hankin, Joshua (Yehoshua). *Ideas on Jewish Colonization in Palestine.* Jerusalem, 1940.
Himadeh, Said. *Economic Organization of Palestine.* Beirut, 1938.
Hooper, C. A. *The Civil Law of Palestine and Trans-Jordan.* Jerusalem, 1936.
Hopwood, Derek. *Russian Presence in Syria and Palestine, 1843–1914.* Oxford, 1969.
Hurewitz, J. C. *Struggle for Palestine.* New York, 1950.
Hyamson, Albert. *The British Consulate in Jerusalem in Relation to the Jews of Palestine, 1838–1914.* 2 vols. London, 1939.
———. *Palestine: A Policy.* London, 1942.
———. *Palestine under Mandate, 1920–1948.* London, 1950.
Kimche, Jon. *There Could Have Been Peace.* New York, 1973.
Kirkbride, Alec Seath. *A Crackle of Thorns.* London, 1956.
Kisch, F. H. *Palestine Diary.* London, 1938.
Klieman, Aaron S. *Foundations of British Policy in the Arab World: The Cairo Conference of 1921.* Baltimore, 1970.
Laqueur, Walter. *A History of Zionism.* New York, 1972.
Lewis, Bernard. *The Emergence of Modern Turkey.* 2d ed. Oxford, 1969.
Luke, H., and Roach, E. Keith. *The Handbook of Palestine.* London, 1922.
Lutfiyya, Abdullah M. Baytin. *A Jordanian Village: A Study of Social Institutions and Social Change.* London, 1966.
McDonnell, Michael F. J. *Law Reports of Palestine, 1920–1933.* 2 vols. London, 1934.
Ma'oz, Moshe. *Ottoman Reform in Syria and Palestine, 1840–1861.* Oxford, 1968.
———, ed. *Studies on Palestine during the Ottoman Period.* Jerusalem, 1975.
Marlowe, John. *Rebellion in Palestine.* London, 1946.
———. *The Seat of Pilate.* London, 1959.
Marx, Emanuel. *Bedouin of the Negev.* Manchester, 1967.
Meinertzhagen, Richard. *Middle East Diary, 1917–1956.* London, 1959.
Migdal, Joel S., ed. *Palestinian Society and Politics.* Princeton, 1980.
Mossek, Moshe. *Palestine Immigration Policy under Sir Herbert Samuel—British, Zionist, and Arab Attitudes.* London, 1978.
Oliphant, Lawrence. *Haifa, or Life in Modern Palestine.* New York, 1887.
———. *The Land of Gilead.* New York, 1881.
Pinner, Ludwig. *Wheat Culture in Palestine.* Tel Aviv, 1930.
Poliak, A. N. *Feudalism in Egypt, Syria, Palestine, and the Lebanon.* London, 1939.
Polk, William R., and Chambers, Richard C., eds. *Beginnings of Modernization in the Middle East.* Chicago, 1968.

Porath, Yehoshua. *The Emergence of the Palestinian Arab National Movement, 1918–1929.* London, 1974.
_____. *The Palestinian Arab National Movement, 1929–1939: From Riots to Rebellion.* London, 1977.
Preuss, Walter. *The Labour Movement in Israel.* Jerusalem, 1965.
Report of the Experts Submitted to the Joint Palestine Survey Commission. London, 1928.
Rose, N. A. *The Gentile Zionists: A Study in Anglo-Zionist Diplomacy, 1929–1939.* London, 1973.
Royal Institute of International Affairs. *Great Britain and Palestine, 1915–1945.* Information papers No. 20. London, 1946.
Ruppin, Arthur. *Memoirs, Diaries, and Letters.* Jerusalem, 1971.
_____. *Three Decades in Palestine.* Jerusalem, 1936.
Rustum, Assad Jibrail. *The Royal Archives of Egypt and the Disturbances in Palestine, 1834.* Beirut, 1938.
Samuel, Edwin. *A Lifetime in Jerusalem.* London, 1970.
Samuel, Horace. *Unholy Memories of the Holy Land.* London, 1930.
Schama, Simon. *Two Rothschilds and the Land of Israel.* New York, 1978.
Sereni, Enzo, and Ashery, R. E., eds. *Jews and Arabs in Palestine.* New York, 1936.
Simson, H. J. *British Rule and Rebellion.* London, 1937.
Stein, Leonard. *The Balfour Declaration.* New York, 1961.
Storrs, Ronald. *The Memoirs of Sir Ronald Storrs.* New York, 1937.
_____. *Orientations.* London, 1937.
Sykes, Christopher. *Crossroads to Israel.* London, 1965.
Taylor, A. J. P. *English History, 1914–1945.* London, 1965.
Tibawi, A. L. *Anglo-Arab Relations and the Question of Palestine, 1914–1921.* London, 1978.
_____. *British Interests in Palestine, 1800–1901.* Oxford, 1961.
_____. *A Modern History of Syria.* London, 1969.
Tute, R. C. *The Ottoman Land Laws with a Commentary.* Jerusalem, 1927.
Viteles, Harry. *The Status of the Orange Industry in Palestine.* Tel Aviv, 1930.
Warriner, Doreen. *Land and Poverty in the Middle East.* New York, 1948.
Wasserstein, Bernard. *The British in Palestine: The Mandatory Government and the Arab-Jewish Conflict, 1917–1929.* London, 1978.
Webb, Beatrice. *Diaries, 1924–1932.* London, 1956.
Weizmann, Chaim. *Trial and Error.* New York, 1966.
Wilson, Reverend C. T. *Peasant Life in the Holy Land.* London, 1906.
Zeine, Zeine. *The Struggle for Arab Independence.* Beirut, 1960.

French and German
Ashkenazi, Tovia. *Tribus Semi-Nomades de la Palestine du Nord.* Paris, 1938.
Auhagen, Hubert. *Beiträge zur Kenntnis der Landesnatur und der Landwirtschaft Syriens.* Berlin, 1907.
Böhm, Adolf. *Die Zionistische Bewegung 1918 bis 1925.* Jerusalem, 1937.
Bonne, Alfred. *Palästina Land und Wirtschaft.* Berlin, 1935.
Cuinet, Vital. *Syrie, Liban et Palestine.* Paris, 1896.

Endres, Franz Carl. *Die wirtschaftliche Bedeutung Palästinas als Teiles der Turkei.* Berlin, 1918.

Ettinger, Jacob. *Konkreter Vorschlag für landwirtschaftliche Kolonisation.* Jerusalem, 1921.

————. *Methoden und Kapitalbedarf jüdischer Kolonisation in Palästina.* The Hague, 1916.

Fischer, Hans. *Wirtschaftsgeographie von Syrien.* Leipzig, 1919.

Granovsky, Abraham. *Bodenbestuerung in Palästina.* Berlin, 1928.

————. *Boden und Siedlung in Palästina.* Berlin, 1929.

————. *Probleme der Bodenpolitik in Palästina.* Berlin, 1935.

Jaussen, P. Antonin. *Coutumes des Arabes au Pays de Moab.* Paris, 1948.

Kremer, Alfred V. *Mittelsyrien und Damascus.* Vienna, 1853.

Latron, André. *La Vie Rurale en Syrie et au Liban.* Beirut, 1936.

Nawratzki, Curt. *Die jüdische Kolonisation Palästinas.* Munich, 1914.

Nord, Erich. *Die Reform des türkischen Liegenschaftsrechts.* Leipzig, 1914.

Oppenheim, Max. *Die Beduinen.* Vol. 2. Leipzig, 1943.

Ruppin, Arthur. *Der Aufbau des Landes Israel.* Berlin, 1919.

————. *Syrien als Wirtschaftsgebiet.* Berlin, 1917.

Shulman, Leon. *Zur türkischen Agrarfrage Palästina und die Fellachenwirtschaft.* Weimar, 1916.

Volney, M. C. F. *Voyage en Syrie et en Egypte.* Vol. 2. Paris, 1781.

Weulersse, Jacques. *Paysans de Syrie et du Proche-Orient.* Paris, 1946.

Arabic and Hebrew

Abramovitz, Z., and Gelfat, Y. *Hameshek Ha'Aravi BeEretz Yisrael VeBearzot HaMizrah Hatikon* (The Arab economy in Palestine and in the countries of the Middle East). Palestine, 1944.

Arlosoroff, Chaim. *Yoman Yerushalaim* (Jerusalem diary). Palestine, n.d.

Ashbel, A. *Shishim Shnot Haksharat HaYishuv* (Sixty years of the Palestine Land Development Company). Jerusalem, 1969.

Assaf, Michael. *HaYahasim ben 'Aravim VeYehudim BeEretz Yisrael, 1860–1948* (The relations between Arabs and Jews in Palestine, 1860–1948). Tel Aviv, 1970.

————. *Hit'orrut Ha'Aravim BeEretz Yisrael VeBerihtam* (The Arab awakening in Palestine and their flight). Tel Aviv, 1967.

Baer, Gabriel. *'Arave HaMizrah Hatikon* (The Arabs of the Middle East). Tel Aviv, 1960.

Bein, Alex. *Toldot Hityashvut HaTziyonit* (The history of Zionist settlement). Ramat Gan, Israel, 1970.

Ben-Gurion, David. *Zichronot* (Memoirs). 2 vols. Tel Aviv, 1971.

Ben Shemesh, Aaron. *Hukay HaKarkar'ot BeMedinat Yisrael* (Land laws in the State of Israel). Israel, 1953.

Darwaza, Muhammad. *Hawla al-Harakah al-'Arabiyyah al-Hadithah* (On the modern Arab movement). Vol. 3. Sidon, 1950.

Dinier, B., et al., eds. *Sefer Toldot Hahaganah* (History of the Haganah). 8 vols. Tel Aviv, 1964.

Doukhan-Landau, Leah. *HaHevrot HaTziyoniot Lerchishat Karka'ot BeEretz Yisrael, 1897–1914* (The Zionist companies for land purchase in Palestine, 1897–1914). Jerusalem, 1979.

Elath, Eliyahu. *Hajj Muhammad Amin al-Husayni—Mufti Yerushalaim leShe'avar* (Hajj Muhammad Amin al-Husayni—the former mufti of Jerusalem). Tel Aviv, 1968.

Frumkin, Gad. *Derech Shofet BeYerushalaim* (The path of a judge in Jerusalem). Tel Aviv, 1954.

Giladi, Dan. *HaYishuv BeTekufat Ha'Aliyah HaReve'et 1924–1929* (The Yishuv in the period of the Fourth Aliya, 1924–1929). Tel Aviv, 1973.

Granovsky, Abraham. *Geulat HaAretz* (Redemption of the land). Jerusalem, 1938.

al-Kayyali, 'Abd al-Wahhab, ed. *Watha'iq al-Muqawama al-Filastiniyyah al-'Arabiyyah didd al-Ihtilal al-Baratani wa al-Sahyuniyyah, 1918–1939* (Documents of Palestinian Arab resistance against British and Zionist occupation, 1918–1939). Beirut, 1968.

Kirk, Ruth. *Toldot Hityashvut BeNegev 'ad 1948* (History and settlement in the Negev to 1948). Israel, 1974.

Milaff al-Witha'iq al-Filastini (Portfolio of Palestinian documents). Cairo, 1969.

Musa, S., and Madi, M. *Tarikh al-Urdun fi al-Qarn al-'Ashrin* (History of Jordan in the twentieth century). 1959.

Nemirovsky, (Namir) Mordechai. *HaMatzav HaKalkali BeEretz Yisrael BeSof Shanat Tarzaq* (The economic situation in Palestine at the end of 1933). Tel Aviv, 1933.

Ruppin, Arthur. *Pirke Hayay* (Chapters of my life). 3 vols. Tel Aviv, 1968.

Sefer Ussishkin (Ussishkin's notebook). Jerusalem, 1934.

Sharett, Moshe. *Yoman Medini* (Political diaries). 3 vols. Tel Aviv, 1971.

Shimoni, Ya'acov. *'Arave Eretz Yisrael* (The Arabs of Palestine). Palestine, 1947.

Smilansky, Moshe. *Prakim BeToldot HaYishuv* (Chapters in the history of the Yishuv). 6 vols. Tel Aviv, 1939–47.

Vaschitz, Joseph. *Ha'Aravim BeEretz Yisrael* (The Arabs in Palestine). Palestine, 1947.

Weitz, Joseph. *'Emek Hefer-Parshah MeToldot Hitahzutaynu* (Wadi Hawarith—chapter from the history of our settlement on land). Jerusalem, 1936.

———. *Hitnahlataynu BeTekufat HaSa'ar 1936–1946* (Our settlement in a period of storm, 1936–1946). Palestine, 1947.

———. *Yomani* (My diary). 5 vols. Ramat Gan, Israel, 1965.

Articles

English

Amiran, D. H. K. "The Pattern of Settlement in Palestine." *Israel Exploration Journal* 3 (1953): 65–78, 192–209, 250–60.

Arian, D. "The First Five Years of the Israel Civil Service." *Scripta Hierosolymitana* 5 (1958): 340–77.

Asfour, J. "Arab Labour in Palestine." *Royal Central Asian Society Journal* 32 (1945): 201–5.

Ashbee, Charles R. "The Palestine Problem Reviewed after Ten Years." *English Review* 61 (November 1935): 529–39.

Baali, Fuad. "Relationship of Man to Land in Iraq." *Rural Sociology* 31 (1966): 171–82.

Baer, Gabriel. "Land Tenure in Egypt and the Fertile Crescent, 1800–1950." In *The Economic History of the Middle East 1800–1914*, edited by Charles Issawi, pp. 79–90. Chicago, 1966.

al-Barguthy, Omar Saleh. "Traces of the Feudal System in Palestine." *Palestine Oriental Society Journal* 9 (1929): 70–79.

Bentwich, Norman. "The Legal System of Palestine." *Middle East Journal* 2 (January 1948): 33–46.

Bergheim, Samuel. "Land Tenure." *Palestine Exploration Fund Quarterly Statement* 26 (1894): 191–99.

Bromberger, E. "Growth of the Population of Palestine." *Population Studies* 2 (1948): 71–91.

Cohen, Michael. "Sir Arthur Wauchope, the Army, and the Rebellion." *Middle Eastern Studies* 9 (January 1973): 19–34.

Dabbagh, Saleh M. "Agrarian Reform in Syria." *Middle East Economic Papers* (1962): 1–15.

Dawn, C. Ernest. "The Rise of Arabism in Syria." *Middle East Journal* 16 (1962): 145–68.

Finn, E. A. "The Fellaheen of Palestine." *Palestine Exploration Fund Quarterly Statement* 11 (January 1879): 33–48.

———. "The Fellaheen of Palestine." *Palestine Exploration Fund Quarterly Statement* 11 (April 1879): 72–87.

Firestone, Ya'acov. "Crop-sharing Economics in Mandatory Palestine." *Middle Eastern Studies* 11, pt. 1 (January 1975): 3–23.

———. "Production and Trade in an Islamic Context: Sharika Contracts in the Transitional Economy of Northern Samaria, 1853–1943." *International Journal of Middle East Studies* 6 (April 1975): 185–209.

Gillon, D. Z. "The Antecedents of the Balfour Declaration." *Middle Eastern Studies* 5 (May 1969): 131–50.

Hoexter, Miriam. "The Role of the Qays and Yaman Factions in Local Political Divisions: Jabal Nablus Compared with the Judean Hills in the First Half of the Nineteenth Century." *Asian and African Studies* 10 (1974): 249–312.

Hoofien, S. "Immigration and Prosperity." *Palestine and Near East Economy Magazine* (1930): 1–55.

Hourani, Albert. "Ottoman Reform and the Politics of Notables." In *Beginnings of Modernization in the Middle East*, edited by William Polk and Richard Chambers, pp. 41–68. Chicago, 1968.

al-Hout, Bayan Nuuweihid, "The Palestine Political Elite during the Mandate Period." *Journal of Palestine Studies* 9 (1979): 85–111.
Hurewitz, J. C. "Arab Politics in Palestine." *Contemporary Jewish Record* 5 (December 1942): 597–619.
Jarvis, Major C. S. "Southern Palestine and Its Possibilities for Settlement." *Royal Central Asian Society Journal* 25 (1938): 204–18.
Kallner, D. H., and Rosenau, E. "Geographical Regions of Palestine." *Geographical Review* 29 (January 1939): 61–80.
Karmon, Y. "The Settlement of the Northern Huleh Valley since 1838." *Israel Exploration Journal* 3 (1953): 4–25.
Karpat, Kemal H. "Land Regime, Social Structure, and Modernization." In *Beginnings of Modernization in the Middle East,* edited by William Polk and Richard Chambers, pp. 69–90. Chicago, 1968.
Kedourie, Elie. "Sir Herbert Samuel and the Government of Palestine." *Middle Eastern Studies* 5 (January 1969): 44–68.
Klat, P. J. "Musha' Holdings and Land Fragmentation in Syria." *Middle East Economic Papers* 4 (1958): 12–23.
──────. "The Origins of Land Ownership in Syria." *Middle East Economic Papers* 5 (1958): 51–66.
Klein, Reverend F. A. "Fellaheen of Palestine." *Palestine Exploration Fund Quarterly Statement* 13 (April 1881): 110–18.
Lambton, A. K. S. "The Evolution of Iqta' in Medieval Iran." *Iran* 5 (1967): 41–50.
"Land Tenure in Palestine." *Palestine* [the organ of the British Palestine Committee] 7 (29 May 1920): 126–27.
Layish, Aharon. "The Muslim Waqf in Israel." *Asian and African Studies* 2 (1966): 41–76.
Lehn, Walter. "Zionist Land: The Jewish National Fund." *Journal of Palestine Studies* 3 (1974): 74–96.
Mandel, Neville. "Attempts at an Arab-Zionist Entente: 1913–1914." *Middle Eastern Studies* 1 (April 1965): 238–67.
──────. "Ottoman Policy and Restrictions on Jewish Settlement in Palestine: 1881–1908—Part I." *Middle Eastern Studies* 10 (October 1974): 312–32.
──────. "Ottoman Practice as Regards Jewish Settlement in Palestine, 1881–1908." *Middle Eastern Studies* 11, pt. 2 (January 1975): 33–46.
──────. "Turks, Arabs, and Jewish Immigration into Palestine, 1882–1908." In *Middle Eastern Affairs,* by Albert Hourani, 4:77–108. St. Antony's Papers, no. 17. Oxford, 1965.
Miller, Ylana. "Administrative Policy in Rural Palestine: The Impact of British Norms on Arab Community Life, 1920–1948." In *Palestine Society and Politics,* edited by Joel S. Migdal, pp. 124–45. Princeton, 1980.
Moghannam, E. Moghannam. "Palestine Legislation under the British." *Annals of the American Academy of Political and Social Science* 164 (1932): 47–54.

Musham, H. U. "Enumerating the Bedouins of Palestine." *Scripta Hiero-solymitana* 3 (1953): 265–80.

Nashashibi, Fakhri Bey. "The Arab Position in Palestine." *Journal of the Royal Central Asian Society* 23 (January 1936): 16–26.

Nielsen, Alfred. "International Islamic Conference at Jerusalem." *Moslem World* 22 (October 1932): 340–54.

Perlman, Moshe. "Chapters of Arab-Jewish Diplomacy, 1918–1922." *Jewish Social Studies* 6 (1944): 124–54.

Post, George. "Essays on Sects and Nationalists of Syria and Palestine—Land Tenure." *Palestine Exploration Fund Quarterly Statement* 23 (April 1891): 99–147.

Potter, Pitman B. "Origin of the System of Mandates under the League of Nations." *American Political Science Review* 16 (1922): 563–83.

Quataert, Donald. "Dilemma of Development: The Agricultural Bank and Agricultural Reform in Ottoman Turkey, 1888–1908." *International Journal of Middle East Studies* 6 (1975): 210–27.

Ro'i, Ya'acov. "The Zionist Attitude to the Arabs, 1908–1914." *Middle Eastern Studies* 4 (April 1968): 198–242.

Rose, Norman. "The Debate on Partition, 1937–38: The Anglo-Zionist Aspect to the Proposal–I." *Middle Eastern Studies* 6 (October 1970): 297–318.

———. "The Debate on Partition, 1937–38: The Anglo-Zionist Aspect—II, The Withdrawal." *Middle Eastern Studies* 7 (January 1971): 3–24.

Schattner, I. "Haifa: A Study in the Relation of City and Coast." *Israel Exploration Journal* 4 (1954): 26–45.

Shapiro, Anita. "The Option on Ghaur al-Kibd: Contacts between Emir Abdullah and the Zionist Executive, 1932–1935." *Zionism* 1 (1980): 239–83.

Sheffer, G. "Intentions and Results of British Policy in Palestine: Passfield's White Paper." *Middle Eastern Studies* 9 (January 1973): 43–60.

———. "The Involvement of Arab States in the Palestine Conflict and British-Arab Relationship before World War II." *Asian and African Studies* 10 (1974): 59–78.

Smilansky, Moshe. "Jewish Colonization and the Fellah." *Palestine and Near East Economic Magazine* 5 (1930).

"Some Bedawin of Palestine." *Moslem World* 20 (July 1930): 302–8.

Stein, Kenneth W. "Legal Protection and Circumvention for Rights of Cultivators in Mandatory Palestine." In *Palestinian Society and Politics*, edited by Joel S. Migdal, pp. 233–61. Princeton, 1980.

Stracey, W. J. "Palestine . . . as It Is and as It Might Be." *Palestine Exploration Fund Quarterly Statement* 12 (October 1880): 241–42.

Strickland, Claude F. "The Struggle for Land in Palestine." *Current History* [published by the *New York Times*] 34 (April 1931): 45–49.

Tannous, Afif I. "The Arab Village Community." *Annual Report of the Smithsonian Institute* (1943): 523–43.

_____. "Land Tenure in the Middle East." *Foreign Agriculture* 7 (August 1943): 170–77.

_____. "The Village Teacher and Rural Reconstruction." *Open Court* 49 (October 1935): 236–40.

Taqqu, Rachelle. "Peasants into Workmen: Internal Labor Migration and the Arab Village Community under the Mandate." In *Palestinian Society and Politics*, edited by Joel S. Migdal, pp. 261–85. Princeton, 1980.

Turkowski, Lucian. "Peasant Agriculture in the Judean Hills." *Palestine Exploration Quarterly* 101 (January 1969): 21–33, 101–12.

Vereté, Mayir. "The Balfour Declaration and Its Makers." *Middle Eastern Studies* 6 (January 1970): 48–76.

Winder, R. Bayly. "The Origins of Representative Government in the Ottoman Empire: An Introduction to the Provincial Councils, 1839–1879." In *Near Eastern Round Table, 1967–68*, edited by R. Bayly Winder, pp. 53–142. New York, 1969.

Zahlan, A. B. "Palestine's Arab Population." *Journal of Palestine Studies* 3 (1974): 32–73.

French and German

Bjorkman, Walter. "Die neuesten Erfolge der arabischen Nationalbewegung." *Zeitschrift für Politik* 27 (1937): 350–66.

Bonne, Alfred. "Die öffentlichen Finanzen des Mandatsgebietes Palästina." *Finanz-Archiv* 46, no. 11 (1929): 90–117.

_____. "Die sozial-ökonomischen Strukturwandlungen in Palästina." *Archiv für Sozialwissenschaft und Sozialpolitik* 63, pt. 1 (1930): 309–36.

_____. "Die sozial-ökonomischen Strukturwandlungen in Palästina." *Archiv für Sozialwissenschaft und Sozialpolitik* 64, pt. 2 (1930): 332–67.

Castel, J. H. "Die Araber in Palästina." *Der Jude* 5 (1920–21): 414–16.

Kohn, Hans. "Zur Araberfrage." *Der Jude* 4 (1919–20): 567–69.

Krichewsky, M. S. "Le Rôle de la Pluie dans la Vie économique de la Palestine." *L'Egypte Contemporaine* 17 (1926): 50–61.

Latron, André. "En Syrie et au Liban: Village Communautaire et Structure Sociale." *Annuales d'Histoire Economique et Sociale* 6 (1934): 225–34.

Montribloux, Hubert. "Palestine 1938: Facteurs économiques et sociaux du Conflit Judéo-Arabe." *Science Politique* 54 (April 1939): 170–93.

Nathan ben-Nathan. "Die Erbpacht." *Der Jude* 4 (1919–20): 25–36.

Rappard, William E. "Zur Soziologie des Mandatssystems." *Zeitschrift für Politik* 18 (1928): 1–8.

Rubaschow, Salman. "Die Privatwirtschaftliche Kolonisation in Palästina." *Der Jude* 6 (1921–22): 212–30.

Ruppin, Arthur. "Das Verhältnis der Juden zu den Araben." *Der Jude* 3 (1918–1919): 453–57.

Steinberg, Fritz. "Die Bedeutung der Araberfrage für den Zionismus." *Der Jude* 3 (1918–19): 147–63.

_____. "Die Bedeutung der Erbpacht für den Neuaufbau in Palästinas." *Der Jude* 3 (1918–19): 555–65.

Tartatakower, Arjeh. "Bodenfrage und Bodenpolitik." *Der Jude* 6 (1921–22): 728–39.

Arabic and Hebrew

Alsberg, Paul. "HaShe'elah Ha'Aravit BeMediniyut HaHanhalah HaTziyonut Lifne Milhemet Ha'Olam HaRishonah" (The Arab question in the Zionist executive's diplomacy before World War I). *Shibat Tziyon* 4 (1956–57): 161–209.

Gerber, Haim. "HaMinhal Ha'Otomani Shel Sanjaq Yerushalaim 1890–1908" (The Ottoman administration of the Sanjaq of Jerusalem, 1890–1908). *HaMizrah Hahadash* 24 (1974): 1–33.

Ghanim, 'Adil Hasan. "Mauqif 'Arab Filastin min al-Yahud wa al-Sahyuniyyah min al-Harb al-'Alamiyyah hatta Idtirabat al-Buraq 1929" (The attitude of Palestine Arabs toward Jews and Zionism from the World War to the 1929 disturbances). *Journal of the Middle East* (January 1974): 213–32.

Luntz, Joseph. "Hamaga'im HaDiplomatiim ben HaTenu'ah Hatziyonit VeHatenu'ah Ha'Aravit HaLeumit 'im Sium Milhemet Ha'Olam HaRishonah" (Diplomatic contacts between the Zionist movement and the Arab national movement at the close of the First World War). *HaMizrah Hahadash* 12 (1962): 212–29.

Ro'i, Ya'acov. "Nisyonotaihem Shel HaMosadot HaTziyoniyim le Hashpi'a 'al Ha'Itonut Ha'Aravit BeEretz Yisrael BeShanim 1908–1914" (The attempts of the Zionist institutions to influence the Arabic press in Palestine in the years 1908–1914). *Zion* 33 (1967): 200–227.

Sela', Avraham. "Sihot VeMaga'im ben Manhigim Tziyonim leben Manhigim 'Aravim Palestinim, 1933–1939, Helek Rishon" (Conversations and contacts between Zionist and Palestinian Arab leaders, 1933–39, part 1). *HaMizrah Hahadash* 22 (1972): 401–23.

Shamir, Shimon. "Temurot BeHanhagah HaKafarit Shel Al-rama" (Changes in the village leadership at Al-rama). *HaMizrah Hahadash* 11 (1962): 241–57.

Yehoshua, Ya'acov. "*Al-Munadi* Ha'Iton HaMuslami HaRishon BeEretz Yisrael" (*Al-Munadi*: The first Muslim newspaper in Palestine). *HaMizrah Hahadash* 25 (1975): 209–15.

———. "Tel-Aviv Be-Raii Ha'Itonut Ha'Aravit BeHamesh HaShanim HaRishonot le Hivasdah 1909–1914" (Tel Aviv as reflected by the Arabic press during the first five years of existence, 1909–14). *HaMizrah Hahadash* 19 (1969): 218–22.

Index